ੴ

JAPJI SAHIB

FiNGERPRINT!

Published by
FiNGERPRINT!
An imprint of Prakash Books India Pvt. Ltd

113/A, Darya Ganj,
New Delhi-110 002
Email: info@prakashbooks.com/sales@prakashbooks.com

Fingerprint Publishing
@FingerprintP
@fingerprintpublishingbooks
www.fingerprintpublishing.com

ISBN: 978 93 5856 400 6

Praise for Japji Sahib, Way to God in Sikhism

"Chahal's objective is to present easily understandable exposition of the lofty spiritual grandeur of Japji to the English-knowing people. The author comprehensively covers the subject. The treatise contains perceptive commentaries and closely reasoned critiques. Idiolectical terms from various languages have been etymologically explained lucidly. The writing is crisp, research impressive, inferences adroit and conclusions sound. It is an accomplishment of sound merit and scholarship."

(Abstracts of Sikh Studies, Chandigarh)

"Maneshwar Singh Chahal's annotation is of great significance. The author uses abundant imagery, so that the annotation creates a cascading effect and the prose flows with each shlok. References intersperse freely with the author's version of the text and you have updates on other learned men's versions of the same phrase. All in all, this book is a labour of love and with the painstaking research that has gone into it, the book may stand the test of time."

(The Tribune, Chandigarh)

"Very little work has been done on the *Banis* in English. Japji Sahib, Way to God in Sikhism by Maneshwar Singh Chahal is a praiseworthy effort in this direction. The 38 pauṛis of the Japji Sahib have been explained very scientifically and their essence spelt out in easy to understand language. As you read the book you feel as if you are ascending step by step closer to the Lord."

(The Ajit, Jullundur, in Punjabi.)

"Maneshwar Singh Chahal has worked on important posts as an IAS officer in both the Center and the State. He has also been CMD Pb and Sind Bank and later a Member of the Pb State Human

Rights Commission. In the midst of these heavy responsibilities he has been deeply religious seeking to understand the Guru's word. His commentary will make it clear that the Japji Sahib is indeed a unique path to God realization."

(Punjabi Digest, New Delhi, in Punjabi)

"Japji Sahib – Way to God in Sikhism", by Maneshwar Singh Chahal (who happens to be a retired bureaucrat) is an in-depth study of the Guru's revelatory message. The Japji encapsulated into thirty eight pauṛis (steps) has been brilliantly captured by the author. His familiarity with the earlier interpretations, combined with his profound insight into the scripture and keen mental perception animate his exposition with a charm and dignity. Chahal's exposition deserves to be ranked as one of the best."

(The Sikh Review, Calcutta)

"The author has put in a lot of hard work in compiling this commentary. In the Foreword he quotes Hew McLeod saying 'The world is poorer for its ignorance of the Sikh scripture.' This is indeed true and one would hope that this book will help bridge the gap. It is well written and both the language employed and the idiom used flow easily. Maneshwar Chahal has collated an extensive array of explanations, views and interpretations on the Japji."

(Studies in Sikhism and Comparative Religion, New Delhi)

Praise for Āsa di Vār

"The intense exploration and research by the author to bring out the essence of *Gurbāṇi* is visible from page one in this well-prepared thesis. The author's earlier book on Japji was equally scholarly. This is a remarkable work, well studied and argued in all subtle details. Strongly recommended for all public libraries and private collections."

(Abstract of Sikh Studies, Chandigarh)

"The translation and explanations are detailed, and Chahal has related some anecdotes that help in understanding the contexts of certain verses. The value of the book is that it should help readers grasp the textual meaning of the *Vār* and possibly encourage them to explore how its contents really underscore the core teachings of this *Vār*. Enjoy the book. It should deepen the ras of *Āsa di Vār* Kirtan the next time you hear it."

(Studies in Sikhism and Comparative Religion, New Delhi)

Praise for Jap Sahib

"Third in the series "Way to God in Sikhism" (the first two being *Japji Sahib* and *Āsa di Vār*), this book is a beautiful production, perhaps the first of its kind in English. Shows the depth to which the author has gone in his study. The book is invaluable for the English-reading public and a worthy addition to the *Gurbāṇi* literature in English."

(Abstract of Sikh Studies, Chandigarh)

The Japji Sahib, Way to God in Sikhism, by Maneshwar Singh Chahal has been approved by the Punjab Government for purchase in all College Libraries vide the following letter:

Memo number 5/2-2006 (Sampadak), dated 23 Jun 2008, from the DPI(Colleges) addressed to the Principals of all Government and Non-Government Colleges.

NOTE ON THE SECOND EDITION

It has been seven years since *'Japji Sahib'*, this first book of the series 'Way to God in Sikhism' first came out. Much energy and thought had gone into the project, and the end product had looked good to me. But, then no mother has ever thought her child was not beautiful! It needed to be seen and evaluated by those who would give it a hard, cold-eyed look and assess its real worth for the reader.

It was with some trepidation that I brought this book to the attention of some noted scholars, and the book editors of some prominent newspapers and magazines. Gradually the book started getting noticed by readers from some of whom I got very positive feedback, and the reviews also started coming in. The book was reviewed in 'The Abstract of Sikh Studies', the official magazine of the Institute of Sikh Studies, Chandigarh. It was also reviewed in the vernacular press in some magazines and newspapers in Delhi and in Jullundur. Sometime later a review also appeared in The Tribune, an English language Newspaper with a large circulation in Punjab, Chandigarh and the neighbouring states. About a year later 'The Sikh Review', published from Calcutta also reviewed the book.

The reviews were for the most part very generous, with the Sikh Review rating it as one of the best commentaries on the subject. By this time the book had also started getting noted through word of mouth reactions. My publisher, Prakash Books, had in the meanwhile taken the initiative and got the book listed on Amazon.co.uk, where some of the readers posted very positive remarks. The book had caught the attention of many who were interested in spirituality and in Sikhism. A second print soon came out. By which time the next two books in the series, the *Āsa di Vār* and the *Jāp Sahib* had also hit the stands and were receiving good response.

The one flaw that some learned scholars pointed out to me was that the phonetics of the Roman text had not been taken care of in the *Japji Sahib*. The text lacked diacritical marks to help with the correct pronunciation of the *Bāṇi* and of the other terms from Gurmukhi that necessarily had to be used. This shortcoming had been addressed in the second book, the *Āsa di Vār*, where I had devised and incorporated a Key to Pronunciation, which was then also followed in the *Jāp Sahib*. This key was based on the system followed by many learned ones in their commentaries on ancient religious texts and by commentators on Sikh scriptures.

Since it was now time to bring out a third printing of this book the publisher thought it would be appropriate to address this flaw and bring the book in conformity with the Key to Pronunciation used in the other two books. It would definitely help make the book more useful for the reader. This has been now been done and the second edition incorporates the correct phonetics for the Roman text.

A few issues had also been raised about the text, or with my interpretation of certain thoughts in the commentary. I found that most of these reactions were born out of some misunderstanding of what I had written, and to these honourable readers I made the effort to personally clarify. I hope they were satisfied. A few of these responses and reactions, I found were based on a radically different perception of what the Guru had said. To these learned ones I humbly replied with the Guru's own word, "*Āp āpnee budhh hai jetee. Barnat bhinn bhinn tuhe tetee*" - The ability to describe the unknowable mystery of the Lord is constrained by the level of our understanding. It is entirely possible that these learned readers could be right, but I must humbly say that this book is the outcome of long hours of thought and study. I, therefore, stand by the interpretation this book offers.

It is entirely possible that I have erred in reaching a particular conclusion while construing some thought in the *Bāṇi*, but whatever I have written is after very careful thought; and after referring to a large number of very learned scholars of Sikhism. At a very few places, however, there was the need to make some minor corrections, or to add a word or two to elaborate or clarify the thought already expressed. This edition incorporates these corrections. I am hopeful gentle reader, that this new edition will enable you to benefit even more from this quintessential *Bāṇi*, and will lead you on the path to spiritual elevation.

KEY TO PRONUNCIATION

Gurmukhi Script	Roman script	Pronunciation
1. ਅ	a	short 'a', as in 'normal', except at the end when it is long as in 'war'
2. ਆ	ā	long a, as in 'war'
3. ਇ, ਿ	i	short 'i' as in 'fit'
4. ਈ, ੀ	ī	long 'i' as in 'meet
5. ਉ, ੁ	u	short 'u' as in 'put'
6. ਊ, ੂ	ū	long 'u' as in 'boot'
7. ਏ, ੇ	e	sharp 'a' as in 'grey'
8. ਐ, ੈ	ai	broad 'a' as in 'fat'
9. ਅੰ, ੰ	[ng]	nasal, short sound, as in sing
10. ਆਂ, ਂ	ā[n]	nasal, long sound as in brand
11. ਸ	s	as in sad
12. ਸ਼	sh	as in sharp, shut
13. ਕ	k	as in kit
14. ਖ	kh	as in *khālsa*, or silk hat (uttered quickly together)
15. ਗ	g	as in good
16. ਘ	gh	as in ghost, or log-hut (uttered quickly together)
17. ਚ	ch	as in chat
18. ਛ	chh	as in Chhatisgarh, or church-hill uttered quickly together
19. ਜ	j	as in just
20. ਝ	jh	as in *jhang*, or hedgehog
21. ਟ	tt	hard sound, as in talk, or curt

22. ਠ	tth	hard sound, as in thakur, or hot-house
23. ਡ	dd	as in dark, or card
24. ਢ	ddh	as in *dholak*, or in red-hot (uttered quickly together)
25. ਣ	ṇ	as in *madhāṇī*
26. ਤ	t	soft 't', as in *talwandī*
27. ਥ	thh	as in thick
28. ਦ	d	soft 'd', as in then
29. ਧ	dh	as in *dhobi*, or breathe hard
30. ਨ	n	as in nun
31. ਪ	p	as in pup
32. ਫ	ph or f	as in phone or fix
33. ਬ	b	as in but, or tube
34. ਭ	bh	as in *Bhagat*, or abhor
35. ਮ	m	as in mat, or time
36. ਯ	y	as in yet
37. ਰ	r	as in rat
38. ਲ	l	as in love
39. ਵ	v,w	as in vent, with
40. ੜ	ṛ	as in *pahāṛ*
41. ਜ਼	z	as in zero

This book is dedicated to
all those who truly seek the One Lord

CONTENTS

FOREWORD

The sublime spiritual beauty of the *Gurbāṇi* is well recognized by all those who have been lucky enough to be exposed to it. Sadly, however, there are many, even among the twenty plus million Sikhs who find the Gurmukhi script a barrier; or more often find the message difficult to understand because the language differs so much from present day Punjabi. As Prof. W.H. McLeod said, "The world is poorer for its ignorance of the Sikh Scriptures." Also, to quote Macauliffe, "The Granth Sahib thus becomes the most difficult work, sacred or profane, that exists, and hence the general ignorance of its contents." He was of course referring to the fact that this sacred writing had employed such a large variety of languages and dialects, and it was hard for any one man to be a scholar in all of those.

Efforts to bring the message to the world in simpler, easier to understand language have often been made. Some European translations exist, especially noteworthy among them being Macauliffe's six volumes: *The Sikh Religion, Its Guru's Sacred Writings and Authors.* There are then detailed commentaries in Punjabi, notably by Prof. Sahib Singh and Bhai Vir Singh. There are dictionaries such as Bhai Sahib Bhai Kahan Singh's *Gurshabad Ratnākar*, more commonly known as the *Mahan Kosh*. Finally, there are verse renderings in English; Prof. G.S. Talib's being notable. All these learned men have tried to make clear the meaning of the *Gurbāṇi*. Our subject here being the *Japji Sahib* we may note that all these have naturally also included their perceptions inter alia, on this, the foremost of the Guru's compositions. Commentaries specifically on the *Japji* in the English language have been few. Generally we find verse translations figuring either as a part of an overall commentary on the Sikh scriptures, or the *Japji* being rendered into poetry in English with a few explanatory footnotes. The Punjabi commentary in greater detail exists but is not accessible to those who do not have an understanding of the Gurmukhi script.

There is, therefore, a large audience, which is aware of the grandeur of this scripture but cannot access it, this being true of the Sikh diaspora with even greater poignancy. There are also many, not necessarily adherents of the Sikh religion but keen seekers of spiritual growth who would like a detailed explanation of the terms used and the thoughts which possibly lay behind those words. It is for all of them that this humble presentation is made. It has been three years in the preparation and the writing, and is based on half a century's personal pursuit of the Guru's Path, however imperfect and lacking in true merit that effort may have been. It owes also a great deal to the many learned commentaries and translations, in Punjabi and in English. A special debt is owed to Prof. Sahib Singh's 10-volume *Sri Guru Granth Sahib Darpan* where he has in Vol. 1 annotated the *Japji Sahib*. Vol. 1 of Bhai Vir Singh's commentary has also been a constant source and guide. Giani Sant Singh Maskin's twenty-cassette audio-commentary on the *Japji* has also been relied on. Osho's twenty-cassette commentary in Hindi and his very readable commentary 'The True Name', on the *Japji Sahib* have also been of help in formulating and shaping these thoughts.

Apart from the above, many other translations, and commentaries, mostly in English and Narain Singh's erudite commentary in Punjabi have also been of great help. This offering refers to all the learned commentaries and then seeks to offer conclusions on how the message of the Guru in the *Japji Sahib* is to be construed. In offering these conclusions effort has been made to steer as close as possible, to the extent the limitations of intellect and knowledge would permit, to the central message of the scripture. Individual words used in the composition have been explained and a line-by-line commentary attempted. This book should therefore be useful to those who would at one single place like the meaning explained and clarified, to help them read and recite this first prayer of the *Nitnem* with better understanding. It should also help direct scholars to the other very much more learned commentaries that are available, some of which we have touched upon above.

May this effort be of some avail, to at least a few, in reaching a better understanding of the message of the Sikh faith. May the learned reader also forgive your humble interlocutor for the many shortcomings that will no doubt be noted here. Be assured that this is placed before you in full awareness of the vastness of the subject, and of the many highly evolved souls in whose hands it will fall.

ACKNOWLEDGEMENTS

Thanks are due to S. Darshan Singh, Chief Engineer (retired), a true devotee of the One Lord. He spared long hours going through the manuscript and made many useful suggestions.

I would also like to extend my gratitude to Sardar M.P. Singh, AGM (retired) of the Punjab & Sind Bank, a good and upright human being who took upon himself the task of personally typing a large part of the draft and who was of much help in bringing this book to the stage of publication.

PREFACE

The context in which the *Gurbāṇi* is to be read is important to know before proceeding to read, understand and then, if the Lord's blessings be on us, to act upon the message and to follow the path the *Sri Guru Granth Sahib* (*SGGS*) prescribes. The approach of the *Gurbāṇi* and the manner in which the message has been presented has obviously been determined by and is rooted in the milieu in which the founder of Sikhism, Guru Nanak Dev *ji* lived. The social, the political and above all the religious factors that prevailed were necessarily going to influence the form in which the message is worded. The Guru's vision is cosmic in scope and in this composition the Guru presents to the common man the mysteries of the Divine, to the extent such mysteries are amenable to presentation within the limitations of human understanding and the constraints of language. Since the message is of the spirit, it had to be couched in language understood by the Guru's audience and in terms that were relevant to their existing religious and spiritual concepts.

The major religions prevalent at that time were Hinduism and Islam. The other religions, like Budhhism and Jainism, though originating from the soil of India were not followed in any significant strength, though Budhhism continued to flourish in large parts of Asia beyond the shores of this country. In this country Budhhism had lost out many centuries ago to a resurgent, and often militant, Hinduism, while Jainism had never really managed to acquire very many adherents. Also, Hinduism with its well known capacity to incorporate and absorb other belief systems had accorded to the Budhha the status of an *avatār*, an incarnation, of Lord Vishnu, and managed thereby to blur the distinctions between the two religions. Islam came into the country gradually, till the raiders of Mahmud Ghaznavi and Mohammad Ghori brought into the country, through the force of arms, a more militant version, in the second millennium. This was followed in quick succession by more conquests from the West and the beginning of a series of Muslim dynasties in India. With this, Islam gained the status of being the ruler's religion and accordingly acquired converts. Such movement into the new religion was also facilitated by the existence of huge inequities that had crept into the Hindu social structure. Islam also gained from the efforts, and the example, of the Sufis whose brand of a kindlier, more spiritual Islam would have attracted large numbers of the more enlightened. This combination of the sword, state power, social inequities of the existing order, and the Sufi saints made Islam strong in India. In spite of all these factors the population continued to be mainly Hindu, by a large majority. The Christian influence was yet very limited.

Thus, when the Guru began his ministry, the seekers, the disciples who thronged the Guru's congregations must have belonged mainly to either the Hindu or the Muslim faith. The language he used and the method of his teaching were bound to be influenced by this circumstance. He would have had to use the idiom that they understood. The path that he delineated for the world was new and different in many ways from both these religious belief systems. Yet, inevitably his presentation, his arguments will be seen to revolve round these existing systems, and from there they proceed to present his new vision, his new way of thinking, his new prescription for God-realization.

In actual fact, the Guru has used the terminology of Hinduism a great deal and has made extensive reference to Hindu mythology and to Hindu customs and rituals. Usually the reference to rituals is meant to point out the futility of relying on these for attaining true spiritual growth or reaching God-realization. The Guru has at other places referred to Muslim practices for the same purpose.

The cosmogony followed by the Guru is almost entirely Hindu. Thus, there is postulated a time horizon measured in *Yugas*; the four *Yugas* – *Satya* (or *Krita*), *Treta*, *Dwāpar* and *Kal(i)*– following in succession over a total period measured as 4.32 million years, lasting each in a proportion of 4:3:2:1 respectively, constituting together a *Mahāyuga* and being repeated in the same cycle. Ruling over these ages is the Trinity of Brahma the Creator, Vishnu the Preserver, and Shiva the Destroyer working in tandem to operate the systems of the universe within the time frame of these *Yugas*. There is Dharamrāj, charged by the Lord with judging the good and the bad that souls practice on this earth, on this field of action which has been provided by the Lord for us to strive so as to improve our spiritual standing, and to prove our worth in the Divine Court; and there is *Chitragupt* who is appointed for recording the deeds of humans and who then presents these to the Dharamrāj. All these find repeated mention in the *SGGS*.

The message of the Guru in its essence is that the Creator is one, and the human soul is a part of Him temporarily separated from Him. This universe has been created by Him in His pleasure, for reasons only He knows, but it is the field of action, the arena in which the separated soul, having reached after a long and hard journey the coveted stage of a human, is to strive to re-attain that union with the Lord. The purpose of human birth is to break down the barrier between the soul and the Creator, to pierce through the veil of falsehood, of illusion, that has caused this separation. This human form is the ultimate stage of the soul's journey through numerous incarnations, believed in the Hindu system to number 8.4 million, and is for that reason extremely precious. We must therefore make the fullest possible use of this rare opportunity offered to us at the end of eons of painful and hard-earned upward movement. It is only after the attaining of this stage that the soul has the chance to climb the path to God-realization, to attain *Moksha* or *Nirvāṇa*, whatever the various belief systems may choose to label it. Even if in any one birth we do not succeed in finding *Moksha* (salvation) yet are our actions in this arena really important. That is because, the Guru tells us, good deeds and righteous action will enable elevation of the soul's status within this world. Equally, bad deeds will cause regression into painful and lowly incarnations; and if those deeds are particularly reprehensible we could regress altogether back from the human stage. In the midst of this flux, of the movement of the soul up and down the spiritual scale, come the opportunities to take the right path whereby, with the help of the right Guru, the right preceptor, the soul could be cleansed of the accumulation of myriad sins and purified to the level where the ever-flowing love and grace of the Lord will enter this human vessel; and by His grace will be removed in a flash the veil of separation. The illusion that surrounds us will be transformed into the shining Reality, the Truth. The moment of that grace will however, says the Guru, come only when the Lord so desires, and is not something to be forcibly snatched or claimed as a right. This is the essence of what the Guru teaches us. He has elaborated on this theme throughout his *Bāṇi*, and in the *Japji Sahib* we can find the message encapsulated into thirty-eight *pauṛis* (steps). Contained herein is a prescription for the cure of all spiritual ills; if only we could learn to read, to understand and then to surrender ourselves to its uplifting, soothing embrace.

JAPJI SAHIB

ੴ ਸਤਿਨਾਮੁ ਕਰਤਾ ਪੁਰਖੁ ਨਿਰਭਉ ਨਿਰਵੈਰੁ ਅਕਾਲ ਮੂਰਤਿ ਅਜੂਨੀ ਸੈਭੰ ਗੁਰ ਪ੍ਰਸਾਦਿ॥	*Ek Onkār Sat Nām Karta Purakh Nirbhau. Nirvair Akāl Mūrat Ajūni Saibhang Gur Prasād.*
ਜਪੁ॥	***Jap(u)***
ਆਦਿ ਸਚੁ ਜੁਗਾਦਿ ਸਚੁ॥	*Ād(i) sach jugād(i) sach.*
ਹੈ ਭੀ ਸਚੁ ਨਾਨਕ ਹੋਸੀ ਭੀ ਸਚੁ॥ ੧॥	*Hai bhi sach Nanak hosi bhi sach.*

Pauṛi 1

ਸੋਚੈ ਸੋਚਿ ਨ ਹੋਵਈ ਜੇ ਸੋਚੀ ਲਖ ਵਾਰ॥	*Sochai soch na hovayi jay sochi lakh vār.*
ਚੁਪੈ ਚੁਪ ਨ ਹੋਵਈ ਜੇ ਲਾਇ ਰਹਾ ਲਿਵ ਤਾਰ॥	*Chupai chup na hovayi jay lāye raha liv tār.*
ਭੁਖਿਆ ਭੁਖ ਨ ਉਤਰੀ ਜੇ ਬੰਨਾ ਪੁਰੀਆ ਭਾਰ॥	*Bhukhia bhukh na utari jay banna purīya bhār.*
ਸਹਸ ਸਿਆਣਪਾ ਲਖ ਹੋਹਿ ਤ ਇਕ ਨ ਚਲੈ ਨਾਲਿ॥	*Sahas syāṇapa lakh hoye ta ik na chalai nāl.*
ਕਿਵ ਸਚਿਆਰਾ ਹੋਈਐ ਕਿਵ ਕੂੜੈ ਤੁਟੈ ਪਾਲਿ॥	*Kiv sachiāra hoīyai kiv kūṛai tuttai pāl.*
ਹੁਕਮਿ ਰਜਾਈ ਚਲਣਾ ਨਾਨਕ ਲਿਖਿਆ ਨਾਲਿ॥ ੧॥	*Hukam rajāyi chalṇa Nanak likhiya nāl.*

Pauṛi 2

ਹੁਕਮੀ ਹੋਵਨਿ ਆਕਾਰ ਹੁਕਮੁ ਨ ਕਹਿਆ ਜਾਈ॥	*Hukmi hovan ākār hukam na kahiya jāyi.*
ਹੁਕਮੀ ਹੋਵਨਿ ਜੀਅ ਹੁਕਮਿ ਮਿਲੈ ਵਡਿਆਈ॥	*Hukmi hovan jīw hukam milai vaddiāyi.*
ਹੁਕਮੀ ਉਤਮੁ ਨੀਚੁ ਹੁਕਮਿ ਲਿਖਿ ਦੁਖ ਸੁਖ ਪਾਈਅਹਿ॥	*Hukmi utam nīch hukam(i) likh dukh sukh pāīay.*
ਇਕਨਾ ਹੁਕਮੀ ਬਖਸੀਸ ਇਕਿ ਹੁਕਮੀ ਸਦਾ ਭਵਾਈਅਹਿ॥	*Ikna hukmi bakshsīs ik hukmi sada bhavāīay.*
ਹੁਕਮੈ ਅੰਦਰਿ ਸਭੁ ਕੋ ਬਾਹਰਿ ਹੁਕਮ ਨ ਕੋਇ॥	*Hukmai andar sab ko bāhar hukam na koye.*
ਨਾਨਕ ਹੁਕਮੈ ਜੇ ਬੁਝੈ ਤ ਹਉਮੈ ਕਹੈ ਨ ਕੋਇ॥ ੨॥	*Nanak hukmai jay bujhai ta haumai kahai na koye.*

Pauṛi 3

ਗਾਵੈ ਕੋ ਤਾਣੁ ਹੋਵੈ ਕਿਸੈ ਤਾਣੁ॥	*Gāvai ko tāṇ, hovai kisay tāṇ.*
ਗਾਵੈ ਕੋ ਦਾਤਿ ਜਾਣੈ ਨੀਸਾਣੁ॥	*Gāvai ko dāt, jāṇai nīsāṇ.*
ਗਾਵੈ ਕੋ ਗੁਣ ਵਡਿਆਈਆ ਚਾਰ॥	*Gāvai ko guṇ vaddiāyia chār.*
ਗਾਵੈ ਕੋ ਵਿਦਿਆ ਵਿਖਮੁ ਵੀਚਾਰੁ॥	*Gāvai ko vidya vikham vīchār.*
ਗਾਵੈ ਕੋ ਸਾਜਿ ਕਰੇ ਤਨੁ ਖੇਹ॥	*Gāvai ko sāj karay tann kheh.*
ਗਾਵੈ ਕੋ ਜੀਅ ਲੈ ਫਿਰਿ ਦੇਹ॥	*Gāvai ko jīw lai phir deh.*
ਗਾਵੈ ਕੋ ਜਾਪੈ ਦਿਸੈ ਦੂਰਿ॥	*Gāvai ko jāpai disai dūr.*
ਗਾਵੈ ਕੋ ਵੇਖੈ ਹਾਦਰਾ ਹਦੂਰਿ॥	*Gāvai ko vekhai hādra hadūr.*
ਕਥਨਾ ਕਥੀ ਨ ਆਵੈ ਤੋਟਿ॥	*Kathna kathi na āvai tott.*
ਕਥਿ ਕਥਿ ਕਥੀ ਕੋਟੀ ਕੋਟਿ ਕੋਟਿ॥	*Kath kath kathi kotti kott kott.*
ਦੇਦਾ ਦੇ ਲੈਦੇ ਥਕਿ ਪਾਹਿ॥	*Denda day lainday thakk pāhe.*
ਜੁਗਾ ਜੁਗੰਤਰਿ ਖਾਹੀ ਖਾਹਿ॥	*Juga jugantar khāhi khāhe.*
ਹੁਕਮੀ ਹੁਕਮੁ ਚਲਾਏ ਰਾਹੁ॥	*Hukmi hukam chalāye rāh.*
ਨਾਨਕ ਵਿਗਸੈ ਵੇਪਰਵਾਹੁ॥ ੩॥	*Nanak vigsai veparvāh.*

Pauṛi 4

ਸਾਚਾ ਸਾਹਿਬੁ ਸਾਚੁ ਨਾਇ ਭਾਖਿਆ ਭਾਉ ਅਪਾਰੁ॥	*Sācha sahib sāch nāye bhākhya bhāu apār.*

ਆਖਹਿ ਮੰਗਹਿ ਦੇਹਿ ਦੇਹਿ ਦਾਤਿ ਕਰੇ ਦਾਤਾਰੁ॥	*Ākhay mangay deh deh dāt karay dātār.*
ਫੇਰਿ ਕਿ ਅਗੈ ਰਖੀਐ ਜਿਤੁ ਦਿਸੈ ਦਰਬਾਰੁ॥	*Pher ke aggai rakhiyai jit disai darbār.*
ਮੁਹੌਂ ਕਿ ਬੋਲਣੁ ਬੋਲੀਐ ਜਿਤੁ ਸੁਣਿ ਧਰੇ ਪਿਆਰੁ॥	*Muhau ke bolaṇ boliyai jit suṇ dharay pyār.*
ਅੰਮ੍ਰਿਤ ਵੇਲਾ ਸਚੁ ਨਾਉ ਵਡਿਆਈ ਵੀਚਾਰੁ॥	*Amrit vela sach nāu vaddiāyi vīchār.*
ਕਰਮੀ ਆਵੈ ਕਪੜਾ ਨਦਰੀ ਮੋਖੁ ਦੁਆਰੁ॥	*Karmi āvai kapṛa nadri mokh duār.*
ਨਾਨਕ ਏਵੈ ਜਾਣੀਐ ਸਭੁ ਆਪੇ ਸਚਿਆਰੁ॥੪॥	*Nanak evai jaṇiyai sabh āpay sachiār.*

Pauṛi 5

ਥਾਪਿਆ ਨ ਜਾਇ ਕੀਤਾ ਨ ਹੋਇ॥	*Thāpiya na jāye kīta na hoye.*
ਆਪੇ ਆਪਿ ਨਿਰੰਜਨੁ ਸੋਇ॥	*Āpay āp niranjan soye.*
ਜਿਨਿ ਸੇਵਿਆ ਤਿਨਿ ਪਾਇਆ ਮਾਨੁ॥	*Jin seviya tin pāyia mān.*
ਨਾਨਕ ਗਾਵੀਐ ਗੁਣੀ ਨਿਧਾਨੁ॥	*Nanak gāviyai guṇi nidhān.*
ਗਾਵੀਐ ਸੁਣੀਐ ਮਨਿ ਰਖੀਐ ਭਾਉ॥	*Gāviyai suṇiyai mann rakhiyai bhāu.*
ਦੁਖੁ ਪਰਹਰਿ ਸੁਖੁ ਘਰਿ ਲੈ ਜਾਇ॥	*Dukh parhar sukh ghar lai jāye.*
ਗੁਰਮੁਖਿ ਨਾਦੰ ਗੁਰਮੁਖਿ ਵੇਦੰ ਗੁਰਮੁਖਿ ਰਹਿਆ ਸਮਾਈ॥	*Gurmukh nāda(ng) gurmukh veda(ng) gurmukh rahiya samāyi.*
ਗੁਰੁ ਈਸਰੁ ਗੁਰੁ ਗੋਰਖੁ ਬਰਮਾ ਗੁਰੁ ਪਾਰਬਤੀ ਮਾਈ॥	*Gur īssar gur gorakh barma gur pārbati māyi.*
ਜੇ ਹਉ ਜਾਣਾ ਆਖਾ ਨਾਹੀ ਕਹਣਾ ਕਥਨੁ ਨ ਜਾਈ॥	*Je hau jāṇa ākha nāhi kehṇa kathan na jāyi.*
ਗੁਰਾ ਇਕ ਦੇਹਿ ਬੁਝਾਈ॥	*Gura ik deh bujhāyi.*
ਸਭਨਾ ਜੀਆ ਕਾ ਇਕੁ ਦਾਤਾ ਸੋ ਮੈ ਵਿਸਰਿ ਨ ਜਾਈ॥੫॥	*Sabhna jiā(n) ka ik dāta so mai visar na jāyi.*

Pauṛi 6

ਤੀਰਥਿ ਨਾਵਾ ਜੇ ਤਿਸੁ ਭਾਵਾ ਵਿਣੁ ਭਾਣੇ ਕਿ ਨਾਇ ਕਰੀ॥	*Tīrath nāva je tis bhāva viṇ bhāṇay kay nāye kari.*
ਜੇਤੀ ਸਿਰਠਿ ਉਪਾਈ ਵੇਖਾ ਵਿਣੁ ਕਰਮਾ ਕਿ ਮਿਲੈ ਲਈ॥	*Jeti sirtth upāyi vekha viṇ karma kay milai layi.*

ਮਤਿ ਵਿਚਿ ਰਤਨ ਜਵਾਹਰ
ਮਾਣਿਕ ਜੇ ਇਕ ਗੁਰ ਕੀ ਸਿਖ ਸੁਣੀ॥
ਗੁਰਾ ਇਕ ਦੇਹਿ ਬੁਝਾਈ॥
ਸਭਨਾ ਜੀਆ ਕਾ ਇਕੁ ਦਾਤਾ
ਸੋ ਮੈ ਵਿਸਰਿ ਨ ਜਾਈ॥੬॥

Mat(i) vich ratan jawāhar maṇik jay ik gur ki sikh suṇi.
Gura ik deh bujhāyi.
Sabhna jia ka ik dāta so mai visar na jāyi.

Pauṛi 7

ਜੇ ਜੁਗ ਚਾਰੇ ਆਰਜਾ ਹੋਰ ਦਸੂਣੀ ਹੋਇ॥
ਨਵਾ ਖੰਡਾ ਵਿਚਿ ਜਾਣੀਐ ਨਾਲਿ ਚਲੈ
ਸਭੁ ਕੋਇ॥
ਚੰਗਾ ਨਾਉ ਰਖਾਇ ਕੈ ਜਸੁ ਕੀਰਤਿ
ਜਗਿ ਲੇਇ॥
ਜੇ ਤਿਸੁ ਨਦਰਿ ਨ ਆਵਈ ਤ ਵਾਤ
ਨ ਪੁਛੈ ਕੇ॥
ਕੀਟਾ ਅੰਦਰ ਕੀਟੁ ਕਰਿ ਦੋਸੀ ਦੋਸੁ ਧਰੇ॥
ਨਾਨਕ ਨਿਰਗੁਣਿ ਗੁਣੁ ਕਰੇ ਗੁਣਵੰਤਿਆ
ਗੁਣੁ ਦੇ॥
ਤੇਹਾ ਕੋਇ ਨ ਸੁਝਈ ਜਿ ਤਿਸੁ ਗੁਣੁ
ਕੋਇ ਕਰੇ॥੭॥

Jay jug chāray ārja hor dasūṇi hoye.
Nava khandda vich jāṇiyai nāl chalai sabh koye.
Changa nāo rakhāye kai, jas kīrat jag lay.
Jay tis nadar na āvayi ta vāt na puchhai kay.
Kītta andar kītt kar dosi dos dharay.
Nanak nirguṇ guṇ karay guṇvantia guṇ day.
Teha koye na sujhayi jay tis guṇ koye karay.

Pauṛi 8

ਸੁਣਿਐ ਸਿਧ ਪੀਰ ਸੁਰਿ ਨਾਥ॥
ਸੁਣਿਐ ਧਰਤਿ ਧਵਲ ਆਕਾਸ॥
ਸੁਣਿਐ ਦੀਪ ਲੋਅ ਪਾਤਾਲ॥
ਸੁਣਿਐ ਪੋਹਿ ਨ ਸਕੈ ਕਾਲੁ॥
ਨਾਨਕ ਭਗਤਾ ਸਦਾ ਵਿਗਾਸੁ॥
ਸੁਣਿਐ ਦੂਖ ਪਾਪ ਕਾ ਨਾਸੁ॥੮॥

Suṇiyai sidh pīr sur nāth.
Suṇiyai dharat dhawal ākās.
Suṇiyai dīp low pātāl.
Suṇiyai poh na sakai kāl.
Nanak bhagta sada vigās.
Suṇiyai dūkh pāp ka nās.

Pauṛi 9

ਸੁਣਿਐ ਈਸਰੁ ਬਰਮਾ ਇੰਦੁ॥
ਸੁਣਿਐ ਮੁਖਿ ਸਾਲਾਹਣ ਮੰਦੁ॥
ਸੁਣਿਐ ਜੋਗ ਜੁਗਤਿ ਤਨਿ ਭੇਦ॥

Suṇiyai īssar barma ind.
Suṇiyai mukh sālāhaṇ mand.
Suṇiyai jog jugat tan(i) bhed.

ਸੁਣਿਐ ਸਾਸਤ ਸਿਮ੍ਰਿਤਿ ਵੇਦ॥	*Suṇiyai sāst simrit ved.*
ਨਾਨਕ ਭਗਤਾ ਸਦਾ ਵਿਗਾਸੁ॥	*Nanak bhagta sada vigās.*
ਸੁਣਿਐ ਦੂਖ ਪਾਪ ਕਾ ਨਾਸੁ॥੯॥	*Suṇiyai dūkh pāp ka nās.*

Pauṛi 10

ਸੁਣਿਐ ਸਤੁ ਸੰਤੋਖੁ ਗਿਆਨੁ॥	*Suṇiyai sat(u) santokh gyān.*
ਸੁਣਿਐ ਅਠਸਠਿ ਕਾ ਇਸਨਾਨੁ॥	*Suṇiyai atth satth ka isnān.*
ਸੁਣਿਐ ਪੜਿ ਪੜਿ ਪਾਵਹਿ ਮਾਨੁ॥	*Suṇiyai paṛ paṛ pāveh mān.*
ਸੁਣਿਐ ਲਾਗੈ ਸਹਜਿ ਧਿਆਨੁ॥	*Suṇiyai lāgai sehaj dhyān.*
ਨਾਨਕ ਭਗਤਾ ਸਦਾ ਵਿਗਾਸੁ॥	*Nanak bhagta sada vigās.*
ਸੁਣਿਐ ਦੂਖ ਪਾਪ ਕਾ ਨਾਸੁ॥੧੦॥	*Suṇiyai dūkh pāp ka nās.*

Pauṛi 11

ਸੁਣਿਐ ਸਰਾ ਗੁਣਾ ਕੇ ਗਾਹ॥	*Suṇiyai sara guṇa kay gāh.*
ਸੁਣਿਐ ਸੇਖ ਪੀਰ ਪਾਤਿਸਾਹ॥	*Suṇiyai sekh pīr pātsāh.*
ਸੁਣਿਐ ਅੰਧੇ ਪਾਵਹਿ ਰਾਹੁ॥	*Suṇiyai andhay pāvay rāh.*
ਸੁਣਿਐ ਹਾਥ ਹੋਵੈ ਅਸਗਾਹੁ॥	*Suṇiyai hāth hovai asgāh.*
ਨਾਨਕ ਭਗਤਾ ਸਦਾ ਵਿਗਾਸੁ॥	*Nanak bhagta sada vigās.*
ਸੁਣਿਐ ਦੂਖ ਪਾਪ ਕਾ ਨਾਸੁ॥੧੧॥	*Suṇiyai dūkh pāp ka nās.*

Pauṛi 12

ਮੰਨੇ ਕੀ ਗਤਿ ਕਹੀ ਨ ਜਾਇ॥	*Mannay ki gat kahi na jāye.*
ਜੇ ਕੋ ਕਹੈ ਪਿਛੈ ਪਛੁਤਾਇ॥	*Je ko kahai pichhai pachhatāye.*
ਕਾਗਦਿ ਕਲਮ ਨ ਲਿਖਣਹਾਰੁ॥	*Kāgad kalam na likhaṇhār.*
ਮੰਨੇ ਕਾ ਬਹਿ ਕਰਨਿ ਵੀਚਾਰੁ॥	*Mannay ka beh karan vīchār.*
ਐਸਾ ਨਾਮੁ ਨਿਰੰਜਨੁ ਹੋਇ॥	*Aisa nām niranjan hoye.*
ਜੇ ਕੋ ਮੰਨਿ ਜਾਣੈ ਮਨਿ ਕੋਇ॥੧੨॥	*Je ko mann jāṇai mann koye.*

Pauṛi 13

ਮੰਨੈ ਸੁਰਤਿ ਹੋਵੈ ਮਨਿ ਬੁਧਿ॥	*Mannai surat hovai mann budh.*
ਮੰਨੈ ਸਗਲ ਭਵਣ ਕੀ ਸੁਧਿ॥	*Mannai sagal bhavaṇ ki sudh.*
ਮੰਨੈ ਮੁਹਿ ਚੋਟਾ ਨਾ ਖਾਇ॥	*Mannai muh chotta na khāye.*

ਮੰਨੈ ਜਮ ਕੈ ਸਾਥਿ ਨ ਜਾਇ॥	*Mannai jamm kay sāth na jāye.*
ਐਸਾ ਨਾਮੁ ਨਿਰੰਜਨੁ ਹੋਇ॥	*Aisa nām niranjaṇ hoye.*
ਜੇ ਕੋ ਮੰਨਿ ਜਾਣੈ ਮਨਿ ਕੋਇ॥੧੩॥	*Je ko mann jāṇai mann koye.*

Pauṛi 14

ਮੰਨੈ ਮਾਰਗਿ ਠਾਕ ਨ ਪਾਇ॥	*Mannai mārag tthāk na pāye.*
ਮੰਨੈ ਪਤਿ ਸਿਉ ਪਰਗਟੁ ਜਾਇ॥	*Mannai pat(i) sio pargatt jāye.*
ਮੰਨੈ ਮਗੁ ਨ ਚਲੈ ਪੰਥੁ॥	*Mannai magg na chalai panth.*
ਮੰਨੈ ਧਰਮ ਸੇਤੀ ਸਨਬੰਧੁ॥	*Mannai dharma seti sanbandh.*
ਐਸਾ ਨਾਮ ਨਿਰੰਜਨੁ ਹੋਇ॥	*Aisa nām niranjan hoye.*
ਜੇ ਕੋ ਮੰਨਿ ਜਾਣੈ ਮਨਿ ਕੋਇ॥੧੪॥	*Je ko mann jāṇai mann koye.*

Pauṛi 15

ਮੰਨੈ ਪਾਵਹਿ ਮੋਖੁ ਦੁਆਰੁ॥	*Mannai pāveh mokh duār.*
ਮੰਨੈ ਪਰਵਾਰੈ ਸਾਧਾਰੁ॥	*Mannai parvāray sādhār.*
ਮੰਨੈ ਤਰੈ ਤਾਰੇ ਗੁਰੁ ਸਿਖ॥	*Mannai tarai tāray gur sikh.*
ਮੰਨੈ ਨਾਨਕ ਭਵਹਿ ਨ ਭਿਖ॥	*Mannai Nanak bhaveh na bhikh.*
ਐਸਾ ਨਾਮੁ ਨਿਰੰਜਨੁ ਹੋਇ॥	*Aisa nām niranjan hoye.*
ਜੇ ਕੋ ਮੰਨਿ ਜਾਣੈ ਮਨਿ ਕੋਇ॥੧੫॥	*Je ko mann jāṇai mann koye.*

Pauṛi 16

ਪੰਚ ਪਰਵਾਣ ਪੰਚ ਪਰਧਾਨੁ॥	*Panch parwāṇ panch pardhān.*
ਪੰਚੇ ਪਾਵਹਿ ਦਰਗਹਿ ਮਾਨੁ॥	*Panchay pāvay dargay mān.*
ਪੰਚੇ ਸੋਹਹਿ ਦਰਿ ਰਾਜਾਨੁ॥	*Panchay sohay dar(i) rājān.*
ਪੰਚਾ ਕਾ ਗੁਰੁ ਏਕੁ ਧਿਆਨੁ॥	*Pancha ka gur ek dhyān.*
ਜੇ ਕੋ ਕਹੈ ਕਰੈ ਵੀਚਾਰੁ॥	*Je ko kahai karai vīchār.*
ਕਰਤੇ ਕੈ ਕਰਣੈ ਨਾਹੀ ਸੁਮਾਰੁ॥	*Kartay kai karṇai nāhi sumār.*
ਧੌਲੁ ਧਰਮੁ ਦਇਆ ਕਾ ਪੂਤੁ॥	*Dhaul dharam daya ka pūt.*
ਸੰਤੋਖੁ ਥਾਪਿ ਰਖਿਆ ਜਿਨਿ ਸੂਤਿ॥	*Santokh thhāp rakhiya jin sūt.*
ਜੇ ਕੋ ਬੁਝੈ ਹੋਵੈ ਸਚਿਆਰੁ॥	*Je ko bujhai hovai sachiār.*
ਧਵਲੈ ਉਪਰਿ ਕੇਤਾ ਭਾਰੁ॥	*Dhawlai uppar keta bhār.*
ਧਰਤੀ ਹੋਰੁ ਪਰੈ ਹੋਰੁ ਹੋਰੁ॥	*Dharti hor parai hor hor.*
ਤਿਸ ਤੇ ਭਾਰੁ ਤਲੈ ਕਵਣੁ ਜੋਰੁ॥	*Tis tay bhār talai kawaṇ jor.*

ਜੀਅ ਜਾਤਿ ਰੰਗਾ ਕੇ ਨਾਵ॥	*Jīw jāt ranga kay nāv.*
ਸਭਨਾ ਲਿਖਿਆ ਵੁੜੀ ਕਲਾਮ॥	*Sabhna likhiya vuṛi kalām.*
ਏਹੁ ਲੇਖਾ ਲਿਖਿ ਜਾਣੈ ਕੋਇ॥	*Eh lekha likh jāṇai koye.*
ਲੇਖਾ ਲਿਖਿਆ ਕੇਤਾ ਹੋਇ॥	*Lekha likhiya keta hoye.*
ਕੇਤਾ ਤਾਣੁ ਸੁਆਲਿਹੁ ਰੂਪੁ॥	*Keta tāṇ suwāliyo rūp.*
ਕੇਤੀ ਦਾਤਿ ਜਾਣੈ ਕੌਣੁ ਕੂਤੁ॥	*Keti dāt jāṇai kauṇ kūt.*
ਕੀਤਾ ਪਸਾਉ ਏਕੋ ਕਵਾਉ॥	*Kīta pasāo eko kavāo.*
ਤਿਸ ਤੇ ਹੋਏ ਲਖ ਦਰੀਆਉ॥	*Tis te hoye lakh darīyāo.*
ਕੁਦਰਤਿ ਕਵਣ ਕਹਾ ਵੀਚਾਰੁ॥	*Kudrat kawaṇ kaha vīchār.*
ਵਾਰਿਆ ਨ ਜਾਵਾ ਏਕ ਵਾਰ॥	*Vāriya na jāva ek vār.*
ਜੋ ਤੁਧੁ ਭਾਵੈ ਸਾਈ ਭਲੀ ਕਾਰ॥	*Ju tudh bhāvai sāyi bhali kār.*
ਤੂ ਸਦਾ ਸਲਾਮਤਿ ਨਿਰੰਕਾਰ॥ ੧੬॥	*Tu sada salāmat nirankār.*

Pauṛi 17

ਅਸੰਖ ਜਪ ਅਸੰਖ ਭਾਉ॥	*Asankh jap asankh bhāo.*
ਅਸੰਖ ਪੂਜਾ ਅਸੰਖ ਤਪ ਤਾਉ॥	*Asankh pūja asankh tapp tāo.*
ਅਸੰਖ ਗਰੰਥ ਮੁਖਿ ਵੇਦ ਪਾਠ॥	*Asankh granth mukh ved pātth*
ਅਸੰਖ ਜੋਗ ਮਨਿ ਰਹਹਿ ਉਦਾਸ॥	*Asankh jog mann rahay udās.*
ਅਸੰਖ ਭਗਤ ਗੁਣ ਗਿਆਨ ਵੀਚਾਰ॥	*Asankh bhagat guṇ gyān vīchār.*
ਅਸੰਖ ਸਤੀ ਅਸੰਖ ਦਾਤਾਰ॥	*Asankh sati asankh dātār.*
ਅਸੰਖ ਸੂਰ ਮੁਹ ਭਖ ਸਾਰ॥	*Asankh sūr muh bhakh sār.*
ਅਸੰਖ ਮੋਨਿ ਲਿਵ ਲਾਇ ਤਾਰ॥	*Asankh maun liv lāye tār.*
ਕੁਦਰਤਿ ਕਵਣ ਕਹਾ ਵੀਚਾਰੁ॥	*Kudrat kawaṇ kaha vīchār.*
ਵਾਰਿਆ ਨ ਜਾਵਾ ਏਕ ਵਾਰ॥	*Vāriya na jāva ek vār.*
ਜੋ ਤੁਧੁ ਭਾਵੈ ਸਾਈ ਭਲੀ ਕਾਰ॥	*Jo tudh bhāvai sāyi bhali kār.*
ਤੂ ਸਦਾ ਸਲਾਮਤਿ ਨਿਰੰਕਾਰ॥ ੧੭॥	*Tu sada salāmat nirankār.*

Pauṛi 18

ਅਸੰਖ ਮੂਰਖ ਅੰਧ ਘੋਰ॥	*Asankh mūrakh andh ghor.*
ਅਸੰਖ ਚੋਰ ਹਰਾਮਖੋਰ॥	*Asankh chor harāmkhor.*
ਅਸੰਖ ਅਮਰ ਕਰਿ ਜਾਹਿ ਜੋਰ॥	*Asankh amar kar jāhe jor.*
ਅਸੰਖ ਗਲਵਢ ਹਤਿਆ ਕਮਾਹਿ॥	*Asankh galwaddh hatiya kamāhe.*
ਅਸੰਖ ਪਾਪੀ ਪਾਪੁ ਕਰ ਜਾਹਿ॥	*Asankh pāpi pāp kar jāhe.*

ਅਸੰਖ ਕੂੜਿਆਰ ਕੂੜੇ ਫਿਰਾਹਿ॥	*Asankh kūṛiyār kūṛay phirāhe.*
ਅਸੰਖ ਮਲੇਛ ਮਲੁ ਭਖਿ ਖਾਹਿ॥	*Asankh malechh mal bhakh khāhe.*
ਅਸੰਖ ਨਿੰਦਕ ਸਿਰਿ ਕਰਹਿ ਭਾਰੁ॥	*Asankh nindak sir karay bhār.*
ਨਾਨਕੁ ਨੀਚੁ ਕਹੈ ਵੀਚਾਰੁ॥	*Nanak nīch kahai vīchār.*
ਵਾਰਿਆ ਨ ਜਾਵਾ ਏਕ ਵਾਰ॥	*Vāriya na jāva ek vār.*
ਜੋ ਤੁਧੁ ਭਾਵੈ ਸਾਈ ਭਲੀ ਕਾਰ॥	*Jo tudh bhāvai sāyi bhali kār.*
ਤੂ ਸਦਾ ਸਲਾਮਤਿ ਨਿਰੰਕਾਰ॥੧੮॥	*Tu sada salāmat nirankār.*

Pauṛi 19

ਅਸੰਖ ਨਾਵ ਅਸੰਖ ਥਾਵ॥	*Asankh nāv asankh thhāv.*
ਅਗੰਮ ਅਗੰਮ ਅਸੰਖ ਲੋਅ॥	*Agam agam asankh low.*
ਅਸੰਖ ਕਹਹਿ ਸਿਰਿ ਭਾਰੁ ਹੋਇ॥	*Asankh kahay sirr bhār hoye.*
ਅਖਰੀ ਨਾਮੁ ਅਖਰੀ ਸਾਲਾਹ॥	*Akhri nām akhri sālāh.*
ਅਖਰੀ ਗਿਆਨੁ ਗੀਤ ਗੁਣ ਗਾਹ॥	*Akhri gyān geet guṇ gāh.*
ਅਖਰੀ ਲਿਖਣੁ ਬੋਲਣੁ ਬਾਣਿ॥	*Akhri likhaṇ bolaṇ bāṇ.*
ਅਖਰਾ ਸਿਰਿ ਸੰਜੋਗੁ ਵਖਾਣਿ॥	*Akhra sirr sanjog vakhāṇ.*
ਜਿਨਿ ਏਹਿ ਲਿਖੇ ਤਿਸੁ ਸਿਰਿ ਨਾਹਿ॥	*Jin eh likhay tis sir(i) nāh(i).*
ਜਿਵ ਫੁਰਮਾਏ ਤਿਵ ਤਿਵ ਪਾਹਿ॥	*Jiv phurmāye tiv tiv pāh(i).*
ਜੇਤਾ ਕੀਤਾ ਤੇਤਾ ਨਾਉ॥	*Jeta kīta teta nāo.*
ਵਿਣੁ ਨਾਵੈ ਨਾਹੀ ਕੋ ਥਾਉ॥	*Viṇ nāvai nāhi ko thhāo.*
ਕੁਦਰਤਿ ਕਵਣ ਕਹਾ ਵੀਚਾਰੁ॥	*Kudrat kavaṇ kaha vīchār.*
ਵਾਰਿਆ ਨ ਜਾਵਾ ਏਕ ਵਾਰ॥	*Vāriya na jāva ek vār.*
ਜੋ ਤੁਧੁ ਭਾਵੈ ਸਾਈ ਭਲੀ ਕਾਰ॥	*Jo tudhh bhāvai sāyi bhali kār.*
ਤੂ ਸਦਾ ਸਲਾਮਤਿ ਨਿਰੰਕਾਰ॥੧੯॥	*Tu sada salāmat nirankār.*

Pauṛi 20

ਭਰੀਐ ਹਥੁ ਪੈਰੁ ਤਨੁ ਦੇਹ॥	*Bharīyai hathh paer tann deh.*
ਪਾਣੀ ਧੋਤੈ ਉਤਰਸੁ ਖੇਹ॥	*Pāṇi dhhotai utrus kheh.*
ਮੂਤ ਪਲੀਤੀ ਕਪੜੁ ਹੋਇ॥	*Mūt palīti kapaṛ hoye.*
ਦੇ ਸਾਬੂਣੁ ਲਈਐ ਓਹ ਧੋਇ॥	*De sabūṇ laīyai oh dhoye.*
ਭਰੀਐ ਮਤਿ ਪਾਪਾ ਕੈ ਸੰਗਿ॥	*Bharīyai mat(i) pāpa kai sung.*
ਓਹ ਧੋਪੈ ਨਾਵੈ ਕੈ ਰੰਗਿ॥	*Oh dhopai nāvai kai rung.*
ਪੁੰਨੀ ਪਾਪੀ ਆਖਣੁ ਨਾਹਿ॥	*Punni pāpi ākhaṇ nāhe.*

ਕਰਿ ਕਰਿ ਕਰਣਾ ਲਿਖਿ ਲੈ ਜਾਹੁ॥	*Kar kar karṇa likh lai jāh(u).*
ਆਪੇ ਬੀਜਿ ਆਪੇ ਹੀ ਖਾਹੁ॥	*Āpay bīj āpay hi khāh(u).*
ਨਾਨਕ ਹੁਕਮੀ ਆਵਹੁ ਜਾਹੁ॥੨੦॥	*Nanak hukmi āwo jāh(u).*

Pauṛi 21

ਤੀਰਥੁ ਤਪੁ ਦਇਆ ਦਤੁ ਦਾਨੁ॥	*Tīrath tap(u) daya dat(u) dān.*
ਜੇ ਕੋ ਪਾਵੈ ਤਿਲ ਕਾ ਮਾਨੁ॥	*Je ko pāvai til ka mān.*
ਸੁਣਿਆ ਮੰਨਿਆ ਮਨਿ ਕੀਤਾ ਭਾਉ॥	*Suṇiya maniya man(i) kīta bhāo.*
ਅੰਤਰਗਤਿ ਤੀਰਥਿ ਮਲਿ ਨਾਉ॥	*Antargat tīrath mul(i) nāo.*
ਸਭਿ ਗੁਣ ਤੇਰੇ ਮੈ ਨਾਹੀ ਕੋਇ॥	*Sabh guṇ teray mai nāhi koye.*
ਵਿਣੁ ਗੁਣ ਕੀਤੇ ਭਗਤਿ ਨ ਹੋਇ॥	*Viṇ guṇ kītay bhagat(i) na hoye.*
ਸੁਅਸਤਿ ਆਥਿ ਬਾਣੀ ਬਰਮਾਉ॥	*Suast āth bāṇi barmāo.*
ਸਤਿ ਸੁਹਾਣੁ ਸਦਾ ਮਨਿ ਚਾਉ॥	*Sat(i) suhāṇ sada mann chāo.*
ਕਵਣੁ ਸੁ ਵੇਲਾ ਵਖਤੁ ਕਵਣੁ ਕਵਣ ਥਿਤਿ ਕਵਣੁ ਵਾਰੁ॥	*Kavaṇ so vela vakhat kavaṇ, kavaṇ thit(i) kavaṇ vār.*
ਕਵਣਿ ਸਿ ਰੁਤੀ ਮਾਹੁ ਕਵਣੁ ਜਿਤੁ ਹੋਆ ਆਕਾਰੁ॥	*Kavaṇ se ruti mah kavaṇ jit hova ākār.*
ਵੇਲ ਨ ਪਾਈਆ ਪੰਡਤੀ ਜਿ ਹੋਵੈ ਲੇਖੁ ਪੁਰਾਣੁ॥	*Vel na pāyīa pandti je hovai lekh purāṇ.*
ਵਖਤੁ ਨ ਪਾਇਓ ਕਾਦੀਆ ਜਿ ਲਿਖਨਿ ਲੇਖੁ ਕੁਰਾਣੁ॥	*Vakht na pāyio kādīya je likhan lekh Korāṇ.*
ਥਿਤਿ ਵਾਰੁ ਨਾ ਜੋਗੀ ਜਾਣੈ ਰੁਤਿ ਮਾਹੁ ਨਾ ਕੋਈ॥	*Thit(i) vār na jogi jāṇai rut(i) māh na koyi.*
ਜਾ ਕਰਤਾ ਸਿਰਠੀ ਕਉ ਸਾਜੇ ਆਪੇ ਜਾਣੈ ਸੋਈ॥	*Ja karta sirtthi kau sājay āpay jāṇai soyi.*
ਕਿਵ ਕਰਿ ਆਖਾ ਕਿਵ ਸਾਲਾਹੀ ਕਿਉ ਵਰਨੀ ਕਿਵ ਜਾਣਾ॥	*Kiv kar ākha kiv sālāhi kiv vārni kiv jāṇā.*
ਨਾਨਕ ਆਖਣਿ ਸਭੁ ਕੋ ਆਖੈ ਇਕ ਦੂ ਇਕੁ ਸਿਆਣਾ॥	*Nanak ākhaṇ sabh ko ākhai ik du ik syāṇa.*
ਵਡਾ ਸਾਹਿਬੁ ਵਡੀ ਨਾਈ ਕੀਤਾ ਜਾ ਕਾ ਹੋਵੈ॥	*Vadda sahib vaddi nāyi kīta jāka hovai.*
ਨਾਨਕ ਜੇ ਕੋ ਆਪੌ ਜਾਣੈ ਅਗੈ ਗਇਆ ਨ ਸੋਹੈ॥੨੧॥	*Nanak je ko āpau jāṇai aggai gaya na sohai.*

Pauṛi 22

ਪਾਤਾਲਾ ਪਾਤਾਲ ਲਖ ਆਗਾਸਾ ਆਗਾਸ॥	*Pātāla pātāl lakh āgāsa āgās.*
ਓੜਕ ਓੜਕ ਭਾਲਿ ਥਕੇ ਵੇਦ ਕਹਨਿ ਇਕ ਵਾਤ॥	*Oṛak oṛak bhāl thakay ved kahan Ik vāt.*
ਸਹਸ ਅਠਾਰਹ ਕਹਨਿ ਕਤੇਬਾ ਅਸੁਲੂ ਇਕੁ ਧਾਤੁ॥	*Sahas atthārāh kahan kateba asloo Ik dhāt.*
ਲੇਖਾ ਹੋਇ ਤ ਲਿਖੀਐ ਲੇਖੈ ਹੋਇ ਵਿਣਾਸੁ॥	*Lekha hoye ta likhīyai lekhai hoye viṇās.*
ਨਾਨਕ ਵਡਾ ਆਖੀਐ ਆਪੇ ਜਾਣੈ ਆਪੁ॥੨੨॥	*Nanak vadda ākhiyai āpay jāṇai āp.*

Pauṛi 23

ਸਾਲਾਹੀ ਸਾਲਾਹਿ ਏਤੀ ਸੁਰਤਿ ਨ ਪਾਈਆ॥	*Sālāhi sālāh eti surt(i) na pāyīa.*
ਨਦੀਆ ਅਤੈ ਵਾਹ ਪਵਹਿ ਸਮੁੰਦਿ ਨ ਜਾਣੀਅਹਿ॥	*Nadīya atai vāh paveh samund na jāṇīye.*
ਸਮੁੰਦ ਸਾਹ ਸੁਲਤਾਨ ਗਿਰਹਾ ਸੇਤੀ ਮਾਲੁ ਧਨੁ॥	*Samund sāh sultān girha seti māl dhan.*
ਕੀੜੀ ਤੁਲਿ ਨ ਹੋਵਨੀ ਜੇ ਤਿਸੁ ਮਨਹੁ ਨ ਵੀਸਰਹਿ॥੨੩॥	*Kīṛi tul na hovni je tis manhu na vīsray.*

Pauṛi 24

ਅੰਤੁ ਨ ਸਿਫਤੀ ਕਹਣਿ ਨ ਅੰਤੁ॥	*Unt na sifti kahaṇ na unt.*
ਅੰਤ ਨ ਕਰਣੈ ਦੇਣਿ ਨ ਅੰਤੁ॥	*Unt na karṇai deiṇ na unt.*
ਅੰਤੁ ਨ ਵੇਖਣਿ ਸੁਣਣਿ ਨ ਅੰਤੁ॥	*Unt na vekhaṇ suṇaṇ na unt.*
ਅੰਤੁ ਨ ਜਾਪੈ ਕਿਆ ਮਨਿ ਮੰਤੁ॥	*Unt na jāpai kiya man(i) munt.*
ਅੰਤੁ ਨ ਜਾਪੈ ਕੀਤਾ ਆਕਾਰੁ॥	*Unt na jāpai kīta ākār.*
ਅੰਤੁ ਨ ਜਾਪੈ ਪਾਰਾਵਾਰੁ॥	*Unt na jāpai parāvār.*
ਅੰਤੁ ਕਾਰਣਿ ਕੇਤੇ ਬਿਲਲਾਹਿ॥	*Unt kāraṇ ketay billāhe.*
ਤਾ ਕੇ ਅੰਤ ਨ ਪਾਏ ਜਾਹਿ॥	*Ta kay unt na pāye jāhe.*
ਏਹੁ ਅੰਤੁ ਨ ਜਾਣੈ ਕੋਇ॥	*Eh unt na jāṇai koye.*
ਬਹੁਤਾ ਕਹੀਐ ਬਹੁਤਾ ਹੋਇ॥	*Bahuta kahīyai bahuta hoye.*
ਵਡਾ ਸਾਹਿਬੁ ਊਚਾ ਥਾਉ॥	*Vadda sahib ūcha thāo.*

ਊਚੇ ਉਪਰਿ ਊਚਾ ਨਾਉ॥	*Ūchay ūpar ūcha nāo.*
ਏਵਡੁ ਊਚਾ ਹੋਵੈ ਕੋਇ॥	*Evadd ūcha hovai koye.*
ਤਿਸੁ ਊਚੇ ਕਉ ਜਾਣੈ ਸੋਇ॥	*Tis ūche ko jāṇai soye.*
ਜੇਵਡੁ ਆਪਿ ਜਾਣੈ ਆਪਿ ਆਪਿ॥	*Jevadd āp jāṇai āp āp.*
ਨਾਨਕ ਨਦਰੀ ਕਰਮੀ ਦਾਤਿ॥੨੪॥	*Nanak nadri karmi dāt.*

Pauṛi 25

ਬਹੁਤਾ ਕਰਮੁ ਲਿਖਿਆ ਨਾ ਜਾਇ॥	*Bahuta karam likhiya na jāye.*
ਵਡਾ ਦਾਤਾ ਤਿਲੁ ਨ ਤਮਾਇ॥	*Vadda dāta til na tamāye.*
ਕੇਤੇ ਮੰਗਹਿ ਜੋਧ ਅਪਾਰ॥	*Ketia mangay jodh apār.*
ਕੇਤਿਆ ਗਣਤ ਨਹੀ ਵੀਚਾਰੁ॥	*Ketia gaṇat nahi vīchār.*
ਕੇਤੇ ਖਪਿ ਤੁਟਹਿ ਵੇਕਾਰ॥	*Ketia khap tutteh vekār.*
ਕੇਤੇ ਲੈ ਲੈ ਮੁਕਰੁ ਪਾਹਿ॥	*Ketia lai lai mukar pāhe.*
ਕੇਤੇ ਮੂਰਖ ਖਾਹੀ ਖਾਹਿ॥	*Ketia mūrakh khāhi khāhe.*
ਕੇਤਿਆ ਦੂਖ ਭੂਖ ਸਦ ਮਾਰ॥	*Ketia dūkh bhūkh sad mār.*
ਏਹਿ ਭਿ ਦਾਤਿ ਤੇਰੀ ਦਾਤਾਰ॥	*Eh bhi dāt teri dātār.*
ਬੰਦਿ ਖਲਾਸੀ ਭਾਣੈ ਹੋਇ॥	*Bund khalāsi bhānai hoye.*
ਹੋਰੁ ਆਖਿ ਨ ਸਕੈ ਕੋਇ॥	*Hor ākh na sakai koye.*
ਜੇ ਕੋ ਖਾਇਕੁ ਆਖਣਿ ਪਾਇ॥	*Je ko khāyak ākhaṇ pāye.*
ਓਹ ਜਾਣੈ ਜੇਤੀਆ ਮੁਹਿ ਖਾਇ॥	*Oh jāṇai jetīya muh khāye.*
ਆਪੇ ਜਾਣੈ ਆਪੇ ਦੇਇ॥	*Āpay jāṇai āpay day.*
ਆਖਹਿ ਸਿ ਭਿ ਕੇਈ ਕੇਇ॥	*Ākhay se bhi keyi kay.*
ਜਿਸ ਨੋ ਬਖਸੇ ਸਿਫਤਿ ਸਾਲਾਹ॥	*Jis no bakhse sift salāh.*
ਨਾਨਕ ਪਾਤਿਸਾਹੀ ਪਾਤਿਸਾਹੁ॥੨੫॥	*Nanak pātsāhi pātsāh.*

Pauṛi 26

ਅਮੁਲ ਗੁਣ ਅਮੁਲ ਵਾਪਾਰ॥	*Amul guṇ amul vāpār.*
ਅਮੁਲ ਵਾਪਾਰੀਏ ਅਮੁਲ ਭੰਡਾਰ॥	*Amul vāpārīye amul bhanddār.*
ਅਮੁਲ ਆਵਹਿ ਅਮੁਲ ਲੈ ਜਾਹਿ॥	*Amul āveh amul lai jāhe.*
ਅਮੁਲ ਭਾਇ ਅਮੁਲਾ ਸਮਾਹਿ॥	*Amul bhaye amula samāhe.*
ਅਮੁਲੁ ਧਰਮੁ ਅਮੁਲੁ ਦੀਬਾਣੁ॥	*Amul dharam amul dībāṇ.*
ਅਮੁਲੁ ਤੁਲੁ ਅਮੁਲੁ ਪਰਵਾਣੁ॥	*Amul tul amul parvāṇ.*

ਅਮੁਲੁ ਬਖਸੀਸ ਅਮੁਲੁ ਨੀਸਾਣੁ॥	*Amul bakhsīs amul nīsāṇ.*
ਅਮੁਲੁ ਕਰਮੁ ਅਮੁਲੁ ਫੁਰਮਾਣੁ॥	*Amul karam amul phurmāṇ.*
ਅਮੁਲੋ ਅਮੁਲੁ ਆਖਿਆ ਨ ਜਾਇ॥	*Amulo amul ākhiya na jāye.*
ਆਖਿ ਆਖਿ ਰਹੇ ਲਿਵ ਲਾਇ॥	*Ākh ākh rahay liv lāye.*
ਆਖਹਿ ਵੇਦ ਪਾਠ ਪੁਰਾਣ॥	*Ākheh ved pātth purāṇ.*
ਆਖਹਿ ਪੜੇ ਕਰਹਿ ਵਖਿਆਣ॥	*Ākheh paṛeh karay vakhiyāṇ.*
ਆਖਹਿ ਬਰਮੇ ਆਖਹਿ ਇੰਦ॥	*Ākheh barmay ākheh ind.*
ਆਖਹਿ ਗੋਪੀ ਤੈ ਗੋਵਿੰਦ॥	*Ākheh gopi tai govind.*
ਆਖਹਿ ਈਸਰ ਆਖਹਿ ਸਿਧ॥	*Ākheh Īssar ākheh sidh.*
ਆਖਹਿ ਕੇਤੇ ਕੀਤੇ ਬੁਧ॥	*Ākheh ketay kītay budh.*
ਆਖਹਿ ਦਾਨਵ ਆਖਹਿ ਦੇਵ॥	*Ākheh dānav ākheh dev.*
ਆਖਹਿ ਸੁਰਿ ਨਰ ਮੁਨਿ ਜਨ ਸੇਵ॥	*Ākheh sur nar mun jan sev.*
ਕੇਤੇ ਆਖਹਿ ਆਖਣਿ ਪਾਹਿ॥	*Ketay ākheh ākhaṇ pāhe.*
ਕੇਤੇ ਕਹਿ ਕਹਿ ਉਠਿ ਉਠਿ ਜਾਹਿ॥	*Ketay kah kah utth utth jāhe.*
ਏਤੇ ਕੀਤੇ ਹੋਰਿ ਕਰੇਹਿ॥	*Etay kītay hor kareh.*
ਤਾ ਆਖਿ ਨ ਸਕਹਿ ਕੇਈ ਕੇਇ॥	*Ta ākh na sakeh keyi kay.*
ਜੇਵਡੁ ਭਾਵੈ ਤੇਵਡੁ ਹੋਇ॥	*Jevadd bhāvai tevadd hoye.*
ਨਾਨਕ ਜਾਣੈ ਸਾਚਾ ਸੋਇ॥	*Nanak jāṇai sacha soye.*
ਜੇ ਕੋ ਆਖੈ ਬੋਲੁਵਿਗਾੜੁ॥	*Je ko ākhay bolvigāṛ.*
ਤਾ ਲਿਖੀਐ ਸਿਰਿ ਗਾਵਾਰਾ ਗਾਵਾਰੁ॥੨੬॥	*Ta likīyai sir gāvāra gāvār.*

Pauṛi 27

ਸੋ ਦਰੁ ਕੇਹਾ ਸੋ ਘਰੁ ਕੇਹਾ ਜਿਤੁ ਬਹਿ ਸਰਬ ਸਮਾਲੇ॥	*So dar keha so ghar keha jit beh sarab samālay.*
ਵਾਜੇ ਨਾਦ ਅਨੇਕ ਅਸੰਖਾ ਕੇਤੇ ਵਾਵਣਹਾਰੇ॥	*Vājay nād anek asankha ketay vāvaṇhāray.*
ਕੇਤੇ ਰਾਗ ਪਰੀ ਸਿਉ ਕਹੀਅਨਿ ਕੇਤੇ ਗਾਵਣਹਾਰੇ॥	*Ketay rāg pari siu kahīan ketay gāvaṇhāray.*
ਗਾਵਹਿ ਤੁਹਨੋ ਪਉਣੁ ਪਾਣੀ ਬੈਸੰਤਰੁ ਗਾਵੈ ਰਾਜਾ ਧਰਮੁ ਦੁਆਰੇ॥	*Gāveh tuhno pauṇ pāṇi baisantar gāvan rāja dharam duāray.*
ਗਾਵਹਿ ਚਿਤੁ ਗੁਪਤੁ ਲਿਖਿ ਜਾਣਹਿ ਲਿਖਿ ਲਿਖਿ ਧਰਮੁ ਵੀਚਾਰੇ॥	*Gāveh Chit Gupt likh jaṇeh likh likh dharam vīchāray.*
ਗਾਵਹਿ ਈਸਰੁ ਬਰਮਾ ਦੇਵੀ ਸੋਹਨਿ	*Gāveh Īssar Barma Devi sohan sada*

ਸਦਾ ਸਵਾਰੇ॥	*sawāray.*
ਗਾਵਹਿ ਇੰਦ ਇਦਾਸਣਿ ਬੈਠੇ ਦੇਵਤਿਆ	*Gāvay Ind indāsaṇ baitthay devtia*
ਦਰਿ ਨਾਲੇ॥	*dar nālay.*
ਗਾਵਹਿ ਸਿਧ ਸਮਾਧੀ ਅੰਦਰਿ ਗਾਵਨਿ	*Gāveh sidh samādhi andar gāvaṇ*
ਸਾਧ ਵਿਚਾਰੇ॥	*sādh vichāray.*
ਗਾਵਨਿ ਜਤੀ ਸਤੀ ਸੰਤੋਖੀ ਗਾਵਹਿ	*Gāvan jati sati santokhi gāveh vīr*
ਵੀਰ ਕਰਾਰੇ॥	*karāray.*
ਗਾਵਨਿ ਪੰਡਿਤ ਪੜਨਿ ਰਖੀਸਰ ਜੁਗੁ ਜੁਗੁ	*Gāvan pandit paṛan rakhīsar jug jug*
ਵੇਦਾ ਨਾਲੇ॥	*veda nālay.*
ਗਾਵਹਿ ਮੋਹਣੀਆ ਮਨੁ ਮੋਹਨਿ	*Gāveh mohṇīya man mohan surga*
ਸੁਰਗਾ ਮਛ ਪਇਆਲੇ॥	*machh payiālay.*
ਗਾਵਨਿ ਰਤਨ ਉਪਾਏ ਤੇਰੇ ਅਠਸਠਿ	*Gāvan ratan upāye tere atthsathh*
ਤੀਰਥ ਨਾਲੇ॥	*tīrath nālay.*
ਗਾਵਹਿ ਜੋਧ ਮਹਾਬਲ ਸੂਰਾ ਗਾਵਹਿ	*Gāveh jodh mahābal sūra gāveh khāṇi*
ਖਾਣੀ ਚਾਰੇ॥	*chāray.*
ਗਾਵਹਿ ਖੰਡ ਮੰਡਲ ਵਰਭੰਡਾ ਕਰਿ ਕਰਿ	*Gāveh khandd manddal varbhāndda*
ਰਖੇ ਧਾਰੇ॥	*kar kar rakhay dhāray.*
ਸੇਈ ਤੁਧੁਨੋ ਗਾਵਹਿ ਜੋ ਤੁਧੁ ਭਾਵਨਿ	*Seyi tudhno gāveh jo tudh bhāvan ratay*
ਰਤੇ ਤੇਰੇ ਭਗਤ ਰਸਾਲੇ॥	*teray bhagat rasālay.*
ਹੋਰੀ ਕੇਤੇ ਗਾਵਨਿ ਸੇ ਮੈ ਚਿਤਿ ਨ	*Hor ketay gāvan se mai chit na āvan*
ਆਵਨਿ ਨਾਨਕੁ ਕਿਆ ਵੀਚਾਰੇ॥	*Nanak kia vīchāray.*
ਸੋਈ ਸੋਈ ਸਦਾ ਸਚੁ ਸਾਹਿਬੁ ਸਾਚਾ	*Soyi soyi sada sach sahib sācha sāchi*
ਸਾਚੀ ਨਾਈ॥	*nāyi.*
ਹੈ ਭੀ ਹੋਸੀ ਜਾਇ ਨ ਜਾਸੀ ਰਚਨਾ	*Hai bhi hosi jāye na jāsi rachna jin*
ਜਿਨਿ ਰਚਾਈ॥	*rachāyi.*
ਰੰਗੀ ਰੰਗੀ ਭਾਤੀ ਕਰਿ ਕਰਿ ਜਿਨਸੀ	*Rangi rangi bhāti kar kar jinsi māya*
ਮਾਇਆ ਜਿਨਿ ਉਪਾਈ॥	*jin upāyi.*
ਕਰਿ ਕਰਿ ਵੇਖੈ ਕੀਤਾ ਆਪਣਾ ਜਿਵ	*Kar kar vekhai kīta āpṇa jiv tis di*
ਤਿਸ ਦੀ ਵਡਿਆਈ॥	*vaddīāyi.*
ਜੋ ਤਿਸੁ ਭਾਵੈ ਸੋਈ ਕਰਸੀ ਹੁਕਮੁ	*Jo tis bhāvai soyi karsi hukam na*
ਨ ਕਰਣਾ ਜਾਈ॥	*karṇa jāyi.*
ਸੋ ਪਾਤਿਸਾਹੁ ਸਾਹਾ ਪਾਤਿਸਾਹਿਬੁ ਨਾਨਕ	*So pātsāh saha pātsāhib Nanak*
ਰਹਣੁ ਰਜਾਈ॥੨੭॥	*rahaṇ rajāyi.*

Pauṛi 28

ਮੁੰਦਾ ਸੰਤੋਖੁ ਸਰਮੁ ਪਤੁ ਝੋਲੀ ਧਿਆਨ ਕੀ ਕਰਹਿ ਬਿਭੂਤਿ॥	*Munda santokh saram pat(u) jholi dhyān ki kareh bibhūt.*
ਖਿੰਥਾ ਕਾਲੁ ਕੁਆਰੀ ਕਾਇਆ ਜੁਗਤਿ ਡੰਡਾ ਪਰਤੀਤਿ॥	*Khinthha kāl kuāri kāya jugat dandda partīt.*
ਆਈ ਪੰਥੀ ਸਗਲ ਜਮਾਤੀ ਮਨਿ ਜੀਤੈ ਜਗੁ ਜੀਤੁ॥	*Āyi panthi sagal jamāti man(i) jītay jagg jīt.*
ਆਦੇਸੁ ਤਿਸੈ ਆਦੇਸੁ॥	*Ādeis tisai ādeis.*
ਆਦਿ ਅਨੀਲੁ ਅਨਾਦਿ ਅਨਾਹਤਿ ਜੁਗੁ ਜੁਗੁ ਏਕੋ ਵੇਸੁ॥੨੮॥	*Ād anīl anād anāhit jugg jugg eko veis.*

Pauṛi 29

ਭੁਗਤਿ ਗਿਆਨੁ ਦਇਆ ਭੰਡਾਰਣਿ ਘਟਿ ਘਟਿ ਵਾਜਹਿ ਨਾਦ॥	*Bhugat gyān daya bhanddāriṇ ghatt ghatt vājay nād.*
ਆਪਿ ਨਾਥੁ ਨਾਥੀ ਸਭ ਜਾ ਕੀ ਰਿਧਿ ਸਿਧਿ ਅਵਰਾ ਸਾਦ॥	*Āp nāth nāthi sabh ja ki ridh sidh awra sād.*
ਸੰਜੋਗੁ ਵਿਜੋਗੁ ਦੁਇ ਕਾਰ ਚਲਾਵਹਿ ਲੇਖੇ ਆਵਹਿ ਭਾਗ॥	*Sanjog vijog doye kār chalāveh lekhay āvay bhāg.*
ਆਦੇਸੁ ਤਿਸੈ ਆਦੇਸੁ॥	*Ādeis tisai ādeis.*
ਆਦਿ ਅਨੀਲੁ ਅਨਾਦਿ ਅਨਾਹਤਿ ਜੁਗੁ ਜੁਗੁ ਏਕੋ ਵੇਸੁ॥੨੯॥	*Ād anīl anād anāhit jugg jugg eko veis.*

Pauṛi 30

ਏਕਾ ਮਾਈ ਜੁਗਤਿ ਵਿਆਈ ਤਿਨਿ ਚੇਲੇ ਪਰਵਾਣੁ॥	*Eka māyi jugut viāyi tin chelay parvāṇ.*
ਇਕੁ ਸੰਸਾਰੀ ਇਕੁ ਭੰਡਾਰੀ ਇਕੁ ਲਾਏ ਦੀਬਾਣੁ॥	*Ik sansāri ik bhanddāri ik lāye dībāṇ.*
ਜਿਵ ਤਿਸੁ ਭਾਵੈ ਤਿਵੈ ਚਲਾਵੈ ਜਿਵ ਹੋਵੈ ਫੁਰਮਾਣੁ॥	*Jiv tis bhāvai tivai chalāvai jiv hovai phurmāṇ.*
ਓਹੁ ਵੇਖੈ ਓਨਾ ਨਦਰਿ ਨ ਆਵੈ ਬਹੁਤਾ ਏਹੁ ਵਿਡਾਣੁ॥	*Oh vekhai ona nadar na āvai bahuta eh viddāṇ.*
ਆਦੇਸੁ ਤਿਸੈ ਆਦੇਸੁ॥	*Ādeis tisai ādeis.*

ਆਦਿ ਅਨੀਲੁ ਅਨਾਦਿ ਅਨਾਹਤਿ ਜੁਗੁ ਜੁਗੁ ਏਕੋ ਵੇਸੁ॥ ੩੦॥	*Ād anīl anād anāhit jugg jugg eko veis.*

Pauṛi 31

ਆਸਣੁ ਲੋਇ ਲੋਇ ਭੰਡਾਰ॥	*Āsaṇ loye loye bhanddār.*
ਜੋ ਕਿਛੁ ਪਾਇਆ ਸੁ ਏਕਾ ਵਾਰ॥	*Jo kichh pāiya su eka vār.*
ਕਰਿ ਕਰਿ ਵੇਖੈ ਸਿਰਜਣਹਾਰੁ॥	*Kar kar vekhai sirjaṇhār.*
ਨਾਨਕ ਸਚੇ ਕੀ ਸਾਚੀ ਕਾਰ॥	*Nanak sachay ki sāchi kār.*
ਆਦੇਸੁ ਤਿਸੈ ਆਦੇਸੁ॥	*Ādeis tisai ādeis.*
ਆਦਿ ਅਨੀਲੁ ਅਨਾਦਿ ਅਨਾਹਤਿ	*Ād anīl anād anāhit.*
ਜੁਗੁ ਜੁਗੁ ਏਕੋ ਵੇਸੁ॥ ੩੧॥	*Jugg jugg eko veis.*

Pauṛi 32

ਇਕ ਦੂ ਜੀਭੌ ਲਖ ਹੋਹਿ ਲਖ ਹੋਵਹਿ ਲਖ ਵੀਸ॥	*Ik doo jībhau lakh hoye lakh hoveh lakh vīs.*
ਲਖੁ ਲਖੁ ਗੇੜਾ ਆਖੀਅਹਿ ਏਕੁ ਨਾਮੁ ਜਗਦੀਸ॥	*lakh lakh geṛa ākhiye ek nām jagdīs.*
ਏਤੁ ਰਾਹਿ ਪਤਿ ਪਵੜੀਆ ਚੜੀਐ ਹੋਇ ਇਕੀਸ॥	*Et rāh pat pavṛīya chaṛīyai hoye ikīs.*
ਸੁਣਿ ਗਲਾ ਆਕਾਸ ਕੀ ਕੀਟਾ ਆਈ ਰੀਸ॥	*Suṇ galla akās ki kītta āyi rīs.*
ਨਾਨਕ ਨਦਰੀ ਪਾਈਐ ਕੂੜੀ ਕੂੜੈ ਠੀਸ॥ ੩੨॥	*Nanak nadri pāyiai kūṛi kūṛai tthīs.*

Pauṛi 33

ਆਖਣਿ ਜੋਰੁ ਚੁਪੈ ਨਹ ਜੋਰੁ॥	*Ākhaṇ jor chupai nāh jor.*
ਜੋਰੁ ਨ ਮੰਗਣਿ ਦੇਣਿ ਨ ਜੋਰੁ॥	*Jor na mangaṇ deiṇ na jor.*
ਜੋਰੁ ਨ ਜੀਵਣਿ ਮਰਣਿ ਨਹ ਜੋਰੁ॥	*Jor na jīvaṇ maraṇ nāh jor.*
ਜੋਰੁ ਨ ਰਾਜਿ ਮਾਲਿ ਮਨਿ ਸੋਰੁ॥	*Jor na rāj māl mann sor.*
ਜੋਰੁ ਨ ਸੁਰਤੀ ਗਿਆਨਿ ਵੀਚਾਰਿ॥	*Jor na surti gyān vīchār.*
ਜੋਰੁ ਨ ਜੁਗਤੀ ਛੁਟੈ ਸੰਸਾਰੁ॥	*Jor na jugti chhuttai sansār.*
ਜਿਸੁ ਹਥਿ ਜੋਰੁ ਕਰਿ ਵੇਖੈ ਸੋਇ॥	*Jis hath jor kar vekhai soye.*
ਨਾਨਕ ਉਤਮੁ ਨੀਚੁ ਨ ਕੋਇ॥ ੩੩॥	*Nanak utam nīch na koye.*

Pauṛi 34

ਰਾਤੀ ਰੁਤੀ ਥਿਤੀ ਵਾਰ।।	*Rāti ruti thhiti vār.*
ਪਵਣ ਪਾਣੀ ਅਗਨੀ ਪਾਤਾਲ।।	*Pavaṇ pāṇi agni pātāl.*
ਤਿਸੁ ਵਿਚਿ ਧਰਤੀ ਥਾਪਿ ਰਖੀ ਧਰਮ ਸਾਲ।।	*Tis vich dharti thhāp rakhi dharam sāl.*
ਤਿਸੁ ਵਿਚਿ ਜੀਅ ਜੁਗਤਿ ਕੇ ਰੰਗ।।	*Tis vich jīw jugat(i) kay rung.*
ਤਿਨ ਕੇ ਨਾਮ ਅਨੇਕ ਅਨੰਤ।।	*Tin kay nām anek anant.*
ਕਰਮੀ ਕਰਮੀ ਹੋਇ ਵੀਚਾਰੁ।।	*Karmi karmi hoye vīchār.*
ਸਚਾ ਆਪਿ ਸਚਾ ਦਰਬਾਰੁ।।	*Sacha āp sacha darbār.*
ਤਿਥੈ ਸੋਹਨਿ ਪੰਚ ਪਰਵਾਣੁ।।	*Tithhai sohan panch parvāṇ.*
ਨਦਰੀ ਕਰਮਿ ਪਵੈ ਨੀਸਾਣੁ।।	*Nadri karm pavai nisāṇ.*
ਕਚ ਪਕਾਈ ਓਥੈ ਪਾਇ।।	*Kach pakāyi othhai pāye.*
ਨਾਨਕ ਗਇਆ ਜਾਪੈ ਜਾਇ।। ੩੪।।	*Nanak gaya jāpai jāye.*

Pauṛi 35

ਧਰਮ ਖੰਡ ਕਾ ਏਹੋ ਧਰਮੁ।।	*Dharam khandd ka eho dharam.*
ਗਿਆਨ ਖੰਡ ਕਾ ਆਖਹੁ ਕਰਮੁ।।	*Gyān khandd ka ākho karam.*
ਕੇਤੇ ਪਵਣ ਪਾਣੀ ਵੈਸੰਤਰ ਕੇਤੇ ਕਾਨ ਮਹੇਸ।।	*Ketay pavaṇ pāṇi vaisantar ketay kān mahes.*
ਕੇਤੇ ਬਰਮੇ ਘਾੜਤਿ ਘੜੀਅਹਿ ਰੂਪ ਰੰਗ ਕੇ ਵੇਸ।।	*Ketay barmay ghāṛat ghaṛīay rūp rung kay veis.*
ਕੇਤੀਆ ਕਰਮ ਭੂਮੀ ਮੇਰ ਕੇਤੇ ਕੇਤੇ ਧੂ ਉਪਦੇਸ।।	*Ketīya karam bhūmi mer ketay ketay dhoo updeis.*
ਕੇਤੇ ਇੰਦ ਚੰਦ ਸੂਰ ਕੇਤੇ ਕੇਤੇ ਮੰਡਲ ਦੇਸ ।।	*Ketay ind chand, sūr ketay, ketay manddal deis.*
ਕੇਤੇ ਸਿਧ ਬੁਧ ਨਾਥ ਕੇਤੇ ਕੇਤੇ ਦੇਵੀ ਵੇਸ।।	*Ketay sidh budh nāth ketay ketay devi veis.*
ਕੇਤੇ ਦੇਵ ਦਾਨਵ ਮੁਨਿ ਕੇਤੇ ਕੇਤੇ ਰਤਨ ਸਮੁੰਦ।।	*Ketay dev dānav, munn ketay, ketay ratan samund.*
ਕੇਤੀਆ ਖਾਣੀ ਕੇਤੀਆ ਬਾਣੀ ਕੇਤੇ ਪਾਤ ਨਰਿੰਦ।।	*Ketīya khāṇi ketīya bāṇi ketay pāt narind.*
ਕੇਤੀਆ ਸੁਰਤੀ ਸੇਵਕ ਕੇਤੇ ਨਾਨਕ ਅੰਤੁ ਨ ਅੰਤੁ।। ੩੫।।	*Ketīya surti sevak ketay Nanak unt na unt.*

Pauṛi 36

ਗਿਆਨ ਖੰਡ ਮਹਿ ਗਿਆਨੁ ਪਰਚੰਡੁ॥	*Gyān khandd meh gyān parchandd.*
ਤਿਥੈ ਨਾਦ ਬਿਨੋਦ ਕੋਡ ਅਨੰਦੁ॥	*Tithhai nād binod kodd anand.*
ਸਰਮ ਖੰਡ ਕੀ ਬਾਣੀ ਰੂਪੁ॥	*Saram khandd ki bāṇi rūp.*
ਤਿਥੈ ਘਾੜਤਿ ਘੜੀਐ ਬਹੁਤੁ ਅਨੂਪੁ॥	*Tithhai ghāṛat ghaṛīai bahut anūp.*
ਤਾ ਕੀਆ ਗਲਾ ਕਥੀਆ ਨਾ ਜਾਹਿ॥	*Ta kīya galla kathhīya na jāhe.*
ਜੇ ਕੋ ਕਹੈ ਪਿਛੈ ਪਛੁਤਾਇ॥	*Je ko kahai pichhai pacchutāye.*
ਤਿਥੈ ਘੜੀਐ ਸੁਰਤਿ ਮਤਿ ਮਨਿ ਬੁਧਿ॥	*Tithhai ghaṛīai surt(i) mat(i) mann budh.*
ਤਿਥੈ ਘੜੀਐ ਸੁਰਾ ਸਿਧਾ ਕੀ ਸੁਧਿ॥ ੩੬॥	*Tithhai ghaṛīai sura sidha ki sudh.*

Pauṛi 37

ਕਰਮ ਖੰਡ ਕੀ ਬਾਣੀ ਜੋਰੁ॥	*Karam khandd ki bāṇi jor.*
ਤਿਥੈ ਹੋਰੁ ਨ ਕੋਈ ਹੋਰੁ॥	*Tithhai hor na koyi hor.*
ਤਿਥੈ ਜੋਧ ਮਹਾਬਲ ਸੂਰ॥	*Tithhai jodh mahābal sūr.*
ਤਿਨ ਮਹਿ ਰਾਮੁ ਰਹਿਆ ਭਰਪੂਰ॥	*Tin meh rām rahiya bharpūr.*
ਤਿਥੈ ਸੀਤੋ ਸੀਤਾ ਮਹਿਮਾ ਮਾਹਿ॥	*Tithhai sīto sīta mahima māhe.*
ਤਾ ਕੇ ਰੂਪ ਨ ਕਥਨੇ ਜਾਹਿ॥	*Ta kay rūp na kathnay jāhe.*
ਨਾ ਓਹਿ ਮਰਹਿ ਨ ਠਾਗੇ ਜਾਹਿ॥	*Na oh maray na tthāggay jāhe.*
ਜਿਨ ਕੈ ਰਾਮੁ ਵਸੈ ਮਨ ਮਾਹਿ॥	*Jin kai rām vasai mann māhe.*
ਤਿਥੈ ਭਗਤ ਵਸਹਿ ਕੇ ਲੋਅ॥	*Tithhai bhagat vaseh kay low.*
ਕਰਹਿ ਅਨੰਦੁ ਸਚਾ ਮਨਿ ਸੋਇ॥	*Karay anand sacha mann soye.*
ਸਚ ਖੰਡਿ ਵਸੈ ਨਿਰੰਕਾਰੁ॥	*Sach khandd vaseh nirankār.*
ਕਰਿ ਕਰਿ ਵੇਖੈ ਨਦਰਿ ਨਿਹਾਲ॥	*Kar kar vekhay nadar nihāl.*
ਤਿਥੈ ਖੰਡ ਮੰਡਲ ਵਰਭੰਡ॥	*Tithhai khandd manddal varbhandd.*
ਜੇ ਕੋ ਕਥੈ ਤ ਅੰਤ ਨ ਅੰਤ॥	*Jay ko kathhai ta unt na unt.*
ਤਿਥੈ ਲੋਅ ਲੋਅ ਆਕਾਰ॥	*Tithhai low low ākār.*
ਜਿਵ ਜਿਵ ਹੁਕਮੁ ਤਿਵੈ ਤਿਵ ਕਾਰ॥	*Jiv jiv hukam tivai tiv kār.*
ਵੇਖੈ ਵਿਗਸੈ ਕਰਿ ਵੀਚਾਰੁ ॥	*Vekhai vigsai karr vīchār.*
ਨਾਨਕ ਕਥਨਾ ਕਰੜਾ ਸਾਰੁ॥ ੩੭॥	*Nanak kathhna karaṛa sār.*

Pauṛi 38

ਜਤੁ ਪਾਹਾਰਾ ਧੀਰਜੁ ਸੁਨਿਆਰੁ॥	*Jat pāhāra dhīraj suniyār.*
ਅਹਰਣਿ ਮਤਿ ਵੇਦੁ ਹਥੀਆਰੁ॥	*Ahraṇ mat ved hathīyār.*
ਭਉ ਖਲਾ ਅਗਨਿ ਤਪ ਤਾਉ॥	*Bhau khala agan tapp tāu..*
ਭਾਂਡਾ ਭਾਉ ਅੰਮ੍ਰਿਤੁ ਤਿਤੁ ਢਾਲਿ॥	*Bhāndda bhāu amrit tit ddhāl.*
ਘੜੀਐ ਸਬਦੁ ਸਚੀ ਟਕਸਾਲ॥	*Ghaṛīyai sabad sachi taksāl.*
ਜਿਨ ਕਉ ਨਦਰਿ ਕਰਮੁ ਤਿਨ ਕਾਰ॥	*Jin kau nadar karam tin kār.*
ਨਾਨਕ ਨਦਰੀ ਨਦਰਿ ਨਿਹਾਲ॥੩੮॥	*Nanak nadri nadar nihāl.*

ਸਲੋਕੁ॥	***Slok***
ਪਵਣੁ ਗੁਰੂ ਪਾਣੀ ਪਿਤਾ ਮਾਤਾ ਧਰਤਿ ਮਹਤੁ॥	*Pavaṇ guru pāṇi pita māta dharat mahat.*
ਦਿਵਸੁ ਰਾਤਿ ਦੁਇ ਦਾਈ ਦਾਇਆ ਖੇਲੈ ਸਗਲ ਜਗਤੁ॥	*Divas rāt doye dāyi dāya khelai sagal jagat.*
ਚੰਗਿਆਈਆ ਬੁਰਿਆਈਆ ਵਾਚੈ ਧਰਮੁ ਹਦੂਰਿ॥	*Changiāyīa buriāyīa vāchai dharma hadūr.*
ਕਰਮੀ ਆਪੋ ਆਪਨੀ ਕੇ ਨੇੜੈ ਕੇ ਦੂਰਿ॥	*Karmi āpo āpṇi kay neṛai kay dūr.*
ਜਿਨੀ ਨਾਮੁ ਧਿਆਇਆ ਗਏ ਮਸਕਤਿ ਘਾਲਿ॥	*Jini nām dhiāyia gaye maskat ghāl.*
ਨਾਨਕ ਤੇ ਮੁਖ ਉਜਲੇ ਕੇਤੀ ਛੁਟੀ ਨਾਲਿ॥ ੧ ॥	*Nanak tay mukh ujlay keti chhutti nāl.*

1

MAN AND THE INFINITE

The soul is eternal, a part of the One Lord, the Deathless One. It separates from Him due to the influence of Māya (illusion) and then passes through numerous stages, incarnating in bodies beginning with the inorganic and culminating at last in the human form. When it reaches this highest level it obtains the rare opportunity of rejoining the One from which it was separated. This is the premise on which the Sikh belief system is predicated. This human birth is therefore priceless beyond all else, and is our opportunity to regain our rightful place of oneness with the Lord. The soul did not have this opportunity till it attained the human form. The importance that the Sikh beliefs give to this stage is obviously because there is something that distinguishes the human form from all the previous stages. This difference is, as we know, in the gift of intellect that mankind has been bestowed with – the ability given to mankind to discriminate between right and wrong; and to choose the path which is righteous. We need to consider as to when humans acquired this faculty. Different religions, and science, come up with different answers.

According to the Hindu belief this faculty has always existed. The world came into existence along with gods and demons and humans at some unknown, and unknowable, date. The universe then moves on its mysterious, and God-determined course strictly according to the Lord's will; and the levels of human spiritual awareness rises and sinks in a cyclical fashion moving through cycles of *Yugas*, each cycle comprising, as we noted above, four *Yugas*, viz., the *Satya Yuga*, the *Treta Yuga*, the *Dwāpar Yuga*, and finally the *Kali Yuga*. The level of righteousness or *Dharma* as it is called in Hinduism, recedes and dwindles in these four *Yugas* sequentially in the ratio of 4:3:2:1. Thus, if *Dharma* be reckoned to have the strength of four in the *Satya Yuga*, that strength would have reduced to just one in the *Kali Yuga*. However, at no time, not even in the worst *Kali Yuga*, does mankind totally lose its discriminative faculties. The nature of each *Yuga* does cause humans to behave in ways of greater or lesser righteousness. They retain always the intellect, the awareness to do right or wrong. In this belief system humans have always had, and will continue to have, the free will to follow the path to Godhead.

In the Judeo-Christian tradition the universe has come into existence at a time less than ten thousand years ago. At that time God over a period of seven days brought the universe into existence through His 'Word', creating first the heaven and the earth. He then created light, and day and night, and thereafter land and the seas. Creation then followed with plant life and then the progressively higher forms of living creatures of various types. The Lord Creator then made man in His own image on the sixth day, and then He rested on the seventh day, the 'Sabbath'. Mankind thus came into existence fully equipped with intellect, but without the knowledge of right and wrong, living in the Garden of Eden in primal innocence. Later, beguiled by an evil entity called the Serpent, Adam and Eve sinned by eating of the forbidden fruit of the tree of knowledge of good and bad. Thus was awareness awakened in them, but with it came the Lord's punishment for disobeying His command. The punishment was exile from the Garden of Eden. The Muslim faith of course also follows the same tradition.

Similarly diverse belief systems exist among mankind on

the earth. The science of archaeology however presents hard evidence of what seems to have been the course of human development over the ages; at least during the present cycle of creation, assuming that the process has repeated itself an infinite number of times in accordance with the Lord's will. The scientific evidence shows that man evolved from a bestial stage over thousands of years. According to it the earliest hominids are 4 to 5 million years old. The bipedal *Australopithecene*, the ape-like ancestors of man, lived at that time as evidenced by the finds in the Rift Valley of East Africa. The earliest stone tools have been dated at 2.5 million years ago, in Hadar in Ethiopia. Man-made shelters at the Olduvai Gorge in Kenya are dated at 1.75 million years. Man's ancestors *Homo Erectus* first existed 1.5 million years ago and some signs of tools, like hand axes, scrapers, etc. have been found around that period. Blades and triangular points for attachment to wooden shafts have been dated about 2 lakh years ago, a lakh being equal to one hundred thousand in the Indian system of numbers. However, the first evidence of modern man – *Homo sapiens* – is only about 1 lakh years ago, in Eastern and Southern Africa. Thus, according to the *Collin's Atlas of Archaeology* called 'Past Worlds' (2003), man rose from the beasts only in the last one lakh years or so.

Jon Gowlett in his *Ascent to Civilization: The Archaeology of Early Man* (Publishers: Alfred A. Knopf, 1984) says that the first positive evidence of fully modern man is only 40000 years ago in Africa and the Middle East. As *Homo Sapiens* were evolving, another branch of humans, Neanderthals, arose in the late Pleistocene about 1.5 lakh years ago but died out about 30000 years ago. He says that evidence exists to show that human progress is not always linear or unbroken. However, about 40000 years ago we have the first positive evidence of fully modern man and an explosive surge that took mankind from Africa to Australia and the New World for the first time with a rapacity which reflects the great cultural changes which were underway. The Stone Age was at that time in full bloom and it lasted till about 7000 years ago. Dynasties occurred since about 5500 years ago and the Bronze Age started about 5000 years ago, with the Iron Age following about 3500 years ago. Language perhaps existed possibly 100000 years ago and maybe even earlier.

Thus, scientists tell us that man in the present form is some 40 thousand to 1 lakh years old. Before that time man was little distinguished from the beast. At what stage did the human form acquire its capacity to think, to meditate on what was not immediately apparent, and to learn the difference between what right is and what is wrong? At some stage man was, according to science, indistinguishable from beasts – but over time he evolved. The cranial cavity increased in size, language developed and so did knowledge. We can take this as the likely and logical course and see what life must have been like for the first men as mankind emerged from beast-hood in the midst of a violent, and possibly frightening, world which men were slowly beginning to learn to cope with.

As mankind rose slowly and steadily to the top of God's creation on this earth, his struggle for survival would no longer need to occupy his entire attention. He would have by then discovered to make himself comfortable and safe from the threat that other creatures could pose. He would also have acquired the means to ensure livelihood with much less effort, leaving him consequently with the time to think, to ponder on the matters of the spirit. The early man would have seen that for all his supremacy in the hierarchy of creatures, he was still a powerless and puny entity when confronted with what he would have daily witnessed - the awesome and overpowering forces of nature all around him. Unable to fully comprehend, we find that primitive man deified all the great forces and attributed godly names and attributes to the individual marvels that he saw. Thus we see practically in all histories and myths that men have ascribed Godhood to all they did not understand. We have in all old mythologies all around the world a Sun God, a God of the Oceans, the Winds, a Fire God, a God of the Netherworlds, and so on. Naturally, the various cultures gave the names and attributes to these divine powers according to their own perceptions, depending upon where they lived and what their surroundings were. Thus, the Norsemen had supernatural entities related to the snows that they lived among. Indian mythology has no such gods but had instead gods of, inter alia, cattle and kine. In all cultures we have also a place where these gods reside – *Swarag* in Indian myth, *Olympus* in Greek mythology and so on, with a ruler over gods, Indra in the case of India, Odin for the Norsemen, and Zeus for the Greeks.

Behind this effort to label and classify these mighty forces in all these millennia, lies man's struggle to find purpose in this universe, to find for himself meaning for his own existence in the midst of these forces. The real reason behind this effort is that man feels overwhelmed and bewildered. Man's efforts have been like the efforts of a drowning man casting about, groping for something solid to hold on to. What essentially underlay this effort to prescribe some order on the forces around him was man's desire to somehow cope with his own sense of pervading terror and awe; and linked inevitably to it is an awareness of his own insignificance, his own powerlessness. From this flowed the realization of a Force, an Entity, a Being that surely must control, and be above the mighty forces that otherwise appeared chaotic. A Force above and beyond what existed in the immediately visible world.

Some early mystic perhaps first had a glimpse of that hidden force and surely he must have tried to express to his kindred what he had experienced, the Grand Design that he must have glimpsed. Since there never have been words to express that unique experience one can imagine that his vision would surely have remained essentially unexpressed. But surely it would nevertheless have succeeded in igniting among at least some of his audience a yearning to understand, an urge to see the principle that underlay and made possible all his gods and the forces around him.

In the millennia that have since elapsed, man has been blessed by the presence, from time to time, of great souls, of achieved personages who have been visited by His grace, and have thus been enabled to glimpse the Unseeable. This could happen only because the Lord loves His creation and makes it possible for all of us to experience Him. When in our ego and our greed for material things we turn our eyes from Him, He sends those who would remind us of what is real. In all cultures and in all parts of the world such souls have been sent so that the beacon of light continues to exist, to shine and to guide.

These great souls have had the almost impossible task of conveying to us that which it is not really possible to put into words. Nevertheless, the great and achieved souls must try and communicate, for that is the purpose of their being. Thus, over all this time we have had these seers laying down for us through prose and verse what they have seen of the Divine. They have tried to, through their written word and through example and persuasion, make it possible for the rest of us to also perhaps perceive, or at least fleetingly experience that ineffable Presence. All these great souls have spoken of the need to set our lives in such fashion, to mould our behaviour and our thought in such direction, as to become worthy of receiving the grace that they know is being constantly showered on this mass of humanity, however unworthy we may be.

The words, the manner in which this message has been couched from time to time, have appeared to be different among these seers. The difference is only superficial and arises from the fact that the message, of necessity, had to be tailored into words that the recipient could understand. The Jew in Palestine, the Arab in the deserts, the Indian in the rich valleys, the Chinese in their vastly different areas and with their different cultural perceptions had to be addressed differently. The uniformity underlying these differences is clear to any discerning mind. That there is one Ruler of this entire creation is clear and recognized in these messages. It is a different matter that many of the followers of these masters have refused to see that message and have chosen instead to go by the formalism that has arisen around the essence. Thus we have strife and struggle for material supremacy rather than the peace and harmony which are bound to prevail if the message were truly understood.

Nevertheless, in the midst of the great chaos the achieved souls have continued to give us the blue print to help us order our lives on the path to realization of the one God. It is the duty of each one of us individually to try and correctly understand what has been laid out for us and to faithfully follow the path our Masters have prescribed. It is also our duty to try and help our fellowmen to see that reality. Limited as most of us are in our perceptions, the best we can do to help is to carefully study what the Masters have laid down, to try jointly to understand what is prescribed and then depending on individual capacity and temperament follow, to the best of our ability, the path prescribed. Whether we reach the desired end will depend upon His grace. When and how it comes, and upon whom it will shine is as the Lord wills. Our duty is to tread the right path and try to make ourselves worthier of that grace.

In an infinite universe, with a Lord who is Immeasurable, Omnipresent, Transcendent and also Immanent, it is reasonable to say that there must indeed be many paths to reach Him. We are each one of us in our own way pilgrims to the same destination. Strife between men over which path to follow is thus meaningless. We are all the creation of the same Supreme Power and for one group to claim superiority, or exclusive rights to that Lord is merely a sign of ignorance. The many Masters who have come to us in the last few millennia – ever since mankind rose from the brutish stage to the present stage where matters of the spirit have begun to be of interest – have all said that the path they prescribe will lead to realization and oneness with the Lord. The paths may often appear mutually contradictory. But if the essence is understood the apparent differences will soon be seen to not matter that much. As long as the aim of the seeker is pure and he is truly focussed on reaching the true realisation the path is not so very material. What is material is that the pursuit of the path is governed by a desire for self-realisation and above all by a love for the Lord's creation. As long as this is so, let each one decide for himself which path of the many will he want to follow. Having so decided he must then wholly and truly be a follower of what that Master has said. True obedience is sure to lead to spiritual upliftment and perhaps, one day to God-realization. These many Masters are all messengers from that one God and are all deserving of veneration and full respect. It would be a big mistake for any seeker to keep changing Masters and shifting paths. That would lead to confusion and a wasted life. Choose your path and be a true and devoted follower. For each seeker his Master has to be the sole beacon, even as all masters are to be accorded respect.

For the follower of the Sikh faith one such Master came to us about six hundred years ago. He lived among us as any other human being for about seventy years and then left for us a prescription, a road map to emancipation, to *Mukti* as we call it in the Sikh religion. Nanak was the name by which He was known, and Guru Nanak is he to us, the Sikhs, who seek to follow that path. The song he sang of love and tolerance, of utter devotion and surrender to His will continues to be the guiding light for the Sikhs.

When he came, what were the circumstances of the country and of its people? What sort of childhood did he have, how did he influence people to follow his new and radical path? All this would be interesting to briefly consider before we proceed to try and understand his message.

2

THE ADVENT OF THE MASTER

Guru Nanak was born in the village of Talwanddi Bhoye, in Punjab on 20 *Vaisakh* 1526, corresponding to 15 April 1469 of the Christian era. In present times his birthday is celebrated on the *purāṇmāsi* (full moon day) of the month *Kārtik*, which spans the months of October and November. The story of how this date got changed is unclear but one explanation given is that at some stage during the various struggles for the succession to Guru Nanak's *gadi* one of the discontented followers intentionally gave the date as the month of *Kārtik* because in some circles it is deemed to be inauspicious. This tradition somehow caught on and has continued. However, research has shown that the correct date is *Vaisākh Sudi* 3, 1526, *Bikrami Samvat* corresponding to 15 April of the year 1469 AD. It is of no great significance as to what the exact date or time of the Guru's advent on this earth was. What does matter is that such a Master did come to us around that time.

His father was Mehta Kalyan Das, a Khatri Hindu of the Bedi sub-caste. Popularly referred to as Mehta Kalu, he was a *Pattwāri*, a Revenue Official under the local chieftain named Rai Bulār. Rai Bulār was the son of Rai Bhoye who had during the period of the Lodhi dynasty carved out a small autonomous principality in western Punjab, in an area now forming part of Pakistan. The village Talwanddi formed part of his realm and came to be known as Talwanddi Bhoye. Fortunately, for the founder of the Sikh faith Rai Bulār, quite unlike the ruling Lodhis of Delhi who were generally an intolerant and bigoted set of rulers who came down hard on any thought they deemed un-Islamic, was a man of a more open bent of mind and also a man who appreciated the spiritual.

Mehta Kalu apart from holding the official position was also the owner of some lands and cattle. Guru Nanak had only one sibling, a sister named Nanaki, four years his elder. She, like most elder sisters with an only brother, doted on him. She not only showered on him all her love but was also to play a significant role in his ministry. She was married to Jairam, an Uppal Khatri belonging to village Khanpur. Jairam was an employee of Nawab Daulat Khan of Sultanpur Lodhi. He had also helped arrange the marriage of the young Guru to Bibi Sulakhni, daughter of Mool Chand who was also a *Pattwāri* of village Pakhokay Randhāwa in the present day district of Gurdāspur, and thus in the same profession as Mehta Kalu. The marriage of Guru Nanak took place in AD 1487 when he was 18 years old. Mehta Kalu decided, after failing to interest his son in any long term commercial venture, to send him to his sister in Sultanpur Lodhi. According to Prof. Sahib Singh's biography of the Guru, this move took place on 30 October, AD 1504, and through Jairam's intercession the Guru was given employment by the Nawab. The young Nanak was to spend considerable time working for the ruler of Sultanpur Lodhi as a stores in-charge. It was also in Sultanpur Lodhi that the Guru was to find his epiphany. But of that, we will discuss later. Let us first look at the early years of the Guru while he was growing up in his father's house in Talwanddi under the watchful but doting aye of his mother Tripta and sister Nanaki.

It is inevitable that hagiography grows around any revered figure, especially when he is the founder of a modern and important religion. His followers see him as divine and ascribe to him many miracles and feats of spiritual greatness. Thus *Janam Sākhis*, literally stories of the birth, exist in large numbers. Many of these are very old and were penned, or at least refer to the recollections of those who were from that period or from the years soon after, by individuals who had worked hard to gather the facts surrounding his early childhood.

Even discounting for this reason some of these stories, the fact shines through that the young Nanak showed the glimpses of his high spiritual attainment from an amazingly young age. The *Purātan Janam Sākhis* abound with such tales. That his nature was compassionate and that he possessed a gravitas and a deep wisdom well beyond his years is uniformly recounted. So persistent is this thread in his life story that it is impossible to dismiss these as merely the work of devotees seeking to exalt their preceptor.

For instance, it is narrated that when Nanak was a tender three years of age a group of mendicant *sadhus* passed through the village. We have to remember that Talwanddi lay in the midst of wooded land somewhat isolated from the world. Today of course like the rest of Punjab, Talwanddi, or Nankana Sahib as it is now called, is part of the open agricultural landscape which characterizes Punjab on both sides of the political divide. Not so at that time, and therefore it was a favourite haunt for sadhus and men seeking spirituality away from the world. This group of sadhus asked for water and the village women drew some for them from the village well. The young Nanak watched the sadhus drink the water in their cupped hands. So moved was this three year old that he ran home and brought a rope used for drawing water from wells and a vessel for drinking water. He offered these to the sadhus and said sweetly that they please use these to draw water whenever they felt the need and not have to make requests of anyone for as essential a thing as water.

This pattern of behaviour was to manifest itself throughout his life. From a very young age, he was forever looking for the needy and the hungry and he would give to them gifts and food from his home. At an age when children are greedy and acquisitive and rarely want to share, this unusual child was giving what belonged to him and his family freely and generously to whoever was in need. This streak of always giving was to show up throughout his lifetime. Before the end he was to give to the needy and the hungry not only the gift of food and of the wherewithal to relieve their material hunger but was to offer to the world a great feast for those who were spiritually starved and show the way to those who had lost their path among the material attractions that constantly draw us away from the path of salvation.

As the young child grew in years, Mehta Kalu like all fathers everywhere, keen to get his child started on a formal course of education, took him to the village *Pandit*. It is said that Nanak was seven years of age then. He had an innate loftiness of the soul and had also by then acquired enough spiritual knowledge through consorting with the sadhus and the holy men who often camped in the wilderness around Talwanddi. In addition he also possessed extraordinary insight and intuitive knowledge of matters spiritual, a fact which came out shiningly in the very first encounter with the *Pandit* who found, to his great consternation, himself being questioned by the young student.

When the *Pandit* asked Nanak to write down as a first lesson the letters of the alphabet, the young Master turned around and questioned him if these letters had any meaning. One can imagine the effect of such a question from a seven-year-old to the teacher who thinks he is dealing with a new student. When the *Pandit*, retaining his cool, tried to say that these were just letters to help learn the language, the Guru not agreeing with that simplistic answer, is said to have composed an acrostic giving a spiritual twist to this first lesson. This acrostic covering each letter from the alphabet is according to the *Janam Sākhis* called the *Ād(i) Bāni*, the 'first utterance'. This acrostic starts with: 'ਸਸੈ ਸੋਇ ਸ੍ਰਿਸਟਿ ਜਿਨਿ ਸਾਜੀ' *sassay soye sristt jinn sāji* and is placed in *Rāg Āsa, Mahla* 1, *Patti likhi*, on page 432 of the *SGGS*. *Patti* is the wooden slate on which children used, in those days, to practice their writing. Each letter in this composition of the Guru has been used to convey a lesson and all 35 letters including the specific *Gurmukhi* letter 'ੜ'. This incidentally should also settle the argument regarding the antiquity of the *Gurmukhi* alphabet. By means of this acrostic the young Guru made the *Pandit* see that true education requires knowledge of the self and that the routine paper learning was of little real value. He is also said at that time to have composed a *Shabad* to this effect which is 'ਜਾਲਿ ਮੋਹੁ ਘਸਿ ਮਸੁ ਕਰਿ ਮਤਿ ਕਾਗਦੁ ਕਰ ਸਾਰੁ' - *Jāl moh ghas muss kar mat(i) kāgad kar sār*, meaning burn false attachments, crush and grind what has been burnt, and make the ink therefrom; and for writing with this special ink use your intellect as the paper. This *Shabad* (composition) is in *Sri Rāg Mahla* 1, page 16 of the *SGGS*, and gives a spiritual lesson analogous to a child learning to write the alphabet. Thus was the lesson on learning to write turned into a spiritual coaching experience. Similar was the experience later with the *Maulvi* who was to teach him Persian. The *Maulvi* also was to similarly witness the astonishing precocity of his young student in matters spiritual.

The *Janam Sākhis* are full of stories how in his brief stay in the school the young Nanak spoke always of things spiritual to his schoolmasters. It was soon clear enough, that this unique child saw the Reality behind the apparent and the obvious. He judged men on the touchstone of the spiritual and not material success or possessions. Empty and superficial show of piety and alms-giving did never impress him. He was able, even as a child, to look into the souls of men, to understand their real worth, and to move them by the force of his own spiritual powers. This aura of purity and of other worldliness manifested itself from his childhood and was distinctly noted by his co-villagers, his teachers and even the frequent travelling holy men who often passed that way or camped in the forest.

There is much to suggest that he interacted with them extensively and thus acquired knowledge of the conditions prevailing in the country, as also the details of the main religious schools and sects prevalent then. These find frequent reference in his *Bāṇi* (compositions). It is to be noted, however, that even where his compositions touch on the harsh political realities and the peculiarities of the sects, there runs through his *Bāṇi* the golden thread of God-realization. Always he concludes each mundane reference by highlighting the pre-eminence of the One Lord. He has answered in his *Bāṇi* the doubts and questions that must have risen naturally from the harshness of these conditions, and then used the answers to prescribe a simple, elegant path to God.

Soon realizing his young son's lack of attachment to worldly matters, Mehta Kalu arranged his marriage to Mata Sulakhni, daughter of Mool Chand of Batala, on the date generally accepted to be *Bhādon Sudi* 7, 1544, corresponding to 24 September 1487, though Prof. Sahib Singh puts this date as 24 *Jetth* 1544 Bk, corresponding to 21 May 1487 AD. Subsequently, many years later, still looking to find his young son some gainful employment, Mehta Kalu decided to send him to Sultanpur Lodhi where the Guru's sister Nanaki and brother-in-law Jairam were happily settled. Nawab Daulat Khan Lodhi agreed to employ him as stores in-charge and it is said that he worked diligently and earned much respect for his clean and efficient handling of duties. His spirituality, however, was not to be diverted by all these activities and he gathered a following of the like-minded. Mardana, a Muslim *rabābi* – rebec player – born in Talwanddi to Mir Badra, a *Mirāsi*, on *Phalguṇ* 1516 Bk and thus about nine years older than the Guru, and an inseparable companion from then on, joined him here.

Then, one day, according to most commentators probably in the year 1507 AD, there was to occur the event that was to drastically change the tenor of the Guru's life. On that fateful day the Guru entered the rivulet named *Bein* and disappeared. This rivulet flows near the city of Sultanpur Lodhi and was commonly used by the populace for bathing. The Guru's entering the water was not therefore unusual. His sudden disappearance certainly was a huge shock for the people of the city. As popular and respected a spiritual leader as Guru Nanak was, the people of Sultanpur, presuming him lost, were naturally much disturbed. There was great turmoil in the town and many parties of townsmen went searching for him but finding no sign of him, believed the worst and presumed he was drowned. Suddenly, after three days, the Guru reappeared from the *Bein*, turning the sorrow of the people into unbelievable joy.

According to the *Purātan Janam Sākhi* the Guru spent this period of three days in the physical presence of the *Akal Purakh* – the One God. The *Sākhis* describe in great detail the manner in which the Guru was received in the Divine Presence and also the details of what transpired there during this period.

Now obviously the narration here pre-supposes an Anthropomorphic God ruling over an organization or place, which can be called an exalted version of a human, earthly organization. Some may want to argue that the Lord Creator that Guru Nanak talks about is a power beyond comprehension, as the Guru himself repeatedly says. How could Guru Nanak have been in a throne room with the Lord seated in the ruler's seat and welcoming the Guru into His presence? For resolving this apparent confusion we need to hear what the Guru has said – that this Power, the Lord, is both Transcendent and Immanent. Such an infinite Omnipotent Power can then easily decide at will to manifest in any way and in any form that it chooses. In dealing with a human, which the Guru always insisted he was, the Lord could well choose the form that would be easiest for a human to comprehend and to respond to – the form of a mighty ruler with all the trappings that go with royalty. In any case it is said that the Lord in His discourse with the Guru commanded the Guru to go back and propagate the Truth among the people and mitigate their enervating ignorance and also wean them away from following the false paths of merely material glory.

Guru Nanak emerged back into this world at the end of this period of three days and the first thing he uttered was, "There is no Hindu and there is no Mussalman." In that pronouncement was not a desire to negate the religions he spoke of. The Guru was instead merely laying down the direction he was then to follow for the next three decades or so of his existence on this earth – the path that was to highlight humanism as the bedrock of his belief system; beyond the false limits and labels of religion, race or caste.

Guru Nanak composed the *Japji Sahib* sometime after his return from this encounter. He laid out therein the path to salvation, the path of surrender to His will and of the total acceptance of His commandments. Before we look more closely into this *Bāṇi*, we need to take a look at the social and political milieu that obtained and which also finds frequent reference in the *Granth Sahib* and which must have influenced the form in which the message of the Guru got formulated.

3

THE MILIEU

As we saw the Guru came to us in 1526 *Samvat*, 1469 of the Christian era. Northern India was under the rule of the Lodhi dynasty with Bahlol Lodhi ruling from AD 1450 to 1488 and his successor Sikandar Lodhi from 1488 to 1517, a period broadly co-terminous with Guru Nanak's sojourn in this world. The conditions for the common man were at that time really deplorable. The Gurus, as also the saintly chronicler Bhai Gurdās, have in their compositions referred to these conditions.

The *Granth Sahib* says in *Rāg Malhār*, page 1288:

'ਰਾਜੇ ਸੀਹ ਮੁਕਦਮ ਕੁਤੇ॥'
Rājay sīhn mukadam kutay—

This line can be translated as: Kings have become rapacious predators and the dispensers of justice are like dogs.

Then again in *Rāg Mājh*, page 145:

'ਕਲਿ ਕਾਤੀ ਰਾਜੇ ਕਾਸਾਈ ਧਰਮੁ ਪੰਖ ਕਰਿ ਉਡਰਿਆ॥'
Kal kāti rājay kāsāi dharam pankh kar uddaria–

Simply translated, this line means: Time is the cutting blade, the rulers are butchers, and righteousness has flown from the world.

Bhai Gurdās also says in the same vein in his *Vār* 1, *Pauṛi* 30:

'ਰਾਜੇ ਪਾਪ ਕਮਾਂਵਦੇ ਉਲਟੀ ਵਾੜ ਖੇਤ ਕਉ ਖਾਈ।'
Rājay pāp kamānvday ultti vāṛ khet kau khāyi

This line broadly translates as: Kings are sinful and the protectors eat up their own protectees.

Justice and fair play were thus not the mark of that age. The Hindus were probably even worse oppressed than the Muslim common man, because the Lodhis were strongly orthodox and discouraged idol worship, sometimes with a strong hand, even to the extent of destroying the Hindu places of worship.

In Punjab the conditions were similar but the Lodhi dynasty was fortunately a somewhat distant problem. The local rulers and chieftains enjoyed considerable autonomy and the quality of life for the common man was determined more by the nature of the immediate ruler. As we have noted, the chieftain ruling over Talwanddi Bhoye was an enlightened man who saw early the greatness of the young Guru and gave him and his family due respect. The Nawab of Sultanpur Lodhi, Daulat Khan was also a comparatively just and even-handed ruler. The employment of Guru Nanak to a fairly responsible official position shows that he did not discriminate merely on the basis of religion. The fact that Jai Ram, the husband of the Guru's sister Nanaki, commanded enough influence with the Nawab to manage a job for his young brother-in-law freshly arrived from Talwanddi also confirms this aspect of Daulat Khan's nature. It can perhaps be taken to be fairly representative of the times for Punjab.

The socio-political conditions being as they were, the material with which Guru Nanak had to work also needs to be considered. The main audience he addressed consisted of the followers of the Hindu and the Muslim faith. That the Hindus were the more down-trodden and religiously oppressed would have meant that more followers would be attracted from amongst them. About the Hindus at that time it would be useful to refer to an early and non-partisan historian of Sikhism, Joseph Davy Cunningham. He writes in his *History of the Sikhs*, on page 34:

"In the beginning of the sixteenth century the Hindu mind was no longer stagnant or retrogressive; it had been leavened with Mohammedanism and changed and quickened for a new development. Ramānand and Gorakh had preached religious equality, and Chaitan had repeated that faith levelled caste. Kabir had denounced images, and appealed to the people in their own tongue, and Vallabh had tāught that effectual devotion was compatible with the ordinary duties of this world. But these good and able men appear to have been so impressed with the nothingness of this life, that they deemed the amelioration of man's condition to be unworthy of a thought. They aimed chiefly at emancipation from priest-craft, or from the grossness of idolatry and polytheism. They formed associations of contented Quietists, or they gave themselves up to the contemplation of futurity in the hope of approaching bliss, rather than calling upon their fellow creatures to throw aside every social as well as religious trammel, and to raise a new people from the debasing corruption of ages. They perfected forms of dissent rather than planted the germs of nations, and their sects remain to this day as they left them. It was reserved for Nanak to perceive the true principle of reform, and to lay those broad foundations which enabled his successor Gobind to fire the minds of his countrymen with a new nationality, and to give practical effect to the doctrine that the lowest is equal to the highest in race as in creed, in political rights as in religious hopes."

The *Encyclopaedia of Sikhism*, Vol. 3 has further to say, on page 169, about the parallel between the religious conditions at that time in the East and the West – the wave of reformation that swept both societies at about the same time. The condition, as the encyclopaedia says, was that: "… for the Hindu community, religious authority rested in the Brahmans as a class. What was required of the common man was the performance of practices laid down for his caste. To this he gave unquestioned obedience. For the Muslim, faith was anchored in the authority of the *Ulema* who interpreted for him his duty. This dominance of religion by authoritarian, ritualistic and morally indifferent formalism was a phenomenon common to both East and West. Also common to both was the beginning of criticism of this situation and a search for an inner, personal faith. Just as Western Christiandom was being awakened by the preaching of Martin Luther and John Calvin, in India an impulse for reconstruction issued from the teachings of Guru Nanak."

Further, it says about the message of Guru Nanak: "Just as important as his attestation of the eternal verities, was Guru Nanak's role in reformation. Earlier Hindu *Bhaktas* and Muslim *Sufis* had proclaimed the ideal of purity of devotion as well as of conduct, and indicated the way to religious reconciliation and regeneration. But it was Guru Nanak who created the means for realizing in a practical way the potential of these developments. In his intuition the spiritual and temporal claims were wrought into a single form and he presented an integrated and substantive view of human destiny. He questioned more effectively the current assumptions and values and, in the mode he had established life seemed to swing from its old ways into the new."

The conditions that confronted Guru Nanak and his approach to handling those become clear from the above – a politically disturbed period with an over-bearing and bigoted overlord in Delhi but with pockets of comparative peace and of tolerance existing in large tracts all over the country. The Hindus, generally oppressed and treated socially as second class, were also getting fairly assimilated into the power structure and getting state patronage by way of jobs, and acceptance as a separate socio-religious entity. In matters of religion the Hindus were suffering the state's heavy hand on many occasions, though gradually a modus vivendi between them and the dominant power structure was emerging. More than the oppression of the state, the Hindus suffered the tyranny of an overpowering and well entrenched priesthood forcing on the common man a rigidly defined ritual that left little room for personal emancipation by an individual soul, and gave the priest the sole say on each man's salvation.

Most oppressed in the polity were the lower castes among the Hindus. They had practically no social or religious position and were the outcast and the deprived of the country. Many turned to Islam but the vast majority continued to suffer, neither wanting to leave their ancestral position in societal hierarchy, even though it was one of pain and deprivation, nor able to make any headway against the strongly entrenched upper classes. The coming of the great souls like Ravidās and Nāmdev from among these castes indicates that not all had accepted their miserable lot in resignation and there was a movement, a struggle to break out of their bondage. There were many masters who had achieved God-realization, belonging to the deprived classes. They preached the lesson of equality of all mankind and of the futility of mere formalism in religion which the Brahmanical order was enforcing so harshly. As Cunningham says, their message was heard, even obeyed but led to no enduring amelioration of the conditions for the under-class. This was so till Guru Nanak came and delivered his message. The message reiterated what many of these saints were already saying but again, to quote Cunningham, it was Guru Nanak who laid the broad foundations for a radically new order which was to lead during the next two centuries to the creation of the Sikh nation, followers of this new religion, that clearly, firmly and unambiguously discarded all forms of discrimination and distinction between man and man, which focussed solely on the spiritual oneness of all mankind and which concludes its daily prayers with an appeal to the Lord to bless the entire mankind.

Over the following decades after Guru Nanak's departure from this world on *Assu vadi* 10, 1596 *Samvat*, corresponding to 7 September 1539 AD, the *Guru Granth* was compiled, installed and finally made the successor to the ten Gurus by Guru Gobind Singh in Nanded just before he passed from this world [see Appendix A]. The *SGGS* is not only the word of Guru Nanak himself but also contains the *Bāṇi* of his successors in whom his spirit resided as per his wishes. Further, it contains the compositions of saints whose message was similar in content and tenor to the message of Guru Nanak. These saints came from all classes and castes and were united only by the uniformity of their vision of God. The *SGGS* is the only Guru a Sikh is supposed to follow though it is enjoined that the saints and exalted souls are to be respected and given honour.

Sometimes doubts arise, even among Sikhs, as to how a book can be the Guru. Some even question the very assertion that the *Granth Sahib* was ever installed as the Guru. The *Encyclopaedia of Sikhism*, Vol. IV, has on pages 243 to 247 spelt out and detailed the history of how and when the *SGGS* was formally anointed the Guru (the extract therefrom can be seen in Appendix A). Sects have come up within Sikhism, which insist on a living Guru, and even some which treat their Gurus as successors in the line of Guru Nanak. Many of these sects are believers in the *Granth Sahib* even though they do not treat it as the Guru. It is not the intention here to argue the merits of such beliefs. Suffice it to say that for many, including non-Sikhs, the *SGGS* is an important teacher and an object of veneration. For the true Sikh, however, it is more than just that and it is in fact the visible form of the Gurus. Its word is, for the true Sikh, the only prescriber of our passage to God-realization.

The *SGGS* comprises 1430 pages of which *Japji* is the first entry from pages 1 to 8. The structure of the Holy Book is by way of recording the *Bāṇi* of the Gurus, the *Bhaktas* and the *Bhatts* in that sequence, with the compositions of the first Nanak recorded first, followed by the other Gurus in sequence. The *Bāṇi* of the *Bhaktas*, the saints, is recorded thereafter. The compositions of the *Bhatts*, the bards, are recorded together towards the end of the *SGGS*. Further, within the *SGGS* the compositions are listed according to the *Rāga*, the musical measure in which it is to be sung. The *Japji Sahib* is inscribed outside of this system and there is no *rāga* prescribed for its recitation. The *Japji Sahib* otherwise also, is uniquely special because in a real sense Guru Nanak has in the *Japji* laid down the key to his entire teaching which was to be enunciated by him in his own lifetime and then added to and elaborated by his spiritual successors, who for that reason do not use their own names. They are instead listed in the *SGGS* as *Mahla* stages, or abodes of the spirit of Guru Nanak. Thus, the second Guru known by the name Angad otherwise will be recorded as *Mahla* 2 implying that Guru Nanak's spirit resided in him. We would therefore refer to him as Nanak the second. This system and form of referring to the later Gurus is followed till the tenth Nanak. The *SGGS* was compiled through the exertions of Guru Arjan, the fifth Nanak who collected the extant compositions of the Gurus and added thereto his own *Bāṇi*. The task was finally completed by the tenth Nanak at which stage some compositions of the ninth Nanak along with one *slok* (stanza), *Bal hoa bandhan chhuttay sabh kichh hote upāye*, which is sometimes attributed to the tenth Nanak, though all do not agree on the issue, were added and the scripture was given its final shape. Any efforts at addition or amendment have strenuously been resisted since then. There are other interesting facts and sidelights about the compilation, the installation thereof in AD 1604 at the Harimandar Sahib in Amritsar, the battles fought to preserve the 'Book' as also the place of its installation, and the conferring on it by the tenth Nanak the status of the Living Guru. It would really require a whole volume to do justice to those stirring events. Let us now return to the subject at hand, the *Japji Sahib*, which we will see has rightly been accorded the pride of place at the very beginning of the *SGGS*. It deserves this honour because it carries in its brief eight pages of the *SGGS*, and its thirty-eight *pauṛis* the very essence of the Guru's message.

The message encapsulated in the *Japji* can then be said to have been elaborated, re-stated and emphasized in the *SGGS*. The nub, the gist, however exists in the *Japji Sahib*. It is important for a Sikh especially, and for any seeker or a student of the path prescribed by the Gurus to try to understand first of all the *Japji Sahib*. Great scholars have expounded on the *Japji Sahib*, learned commentaries have appeared and millions have benefited from them.

When an achieved soul speaks out in rapture of his experience of Godhood, the rest of us can but hope to at best see some glimpse of the Eternal Truth being recorded. Any commentary on, or effort to, elaborate on or explain what the Master said is bound to be limited, constrained and circumscribed by our inability to really share that mystical experience. Words, human language, are after all a very poor substitute for a direct extra-sensory experience. Description becomes an impossible task. As the Master says in the *SGGS,* the effort to describe this experience is like a speech-deprived man trying to explain the taste of a delicious sweet. Nevertheless, the effort needs to be made. One's understanding is necessarily limited and even the study of the various commentaries by truly learned souls reveals the enormity of the task, because even great scholars differ, however subtly, on the true meaning of the words of the Gurus. In all humility and in full knowledge of the difficulty and the magnitude of the task, this offering is attempted with a prayer to our Master to guide it to the right conclusion.

As we noted, one is greatly handicapped in such an endeavour. The Guru brought to us the word of God born out of his own enlightenment. In doing so he was inevitably constrained by the limits of human understanding and language of his audience. Beyond that inherent difficulty for any seeker is the further constraint imposed by the fact that the Guru chose to use poetry for his composition. Poetry being a vehicle for the finer feelings, the Guru perhaps deemed it the right medium.

For the seeker the problem of understanding becomes just that little bit harder. Just look at how many volumes of critical analysis exist on any ordinary piece of literature. Reams of paper, for instance, can be found merely interpreting a poem by Shakespeare, and even those interpretations, will be seen to differ. Imagine how much harder the task is going to be when dealing with matters mystical.

Similarly, both because of the limits imposed by the poetic form and much more so because of the nature of the subject itself, the Guru's *Bāṇi* could also have somewhat differing connotations for the seeker depending on the way he is able to interpret and understand. As we noted, men of great intellect and high spiritual attainment will be seen sometimes to interpret the same words differently. The differences of interpretation we will see are not of any great significance mainly because fortunately, so strong is the underlying theme, so intensely uni-focused the direction of the Guru's message that the essentials would get through even to our imperfect minds.

Among the many great commentators referred to during this endeavour are Bhai Vīr Singh, a mystic poet and thinker of great spiritual attainment; Prof. Sahib Singh, a scholar with a thorough grasp of his subject and specially of the Punjabi grammar; Bhai Sahib Bhai Kāhan Singh of Nabha, a man of great intellect and a prolific author with attainments in not only the field of spirituality but also diplomacy and administration, was a man who commanded respect from all, commoners and princes alike.

That ancient scholar, mystic and companion of the Gurus, Bhai Gurdās has in his poetic compositions expatiated on the theme of the Guru's *Bāṇi* and his writings are rightly called the 'Key' to the *SGGS*. Reference has been made to his works also in trying to put together this humble offering.

4

MOOL MANTRA

When and how was the *Japji Sahib* compiled or composed? According to the *Purātan Janam Sākhi*, which is estimated to have been written around AD 1635-1645 and is one of the earliest references, the *Japji* is the first composition of Guru Nanak after his encounter with the Divine following his immersion in the *Bein* rivulet sometime when he was thirty years of age and residing in Sultanpur Lodhi. Iqbal Singh has referred to W. H. Mcleod's *Early Sikh Tradition* and *Japji* by Prakash Singh (Amritsar: Singh Brothers, 1978), pp. 13-14, who, he says, quotes Mohan Singh's *Punjābi Bhāsha Vigyān Atay Gurmat Gyān*. According to this, Guru Nanak, after he was commanded by the Lord during his three-day Divine communion to spread His name and word, uttered the 'Mool Mantra' and the *Japji Sahib*. Osho in his *The True Name* and Giani Sant Singh Maskin have both held this view.

However, Kavi Santokh Singh in his *Gurupartāp Suraj Granth*, written in 1823, holds that the different *pauṛis* had been composed at different times over many years. When the Guru settled down at Kartārpur after his travels, these stanzas were compiled at the request of his disciple Lehṇa known later as Guru Angad, Nanak II. This text then acquired scriptural status because it was prescribed to be recited at dawn everyday in the daily congregations. Another view is that of Bhai Mani Singh who held that it was composed as a full text after Guru Nanak's composition known as *Sidh Goshtt(i)* – dialogue with the *Sidhs*. Prof. Sahib Singh in his *Gurbāṇi tay itihās bāray* has concluded that Guru Nanak himself inscribed his *Bāṇi* as he composed it and this was then passed on intact to his successors. In this light the *Japji Sahib* could also be said to have been so handed over to his close disciple Bhai Lehṇa at Kartārpur after the Guru settled there and was joined by his disciple in or around AD 1531.

It is easy to believe that this *Bāṇi* could not have been culled out from different places because the thematic structure is quite cohesive, revolving as it does around the theme *Kiv sachiāra hoiyai kiv kūṛay tuttai pāl* occurring in the first *pauṛi*. It is also true that this *Bāṇi*, unlike the other compositions of the Gurus, is not ascribed a *rāga* or a number and is placed right at the beginning of the *SGGS*. It also consists of *pauṛis* of greatly unequal length and seem addressed to different categories of persons and possibly at different times. For instance *Pauṛi* 22 is generally believed to have been addressed to a Muslim audience in Baghdad. *Pauṛis* 28 and 31 are clearly addressed to the *Jogis*, or *Nāths* or *Yogis*, as they were called. It really is of no great spiritual significance to a seeker whether it was composed at one sitting or culled out from different compositions. What is really material is the message it conveys, the path it delineates.

Whatever the real facts behind the timing or the sequencing of its composition, there is little doubt that it is indeed Guru Nanak's composition, whether uttered at one sitting to Baba Lehṇa, handed over to him or compiled by the latter and got approved from Guru Nanak. It clearly was extant in its present form during Guru Nanak's time and already constituted part of the liturgy for the Sikhs. The proof of it is in the *Vārs* of Bhai Gurdās, who writes in his *Vār* 1, *Pauṛi* 38 'ਸੋਦਰ ਆਰਤੀ ਗਾਵੀਐ ਅੰਮ੍ਰਿਤ ਵੇਲੇ ਜਾਪ ਉਚਾਰਾ।' - *Sodar ārti gāviyai amrit velay jāp uchāra*), the Sikhs would recite the *sodar* and *ārti* at dusk, and in the *Amrit vela* (ambrosial hour) which refers to the early morning hours, they would recite the *Japji*. Thus, while the time of its composition or compilation may be debated, no doubts exist regarding Guru Nanak and not someone at a later date, being the author.

The *Japji Sahib* in its structure consists of the *Mool Mantra*, two *sloks*, one each at the beginning and at the end with thirty-eight *pauṛis* in between. A *pauṛi* literally means a step. We can therefore call the *Japji Sahib* the thirty-eight stepped ladder to God-realization.

We start our study by looking at the *Mool Mantra*, with which the Guru commenced this composition. Literally it means the 'basic creed'. It says:

'ੴ ਸਤਿਨਾਮੁ ਕਰਤਾ ਪੁਰਖੁ ਨਿਰਭਉ ਨਿਰਵੈਰੁ ਅਕਾਲ ਮੂਰਤਿ ਅਜੂਨੀ ਸੈਭੰ ਗੁਰ ਪ੍ਰਸਾਦਿ॥'
(*Ek Onkār Sat Nām Karta Purakh Nirbhāu. Nirvair Akāl Mūrat Ajūni Saibhang Gur Prasād*)

Simply translated the *Mool Mantra* means The One Lord, The Eternal Reality, Creator, Immanent, Without Fear, Without Enmity or Rancour, The Form Beyond Time or Death, Beyond the trammels of Birth or Incarnation, Self-Existent, [Realized] Through the Grace of the Guru.

The *Mool Mantra* occurs in the *SGGS* not only at the beginning but repeatedly as the chapters according to the *rāgas* unfold. It is also the most commonly recited line for a Sikh and in some ways can be compared to the *Kalma* for a Muslim.

This *Mool Mantra* is here offered by the Guru as an invocation before the commencement of the 'Holy Book'. As we noted, the *Japji Sahib* is the first *Bāṇi* recorded in the *SGGS*. Before the composition proper commences the Guru has offered this invocation. It is customary in the Indian culture to commence any holy or otherwise important undertaking with an invocation to a deity. This is meant to seek blessings for the trouble-free completion of the task being undertaken. It is usual amongst the followers of the Hindu 'Dharma' to invoke the blessings of Lord Ganesha, the elephant-headed son of Lord Shiva. Ganesha is called the *Vighneshwara* (remover of all obstacles) and thus the facilitator of human endeavours. Guru Nanak, however, in keeping with his new vision which was beyond any denomination and unrestricted by any dogma, chose instead an invocation to the Creator Himself, the Timeless One, the Lord of all the Gods.

Immediately, one will notice that the Master comes up against the problem he will often refer to in the *SGGS* itself – the difficulty of describing the indescribable. He had personally experienced and had known the Unknowable. How is he now to convey to the rest of us that Great Reality? So the Guru starts by stressing the foremost of the infinite attributes of the Lord, that He is 'One'. And he is the 'Word', pronounced in Indian languages as *Aum*.

The concept of the 'Word' as Creator is not limited to Sikhism alone. Hindu thought describes *Aum* or *Om* as the underlying principle of our universe – the Creator Himself. The Guru in his language calls it *Onkār*, but where he sharply delineates the contours of his distinct vision is in adding here the prefix *ek* meaning one or, here, unique. In this lies the bedrock of the Sikh faith, that there is but one God, One Creator and there is none else to whom worship is to be accorded.

The Guru is thus saying that the Lord is the Prime Cause and all that exists is His doing. However, says the Guru, He as Creator is not outside or distinct from His creation – He also permeates it. The concept put forth by the Guru is thus of a Creator who has made all that exists and is in that context Transcendent. However, He is not merely some amorphous concept beyond all creation. No, He also permeates every pore of the universe and exists in each and every part of this creation. He is thus also immanent.

There is thus One God, unique in Himself and there can be nothing else like Him. He is the 'Word' - *Shabad* or *Logos*. He is *Satnām*, the only Truth, the underlying Reality of the visible world. As the fifth Nanak says in the *Sukhmani Sahib*, on page 284, *Nām kay dhāray saglay jant, Nām kay dhāray Khandd brahmandd*, meaning that all created beings and the created universe are sustained by the *Nām*. This is, in the Guru's concept, by no means meant to deny the reality of the universe. It is meant only to highlight the Prime Cause behind that reality. He is *Karta Purukh*, the Creator who also exists in His creation, the Immanent Lord of the real universe who is also its Transcendent Creator.

The Guru then goes on to try and describe this Creator to us mortals by ascribing to Him qualities and traits which the human mind in its inherent limitations could relate to. The Creator is *Nirbhau*- the one without fear, *Nirvair* - the one without enmity or rancour, *Akāl Mūrat* - unbound by the trammels of time and thus untouched by death, *Ajūni* - the un-incarnated, hence not subject to the eternal cycle of death and rebirth, *Saibhang* – Self Created. Obviously, the one and only Lord God cannot have another who would create Him. By definition the One God is Self-Created. Finally, the *Mool Mantra* concludes with *Gur Parsād* – by the Grace of the Guru. This phrase is described as meaning, "through the Grace of the Guru" by Bhai Vir Singh as also Prof. Sahib Singh. The Shiromani Gurdwara Parbhandak Committee (SGPC) in its four-volume *Shabdarth* also translates the phrase in this way. However, Dr. Sangat Singh in his *Japji* argues that since the Guru is describing the Lord in monosyllables giving his attributes, this phrase must also be read as two separate words *Guru* and *Parsād*. He translates these as 'Enlightened' and 'Bountiful'. Keeping in view the constant stress the *SGGS* places on the importance of the Guru, the meaning as also recognized by the SGPC seems the more appropriate. The Guru is telling us that the Lord is to be realized through the grace of the *Guru*, which in the modern context for the Sikhs will mean the *SGGS* embodying the Gurus in living form [see Appendix-A].

The essence of the above description is quite close to Sankara's *Advaitism*, and perhaps, even closer to Ramanuja's *Vishishtta Advaitism*. Sankara holds that the Creator is the only Reality and all else that we see is but Māya and a result of our

Avidya – our lack of comprehension. Ramanuja's *Vishishtta Advaitism* also says that the Lord is the Reality but holds that the material world and the created beings are also real to an extent, being created and sustained by Him. The world, its Creator and the self are not separate or distinct, but are all one and the same, and the created universe has existence to the extent the Lord is Immanent in it. The Immanence of the Transcendent Creator is stressed repeatedly. Mankind is thus but a form and manifestation of the Creator. Put in other words man is truly the child of God.

The realization of this relationship should surely bring to any seeker's mind great reassurance. In practical terms it gives all of us the means to rise above over petty quotidian concerns. No fears need exist of the powerful. No need to fear death for it is only re-merger with the source from which one came. If we are but a reflection of the Eternal then it is clearly absurd to have fear of any earthly powers. In this world, greed, dread of dying, rancour, enmity, and jealousy can only exist because we have failed to understand our true relationship with the Eternal. The moment one can do so, all negative human thoughts and frailties will vanish. To reach that realization it is in Sikhism enjoined upon us to recite His name – 'JAP'. The *Japji Sahib* lays down for us a step-by-step guide towards this goal. While doing 'Jap' what is our mind to focus on, through what stages should we expect to move and what shall be the end result is beautifully, thoroughly, yet very succinctly prescribed in the *Japji Sahib*. We will by following this road map reach our goal – by the Guru's grace.

Since the Guru occupies such an important place in the Sikh system it would be worthwhile to see what it is intended to mean. There are many wise and good men who have picked on this theme to say that according to the *Granth Sahib* God-realization can come only through following a Guru – who in their view must be alive in front of you to provide you the needed guidance throughout your life and then bestow on you the grace which will bring you to your epiphany. This line of thinking has of course ensured the existence of some very wealthy *Deras* (religious seminaries), though literally the word *Dera* translates as 'camp'. Each of these is headed by exponents of this line of thought, the propounders of the living Guru proposition. While in all fairness it must be said that many of these religious leaders are genuine teachers and guides who will selflessly lead you to spiritual elevation, however inevitably, around such centres there develops a coterie of self seekers and power brokers. The *Deras* in most cases are wealthy and powerful and their heads live lives of royal splendour. The material gets prominence of place and importance is counted by the number of followers, the volume of the donations, the grandeur of the place and the strength of connections that develop around the *Dera*. Politicians curry favour and in a display of mutual back-scratching, strengthen one or the other centre depending on electoral considerations. It is only too frequent that the emphasis shifts from spiritual guidance to more material things.

Unfortunately, leaving aside the few true and genuine spiritual leaders, taking shelter behind the same 'living Guru' philosophy, a horde of mercenaries merely posing to be spiritual have come into existence. It has in many cases become an easy route to wealth and worse. It is extremely difficult for the innocent initiate and seeker to be able to sift his way through this plethora of Gurus. Such a seeker would waste valuable time of his all too short existence on this earth, searching vainly for the true teacher. What is worse, it is very possible that the innocent seeker would be ensnared by one of the many false Gurus and be put on the wrong path altogether. The Sikh faith has overcome this dilemma by Guru Gobind Singh, the tenth Nanak, bestowing the 'Guruship' on the *Granth Sahib* [see Appendix-A]. The simple and sublime language, the use of the everyday idiom and repeated examples and stories to highlight the one Basic Truth makes it possible for even the simplest soul with the least erudition to find his way to the realization of Godhood in oneself.

The *Gur Prasād* at the end of the *Mool Mantra* is to be read and understood in this context. As we begin our journey to the ultimate goal of spiritual enlightenment through reading and understanding the truth spelt out in the *SGGS*, the *prasād* (the holy fruit) of our labour will begin to appear, but not by mere effort on our part – it will come through the Guru, which for the Sikh is the *SGGS*. Here will be found the pathway; the road map laid down by the Guru, which when sincerely followed will bring to us the inevitable fruit, the attainment of God-realization. For that the first step is spelt out now by him. Thus, the Guru at the very outset lays upon us the injunction 'Jap'. He says, recite His name.

'Jap' is the title of this composition. It is, as we noted, not set to any musical meter and is not to be sung to any *rāga* unlike the most of the compositions in the *SGGS*. This *Bāṇi* is traditionally recited as the first of the five *Bāṇis* prescribed for the devout in the *Nitnem* (daily routine), as indicated in Article IV of Chapter III of the *Sikh Rehat Maryāda* (*The Code Of Sikh Conduct & Conventions*) issued by the SGPC, the body created for managing 'Gurdwaras' in the state of Punjab. Appendix C reproduces the relevant part of the code. It is said by Bhai Gurdās that the 'Jap', to which the honorific 'ji' has been added as a sign of respect, was part of the daily routine of the early congregation that gathered around Guru Nanak after he had settled at Kartārpur on the banks of the river Rāvi, in the year 1521 AD, where he was to remain till his departure from this world in September 1539 AD. Before that, till 1521 and starting some fifteen years earlier the Guru had undertaken extensive travels which are believed to have taken him to all the four corners of the country, and beyond its borders into Tibet and China and West into what is now the Middle East. From AD 1521 onwards he did not travel any great distance away and during this time proceeded to create a bustling community of disciples of whom Bhai Lehṇa, a Trehan Khatri, born in Mati Ki Sarāi in district Muktsar, part of the present Indian Punjab, in March 1504, was the closest to him. Equally prominent was Bhai Buddha, a Randhāwa Jatt from district Amritsar. Bhai Lehṇa ultimately was chosen the successor just before Guru Nanak moved on to *Sach khandd*, the Heavenly Abode, in AD 1539. The Sikh faith was just taking shape and the routines were beginning to be established. Regular prayer, hard work during the day and community eating where all sat together in the *Pangat* (in a community row) without regard to rank, caste, or status, were the hallmark of Sikh practices. Meditation on the Lord's name and reciting the *Bāṇi* was the central part of the prayers, and as Bhai Gurdās has recorded the *Sodar* and the *Ārti*, as evening prayers, and the 'Jap', as Morning Prayer, were recited regularly as part of the daily routine by the congregation – the *Japji* being recited at what is called the 'Ambrosial Hour'. Subsequently, two more *Bāṇis*, the *Jāp Sahib* and the *Amrit Sawayye* of the tenth Nanak were in due course added to complete the five *Bāṇis* of the presently precribed daily routine.

The *Japji* has thus been the first of the liturgical prayers each true Sikh has recited in the five hundred years or so since then, and always at *Amrit Vela* - the Ambrosial Hour- as prescribed in the *SGGS* also. This hour is traditionally counted as the two hours before sunrise, or more accurately the four *ghaṛis* before sunrise. A *ghaṛi* is defined in the *Jyotish Prabhākar* as a period of twenty-four minutes according to the *Mahan Kosh* of Bhai Kahan Singh This prescription about *Amrit Vela* has also later on been incorporated in the *Rehat Maryāda*, the 'Code of Conduct' prescribed for the followers of Sikh faith.

The *Japji Sahib* starts after the *Mool Mantra*. As we noted, it consists of an opening *slok*, thirty-eight *pauṛis*'and a concluding *slok*. There is no formally prescribed structure for the *pauṛis*. However, the common theme, the golden thread that runs through and shapes the composition is to be found in the very first *pauṛi*.

It is *Kiv Sachiāra hoiyai* – how to pierce the veil of illusion, how to breakdown the dividing wall of falsehood that separates man from His Lord, and it occurs in the fifth line. How is the sequence of the *pauṛis* structured? A broad categorization attempted by Prof. Sahib Singh in the *Sri Guru Granth Sahib Darpan* is:

Pauṛi 1 to 3	How to bridge the gap with the Lord; importance of *Hukam*
Pauṛi 4 to 7	The Lord's pre-eminence and importance of *Nām Simran*
Pauṛi 8 to 11	Listening and imbibing the Lord's word
Pauṛi 12 to 15	True believing in what has been listened to and imbibed
Pauṛi 16 to 19	The chosen ones from among the Lord's servants good or bad; and places
Pauṛi 20 to 27	The Lord's creation and impossibility of knowing all of Him
Pauṛi 28 to 33	Discourse to Yogis, of the Lord Eternal
Pauṛi 34 to 38	The *Khandds* of spiritual growth, completion of lesson

Iqbal Singh in his *Japji and other Sikh Scriptures* sees four broad parts of the *Japji* which he broadly lists as:

Pauṛi 1 to 7	Define and focus on difficulties of a devotee
Pauṛi 8 to 27	Progressive movement towards the vision of the Great Reality
Pauṛi 28 to 31	Attributes of the person who has experienced Divine Grace
Pauṛi 32 to 38	Process of attaining union with the Divine, and stages of spiritual development

Narain Singh in his *Japji Sahib* lists a much longer categorization with almost each *pauṛi* except for the group 7 to 11, 12 to 15, 28 to 31 and 34 to 37 being separately taken. The short point here is that the theme is coherent and any such attempt at grouping is not really of any great importance.

After the 38 *pauṛis* comes the concluding *slok* which underlines and re-states the theme that in the Lord's presence shall your good and bad deeds be judged. That judgement shall determine whether we earn the right to stay in the blissful vicinity of the Lord or are we to suffer distance or even banishment from Him. Those who have truly fixed their minds on the Lord and have recited His name in meditation, their labour will be accepted and, as the Guru will tell us in the concluding *slok*, their faces shall shine in glory. At the conclusion of the *Mool Mantra* is recorded the title of this composition, 'Jap'. The *Japji Sahib* then commences with the first *slok* followed by the thirty-eight *pauṛis* and concluding with the last *slok*.

Let us now look at our subject in more detail starting with the opening *slok*.

5

THE FIRST GLIMPSE OF THE LORD

ਜਪੁ	*Japp*
ਆਦਿ ਸਚੁ ਜੁਗਾਦਿ ਸਚੁ ॥	*Ād(i) sach jugād(i) sach.*
ਹੈ ਭੀ ਸਚੁ ਨਾਨਕ ਹੋਸੀ ਭੀ ਸਚੁ ॥ ੧ ॥	*Hai bhi sach Nanak hosi bhi sach.*

Brief glossary

ਆਦਿ	*Ād(i)*	The beginning
ਜੁਗਾਦਿ	*Jugād(i)*	Through the ages
ਸਚੁ	*Sach*	Eternal Truth, the Ultimate Reality

Simply translated this *slok* means: "[The Lord] was True in the beginning, He is True through the ages, He is True today, He shall be Eternally True."

In this, what we can call the opening statement, the Guru re-affirms and emphasizes the essence of the theme put forth in the *Mool Mantra*. The Guru is adding for us another perspective to our understanding of the Divine. The attributes spelt out in the *Mool Mantra* necessarily could give but a limited glance of the infinite. The Guru now states that the "Lord was the Truth in the beginning; He shall so remain the Truth throughout all eternity. He is the Truth and shall forever be the Truth."

The concept is of course in complete consonance with the proposition in the *Mool Mantra* that there is but One Creator and

He is the only Truth. Being outside of time and not bound by the tyranny of birth, death and rebirth – the cycle imposed on mortals from which we all have to strive to be freed – the Lord is always the same, the Eternal and the only Truth.

The word 'Truth' is sometimes confused with the term 'correct' or 'right' by some of us when we begin the exercise of training ourselves towards seeking the Lord. It is here not intended in that limited sense. As Osho puts it, the difference between Truth and Untruth here is that the latter is something which at some stage was not, then it existed and in the course of time it faded to nothingness. Untruth is like a dream, it is while we sleep but is not before we fell asleep or after we woke up. This body similarly was not, then some years ago it came into existence and will soon cease to be. So is anger, or power or wealth, all Untruths. That which in the midst of all the flux is unchanged is then the only Truth, the only Reality. The Guru says God alone is the Truth. This world has assumed this form, this existence only by His will, and His Immanent Presence permeates each particle of this creation. If it were somehow possible to abstract from this creation His Presence, what is left behind would be nothing but a lie, a mirage, sheer falsehood. In this sense is the Lord the only Truth.

Since He is beyond time, obviously no period or date could be assigned to when exactly it was that He became the Truth. Lord Krishna addressing Arjuna in the *Bhagvad Gita* states, "Before Time was I am." This obviously is not a syntatic or grammatical error as it may seem to some. It is merely the Lord describing His relationship to time. He says He has existence since before time itself came into existence. Time is thus a construct and not an eternal verity. The rest of this creation is under the control of time and will in due course change, or grow, or even cease to exist. Time, as well as all creation, exists within the *Hukam*, the will of the Lord. Outside of the Lord time cannot exist. The Lord is the only Reality and only He can, and does, exist outside of time. He is forever; He is today and will always be. All else that we see or perceive is a dream and will go away with time.

To sum up, the Guru by way of an opening statement, seeks to make us aware of the One Lord whom we are seeking and for which the Guru prescribes for us the golden rules in the thirty-eight steps that follow, which will, if properly understood enlighten us gradually, and if we succeed in correctly observing the discipline laid down, one day take the true seeker to the True Lord. Here the Guru tells us the Lord is beyond the reach of time. His self-created existence is the root from which the entire material universe, even time itself has originated.

6

THE FIRST STEPS TOWARDS HIM

Pauṛi 1

ਸੋਚੈ ਸੋਚਿ ਨ ਹੋਵਈ ਜੇ ਸੋਚੀ ਲਖ ਵਾਰ॥	*Sochai soch na hovayi jay sochi lakh vār.*
ਚੁਪੈ ਚੁਪ ਨ ਹੋਵਈ ਜੇ ਲਾਇ ਰਹਾ ਲਿਵ ਤਾਰ॥	*Chupai chup na hovayi jay lāye raha liv tār.*
ਭੁਖਿਆ ਭੁਖ ਨ ਉਤਰੀ ਜੇ ਬੰਨਾ ਪੁਰੀਆ ਭਾਰ॥	*Bhukhia bhukh na utari jay banna purīya bhār.*
ਸਹਸ ਸਿਆਣਪਾ ਲਖ ਹੋਹਿ ਤ ਇਕ ਨ ਚਲੈ ਨਾਲਿ॥	*Sahas syāṇapa lakh hohe ta ik na chalai nāl.*
ਕਿਵ ਸਚਿਆਰਾ ਹੋਈਐ ਕਿਵ ਕੂੜੈ ਤੁਟੈ ਪਾਲਿ॥	*Kiv sachiāra hoīyai kiv kūṛai tuttai pāl.*
ਹੁਕਮਿ ਰਜਾਈ ਚਲਣਾ ਨਾਨਕ ਲਿਖਿਆ ਨਾਲਿ॥ ੧॥	*Hukam rajāyi chalṇa Nanak likhiya nāl.*

Brief glossary

ਸੋਚੈ	*Sochai*	By purification (through rituals)
ਚੁਪੈ	*Chupai*	By stilling of the mind, literally by silence
ਲਿਵ ਤਾਰ	*Liv tār*	The string of single-minded devotion
ਭੁਖ	*Bhukh*	Hunger, avārice
ਪੁਰੀਆ ਭਾਰ	*Purīya bhār*	Material wealth of the worlds
ਸਚਿਆਰਾ	*Sachiāra*	True

ਕੂੜ	*Kūṛ*	Falsehood, illusion
ਪਾਲਿ	*Pāl*	Wall or partition

Simply translated this *pauṛi* means: 'Purificatory rituals will not allow us to comprehend Him. Long spells of meditation will not bring God-realization. Possessions cannot bring satiety even if the wealth of whole worlds were to become ours. Human wisdom multiplied a hundred thousand times is unavailing in reaching God. How are then we to reach the status of the True One and how shall the veil of illusion and falsehood be pierced? Only by accepting His Command – His *Hukam*, and moulding our lives into a non-resisting path, always gladly accepting that which He chooses to bestow on us. Let us now look at it in more detail and also see what the learned commentators have said.

In this first *pauṛi* the Guru has raised the very fundamental question, which he of course proceeds to then answer throughout his discourse. The question is: "How is one to realize the Godhead within oneself and thus become True". In other words, how to reach God. The Guru poses the question and then in startlingly simple fashion provides us the golden key to this poser.

Before discussing the issue further let us look at the words used here, of which the brief glossary we have seen above. The Guru has in the beginning of the *pauṛi* listed out some of the methods which he says will not help achieve the aim for us. The methods for seeking spiritual growth which were then the most prevalent; he discusses and then simply discards them as not suitable vehicles for our journey. What were these methods? The first was *Soch*. The word 'ਸੋਚ' -*Soch* translates both as 'cleanliness' as well as 'thought'. In either sense the phrase conveys the message quite fully. We can see right here the first example of how in the interpretation of the *Gurbāṇi* wise and learned men can differ widely. The word *Soch* is rendered by Dr. Gopal Singh in his versified translation as 'thought', which is how Macauliffe had also construed it. Dr. Sangat Singh gives both translations, i.e., thought and cleanliness, equal weight in his rendering in verse of the *Japji Sahib*. Prof. Sahib Singh, Prof. Talib and Bhai Vir Singh however render it to mean 'cleanliness'. The *Faridkot wala Tīka*, one of the earlier commentaries on the *SGGS* commissioned by the Maharaja of Faridkot in the early twentieth century also renders it as 'cleanliness', as do most other commentators. Thus, both meanings have appealed to learned men. However, the interpretation by Bhai Vir Singh *et al.* seems more appropriate and also stands the test of reason. At the time and in the milieu of this *Bāṇi,* cleansing rituals were highly in vogue, among the Hindus especially. So much so that the mere ritual of taking a bath at a particular place or on a particular occasion was deemed adequate for cleansing the soul of its stains in the form of sins. It is more likely that the Guru is referring to this practice. This view of the matter is further strengthened if we note that in the same *pauṛi*, just two lines later the Guru has referred to the inadequacy of the 'intellect' as a means of reaching Him. The first line therefore could not be referring to the intellect, or thought and is obviously meant to tell us that cleansing rituals will not allow us to comprehend Him though we perform these a hundred thousand times.

In the second line the Guru refers now to the other prevalent practice, that of going into long spells of meditation to still the mind. He says that trying to build a linkage with the Lord through this practice, supposedly for achieving inner silence, will also not succeed however long may we seek to maintain such absorption.

In the third line the Guru says that acquiring of great wealth will not be able to bring us satiety even if the wealth of whole worlds becomes ours. The futility of striving to acquire wealth and power as a step towards satiating the inner hunger for reaching the Lord is here highlighted.

In the fourth line the Guru now turns to the role of intelligence or wisdom – *Syāṇap* (ਸਿਆਣਪ). He says you may possess the wisdom thousand-fold of a man, nay a hundred-thousandth folds, but it shall be unavailing in reaching your destination of God-realization.

Thus we see the Guru has pointed out the non-applicability of all the methods men customarily follow – observing religious rituals of purification, practices of austerities for stilling the mind, striving for greatness through acquisition of wealth and power, and finally relying on the force of the intellect. He then poses the question that follows naturally and asks in the fifth line, "How are we to reach the status of the True One and how shall this veil of illusion and falsehood be pierced?"

We must pause here once more, to note that this is the fundamental question for any true seeker, whichever belief system he may follow. Our existence in this world is meant for the sole purpose of trying to achieve acceptance in the eyes of the Lord, and in Sikhism this means to somehow pierce this veil of Māya and to be able to see the Reality behind the illusion. At the outset the Guru has rejected the conventionally accepted methods and paths prescribed. The Guru will be later in the *SGGS* telling us ਭਈ ਪਰਾਪਤਿ ਮਾਨੁਖ ਦੇਹੁਰੀਆ॥ ਗੋਬਿੰਦ ਮਿਲਣ ਕੀ ਇਹ ਤੇਰੀ ਬਰੀਆ। - *Bhayi prāpt mānukh dehurīya. Gobind milan̲ ki eh teri barīya*, *Rāg Āsa Mahla* 5, on page 12 of the *SGGS* and again on page 378. It translates broadly as: "You have been blessed with this human body. This is your chance to achieve oneness with the Lord." It is part of the Sikh faith that the human soul moves through 8.4 million forms of creation from the lowest, through the semi-sentient to the status of man. References to this are frequent in the SGGS, for instance at *Rāg Gaur̲i, Mahla* 3, p 162; *Rāg Māru Mahla* 1, p1034; *Rāg Māru Mahla* 5, p1100; *Rāg Bhairo Bhagat Kabir*, p1161; and numerous other places. The human form is for the soul the culmination of a long and arduous journey and it is our sole opportunity after that very long chain of transmigrations to now reach our Lord and break the chain thus achieving salvation. Only in the human form will this opportunity come, for the beasts have not the gift of singing His praises or meditating on Him.

How, the Guru poses the query, are we to achieve that state. And the Guru provides us the simple and elegant answer in the sixth, the concluding line: *Hukam rajāyi chalṇa* (Mould your very existence into a non-resisting path. Accept and be in complete tune with His *Hukam*). The path prescribed is of complete surrender to His will, of always accepting that which He chooses to bestow on us.

The tradition of complete surrender is of course known to many religions and has been part of the wisdom imparted by a number of great seers, revered in various parts of the world. Christianity teaches 'Thy Will be done' as an important postulate. This obviously implies complete submission and a lack of resistance to His command. Similar is the position in Islam where the very word translates as 'submission'. Even Hindu thought from the Vedic times onwards has had an implicit component of surrender of the self as a means to salvation. Guru Nanak also adopted the concept, but then he went on to revolutionize the approach to religion as it then existed. He preached and then successfully achieved an upheaval in the practice of religion. His way – Sikhism as it came to be known – was a virtual revolution against the empty formulism and the empty pursuit of rituals that was at that time widely practiced. He taught us to be fully participative in life and not run away to seminaries – *Matths* – or to jungles. Rather, he said be *Grahsta māhay udāsa* (Live the life of the householder but be detached from materialism). Rising above caste he said: *Chahu Vārṇa ko deh updes, os pandit ko sada ādeis* (Praise is due to that *pandit* who equally gives the message of God to all the four *Varṇas*; these being the division in Hinduism of humans into four hierarchically defined castes). Thus was his message unique and revolutionary, but the concept of "complete surrender to the Lord's will", of seeking to lose one's "sense of self" provided the solid underpinning.

In Sikhism this sense of the self is referred to as *haumai*. The word also translates as ego, self pride, arrogance in oneself in the everyday use of the word. Obviously the *haumai* in man breeds these evils and the two meanings have thus coalesced. This *haumai* is as per the Guru at the very root of man's distance from his Lord, and the day man realizes God, *haumai* will vanish – the two situations cannot co-exist. Conversely, if we strive and succeed in suppressing our *haumai* we will immediately realize God.

Thus, the *pāl* (veil) separating the self from the Reality is only this *haumai*. This sense of the self makes us relate more and more strongly to the material world, puts us under the sway of Māya, and increases our distance from the spiritual. In a vicious circle our selfness makes us more and more entangled in the frivolities around us. As we acquire greater wealth and power our attachment to the world increases and continuous pandering to our senses becomes the most important goal for us. This further feeds our *haumai* and we are inevitably led down the seductive but destructive path where mere acquisition of greater wealth or power becomes the sole measure of our success or failure. As we crave for more we inevitably begin to envy and covet what some others may have acquired. This unfortunate spiral continues downwards. Thus, from *haumai* are born avarice, anger, rancour, fear and all the evils that accompany material success.

We who are a manifestation of the Divine, who carry that divine spark inside all of us, acquire qualities that are more and more un-Godly. As we noted in the *Mool Mantra,* the Lord is *Nirbhau* (free of all fear) and *Nirvair* (without antagonism or rancour) towards anyone. These are the ideals we have to try to reach. Our mindless pursuit of material wealth however will take us in just the opposite direction.

The way out is clearly spelt out – *Hukam rajāyi chalṇa* – to mould our daily life along the path of accepting His will. To be happy and content in whatever state He may choose to keep us is to be our ideal – and is to be our pathway to God-realization or salvation – *Moksha*. In a state of full and uncomplaining acceptance our inner-self will come to the level of serenity and purity necessary for the awakening of the soul.

As the *SGGS* will clarify for us, it is not by mere observance of this rule – of surrender – that we can claim to have acquired a right to be accepted in the Lord's presence. For that it will still be necessary for us to wait patiently for *Nadar* (His grace, His blessing). It is only He who will one day suddenly awaken us to Himself. The effort enjoined upon us is to be prepared and be worthy. The strenuous effort called for from us is to purify ourselves. Living in total surrender to Him is the one precondition. Training our mind, our body, our senses; forever controlling the urge towards the material and forever seeking the right path, are all enjoined upon us. As the Guru says, as soon as the vessel is ready the *Amrit* (Nectar) of His name will come flooding into us. We have to just be ready and be capable of receiving that magnificent and overwhelming gift. It will come when He so decides, if only we strive to make ourselves fit for it. As the Guru says in *Gūjri Mahla* 1, page 504, SGGS ਊਂਧੈ ਭਾਂਡੈ ਕਛੁ ਨ ਸਮਾਵੈ ਸੀਧੈ ਅੰਮ੍ਰਿਤੁ ਪਰੈ ਨਿਹਾਰ – *Ūndhai bhānddai kuchh na samāvai sīdhai Amrit parai nihār*. The lines can be translated as: When the vessel is inverted it cannot receive anything. As soon as it becomes right side up nectar flows into it.

The attainment of the divine grace thus requires of us only the effort of keeping the vessel – our selves, bodies and minds – clean and pure and then awaiting in a state of total surrender for His kindly eye of Grace to turn towards us and fulfil our existence by the highest possible gift – that of His Divine Grace.

7

THE DIVINE ORDINANCE

Pauṛi 2

ਹੁਕਮੀ ਹੋਵਨਿ ਆਕਾਰ ਹੁਕਮੁ ਨ ਕਹਿਆ ਜਾਈ॥	*Hukmi hovan ākār hukam na kahiya jāyi.*
ਹੁਕਮੀ ਹੋਵਨਿ ਜੀਅ ਹੁਕਮਿ ਮਿਲੈ ਵਡਿਆਈ॥	*Hukmi hovan jīw hukam milai vaddiāyi.*
ਹੁਕਮੀ ਉਤਮੁ ਨੀਚੁ ਹੁਕਮਿ ਲਿਖਿ ਦੁਖ ਸੁਖ ਪਾਈਅਹਿ॥	*Hukmi utam nīch hukam(i) likh dukh sukh pāīay.*
ਇਕਨਾ ਹੁਕਮੀ ਬਖਸੀਸ ਇਕਿ ਹੁਕਮੀ ਸਦਾ ਭਵਾਈਅਹਿ॥	*Ikna hukmi bakshsīs ik hukmi sada bhavāīay.*
ਹੁਕਮੈ ਅੰਦਰਿ ਸਭੁ ਕੋ ਬਾਹਰਿ ਹੁਕਮ ਨ ਕੋਇ॥	*Hukmai andar sab ko bāhar hukam na koye.*
ਨਾਨਕ ਹੁਕਮੈ ਜੇ ਬੁਝੈ ਤ ਹਉਮੈ ਕਹੈ ਨ ਕੋਇ॥ ੨॥	*Nanak hukmai jay bujhai ta haumai kahai na koye.*

Brief glossary

ਹੁਕਮੁ	*Hukam*	The Divine Command, Order, the Operating Principles of the universe
ਆਕਾਰ	*Ākār*	Form, creation
ਵਡਿਆਈ	*Vaddiāyi.*	Exaltation, greatness
ਬਖਸੀਸ	*Bakhsīs*	Favour, grace
ਹਉਮੈ	*Haumai*	The sense of selfness, ego, arrogance

This *pauṛi* tells us that the Lord, having created the universe, has set in place His ordinance which now inexorably keeps the various components of this vast and mysterious creation functioning in perfect harmony. It is within this parameter that the world functions. In accordance with it does matter take shape, living beings come to exist; and then attain greatness or face suffering. There is no person and no material thing which is beyond the reach or control of this *Hukam*. Let us now look at the message in more detail.

Having in the first *pauṛi* laid down that the path prescribed for us is to move according to, and in step with, His *Hukam*, and to always accept in full surrender His will, the Guru now expounds on the concept further. The Guru says in the first line that only through His *Hukam* has this creation come into existence. The Guru says, it is not possible for us mortals to know or to understand what exactly this *Hukam* is, nor is it possible for it to be explained. However, it is only through *Hukam* that the business of this universe, of creation is carried on. In the second line the Guru says that all beings are created through His *Hukam* and any honour or greatness that we attain will only come from this *Hukam*. On our own there is nothing we could achieve. The Guru here is obviously addressing the many we see striving and struggling for high position and wealth. The amount of struggle, the zeal of the pursuit is the same for the many, but the fruit of that effort will come only to a few – as the *Hukam* of the Lord may ordain.

The third line says that humans become superior or inferior according to His *Hukam*, and the bestowal of suffering and joys on human beings is also by His *Hukam*. Continuing in the fourth line on the same theme the Guru says that by His *Hukam* on some is showered His blessing while for another there is the continuing cycle of death and rebirth. In the fifth line the Guru says there is none who is exempt from or beyond the reach of His *Hukam*. Finally, he says that the one who truly recognises the *Hukam* will automatically and immediately lose his *haumai* – his sense of selfness, of ego, his feeling of being separate from the Creator.

This *pauṛi* firstly spells out for us some of the contours of this *Hukam* which we are to comply with so as to be able to break through the veil of ਕੂੜ – *Kūṛ* – falseness and illusion. The Guru explains to us how our everyday life is governed by the *Hukam*; our successes and our failures, our greatness and our fame all are governed by the *Hukam*.

There may perhaps be detected a touch of determinism in this postulation. If all is merely *Hukam* then where do our efforts and our striving come in? Should we just sit down inert and passive and let the *Hukam* have its way with us? Our actions will in this view seem futile and the world meaningless. Why put mankind here at all if all we can do is fatalistically wait for our fate to unfold till listlessly we reach the end of this pointless journey?

Seen carefully and examined more fully in the context of the Guru's message as expounded further in the *Gurbāṇi* it will become clear that man's journey through this life is full of purpose and meaning. There is a clear, and very tough, task spelt out by the Guru himself – the task of trying to reach oneness with the Lord. There is absolutely no contradiction or anomaly in the message here. Everything indeed is under His *Hukam*. The universe has come into existence by His *Hukam*; the riches of the world, the myriad species that exist in such splendid variety in this universe are all so placed in accordance with His *Hukam*. In the midst of it all yet is man endowed by the Lord with free will.

The Lord has bestowed on mankind the freedom to choose evil or to choose good. It is within man's domain to use these God given gifts of intellect and free will to strive to understand that he is under a veil of illusion and he needs to make the hard effort to somehow break through this veil. It is man's choice to seek a return to his Creator by choosing the right path to help him break through this veil and see the Truth. Man can exercise his own will and choose to be either a *Manmukh* or a *Gurmukh* – be ego-centred and looking away from God, or to centre his vision on God's path and to live life as prescribed by the Lord's messengers, the Gurus. In the case of the Sikhs the *SGGS* is the preceptor, the Guru and it is therein that the road map is to be found for this path.

The Guru exhorts us repeatedly that in order to be worthy of the Lord's blessing we have to follow the path laid down by him. He tells us that by following this path we can achieve the desired oneness. It is however entirely the individual's free choice if he will follow this path whole-heartedly, partially or not at all. Inevitably the consequences will accordingly follow, but the choice exists. Inspite of knowing the evil outcome in the long run, so many of us are enticed by the momentary joys of worldliness that we make no effort to follow the Guru's injunctions. Literally *Manmukh* translates as 'facing one's own self' and *Gurmukh* as 'facing the Guru, looking towards the Guru'. This in other words means following the Guru and the path laid down by the Guru. This choice will make us move closer to the moment, whether in this incarnation or the next as the *Hukam* may prescribe for us, when we will be blessed with a breakthrough from our state of ignorance and suddenly the veil of illusion will be sundered. As soon as this veil is pierced the wall of separation between us and the innate reality within us will tumble. Thus will the purpose of our sojourn be fulfilled and thus will we find salvation. The choice is open to us.

The other choice - that of the *Manmukh* – is also equally available. By following our own mind, our own ego, our own self, rather than following the Guru's path, we can just as easily waste this opportunity and move ever further from salvation. The followers of this path will chase after material wealth, power over others and ceaseless activity for gratifying the senses. In all probability they will succeed in acquiring more and more of these things until one day perhaps realization will dawn about the utter futility of this path. They will, if they are lucky, learn that amassing more and more possessions only enhances the hunger for more of the same. There is no end to such endeavour. Such actions can never bring lasting peace or enduring happiness for the soul. Such *Manmukhs* will forever be restless and hungry. The relentless pursuit of the material, wealth, power and possession will soon become apparent as a totally meaningless activity. Such will be the path of the *Manmukh*.

The *Manmukh* will continue to strive along this path until the lucky day they realize their folly and turn to the Guru, and stop being *Manmukh*. When that fortunate day arrives they will be enabled to see that the path of self-discipline, of controlling the mind and reaching internal contentment is the more desirable, and in the long run the much more satisfying path. This is the path which the *Gurmukh* always pursues. A day will come in the life of the *Manmukh* when this realization will dawn and he will, like the *Gurmukh,* be able to see that everything moves by His *Hukam* and that the *Hukami* – the Lord, the Creator, permeates every pore of the *Gurmukh*. Instantly his *haumai* will vanish and Divine Reality will cast its glorious light all around. The gap between the self and the Creator will cease to exist and the purpose of this life will have been fulfilled.

8

SEEKING THE UNKNOWABLE

Pauṛi 3

ਗਾਵੈ ਕੋ ਤਾਣੁ ਹੋਵੈ ਕਿਸੈ ਤਾਣੁ॥	*Gāvai ko tāṇ, hovai kisai tāṇ.*
ਗਾਵੈ ਕੋ ਦਾਤਿ ਜਾਣੈ ਨੀਸਾਣੁ॥	*Gāvai ko dāt, jāṇai nīsāṇ.*
ਗਾਵੈ ਕੋ ਗੁਣ ਵਡਿਆਈਆ ਚਾਰ॥	*Gāvai ko guṇ vaddiāyia chār.*
ਗਾਵੈ ਕੋ ਵਿਦਿਆ ਵਿਖਮੁ ਵੀਚਾਰੁ॥	*Gāvai ko vidya vikham vīchār.*
ਗਾਵੈ ਕੋ ਸਾਜਿ ਕਰੇ ਤਨੁ ਖੇਹ॥	*Gāvai ko sāj karay tann kheh.*
ਗਾਵੈ ਕੋ ਜੀਅ ਲੈ ਫਿਰਿ ਦੇਹ॥	*Gāvai ko jīw lai phir deh.*
ਗਾਵੈ ਕੋ ਜਾਪੈ ਦਿਸੈ ਦੂਰਿ॥	*Gāvai ko jāpai disai dūr.*
ਗਾਵੈ ਕੋ ਵੇਖੈ ਹਾਦਰਾ ਹਦੂਰਿ॥	*Gāvai ko vekhai hādra hadūr.*
ਕਥਨਾ ਕਥੀ ਨ ਆਵੈ ਤੋਟਿ॥	*Kathna kathi na āvai tott.*
ਕਥਿ ਕਥਿ ਕਥੀ ਕੋਟੀ ਕੋਟਿ ਕੋਟਿ॥	*Kath kath kathi kotti kott kott.*
ਦੇਦਾ ਦੇ ਲੈਦੇ ਥਕਿ ਪਾਹਿ॥	*Denda day lainday thakk pāhe.*
ਜੁਗਾ ਜੁਗੰਤਰਿ ਖਾਹੀ ਖਾਹਿ॥	*Juga jugantar khāhi khāhe.*
ਹੁਕਮੀ ਹੁਕਮੁ ਚਲਾਏ ਰਾਹੁ॥	*Hukmi hukam chalāye rāh.*
ਨਾਨਕ ਵਿਗਸੈ ਵੇਪਰਵਾਹੁ॥ ੩॥	*Nanak vigsai veparvāh.*

Brief glossary

ਤਾਣੁ	*Tāṇ*	Power, might, capability
ਦਾਤਿ	*Dāt*	Gift, blessings, grace
ਨੀਸਾਣੁ	*Nisāṇ*	Sign, indication, mark
ਗੁਣ	*Guṇ*	Qualities
ਚਾਰ	*Chār*	Beautiful
ਵਿਦਿਆ	*Vidiya*	Learning, knowledge

ਵਿਖਮੁ	*Vikham*	Difficult, hard, tough
ਵੀਚਾਰੁ	*Vīchār*	Wisdom, thought
ਸਾਜਿ	*Sāj*	Create, make
ਜੀਅ	*Jia or jīw*	Life, body
ਲੈ ਫਿਰਿ ਦੇਹ	*Lai phir deh*	Takes away and then gives again
ਹਦੂਰਿ	*Hadūr*	Presence
ਕੋਟੀ	*Kotti*	Literally ten million, limitless
ਵਿਗਸੈ	*Vigsai*	Blooms, flourishes, grows
ਵੇਪਰਵਾਹੁ	*Veparvāh*	Without worry, free from tension

Simply understood this *pauṛi* tells us the different ways in which we perceive God. Those with power see Him in that form, others see Him as the Bestower of gifts. Yet others see Him as the epitome of good qualities. The learned ones see Him as the Personification of the most esoteric and complicated of Knowledge. He is seen as the Creator, and also as the Destroyer, the One who gives and then takes away. Some see Him as far away, others as intimately near. There is no end to these descriptions even though countless people have tried to describe Him. The Lord bestows His bounty limitlessly and the recipient may tire of taking; through the ages have we partaken of His munificence. Through His *Hukam* does He operate the universe and in doing so He takes joy even as He seems to show an apparent unconcern. Let us now look in more detail at these concepts and also see what has been the view of various learned ones.

As seen above, in this *pauṛi* the Guru describes the various ways in which humans perceive the Creator. The meaning of these lines has again been interpreted in different ways by many learned commentators. The version put out by the SGPC in its *Shabdarth* has it one way while a number of other commentators have a different interpretation. The reason for this differing perception lies in the word *gāvai* with which the first few lines of the *pauṛi* commence. It is amenable to being construed as a straight-forward statement meaning 'sings'. It can also be read as denoting a query, especially when read together with the next word which is *ko*. In this construction it can mean, 'who can?' Thus, some translators will say these lines are statements and refer to persons who have these particular qualities. Others will say these are queries and are to be construed as meaning, "Who could have the capacity," for instance, to dare sing of the Lord's power, and similarly for the other qualities referred to in these lines.

The more appealing interpretation is the one adopted by the *Shabdarth*. This is also followed by most commentators. The Guru is saying that those to whom the Lord has granted power sing of the Lord as Power. There are others who, according to their aptitude, sing of Him as the Giver, the Provider. There are others yet who experience Him as the possessor of great and numerous qualities. Yet others sing of Him as Knowledge of which attainment is very difficult. Some others sing of Him as one who creates these bodies and then destroys them. Some perceive Him as being very far away and beyond reach while others see Him as pervading everything and being ever nearby and within reach. Thus humans in their myriad songs, sing of Him in His various characteristics in their own ways determined by and limited to their own perceptions and capacities. Though the opening lines have been interpreted in these differing fashions, there are no differences when it comes to the last four lines. All are agreed that the Guru in the last four lines says that while all the various men sing variously His praises, yet even billions of such recitations cannot bring Him within the boundaries of physical description. In the midst of all this, says the Guru, the Lord Creator ceaselessly keeps giving to His creation from His limitless bounties until those who are the recipients of this munificence get satiated. This has been so from the very beginning of creation. The *Hukmi* – the Lord Creator – continues to run the universe by and in accordance with His *Hukam*. The pre-ordained march of events and time continues inexorably, and the Creator watches it all, free from worry.

This concept, of the Lord watching unconcerned, needs to be clearly understood. Is the Guru saying that having created the universe and having given so much of His bounties to us, the Lord is not any longer bothered about His creation and He disinterestedly is watching events unfold? That having set things in motion He has now become tired of it and indifferent – *vepravāh* – meaning without worry or concern about what may now happen. This is obviously not consistent with the concept of the Lord as the loving father, as the indulgent Bestower of bounty, as the one who is constantly showering love on His creation. An imperfect analogy may here make it easier to understand. Assume a very good, very caring doctor. Patients come to him by the hundred. He sees their troubles and prescribes medicine and other ways of alleviating their troubles. He does this to the best of his ability and he cares for the outcome in each case hoping he has been able to help ease the patient's troubles. Is he however to completely sink himself in each patient's tale of woe? If ever he did that he would go emotionally unstable and become unable to serve the other patients effectively. So he develops an attitude of concern and care for each while at the same time maintaining a certain detachment, a certain distance so that he can see the problem and unemotionally be able to determine the best course for treating the trouble. Could we say the doctor was unconcerned or not involved enough? By ensuring the distance so that he does not himself get emotionally involved and distressed, the doctor is in fact showing a true love and care for his patients. As we noted, the analogy is imperfect. There is no way any human situation can really be equated to the Lord's relationship with His creation.

What we can see from the above example is that even among humans it can be possible to have an unconcern which is deeply imbued with compassion and care and a desire to help. On a much vast and more exalted, cosmic scale the Lord's attitude can be thus understood. The Lord sees and takes fond delight in His beings. He is watchful of what they do and He is ever-loving, ever-giving. Yet in this process there is apparent unconcern on His part because He lets the world proceed on its course and He lets individual souls make their own lives as they choose – earning good *Karma* or bad. He does not intervene in each little action or in the results that ensure from the merits of such action – or its demerits. He watches as the individual soul develops and progresses on the path to God-realization. He equally watches as we regress or turn to material pursuits. The Guru will again, in *pauṛi* 37, return to this concept of the Lord watching over His creation and being pleased where he says: "Yet the Lord sees all, ponders over His creation – *vekhai vigsai kar vīchār* – and He is pleased." The term *vigsai* literally means to develop, bloom or grow – attributes which really are meaningless when applied to the Ultimate, who after all is the Bestower of all that exists, and could hardly be said to be developing. The context here thus requires the word to be read as 'pleasure' or 'delight'. *Nanak vigsai vepravāh* here has to mean that the compassionate, loving Lord, even as He may seem unconcerned, takes pleasure in watching over His creation.

In the above light we can now look at the *pauṛi* line by line. While doing so we will follow the interpretation given by the SGPC. In doing so we will ignore some other versions among which is an interesting one by a learned commentator who in his *Japji* translates the word *gāvai* in these first lines as an exhortation by the Guru to recite that the Lord has these qualities, treating the word *gāvai* as two words *ga* and *vay*; *ga* meaning sing and *vay* meaning 'hey you'. We may note that in either approach to the understanding of this *pauṛi,* the end result will not be too different. The short point is that the Lord Creator possesses all power, is the Giver of all blessings and so on. His creatures all sing of Him in His multifarious forms and manifestations. They wonder if He is close or far. The Lord watches over all His creation is compassionate pleasure and bestows His gifts forever and ever. So endless and infinite is His bounty that it is never exhausted while we who receive it may live and be satiated.

In the first line the Guru says if someone has been endowed with power – *tāṇ* – he will sing of the Lord as a manifestation of Power, or as Power Incarnate. In line 2 he is saying that others who have been the recipient of much largesse – *dāt* – see His vast bounties and see in these His Form and sing of Him in that way. In the third line is the reference to those who are bestowed with good qualities – *guṇ* – and sing of the Lord as the epitome of all splendid qualities. In line 4 is the mention of those wise and learned ones who see in Him mystical knowledge –*vidya* – and sing of Him as Knowledge Incarnate the understanding of which is – *vikham* – extremely tough.

In line 5 are mentioned those who see the Lord as – *sāj karay tann kheh* – the Creator of life and also the Destroyer; and in line 6 are those mentioned who see Him as - *jīw lai phir deh* - the one who moves the souls from body to body. Accordingly do they sing of Him!

In lines 7 and 8 is the reference to another distinction humans varyingly experience. This is with regards to the perception of Him as someone distant and unreachable, as against the perception many others have of Him being an ever present companion. There are both categories of men and they sing of Him in the light of their own understanding.

In lines 9 and 10 the Guru sums up this listing of the various categories and says there is no end to these narrations of the Lord and limitless is the number of those who thus sing of Him, or in other words narrate their experience and personal perception of Him. Since the Lord is Eternal and Infinite, obviously no amount of such narrations can fully describe Him or explain Him to mere mortals.

In the lines 11 and 12 the Guru reminds us that all that exists is the Lord's bounty. He says *denda day lainday thakk pāhe* – He has since eternity been giving to His creation, so much that the recipient may tire of receiving but the Lord's bounties will not cease. Since time began, this giving and taking has been going on. In other words, the Lord is the Eternal Bestower and we are eternally the recipients, the consumers of His limitless bounty.

In the last two lines, the Guru says *Hukmi hukam chalāye rāh* – the Lord's ordinance, His command, prevails forever and the system of the universe operates according to it. The Lord thus having brought into existence this vast and mysterious universe has then laid upon it His *Hukam* and the universe now moves for ever on its ordained path, in accordance with this ordinance. The Lord watches over this entire activity and is pleased even as He watches *veparvāh* (free of any concern). Thus in these concluding four lines has the Guru summed up that the Lord watches over all His creation in compassion and love and bestows His gifts forever and ever. So unending and infinite is His bounty that it is never exhausted while we who receive it may tire and be satiated.

9

BY HIS GRACE ALONE

Pauṛi 4

ਸਾਚਾ ਸਾਹਿਬੁ ਸਾਚੁ ਨਾਇ ਭਾਖਿਆ ਭਾਉ ਅਪਾਰੁ॥	*Sācha sahib sāch nāye bhākhya bhāu apār.*
ਆਖਹਿ ਮੰਗਹਿ ਦੇਹਿ ਦੇਹਿ ਦਾਤਿ ਕਰੇ ਦਾਤਾਰੁ॥	*Ākhay mangay deh deh dāt karay dātār.*
ਫੇਰਿ ਕਿ ਅਗੈ ਰਖੀਐ ਜਿਤੁ ਦਿਸੈ ਦਰਬਾਰੁ॥	*Pher ke aggai rakhiyai jit disai darbār.*
ਮੁਹੌਂ ਕਿ ਬੋਲਣੁ ਬੋਲੀਐ ਜਿਤੁ ਸੁਣਿ ਧਰੇ ਧਿਆਰੁ॥	*Muhau ke bolaṇ boliyai jit suṇ dharay pyār.*
ਅੰਮ੍ਰਿਤ ਵੇਲਾ ਸਚੁ ਨਾਉ ਵਡਿਆਈ ਵੀਚਾਰੁ॥	*Amrit vela sach nāu vaddiāyi vīchār.*
ਕਰਮੀ ਆਵੈ ਕਪੜਾ ਨਦਰੀ ਮੋਖੁ ਦੁਆਰੁ॥	*Karmi āvai kapṛa nadri mokh duār.*
ਨਾਨਕ ਏਵੈ ਜਾਣੀਐ ਸਭੁ ਆਪੇ ਸਚਿਆਰੁ॥੪॥	*Nanak evai jaṇiyai sabh āpay sachiār.*

Brief glossary

ਸਾਚਾ	*Sācha*	The True One
ਸਾਚੁ	*Sāch*	The reality, essence, truth
ਨਾਇ	*Nāye*	Rule, justice. Also name
ਭਾਖਿਆ	*Bhākhya*	Language
ਭਾਉ	*Bhāu.*	Love, regard
ਅਪਾਰੁ	*Apār*	Unlimited

ਆਖਹਿ	*Ākhay*	Asking
ਮੰਗਹਿ	*Mangay*	Requesting, demanding
ਦੇਹਿ	*Deh*	Give, bestow
ਦਾਤਿ	*Dāt*	Gift, blessing
ਅੰਮ੍ਰਿਤ ਵੇਲਾ	*Amrit Vela*	The ambrosial hour, the time when the mind is fixed on the Lord, generally early hours before the sunrise
ਕਰਮੀ	*Karmi*	Here through actions, *karam* in Persian means benediction
ਕਪੜਾ	*Kapṛa*	Apparel, here the natural body in which the soul resides
ਨਦਰੀ	*Nadri*	Through His grace, His benevolent glance
ਮੋਖੁ	*Mokh*	Salvation, liberation
ਦੁਆਰੁ	*Duār*	Gate, entrance

Simply translated this *pauṛi* tells us that He is the only Reality, His law is true and He is addressed in the language of adoration, of unbounded love. We beg of Him for His bounty and He is always giving to us. What could we offer to Him (since all we have in any case belongs to Him) that we may be blessed with a glimpse of the Divine Court? What words could we utter to please Him? The answer is, fixing your mind during the *Amrit Vela* (the early morning hours), on His name, ponder and meditate on His greatness. The good actions will earn us merit enough to give us re-birth into good lives but salvation can come only through His glance of grace (and not as a right). (Guru) Nanak says know that He is the only reality. Let us now discuss this at more length and also see what the various learned commentators have to say about it.

The Guru here expounds further on the description of the Creator. He says in the first line that the Lord is the sole Truth, the only Reality. So is the system created by Him. The word *nāye* is translated as law, or rule. This is the sense in which Prof. Sahib Singh has construed it. Many other learned commentators have, however, translated it in the sense of 'name', saying thereby that the line means, "True is the Lord, and True His Name". They take support from the fact that the term *nāye* has been elsewhere in the *Gurbāṇi* used in this sense. Prof. Sahib Singh, however, drawing upon his awesome mastery of grammar has in his commentary argued why the correct sense has to be "Rule, or Law, or System". Even otherwise, in the context here, the construction as it referring to the governing system within which the universe operates is more appealing, more in tune with the Guru's message. The postulate here is that the Lord, having created this entire universe does not sit micro-managing each event. Rather does the system put in place by Him keep the universe functioning, of course entirely in accordance with His *Hukam*, the eternal operating principle He has prescribed. This operating principle being also the Lord's creation, the Guru says, also carries in it the same immaculate perfection that exists in the Lord Himself. The Guru now refers to the way of addressing that Lord. He then tells us that the only language that can work is of unbounded love. In the second line he adds that His creation is forever asking, demanding more and more from Him, and He keeps bestowing His bounty. He is thus the source of all that we may possess, all that exists. No human is the real owner or possessor of anything on this earth.

The Guru in lines 3 and 4 then asks what can a poor human offer to such a Lord that could earn him even a glimpse of the Divine Abode. What words can a human mouth utter that could awaken in the Lord some special love for the seeker. The answer obviously is – there is no such thing or offering. It is absurd to even think that by offering some little bauble to the Lord we can earn His gratitude. Any earthly bauble we may seek to lay before Him will obviously be as nothing before the limitless bounty that the Lord has so richly been showering on us through all eternity.

And in any case it could have come to its human owner from the very source, which is the Lord Himself. Giving back a portion of those gifts to the very Donor is indeed laughable. Similarly, human wit or wisdom or intelligence can shape no prayer, no words which could impress the Infinite Lord. This is a concept already laid down in *paur.i* 1 where the Guru talks of *Sahas syān. apa lakh hoye ta ik na chalai nāl* - Not by force of intellect is He to be approached.

The Guru is thus stressing the helplessness of mere mortals in trying to entice or impress the Lord into a loving relationship. The Guru probably had in mind the common practice of the rich making large offerings to religious centres, which unfortunately continues to be in vogue even to this day. We have the unsavoury instances of the rich making donations and getting their names inscribed on stone plaques at religious places, or having announcements made of their munificence. Deluded fools, they do not realize that the wealth of which they are indirectly boasting has come to them from the same Lord before whom they want to be proclaimed as great and holy donors. The very Creator, the Source and the Bestower of all worldly goods and wisdom can obviously not be won over by offering back to him portions of these very things. Imagine a penurious man gifted large wealth by a king trying to offer a few coins in obeisance to the same king and expecting that this earn him sufficient favour. Ridiculous as such an endeavour would be, infinitely more ridiculous is the sight of men offering money and things to God – the King of all kings – and hoping that it will give them merit in the Lord's accounts.

Having stressed the obviously ridiculous nature of such efforts, the Guru then in the fifth line gives us the right key. He does not end with the discouraging conclusion that there is nothing that we humans can offer to the Lord. He instead goes on to prescribe the one method which will work. And that method is *Amrit vela sach nāu vaddiāyi vīchār* - Fix your consciousness, your mind on the True One when *Amrit Vela* comes, and meditate on

His Greatness. The importance of *Amrit Vela* is thus very high. The term translates as 'The Ambrosial Hour'. The Guru says that it is the correct hour, the right time to meditate on the True One. In this light we can look a bit more closely at this concept.

Amrit Vela by tradition is deemed to be the period starting two hours before sunrise and ending an hour after sunrise. The *Mahan Kosh* explains it as the four *gharịs* before sunrise. The second meaning it gives is the time at which *Mukti* or salvation comes. It then defines *gharị* as varyingly understood but meaning the sixtieth part of the day according to the *Jyotish Prabhākar*, a treatise on the Indian system of astrology. In this light the *Amrit Vela* would commence 96 minutes before sunrise. It is customary for Sikhs to rise at this hour, complete their ablutions and having bathed, sit down to meditate on, or to sing the praises of the Lord. The importance of *Amrit Vela* has been known since ancient times and predates Sikhism. Hinduism has its own prescribed prayers for the dawn and sunset times. Muslim practices also require some of the prayers to be at daybreak. The Sikhs certainly have been practicing it since the time Guru Nanak settled in Kartārpur on the banks of the river Rāvi, in 1521. The followers who settled with him on a piece of land donated by a wealthy follower constituted the first formal congregation. It was the practice for all of them to gather before dawn and join the Guru in meditation and singing of hymns. There is certainly something about this early hour, before the world wakens and before the air is filled with the hubbub of everyday life, which moves the mind naturally to spirituality. It is always easier in such surroundings and in that atmosphere to forget the material and to ponder on the greater mysteries of creation.

There is also, one may note, a very practical aspect to this practice. The times when these prescriptions were laid down were the early historic times, and when the Guru's Sikhs adopted it in the medieval times the circumstances prevailing required that a certain routine be adopted. It will be recalled that we are here speaking of the sixteenth century, much before electricity was discovered and harnessed. The daily routines therefore necessarily were required to be moulded to natural daylight. The hours during the day had to be utilized in attending to life's needs. Simple though these needs were yet they must have required considerable time and labour, since labour-saving devices were also yet sometime in the future. In the middle of the daily grind it would obviously have been difficult for the ordinary man to bring his mind around to prayers and spirituality. It was therefore even otherwise practical to reserve some special time for this essential activity. What better time than the early morning hours – hours that were free and peaceful and were traditionally accepted as the time for prayers.

So we see that the Guru's prescription of a time for prayers was practical and most suited to his followers, the bulk of whom were from the peasantry whose workday in the fields had to start with sunrise and to end with sundown. It was best to set apart for them time in the morning before they got stuck in the quotidian chores. We also see that practicality apart, the mind is certainly at its freshest and the body most rested and the whole person most at peace at that early morning hour. The beasts and the birds, the world at large is still asleep and there is an ethereal quiet on the landscape that greatly reinforces any effort towards spirituality. So, meditating on the True One at the ambrosial hour would bring greater benefit and bear more fruit.

Above all, the ambrosial hour is really that when your mind frees itself from the useless striving for material wealth and worldly goods and turns itself towards the Lord. When the Guru says to meditate on the greatness of the Lord at the ambrosial hour, he is obviously not restricting us to such effort only at that particular hour. Meditation, the *Sri Guru Granth Sahib (SGGS)* tells us, should so become part of us that with each breath and with each morsel of food we take in, we should take His name. In short whenever worldly entanglement is loosened and the mind turns towards the spiritual – then is the ambrosial hour. It would do more good if this meditation were done in the early hours of the morning at the traditionally prescribed times, but it is equally efficacious if at any time at all the mind were persuaded to turn away from the everyday rut and were fixed on the Lord. In this context *A Popular Dictionary of Sikhism* by W. Owen Cole and Piara Singh Sambhi gives a broader meaning to the phrase through a reference to the *shabad* of the third Nanak, known to us also as Guru Amar Das, recorded in the *SGGS*, page 35, "*Jay vela vakhat vīchāriyai ta kit vela bhagat hoye*". This broadly translates as: "Those who engage in devotion do not wait to enquire when the hour will be auspicious; what kind of devotion is it which puts the beloved out of mind even for an instant." Bhai Vir Singh in his commentary has translated this phrase - *Amrit Vela* - as meaning that time which is as spiritually invigorating as Nectar and which avails to carry us closer to the Lord, though he also says that in the *Japji Sahib* the Guru's hint is towards the early morning hours. Thus we must desist from the temptation to give a ritualistic connotation to this situation, while accepting the importance of those precious morning hours.

Here we need again to pause and to consider that in laying down these prescriptions the Guru also is showing us that man, in the midst of the Lord's fixed commands, has yet the gift of free will. The choice on when or whether at all to meditate is entirely ours. The effort of picking up the right option for our actions has to be made by us. It is also open to us to ignore this choice altogether and decide instead to drift through life. If however we do make the right choice the rewards will immediately follow. This the Guru spells out for us in the very next line. The Guru very much wants us to decide correctly, so he tells us the consequences of our choice, as we shall see in the next line.

The Guru says in the sixth line, "*Karmi āvai kapṛa nadri mokh duār*". The assured reward to the follower of the right path is to be blessed with a deserving *kapṛa.* This word translates literally as apparel, cloth or dress. Here it is of course used for the human body, which indeed is the attire for the soul in this world. The soul inside each living being is but a part of the Divine. It is in a state of separation from the Lord and has been sent to this world to work its way to reunion. That is the simple hypothesis behind the Guru's teaching. The soul can obviously not exist in the material world in its immaterial form by itself, so the Lord while sending it to this world of mortals ordains that it be clad in a body. The type of body that falls to its lot can by itself be a major determinant of how easy the soul's passage to that reunion with the Lord will be.

In the first place, we have been told that the soul in its passage has, according to the Guru, to progress through various pre-animal semi-sentient, and then animal stages till it has earned enough merit to earn a human incarnation. Now within this stage starts a new and equally time-consuming and difficult struggle. As the Guru says elsewhere, "*Bhayi prāpat mānukh dehurīya, Gobind milan̥ ki eh teri barīya*" (*Asa Mahla* 5, *SGGS*, page 12), meaning, "You have at last been blessed with a human body to your good fortune; this is your chance to attain union with the Lord." It is for this stage of the soul's passage through this mortal world that the great seers have prescribed paths for movement towards the Lord. It is for this that Guru Nanak has spelt out the message of the *Japji.* And it is here that the importance of following that path with discipline and devotion becomes vital.

The more faithfully we observe the discipline prescribed by the Guru, the more sincere and devout is our effort, the better is the *Kapṛa* to which we can hope to be given. How does it matter as to what *Kapṛa* this soul is wearing? The release from this worldly existence – this separation from the Lord will come only when the Lord's glance of grace turns on us. Till then we will have to move between one human body and the other. Depending on our deeds, the *Karma* that we earn through our actions the movement can be upward to a body with a higher spirituality or downward into a brutish existence.

We can easily imagine how much easier it is to follow the path of self-discipline and spiritual growth if we were born into an environment which encourages such growth, say a religious, God-fearing family where the natural encouragement is towards Godliness. A family where material needs are comfortably met and energy need not be squandered in merely making up the wherewithal for everyday existence; where there is also no excess of material wealth such as to lure the mind away from the path of righteous living. See how much easier the pursuit of the right path would be in such surroundings.

Now imagine the opposite. What if our *Karma* lands us into either extreme? What if there is too much wealth where acquisitions and power are the sole aim, where energy is channelled into only such pursuit. How could, in such circumstances, a soul even attempt a path to the humility, serenity and the righteous behaviour required by the Guru's prescription? Equally, if existence required continuous struggle for the basics of livelihood, if the atmosphere were full of anger and worry and tension, how would it be possible to find time or even the space to concentrate on what is required for self-discipline?

There may be some who, in spite of these huge handicaps find the way out. The large majority will however succumb to the pressure and will struggle to find the right path. Such souls deprived of the opportunity to live the right life may then tend to regress further. In short, incongenial surroundings can be a millstone round the neck of the seeker, hard to carry and dragging him downwards away from the Lord. If a soul fails to overcome and keeps sliding back, a day may come when it moves back to an animal existence. As Bhagat Kabir says in *Rāg Gūjri*, *SGGS* page 524, *Chār pāv duye sing gung mukh tubb kaisay guṇ gayi hai,* meaning "Take the Lord's name now when He has given you this golden opportunity, because when you inhabit an ox's body and your shoulders ache from pulling and your nostril is split by the bit and you have no means of speaking, how will you sing praises of the Lord." Kabir ji is of course referring to the movement of the soul through a series of births which will one day also include rebirth as a bullock pulling some plough.

The immediate benefit that accrues from our good actions, our right living is that the Lord bestows on us a better *Kapṛa* thus making it possible and easier for the soul to continue its path upwards to follow the right path, to purify ourselves, to make ourselves worthier of receiving His grace, till one fortunate day the Lord God chooses to bless us and we attain oneness with Him, we realize the Lord Immanent in all creation, we reach salvation - *Moksha*.

Here we may note that the term *karmi* can also be construed as 'through His Grace'. This is because the word *karam* means both 'action' in Sanskrit; and 'benediction' or 'blessing' in Persian. Bhai Vir Singh has used it in the sense of 'action'. Prof. Sahib Singh uses it as 'benediction'. Different commentators have used either connotation. The SGPC's *Shabdarth*, as also Dr. Gopal Singh in his commentary, follow the sense as used by Bhai Vir Singh. It also stands to reason otherwise. If the Guru had meant to use it as 'benediction' then the word *Nadri* which also means 'through His grace' would not have been used in the same line. The meaning of *karam* here should more appropriately be taken as 'action'. The Guru is enjoining upon us to keep our conduct righteous and is affirming that commandment by telling us the advantage we can expect to gain from it.

The Guru in the seventh, the last line of this *pauṛi* says: *Nanak evai jaṇīyai*. This has been translated by Prof. Sahib Singh as: "Thus is the Lord to be experienced." Prof. Talib however renders the line as: "Nanak! Know the All-holy (*sachiār*) to be Almighty, Absolute." Bhai Vir Singh renders it as: "When the door to salvation opens, through His Grace, as the Guru has said in the 6th line, then the knowledge immediately dawns that the Lord is the only Reality."

Thus we see that in this *pauṛi* the Guru is telling us that by the observance of the steps laid down in the previous lines will we be enabled to be enlightened to the fact that He is 'ਸਾਚਾ ਸਾਹਿਬ' - *Sācha Sahib* - the True Lord who can be addressed only through 'ਭਾਖਿਆ ਭਾਉ' - *Bhākhia bhāu* - the language of love. He is 'ਅਪਾਰੁ' – *Apār* - limitless, unbounded. He is eternally the Giver to His creation who are forever asking and demanding and who are given so much by that limitless Giver that they will be satiated and will one day get tired of asking. He is to be reached through proper meditation, as prescribed by the Guru. In the last line the Guru concludes by reiterating that the Lord is the only Truth.

10

THE LORD OF ALL

Pauṛi 5

ਥਾਪਿਆ ਨ ਜਾਇ ਕੀਤਾ ਨ ਹੋਇ॥	*Thāpiya na jāye kīta na hoye.*
ਆਪੇ ਆਪਿ ਨਿਰੰਜਨੁ ਸੋਇ॥	*Āpay āp niranjan soye.*
ਜਿਨਿ ਸੇਵਿਆ ਤਿਨਿ ਪਾਇਆ ਮਾਨੁ॥	*Jin seviya tin pāyia mān.*
ਨਾਨਕ ਗਾਵੀਐ ਗੁਣੀ ਨਿਧਾਨੁ॥	*Nanak gāviyai guṇi nidhān.*
ਗਾਵੀਐ ਸੁਣੀਐ ਮਨਿ ਰਖੀਐ ਭਾਉ॥	*Gāviyai suṇiyai mann rakhiyai bhāu. (5)*
ਦੁਖੁ ਪਰਹਰਿ ਸੁਖੁ ਘਰਿ ਲੈ ਜਾਇ॥	*Dukh parhar sukh ghar lai jāye.*
ਗੁਰਮੁਖਿ ਨਾਦੰ ਗੁਰਮੁਖਿ ਵੇਦੰ ਗੁਰਮੁਖਿ ਰਹਿਆ ਸਮਾਈ॥	*Gurmukh nāda(ng) gurmukh veda(ng) gurmukh rahiya samāyi.*
ਗੁਰੁ ਈਸਰੁ ਗੁਰੁ ਗੋਰਖੁ ਬਰਮਾ ਗੁਰੁ ਪਾਰਬਤੀ ਮਾਈ॥	*Gur īssar gur gorakh barma gur pārbati māyi.*
ਜੇ ਹਉ ਜਾਣਾ ਆਖਾ ਨਾਹੀ ਕਹਣਾ ਕਥਨੁ ਨ ਜਾਈ॥	*Je hau jāṇa ākha nāhi kehṇa kathan na jāyi.*
ਗੁਰਾ ਇਕ ਦੇਹਿ ਬੁਝਾਈ॥	*Gura ik deh bujhāyi. (10)*
ਸਭਨਾ ਜੀਆ ਕਾ ਇਕੁ ਦਾਤਾ ਸੋ ਮੈ ਵਿਸਰਿ ਨ ਜਾਈ॥੫॥	*Sabhna jiā(n) ka ik dāta so mai visar na jāyi.*

Brief glossary

ਥਾਪਿਆ	*Thāpiya*	Established, set up
ਕੀਤਾ ਨ ਹੋਇ	*Kīta na hoye*	Cannot be fashioned or made
ਨਿਰੰਜਨੁ	*Niranjan*	Free from taint. Anjan means kohl, *surma*, used in India to line the ayes.

ਸੇਵਿਆ	*Seviya*	Served
ਮਾਨੁ	*Mān*	Honour, respect
ਗਾਵੀਐ	*Gāviyai*	To sing, here paeans of praise to the Lord
ਨਿਧਾਨੁ	*Nidhān*	Treasure
ਭਾਉ	*Bhāu.*	Love, here an awe-struck adoration
ਦੁਖ ਪਰਹਰਿ	*Dukh Parhar*	To remove all woes
ਘਰਿ	*Ghar*	Home, here the heart
ਗੁਰਮੁਖਿ	*Gurmukh*	Facing the Guru. From the mouth of the Guru; here his word, his 'Bāṇi'
ਨਾਦੰ	*Nād*	Sound, here the divine music
ਵੇਦੰ	*Ved*	Knowledge
ਰਹਿਆ ਸਮਾਈ	*Rahiya samāyi*	Pervades all existence
ਈਸਰੁ	*Īssar*	A name for Lord Shiva
ਬਰਮਾ	*Barma*	Lord Brahma
ਪਾਰਬਤੀ ਮਾਈ	*Pārbati Māyi*	Mother Parvati (Shiva's consort), or Parvati and Māyi (Lakshmi, Vishnu's consort)
ਹਉ	*Hau*	Myself
ਦੇਹਿ ਬੁਝਾਈ	*Deh bujhāyi*	Made to understand, made understood

Here we are told that the Lord is not something you could install or create; He is self-existent and beyond any taint. Those who serve Him with true devotion earn honour. We should sing paeans to that storehouse of virtues. We should sing to Him, listen to laudation of Him, and fill our mind and heart with love, awe and adoration for Him. Thus will our woes be shed and joy will come to us. The Guru's *bāṇi* – his word – contains within it the sum total of all existence and the Lord Himself is manifest in His *bāṇi*. The Lord, however, is really unknowable and it is not within human capacity to attempt His description. In conclusion, the Guru prays to the Lord to grant him the continuing understanding that the Lord is the sole giver, the One Source of all that we have. Let us now look in more detail as to what the learned men of God have to tell us.

As we have briefly seen, the Guru in this *pauṛi* elaborates on the attributes of the One Lord. In the first and second lines he says the Lord cannot be installed, nor fashioned. He the Faultless, Immaculate One is self-existent. *Thāpiya* is from the Sanskrit *sthāpit*, a term used for establishing something and commonly used for the ritual installation of an idol of the deity in a Hindu temple. Referring obliquely to this practice, the Guru, who did not endorse idol worship at all, says the Lord is not subject to such ritual installation. Simultaneously, he reiterates through this example the primacy of the Lord as the self-created – 'ਸੈਭੰ' - *Saibhang*. He adds that nor is the Lord to be fashioned, created or made by any outside agency. He Himself is His own Creator, His own Maker. Further He is *Niranjaṇ*, free from taint. The Lord as the sole power in the entire universe which is beyond the control of Māya is referred to here. The rest of creation suffers from the effects of Māya (illusion). This taint is carried by all created beings. Only the self-created Lord is free from this taint. He is thus described as beyond the limits of time and space and unique, all by Himself.

In the third and fourth lines the Guru turns to the other recurring theme of this discourse; that since true honour can be earned only through serving Him, therefore sing His praises for He is the treasure-house of all that is good. Serving the Lord is obviously not through mere physical action qua some material person or body. Serving Him is through acquiring love and devotion for Him and His creation, and through constantly meditating on His name while living a life of self-discipline and control over the senses. The only contact we have with the Lord is through our minds, our inner-selves, or through His created beings and things in the midst of which we exist. Thus, service to Him can also be achieved only through these channels. Love His beings, hurt no heart, help those in need and provide to those who lack. While doing all this on the material plane, fight also the inner battle, of discipline, self-control and single-mindedly fixing your mind on Him and singing of His praises. Thus is He served, and those who do serve Him will win true honour. This honour may even come in this world but certainly will it be our due in His presence. The only real treasure to seek is His approval, His glance of grace. He is the treasure-house from which all gifts, even the mundane ones, will come to us; He is *guṇi nidhān*, literally the 'Treasure house of Virtues'.

In lines 5 and 6 the Guru says when we sing of Him and hear such laudation, while in our hearts we carry the love and adoration for Him, our woes will vanish and all bliss will be bestowed on us. The injunction *gāviyai suṇiyai* (singing and listening) occurs often in the *Gurbāṇi.* Sing His praises, not because He is very fond of sycophantic language, but because in the process of such single-minded and devoted singing, our own inner-selves will get washed clean of all accumulated sins. Not only must we sing to Him, we must also hear His praises. This obviously requires that we keep the company of those who sing to him. The keeping of the company of 'Sādhus and Saints' - true devotees - is also repeatedly enjoined on the seeker. In *Sādh sangat* (company of the pious, the saintly), our own selves will undergo purification. Thus we are told to sing to Him, and also hear those singing to Him. While we do this the state of our mind must also be properly modulated. There must be no doubt, no scepticism, no questioning. Let the mind be filled with love, awe and adoration for Him. This discipline will result in, the Guru says, ridding us of all our woes, and ushering into our selves all bliss.

Lines 7 and 8 have been rendered somewhat differently by various commentators. The word *Gurmukh* in line 7 has been translated by Prof. Sahib Singh as: (i) By turning one's face towards the Guru, (ii) One who has his face towards the

Guru, and (iii) Through the Guru. Prof. Talib renders it as "Preceptor's word". Iqbal Singh renders it as the "Guru's word", as does the SGPC's *Shabdarth*. Dr. Sangat Singh translates it as 'God'. Literally the word *Gurmukh* combines 'Guru' and 'mukh' meaning the 'preceptor' and 'face'. A person who obeys the Guru and heeds his commands is said to be *Gurmukh* – facing the guru – as opposed to *Manmukh* – facing his own egoistic self. Narain Singh has another view and sees *Gurmukh* as meaning the chief of the Gurus, from using the word *mukh* in the sense of *mukhya* meaning 'main' or 'chief'. He thus translates it as 'God'. Since here, in line 8, the word used is 'Guru' so it would be consistent to see the two lines as referring to God whose further attributes the Guru is describing here. Viewed another way, the Guru's word is *Gurbāṇi* which is viewed by the true seeker as God incarnate. The difference between calling it *Gurbāṇi* or 'Guru, the Lord' is thus only in the semantics. Viewed thus, these lines mean that the word of the Guru is that mystical 'Word' – the Divine Sound, the music of the spheres. The 'Word' is also the sum of all knowledge. *Nād* is literally musical sound and *Ved* is derived from *Vidya* (knowledge). *Ved* here is not used for the scriptural four *Vedas* of Hinduism, but for all knowledge. The 'Word' is thus the divine music, the sum of all knowledge and it pervades all creation. *Rahiya samāyi* means 'permeates everything'. The eighth line states that this Guru – God Himself – contains within Himself Īssar, Vishnu, Brahma and the goddesses Pārbati, Lakshmi and Saraswati. What the Guru intends us to see is that there is but one 'God' and various deities, goddesses, or repositories of knowledge have no independent existence outside of Him. The oneness of the Creator, His uniqueness and His Primacy is being explained. Īssar is one of the names used for Lord Shiva; Gorakh (protector) from *goe* - earth, and *rakh* – protect, means literally 'protector of the earth' and refers here to Lord Vishnu; and Lord Brahma is of course the third part of the Trinity, believed in Hinduism to rule the universe. Pārbati is

Pārvati, the consort of Lord Shiva and also the personification of the Female Principle of the Divine. *Māyi* can mean 'mother'. Some scholars however split up *Māyi* into *Ma* meaning Lakshmi, the consort of Lord Vishnu and *i* meaning Saraswati, the consort of Lord Brahma. Thus in this construction the reference covers all the main goddesses together. However, even construed thus the reference is again to the Female Divine Principle and the sense of these lines does not change. The Lord is manifest in the Guru and the *Gurbāṇi*, which for the Sikh are interchangeable really, because the *Gurbāṇi* is the Guru and the Guru is the Lord Himself. The same concept of the *Gurbāṇi* being the sum total of everything occurs again at *Rāmkali Mahla* 1, SGGS, page 879, where the Guru says, "*Sabh nād beid gurbāṇi* …", meaning that the *Gurbāṇi* is the 'Divine Word'; it is the sum of all knowledge.

In line 9 the Guru adds that the Lord is really unknowable and even if one were to come to know of Him, it would be impossible to put that knowledge into words that could really express the experience. So the difficulty is two-fold here. Firstly knowing Him is beyond human power. The Guru repeatedly says that His Extent, His Limits and His Power are so infinitely beyond human ken that none may boast of having measured Him. Further, if by some divine intervention this knowledge were to be bestowed on one, the description of that Divine presence, of that experience, would find a man powerless to put it into words. As Prof. Talib puts it in his commentary, this line says, "Were I to realize His true greatness, how may I utter it? By what power may I express it?" And as Iqbal Singh says, "Were I to attain some understanding of Him, how do I describe Him? For, he cannot be narrated in words." As the *Gurbāṇi* tells us more than once, the experience of the infinite is a rare event for the human race and when the experience does happen the description is as impossible as the dumb man describing the taste of a very sweet and tasty dish. Words are totally inadequate for such an experience.

The last two lines are seen differently by learned commentators, specially the tenth line. The words *Gura ik deh bujhāyi* are rendered as "Oh Guru (the Lord Himself) it is my prayer to you", by Prof. Sahib Singh, and Bhai Vir Singh sees it the same way. Prof. Talib, on the other hand, puts it as: "My Master thus has enlightened me." He says it is meant as a prayer to the Guru to give us this understanding. The tenth line is translated by Narain Singh as: "O my Guru, give me but one understanding." Iqbal Singh follows Prof. Talib's rendering. So, it is either seen as a direct statement by the Guru describing what the Lord has already bestowed on Him, namely, the understanding of the basic truth that there is but one Provider who is forever giving to all the beings in this world. Alternatively, it is seen as a prayer by the Guru beseeching the true Guru, the *Satguru*, the Lord Himself, to always grant him the understanding. Since the Guru has throughout this composition approached the Lord as a humble seeker, the latter rendering seems to be the correct one. The Guru here prays to the *Satguru* to always grant to him the continuing understanding of the status of the Lord as the Sole Giver, ending with the further prayer that never may the seeker forget Him.

A point that emerges in this *pauṛi* is the importance given to the concept of Guru. The *Gurbāṇi* will repeatedly tell us that without the Guru no man may hope to reach Him. The Guru is given the status of all deities and divine power by Guru Nanak. The seeker's consciousness will get awakened only through exposure to the teachings of the Guru and none may hope on his own to reach beyond the veil of falsehood. This strongly repeated theme, as noted earlier, has been seized upon by many to press the claim of human Gurus as the bestowers of the divine knowledge. It is entirely possible that there do exist enlightened individuals who have indeed this divine light that they can pass on to the seeker. It is also enjoined upon the Sikh that those who are god-fearing and moving on the path of Godliness are to be respected and their company actively sought. However, the Sikh has but one Guru, the *Sri Guru Granth Sahib* – the visible form of the Gurus.

Ever since AD 1708 when the tenth Nanak, Guru Gobind Singh, passed on the divine light to the *Granth Sahib* and commanded his Sikhs to keep faith in it and treat the book as the living Guru, the Sikh cannot repose faith in any other Guru. The lessons of how to bring order to one's life and of transcending the veil of illusion are contained therein and while the Sikh must seek the company of the men of God of whatever faith or religion, no practices contrary to the *SGGS* must be followed and the true Sikh must strictly order his life in accordance with this path and never let himself be distracted lest he lose himself in confusion between paths and waste this most precious human incarnation.

11

THE JEWELS WITHIN

Pauṛi 6

ਤੀਰਥਿ ਨਾਵਾ ਜੇ ਤਿਸੁ ਭਾਵਾ ਵਿਣੁ	*Tīrath nāva je tis bhāva viṇ bhāṇay*
ਭਾਣੇ ਕਿ ਨਾਇ ਕਰੀ।।	*kay nāye kari.*
ਜੇਤੀ ਸਿਰਠਿ ਉਪਾਈ ਵੇਖਾ ਵਿਣੁ	*Jeti sirtth upāyi vekha viṇ karma kay*
ਕਰਮਾ ਕਿ ਮਿਲੈ ਲਈ।।	*milai layi.*
ਮਤਿ ਵਿਚਿ ਰਤਨ ਜਵਾਹਰ ਮਾਣਿਕ ਜੇ	*Mat(i) vich ratan jawāhar maṇik jay*
ਇਕ ਗੁਰ ਕੀ ਸਿਖ ਸੁਣੀ।।	*ik gur ki sikh suṇi.*
ਗੁਰਾ ਇਕ ਦੇਹਿ ਬੁਝਾਈ।।	*Gura ik deh bujhāyi.*
ਸਭਨਾ ਜੀਆ ਕਾ ਇਕੁ ਦਾਤਾ	*Sabhna jia ka ik data so mai visar*
ਸੋ ਮੈ ਵਿਸਰਿ ਨ ਜਾਈ।। ੬।।	*na jāyi.*

Brief glossary

ਤੀਰਥਿ	*Tīrath*	Place of pilgrimage, literally a river fording place
ਸਿਰਠਿ	*Sirtth*	World, here entire creation
ਵਿਣ ਕਰਮਾ	*Viṇ Karma*	Without the Lord's grace
ਕਿ ਮਿਲੈ ਲਈ	*Kay milai layi*	Who can obtain
ਮਤਿ ਵਿਚਿ	*Mat(i) vich*	In the intellect, in the mind
ਮਾਣਿਕ	*Māṇik*	Pearls, jewels

Simply translated this *pauṛi* tells us that ritual baths at places of pilgrimage are meaningless, and would only matter if our actions were to please the Lord. Any action that pleases not the Lord is fruitless. In the entire creation there is nothing that could be acquired without His benediction. If we follow the path shown by the Guru then the jewels, pearls and rubies of enlightenment will shine forth within our minds. The Guru then prays for the continuing understanding that the Lord is the sole source of all that we may have. We can now look at the message in more detail and also see what the men of learning have to tell us on this issue.

In the first line the Guru says: "I would bathe at a *Tīrath* but only if it were to please Him but what use are such rituals if our actions do not please Him." The pilgrimage to a holy place is an old established tradition in almost all religions and parts of the world. As the *Oxford Dictionary of World Religions* tells us, *Tīrath* in Sanskrit literally means a ford – a crossing place, where streams or rivers are shallow and hence fordable. It becomes an allegory for the crossing by the soul from this world to the next. In religious parlance in India it has taken the meaning of 'holy place'. Such places would naturally have been placed along the banks of streams which would encourage habitation in view of the ready availability of drinking water, and also along well-travelled paths traversed by the people seeking to cross over streams because bridges would be rare in those days. The intersections of the river and the road, the fords, thus would naturally become the ideal locations for congregation. At all such important places holy traditions developed over long periods of time due to either the associations with a great seer or due to mythical tradition. There are of course many holy places that are not located on a river – the Darbār Sahib at Amritsar or the city of Jerusalem come to mind as the most obvious examples. However, the word *Tīrath* now applies to all such places. In India even the*Tīraths* not located on a river will usually have attached to it a lake, natural or man-made. This is to enable the pilgrim to take the ritual purificatory bath which was supposed to wash away all earthly sins. This also, as we noted above, is supposed to have a bearing on the spirit's journey from the earthly shore, which is this mortal world, to the other shore – the eternal abode of the spirit. A symbolic cleansing of the body at these *Tīraths* signified the purification of the soul within to prepare it for making the crossing from this world, full of woes, to the Lord's presence where eternal bliss prevails.

The Guru here is giving us all a universal message applicable not only to the Hindu culture with its stress on visits to *Tīraths*. The Muslims stress on pilgrimages to Mecca and Medina, the Christians on visiting the shrines, the Jew visiting Jerusalem and so on regardless of religious affiliation can look at this message and gain from its profundity. While it is never the Guru's style to openly or sharply condemn the other person's belief, he misses no opportunity to gently bring home the futility of any ritualistic practice that does not focus essentially on the elevating of his interlocutor's spirituality. Here again we see how the Guru without as such bluntly condemning the practice of pilgrimage with its purificatory expectations drives home the true meaning of the ritual. In doing so he makes it clear that the ritual as such is of no avail. He brings home to us as to what is the real pilgrimage or purificatory bath.

The Guru says that the real pilgrimage is within us. It consists not of going off to a *Tīrath* and indulging in purificatory immersions of the body. Rather it consists of regulating our existence strictly in accordance with the Lord's will, living the righteous life and indulging only in such action as would please the Lord. If we can thus please Him, we would have carried out the right pilgrimage and taken the real purificatory bath. The ritual of pilgrimage and purificatory bath by itself is of no utility. It is fruitless therefore to assume that mere visits to holy places and purificatory baths therein can wash one's sins away. In other words, living according to the Lord's will and indulging in righteous actions is the real pilgrimage and only that can suffice to produce the purification which the misguided pilgrim vainly seeks at these *Tīraths*.

In the second line the Guru points to the great bounty of the Lord in the form of the entire creation in the midst of which man has been placed. The Guru then poses the question, whether there is anything which has been attained without His grace? The Guru is telling us that the creation that surrounds us is the Lord's gift of love to us. There is none who on his own merit could earn any part of it. By our own action or will we cannot attain even an iota of this endless universe. This line also lends itself to another interpretation arising from the two different meanings of the word *Karam*, the Persian 'benediction' and the Sanskrit 'action'. Prof. Talib renders it as: "No one out of God's creation finds fulfilment except by His Grace." Prof. Sahib Singh follows the same line. Bhai Vir Singh however sees *Karam* here as meaning the results of our actions which he says is also dependent on the Lord's grace. This broad line is followed by some others too. In either construction the sense changes only marginally. Thus is this entire creation a gift to us out of the Lord's benediction; or it is a gift to us as a reward from the Lord consequent upon our good actions – good *Karma*. There is none who could assert that he has earned any of it as a matter of right. Merely by our own actions or our own will we cannot attain even an iota of this infinite universe.

On the other hand, says the Guru in the third line, as soon as we acquire the true knowledge by following the correct path we will discover that the richest gems and jewels of this world, that is the knowledge of the Divine and the Divine qualities have appeared within ourselves. Another construction could be that all the pearls, rubies and gems of the world are not the equal of the riches that the mind acquires when we follow the correct path as laid down by our Guru. Since the words used by the Guru are *mat(i) vich*, meaning 'within our mind, our intellect', the first interpretation seems the more appropriate, that is to say that the discipline of truly listening will awaken our minds. In the concluding part, in lines 4 and 5, the Guru again speaks of his Master – the Lord Himself – and says that he prays that the Master may so enlighten us that we may always recognise and understand that the Lord alone is the Provider of all; may we never put Him out of our mind. This part is of course repeated from the fifth *pauṛi*, where we had discussed it in detail.

In short, in this *pauṛi* the Guru has laid further stress on following the path shown by the Guru – which for a Sikh today means none else than the *SGGS* – and not be a believer in the rituals such as purificatory baths at the holy *Tīraths*. There is none who has attained even a tiny fraction of the Lord's great bounties by his own action or volition. All that comes to us comes through His grace. In fact if we follow the path shown to us by the Guru the enlightenment of the mind that is sure to follow will make meaningless any earthly riches, and will show us that no such riches can be the equal of that wealth of the mind. The *pauṛi* is quite in consonance with the entire thrust of the *Japji* which is that mere observances of rituals and purificatory rites, or following the path of yogic practices called *sādhanas,* or Jain austerities cannot help us attain the True Knowledge. This can only be attained through a total acceptance of and surrender to His will. Once that state of mind is attained the rest does not matter. Regardless of which religion you follow or what rituals you choose to perform, you can succeed as long as your actions are infused totally by surrender and acceptance of the Lord's will.

In the last lines the Guru pleads for but one blessing, that the Lord may grant him the constant awareness of the Lord – the only True Reality who is the only source of all creation, and may he always remember the True Lord.

12

SEEK TO PLEASE ONLY HIM

Pauṛi 7

ਜੇ ਜੁਗ ਚਾਰੇ ਆਰਜਾ ਹੋਰ ਦਸੂਣੀ ਹੋਇ॥	*Jay jugg chāray ārja hor dasūṇi hoye.*
ਨਵਾ ਖੰਡਾ ਵਿਚਿ ਜਾਣੀਐ ਨਾਲਿ ਚਲੈ ਸਭੁ ਕੋਇ॥	*Nava khandda vich jāṇiyai nāl chalai sabh koye.*
ਚੰਗਾ ਨਾਉ ਰਖਾਇ ਕੈ ਜਸੁ ਕੀਰਤਿ ਜਗਿ ਲੇਇ॥	*Changa nāo rakhāye kai, jas kīrat jag lay.*
ਜੇ ਤਿਸੁ ਨਦਰਿ ਨ ਆਵਈ ਤ ਵਾਤ ਨ ਪੁਛੈ ਕੇ॥	*Jay tis nadar na āvayi ta vāt na puchhai kay.*
ਕੀਟਾ ਅੰਦਰ ਕੀਟੁ ਕਰਿ ਦੋਸੀ ਦੋਸੁ ਧਰੇ॥	*Kītta andar kītt kar dosi dos dharay.*
ਨਾਨਕ ਨਿਰਗੁਣਿ ਗੁਣੁ ਕਰੇ ਗੁਣਵੰਤਿਆ ਗੁਣੁ ਦੇ॥	*Nanak nirguṇ guṇ karay guṇvantia guṇ day.*
ਤੇਹਾ ਕੋਇ ਨ ਸੁਝਈ ਜਿ ਤਿਸੁ ਗੁਣੁ ਕੋਇ ਕਰੇ॥੭॥	*Teha koye na sujhayi jay tis guṇ koye karay.*

Brief glossary

ਜੁਗ	*Jugg*	A *yuga*, a cosmological division of time in Hinduism
ਆਰਜਾ	*Ārja*	Lifespan
ਦਸੂਣੀ	*Dasūṇi*	Ten-fold
ਨਵਾ ਖੰਡਾ	*Nava khandda*	The nine quarters of the world as per Hinduism
ਜਸੁ ਕੀਰਤਿ	*Jas kīrat*	Honour, high esteem
ਵਾਤ	*Vāt*	Consideration

ਕੀਟੁ	*Kīt*	Insect
ਨਿਰਗੁਣਿ	*Nirguṇ*	Without merit, lacking any redeeming qualities

Simply translated, the futility of human endeavours when it is unredeemed by a surrender of the will to the Lord is further elaborated by the Guru in this *pauṛi* which speaks to us of some of the commonly coveted wishes that we all nurture. In the first line is referred the desire for a long life-span and the Guru says that let someone be granted a life-span equal to the four *Yugas*, nay ten times that. With such long life, let him also be granted the other common wish, fame such that it resounds in all the nine quarters of the world, meaning the whole world. Beyond that let all obey the commands of such a person. Let him also have the fulfilment of another common desire, that of great renown and great honour and credit. Let there be all this, says the Guru in the first three lines and then proceeds in the fourth line to puncture the balloon of this futile pursuit. He says it would all be of no worth if the Lord's grace and blessings were not yours. Without that blessing, adds the Guru in the fifth line, the worth of such a person is no more than the worth of an insect, and he will find himself accused even by reprobates. The Lord only can confer merit, says the Guru in the sixth and seventh lines – even on those who lack any good qualities, and He can enlighten further those who have some merit. There is, however, none existing who could add any qualities to the Lord. Let us now examine the various commentaries on this.

It is every man's desire that he may live a long life and during that life he may gain honour and fame in the world of men. The Guru touches on this theme and then concludes by re-emphasizing the main thrust of the *Japji*. About this urge for a long life the Guru says, as we saw above, let your life be equal to the four *Yugas* – the *Yuga* being a period defined in the Hindu cosmogony. For details about the *Yugas* see Appendix-B.

In this *pauṛi* the Guru is saying to us that being granted a long life, even equal to ten *Mahāyugas*, which are equal to 4.32 million years each, is in itself futile. Similarly, great fame, such that you are acknowledged mighty in all the nine quarters which are supposed to constitute together the whole world; and in addition having all humans under your command is equally meaningless. The Guru says even if all this were to happen yet is your worth as nothing if the Lord's blessing and grace were not yours. All these attainments when weighed against the Lord's blessing are but dust. The weight and worth of such a person in the Lord's presence is no more than the worth of any meritless person whom no one honours. A man without the Lord's blessing is but an insect among insects, a worm among worms. Far from being worthy of honour in the divine accounting, such a person will be accused by even those who themselves are reprobates. Such a man who has spent his energies in acquiring wealth and power and never sought to tune himself to the will of the Lord will find himself shunned and given no honour in the Lord's presence, and all his worldly possessions and achievements will in that moment be as nought.

In the last line the Guru says that all earthly and other-worldly merits proceed from the Lord. He is the only Power that can confer merit on those who lack it. The ones who do have some worth have only the Lord to thank for it. There is none to be seen who can grant these gifts and virtues in turn to the Lord.

In short, the Guru in this *pauṛi* presses further the lesson he is trying to make us understand throughout this sublime composition. The insignificance of worldly achievements, the futility of wishing for long existence so as to use it for acquiring more power, wealth and dominion over others is starkly brought out. The extreme of such wishfulness, i.e., a life-span of cosmic proportions and dominions equalling the entire universe are cited by the Guru as being nothing without the grace of the Lord. We are thus told to have all our actions and wishes to be always infused with a devout sense of it all being a gift from the Lord. We will note that the Guru is not telling us to stop wishing for or acquiring worldly things. It is, in other words, not a prescription for doing nothing except sitting and singing praises of the Lord and idly waiting for His gifts to flow to us.

No, the Sikh way is one of action and effort. It is a way which requires of us to work hard and to honestly earn a good living. It then of course requires us to share it with those less fortunate, and to always hold the Lord's creatures in affection, to see Him in all His creation. While striving to earn and acquire we have constantly to be aware that the results that ensue from our efforts are not in our hands – those only the Lord will determine. Our efforts, our striving has to be whole-hearted but it must never flow from the ego. We must remember that we are not the ultimate deciders and that whatever we do achieve from our efforts is as the Lord wills. If success has not come our way then the only thing we have to do is stop and assess whether our efforts were lacking or misdirected. If we made our full effort and yet the Lord has chosen to grant us results which are below what we wanted, yet must we be fully content and thankful to Him.

It will be noted how close that message is to what Lord Krishna told Arjuna on the battlefield of Kurukshetra: "Surrender your will to Me because in your hands lies only the action. The results will lie in My Hands alone." Remember how that message succeeded in freeing Arjuna from the paralysis of will to which he had succumbed on seeing that the battle he was about to join would involve fighting against, and possibly killing, the very persons whom he adored the most. He would rather not attempt the task because it was so hard and unpleasant. Thus, he would have to continue living with the injustice and ignominy which his dear and near ones on the *Kaurava* side had so ruthlessly inflicted on him. Lord Krishna removed Arjuna's doubts with the resounding and noble sermon he delivered on that battlefield. That famous sermon has come down to us in the form of the *Bhagvad Gita.* Never desist from righteous action, says he, however hard or nasty the task might appear. Let your actions be thoroughly imbued with the spirit of total surrender of your ego and your selfness to the Lord. Act, and involve yourself whole-heartedly in worldly activity, but while doing so leave the fruits of your actions to the Lord to determine and bestow on us what He wills. From Him alone flows all power and merit. Away from Him all our efforts may bring some worldly wealth and power, but we will be no better than the meanest of worms and no purer than the worst reprobate and sinner.

Thus, we have seen that in the first seven *pauṛis*, and the *Mool Mantra*, the Guru has spelt out for us the greatness of the Lord, the incomparable grandeur and the unreachable power and might, and also the difficulty of trying to understand Him. While spelling out, to the extent words can do so, the position and the characteristics of the Lord, the Guru has also simultaneously laid out man's relationship to the Lord and to this universe. He has also told us how are we to proceed to reach Him, to pierce the veil of illusion which keep us from seeing the True Reality. The Guru tells us of the need to act always in the full consciousness of the Lord's will, to surrender ourselves, our egos, to always accept and be content with what He chooses to give us. He tells us that the knowledge of the Lord will come to us from within if we follow the path the Guru lays down for us. The importance of following the path, of disciplining ourselves so as to control our baser instincts and fixing our minds on the Lord is enjoined upon us.

13

HEAR WITH THE HEART

Pauṛi 8 to 11

Having established for us the basic structure of the Lord's relationship with man and given us the key to how man is to conduct himself through this journey he now in the next four *pauṛis* goes into more detail of how we should proceed. The first step he says is to really listen. Not merely hearing the Guru's message but by truly absorbing it and by attuning the mind can the right message sink into us. The difference between merely hearing the words and hearing the message needs to be comprehended here. The Guru gives us the message, but it is only when we have truly heard him that we will begin to comprehend the need for not just understanding the Roadmap but making it an integral part of our life. When our hearing is at that deeper level we will gain the benefits the Guru has intended for us. With this background let us look at each of these four pauris. In the first of these, pauri number 8, the Guru tells us: -

Pauṛi 8

ਸੁਣਿਐ ਸਿਧ ਪੀਰ ਸੁਰਿ ਨਾਥ॥	*Suṇiyai sidh pīr sur nāth.*
ਸੁਣਿਐ ਧਰਤਿ ਧਵਲ ਆਕਾਸ॥	*Suṇiyai dharat dhawal ākās.*
ਸੁਣਿਐ ਦੀਪ ਲੋਅ ਪਾਤਾਲ॥	*Suṇiyai dīp low pātāl.*
ਸੁਣਿਐ ਪੋਹਿ ਨ ਸਕੈ ਕਾਲੁ॥	*Suṇiyai poh na sakai kāl.*

ਨਾਨਕ ਭਗਤਾ ਸਦਾ ਵਿਗਾਸੁ ॥	*Nanak bhagta sada vigās.*
ਸੁਣਿਐ ਦੂਖ ਪਾਪ ਕਾ ਨਾਸੁ ॥ ੮ ॥	*Suṇiyai dūkh pāp ka nās.*

Brief glossary

ਸੁਣਿਐ	*Suṇiyai*	To hear, listen
ਸਿਧ	*Sidh*	A *yogi* who has earned control over miracles
ਪੀਰ	*Pīr*	A religious head, a spiritually exalted person
ਸੁਰਿ	*Sur*	The *devtas*, gods
ਨਾਥ	*Nāth*	A head of a *yogi* sect
ਧਵਲ	*Dhawal*	The bull (on whom the earth rests)
ਦੀਪ	*Dīp*	Sanskrit *dweep* - continent. One of the seven parts of the world as per the Hindu belief system
ਕਾਲੁ	*Kāl*	Time, period, death
ਵਿਗਾਸੁ	*Vigās*	Growth, bloom, happiness

This *pauṛi* says if we truly learn to listen we can acquire the high status of the *Sidh*, the *Pīr*, and the *Nāth*. We can learn the mysteries of the earth, the heavens, and also what supports this world. The mysteries of the world and also the nether regions are revealed. Death cannot touch the one who truly listens. The devotees are ever in an exalted state and by truly listening, all sorrow and all evils are removed. Let us now look at it in detail and also see what the learned ones have to tell us.

Suṇiyai, the recurring command in these four *pauṛis*, is here not merely in the sense of listening or hearing, which happens to be the literal meaning. It is not just the sound reaching the ears. It is rather much beyond that. In the true sense of *Suṇiyai* is also implied the understanding and absorption of what is heard. Truly hearing in this sense will gradually turn the mind towards the Lord. This attunement will bring with it the rewards that are illustratively listed in these four *pauṛis.*

The Guru says in the first line that such a state of mind will bring to us *Sidhis*, which are otherwise earned through hard practices and austerities. It was the practice among ascetics to undergo severe austerities until they reached a level of self-discipline and control over their minds that they could perform the various types of miracles which are described in the various Hindu texts. Such achieved ascetics were called *Sidhas* and were respected as men of high spiritual standing. The Guru always preached against such practices and the *Gurbān.i* tells us *ridh sidh awrā sād* (These attainments are a false satisfaction) in the 29th *paur.i* as we shall later see. A *Pīr*, especially among the Muslims, again meant a religious teacher who had attained an exalted spiritual level. *Pīrs* were also believed similarly to be able to perform miracles and were similarly admired and respected. *Sur* means literally gods. In the Hindu pantheon there are, at the apex, the top three supregods, the gods of gods, the Holy Trinity – Brahma, Vishnu, Mahesh (Shiva) – through whom the Lord operates the cycle of creation, preservation and destruction. Much below them come the other gods of whom Indra is the king. He is also the thunder wielder and the Lord of Rains. With him are the other gods with powers over certain specific elements. Thus, Vāyu is Lord of the Winds, Agni the Lord of Fire, Vārun.a the Lord of the Oceans, and so on. Below them are the numerous lesser gods, the total number of whom is believed to be 33 crores (330 million).

They are all of them in varying degrees superior to man and are thus accorded worship. *Nāth* is the term used for the heads of the various sects of yogis. The *yogis* were a numerous lot in the ages when the Guru gave us his message. They were divided into sects each functioning from a *matth*. The *matth* was not only the seminary but also the headquarters of the individual sect. Ruling each *matth* was a *Nāth*. These were obviously men of learning and were accorded great respect. All these highly regarded personages and the semi-divine and divine powers, says the Guru, will not rank as greater, or wiser, than the one who truly listens.

In the *Shabdarth* put out by SGPC the first line is explained as meaning that by truly listening to the Guru's message the listener will get to understand just how much are the *Sidhas*, the *Pīrs* and the *Nāths* worth, and therefore how much weight should be given to their teaching when they talk of the mysteries of the earth and heavens, etc. This however does not seem quite in consonance with the thrust of the message so far. The Guru is explaining to us the greatness of the Lord, our relationship to Him and His creation and the method for attaining God-realization. In that context this *paur.i*, and the next three from 9 to 11, can only be meant to tell us what next to do, what further discipline to adopt to bring our minds under control. Singing praises of Him and meditating on His greatness has been spelt out for us. The next step would be truly listening to the Guru's message. This is also the sense in which most commentators, Prof. Sahib Singh and Prof. Talib included, have taken these four *paur.is*. It certainly seems the more appealing interpretation.

In the second line the Guru says that by truly listening shall we be enlightened regarding the true nature and mystery of the world, of the power that sustains it and of the heavens above. *Dhawal* literally means a white bull. It is a mythic belief in Hinduism that the Lord's creation, this world, is supported on the horns of a Cosmic Bull. Earthquakes in this myth are explained by the bull shifting the load from one horn to the other. While the Guru later in the *Japji* debunks this myth, yet here it is referred to the broad sense of the Power which supports the existence of the world. These esoteric mysteries will remain secret no more to one who listens, and of course truly absorbs.

In the third line on the same theme the Guru says that the knowledge of the *deep – dweep* in Sanskrit meaning island literally but here meaning a part or sector of the world – the *low*, the inhabited portions of the world, and *pātāl,* the nether regions, is revealed to the one who listens. Having in the second line spoken of the heavens, their counterpart, the nether regions are now mentioned. *Low* means literally the world but here it is in the sense of the regions which are inhabited by humans. As we saw the world has already been referred to as *dharat* in the first line. Thus, every part of the visible and hidden creation, the world (*dharat*), the mythical support of the world (*dhawal*), the heavens (*ākās*), the continents (*dweep*), the inhabited portions (*low*) and the nether regions (*pātāl*) is here spoken of, obviously to drive home the point that nothing would remain hidden from one who truly listens and is attuned totally to the Lord.

The Guru goes further and in the fourth line says that the true listener will be able to transcend the boundaries of, and go beyond the reach of time, and death, itself. As we know there is none except the Lord Himself beyond the reach of *Kāl*, of time and death. The Guru is thus telling us that the person with his mind attuned to the Lord and listening to the Cosmic Word will have become one with the Lord, and therefore like the Lord Himself. Complete awareness of all the mysteries of creation in all its various components – the world itself, the nether regions, the heavens, the power that supports and sustains – will immediately follow once you learn to listen and attune yourself. In that state you will cross the boundaries of death and time and be one with the Lord.

The last two lines, the fifth and sixth, are repeated at the conclusion of each of the three succeeding *paur.is.* The Guru says in these lines that those who are thus devoted to the Lord and try to listen in such fashion, he calls them *Bhagats*, remain forever in a state of high spirits and joyful growth. They are always in an exalted state and all their sorrows and their sins are removed by such listening. That man is prone to sorrow and by his very nature will also acquire sinful *karma* as he wends his way through this mortal world is an inevitable part of human existence. The cleansing of these sins will come about, if we recite His name, as the Guru will later tell us in the *Japji*. Here he says these sins are washed away by listening to the Guru and truly attuning yourself to the message.

14

BE A TRUE LISTENER

In the next *pauri* the Guru continues with the lesson of what we can gain when we truly listen to the Guru's teaching. The Guru expounding further on the theme, says:

Pauṛi 9

ਸੁਣਿਐ ਈਸਰੁ ਬਰਮਾ ਇੰਦੁ ॥	*Suṇiyai īssar barma ind.*
ਸੁਣਿਐ ਮੁਖਿ ਸਾਲਾਹਣ ਮੰਦੁ ॥	*Suṇiyai mukh sālāhaṇ mand.*
ਸੁਣਿਐ ਜੋਗ ਜੁਗਤਿ ਤਨਿ ਭੇਦ ॥	*Suṇiyai jog jugat tan(i) bhed.*
ਸੁਣਿਐ ਸਾਸਤ ਸਿਮ੍ਰਿਤਿ ਵੇਦ ॥	*Suṇiyai sāst simrit ved.*
ਨਾਨਕ ਭਗਤਾ ਸਦਾ ਵਿਗਾਸੁ ॥	*Nanak bhagta sada vigās.*
ਸੁਣਿਐ ਦੂਖ ਪਾਪ ਕਾ ਨਾਸੁ ॥੯॥	*Suṇiyai dūkh pāp ka nās.*

Brief glossary

ਈਸਰ	*Īssar*	A name for Lord Shiva
ਬਰਮਾ	*Barma*	Lord Brahma
ਇੰਦੁ	*Ind*	Lord Indra, king of gods
ਸਾਲਾਹਣ	*Sālāhaṇ*	Praise (of God)
ਮੰਦ	*Mand*	Bad one
ਜੋਗ ਜੁਗਤਿ	*Jog jugat*	Technique, skill of Yoga
ਤਨਿ ਭੇਦ	*Tan(i) bhed*	Secrets of the body
ਸਾਸਤ	*Sāst*	The *Sastras*, the scriptures
ਸਿਮ੍ਰਿਤਿ	*Simrit*	The *Smritis*
ਵੇਦ	*Ved*	The *Vedas*. The *Shāstras*, *Smritis*

and the *Vedas* are all Hindu holy books, containing spiritual knowledge

Simply translated this *pauṛi* says by truly listening, one's consciousness is raised to the level of the gods Shiva, Brahma and Indra. By truly listening even lowly ones will learn to sing His praises. The knowledge of the mysteries of the human body that yogic practices claim to bring will come through truly listening. The sum total of *Shāstras*, *Smritis* and the *Vedas* will come intuitively to us by truly listening. The devotees are ever in a state of exaltation, and a cessation of all sorrows and all evils will come through truly listening. We can now look at the message in more detail and also see what learned commentators have said on the issue.

Further to the attainments listed in *pauṛi* 8 which comprehensively spoke of the creation and its various parts and divisions, the Guru here tells us more of what awaits the one who trains himself to be a true listener.

The Guru says in the first line that by listening is one raised to the level of Shiva, Brahma and Indra, the first two being part of the Trinity of the deities believed in Hinduism to be charged with the control and functioning of the Lord's creation; Indra being the king of the gods in the Hindu pantheon.

This line is however interpreted differently also in some commentaries. One such interpretation is that the great deities like Lord Shiva (Īssar), Lord Brahma and Indra, the king of the gods, have reached their exalted stations by following this path of listening to the word of the Lord. The SGPC's *Shabdarth* offers another slightly different version saying that by listening, the reality of the deities such as Shiva, Brahma or Indra becomes clear and known and the devotee will then leave the worship of these and will instead start to worship only the One True Lord. As we have discussed in the previous chapter also, the more acceptable meaning seems to be that the Guru is listing out for us some more of the good results that we can expect to achieve from this discipline.

The short point is that interpreted either way the message of this *pauṛi* is that man can expect to have wondrous attainments by listening and attuning himself to the Lord's word.

In the second line the Guru says that even those unworthy of the Lord will sing His praises when they learn to listen. This line is also rendered by some learned ones to mean that by listening, the devotee's face – *mukh* – becomes praiseworthy. In other words, the one who learns to truly listen will "be invested with all praiseworthy qualities", as Prof. Talib puts it, in his translation. Dr. Sangat Singh renders it to say that such a person "is praised by high and low". Dr. Gopal Singh has another take on it and says that *mand* here refers to the Sanskrit *Mantra*, and thus he renders this line as: "… (they) utter: 'Praise be to Him', the Mantra." The more often followed and the more appealing interpretation here is that *mand* here means the vile and lowly ones, as we have also noted above.

In the third line the Guru gives further details of the gifts awaiting the true listener. He says by listening, the true nature of the body, that is to say the mystery of its functioning, becomes known. The techniques that the yogis learn are also made automatically known to the true listener. This is a reference to the practices of *Hattha Yoga* where the esoteric knowledge of the *chakras* or lotuses of energy within the body is sought to be acquired. The body according to this belief is not merely a collection of organs functioning in interdependency to keep the life-cycle going. It has within this physical body a mystical system of energies which is the real reason that we can exist. The Hindu belief system postulates certain foci of this mystical energy within the body and the yogic practices are tailored to understand, release and control these energies which really determine the functioning of the body. The Guru is not by any means recommending any such practice – for his entire teaching is to the effect that rituals, austerities and esoteric practices are of no real avail. Instead, he stresses repeatedly on surrender to the Lord and extinguishing the selfness – the *haumai*, the ego. What the Guru is telling us here is that by listening to the Lord's word we can acquire the same intimate knowledge of this mysterious body as the *yogis* seek to acquire through the techniques prescribed in *Hattha Yoga*. That the mysteries of the body were known to and its functioning understood even in ancient times by the *rishis* of India and other similar mystics elsewhere is clear from the various ancient systems of healing that have been passed down to us. They were developed much before the modern tools of science became available, before we could see into bodies and its organs. There was definitely great intuitive knowledge at work, which could have been learnt quite possibly through such practices. For the follower of the Guru, however, all this is quite unnecessary and the benefits of acquisition of any such lore will instead come through the practice of true listening as explained by the Guru.

By truly listening, says the Guru in the fourth line, the sum total of all knowledge as contained in the *Shāstras*, *Smritis* and *Vedas* can become ours. A *Shāstra* is a compilation of teachings on a subject and served as aids for teaching since the ancient times. The *Smritis* are collections of common lore collected from what great seers had said or prescribed. The *Vedas*, numbering four, are the hallowed scriptures that have guided the Hindu faith since the last almost four thousand years. These are believed to be of divine origin having issued from the mouth of Brahma, the creator component of the Holy Trinity in Hinduism. Prescribed in the *Vedas* are the rituals and disciplines for governing the entire life-cycle of the believer and meant to lead him to salvation ultimately. Taken together the *Vedas*, *Smritis* and *Shāstras* contain all that is known in this world. Few can hope to acquire all the sum total of knowledge in these at the same time. The Guru says that by listening truly and attuning with the True One this knowledge will come automatically to you. The short point is that such attunement through true listening raises the consciousness to a level where the veil of illusion slips away and reality shines through. When through slow and steady practice of this discipline the seeker has reached the proper stage, the knowledge of the entire creation comes, by His grace, in a single flash.

The last two lines, the fifth and sixth, are the same as the last two lines in the previous *pauṛi* and we have discussed these already. In these lines the Guru says that the *Bhagats* of the Lord are forever in a state of exaltation and all woes and all sins are removed once we learn to listen, not merely with the ears but with our hearts.

15

LISTEN AND ALL KNOWLEDGE IS THINE

Pauṛi 10

ਸੁਣਿਐ ਸਤੁ ਸੰਤੋਖੁ ਗਿਆਨੁ ॥	*Suṇiyai sat(u) santokh gyān.*
ਸੁਣਿਐ ਅਠਸਠਿ ਕਾ ਇਸਨਾਨੁ ॥	*Suṇiyai atth satth ka isnān.*
ਸੁਣਿਐ ਪੜਿ ਪੜਿ ਪਾਵਹਿ ਮਾਨੁ ॥	*Suṇiyai paṛ paṛ pāveh mān.*
ਸੁਣਿਐ ਲਾਗੈ ਸਹਜਿ ਧਿਆਨੁ ॥	*Suṇiyai lāgai sehaj dhyān.*
ਨਾਨਕ ਭਗਤਾ ਸਦਾ ਵਿਗਾਸੁ ॥	*Nanak bhagta sada vigās.*
ਸੁਣਿਐ ਦੂਖ ਪਾਪ ਕਾ ਨਾਸੁ ॥ ੧੦ ॥	*Suṇiyai dūkh pāp ka nās.*

Brief glossary

ਸਤੁ	*Sat(u)*	Truthfulness, also 'giving' or 'charity'
ਸੰਤੋਖੁ	*Santokh*	Contentment
ਗਿਆਨੁ	*Gyān*	Knowledge
ਅਠਸਠਿ	*Atth Satth*	Sixty-eight, the *Tīraths* known in Hinduism
ਪੜਿ ਪੜਿ	*Paṛ paṛ*	Repeated studying
ਮਾਨੁ	*Mān*	Respect, honour
ਸਹਜਿ ਧਿਆਨੁ	*Sehaj dhyān.*	Concentration in meditation, knowledge of the other worldly condition

Simply rendered this *pauṛi* says that by truly listening, the qualities of truthfulness, contentment and knowledge can be gained. The merits supposed to accrue from bathing at the 68 holiest places of pilgrimage are acquired by truly listening; the honour that comes from erudite studies can be had by truly listening. The mind will be concentrated in meditation. In the two lines of the refrain the Guru says the devotees are ever in a state of exaltation, and all woes and all evils are removed by truly listening. We can now see in detail what the message here is and what the men of learning have said about it.

The Guru says in the first line that by true listening we can achieve a condition of truthfulness, contentment and knowledge. In the previous two *pauṛis* were listed by the Guru, firstly knowledge of the physical part of creation of the world, the heavens and the nether regions. Secondly, the knowledge contained in all the scriptures and the knowledge of the body and its functioning. Here the Guru lists the personal qualities which will emerge in us if we listen. Knowledge, in the sense of enlightenment, will emerge, as also contentment, a quality greatly regarded by the Guru and repeatedly stressed in the *Gurbāṇi.* The term 'ਸਤੁ' – *sat(u)* – is rendered differently by commentators. Dr. Sangat Singh in his *Japji* translates it as truthfulness, and Prof. Talib uses the same formulation. Others have translated it as charity or philanthropy. Prof. Sahib Singh expounding at some length the etymology of the word which he says is from the Sanskrit root *Uss,* meaning letting go, renders it as philanthropy. The rendering as 'Truth' is however the more appealing here, and this is how the *Mahan Kosh* of Bhai Sahib Bhai Kahan Singh also translates it.

In the second line the Guru says that by listening we acquire the merit of having bathed at the 'Sixty-Eight'. This number refers to the traditionally recognized places of pilgrimage in Hinduism which are said to be sixty-eight. There are of course numerous other places where people go for a pilgrimage but those are supposed to be minor and of lesser religious significance. These sixty-eight are the main recognized centres. It is believed that if one can complete this cycle of pilgrimages, the merit achieved is such as to wash away all sins and lead us to salvation. The Guru here is not recommending that we follow this course and carry out the visits … quite the opposite in fact. The Guru is telling us that we need not carry out this ritual. Instead we need just to open our mind to the Lord's message as given to us by the Guru – to listen and to attune ourselves. This by itself will bring to us the merit that we were hoping to acquire through our pilgrimages. It may be of interest that the number of *Tīraths* differs in the various *Purāṇas*. The *Mahan Kosh* says that the twenty-second chapter of the *Shrādh Kalpa* mentions 222 *Tīraths*. However, the *Bhavishya Purāṇa* gives this number differently, in chapter 102. The *Kapil Tantra* does list 68 *Tīraths*, the list of which the *Mahan Kosh* then adds. The traditionally accepted number however is definitely 68. The Guru of course talks of it only to stress the opposite, that no such ritual need be observed; instead hearken to the Guru's word.

In the third line the Guru turns to the area of scholastic learning. He tells us that by truly listening we can expect to gain the same honour that we would have gained by way of the highest scholastic endeavour for acquiring learning. This line is rendered as, "He obtains scholastic honour," by Dr. Sangat Singh. Prof. Sahib Singh says it means that the true listener acquires through this practice the same knowledge that the learned ones reach through repeated study. This is also the sense taken by Bhai Vir Singh. Since, as we may notice, the Guru is listing out what all is gained through true listening, the interpretation taken by Prof. Sahib Singh and Bhai Vir Singh would seem the more appropriate one. The fourth line says that by truly listening the mind will be concentrated on meditation – *lāgay sehaj dhyān*. Here we need to pause and try to understand what the *sehaj* state is. The *Mahan Kosh* defines it as 'that with which we were born', and prof. Sahib Singh has the same view. It has a number of other meanings too, the other important one being 'with ease', or 'without effort'. It is a recognised reality that all seekers who try to fix their minds on the Lord and try to meditate will have to exert hard to control their wandering thoughts and the natural urges of the body and the mind to be able to concentrate their attention for that. According to this meaning of the word, the state of *sehaj* is that stage, beyond the mundane, where the mind is effortlessly and constantly fixed on the Lord. This is in fact the state in which the soul came to this world, and was thus born with us. It is the innate state of mind of the newly- born, which with time and the effect of Māya in this world is then gradually lost. After the soul has been exposed to the effects of this existence on this mortal world, the three *Guṇas,* that of *Rajas, Tamas* and *Sattva*, which combined together constitute the material world, or Māya, start to act upon the soul. Each soul then acquires these three *Guṇas* in varying proportions depending upon the previous *Karma* and the way we order our lives during our present births. It is when we are able to raise ourselves, our souls, above and beyond these three *Guṇas* and re-attain the original pristine condition that we can claim to have entered the *sehaj state*. It is greatly desired by all true devotees and the Guru says it is yours if you will learn to truly listen. The term has been also defined in the *Encyclopedia of Sikhism* which calls it: "A state of mental spiritual equipoise without the least intrusion of the ego; unshaken natural effortless serenity attained through spiritual discipline." Most commentators have used it to denote that meditation is easy to do if you truly learn to listen. That is also not entirely incorrect, but the more appropriate meaning should be that if we follow this discipline of listening then we will acquire again the lost state of pristine oneness with Him and without any effort or struggle will our attention remain focussed on the Lord.

The last two lines, the fifth and the sixth, are the refrain of these four *pauṛis* as we have seen and discussed already. These say that by truly listening we can get rid of all sorrows and sins and that the true *Bhagtas* live ever in a state of exaltation.

16

LISTEN AND ALL VIRTUES ARE THINE

Pauṛi 11

ਸੁਣਿਐ ਸਰਾ ਗੁਣਾ ਕੇ ਗਾਹ ॥	*Suṇiyai sara guṇa kay gāh.*
ਸੁਣਿਐ ਸੇਖ ਪੀਰ ਪਾਤਿਸਾਹ ॥	*Suṇiyai sekh pīr pātsāh.*
ਸੁਣਿਐ ਅੰਧੇ ਪਾਵਹਿ ਰਾਹੁ ॥	*Suṇiyai andhay pāvay rāh.*
ਸੁਣਿਐ ਹਾਥ ਹੋਵੈ ਅਸਗਾਹੁ ॥	*Suṇiyai hāth hovai asgāh.*
ਨਾਨਕ ਭਗਤਾ ਸਦਾ ਵਿਗਾਸੁ ॥	*Nanak bhagta sada vigās.*
ਸੁਣਿਐ ਦੂਖ ਪਾਪ ਕਾ ਨਾਸੁ ॥੧੧॥	*Suṇiyai dūkh pāp ka nās.*

Brief glossary

ਸਰਾ	*Sara*	Reservoir, *sarovar*
ਗੁਣਾ	*Guṇa*	Good qualities
ਗਾਹ	*Gāh*	Knowledge, awareness
ਸੇਖ	*Sekh*	Sheikh, a chief and leader
ਅੰਧੇ	*Andhay*	Blind, here the spiritually bankrupt
ਰਾਹੁ	*Rāh*	Path, passage
ਅਸਗਾਹੁ	*Asgāh*	Deep ocean

Simply translated this *pauṛi* says by truly listening the reservoirs of good qualities are tapped. The high state that *Sekhs*, *Pīrs* and Emperors command is ours if we truly listen. The blind can find their path if they listen truly. The deep mysteries of the world are understood by truly listening. The woes and evils are removed and the devotees are ever in an exalted state. Let us now see what learned commentators have said on this issue.

Concluding with this, the fourth *pauṛi* of the quartet of *pauṛis* with the refrain *Suṇiyai*, the Guru lists some more wonders that would follow the discipline of truly listening. The Guru says in the first line that by truly listening the reservoirs of good qualities get tapped. In other words, the deep spiritual truths that lie stored but unfortunately unheeded within us will come within the capacity of our conscious mind to tap and to understand. This is the broad sense in which Prof. Sahib Singh, Bhai Vir Singh and almost all commentators have taken it. In fact one notices little difference of interpretation among scholars in construing this *pauṛi*.

In the second line the Guru refers to another human desire, that of commanding high status. He lists out what awaits those who will learn to truly listen. He says if you follow this path you will command the stature as of the *Sheikh*, the *Pīr* and the *Pātsāh*. *Sheikh* is a person who is a leader, a ruler of men but is also at the same time a person rich in learning and spirituality. A *Pīr* as we have noted in the eighth *pauṛi* also is a religious head, a spiritually exalted person. *Pīrs* are, among Muslims, given high respect and sometimes even accorded some worship. *Pātsāh* is the common form of *Pātshāh*, or the Persian *Pādishāh*, a great ruler, an emperor. Thus, the Guru is saying that listening will bring to us great holiness, a royal status and a *Sheikh*'s position of leadership in both spheres.

In the third line the Guru says that in this way even the blind can find their way. The reference obviously is to the spiritually bankrupt, those whose eyes are blind to everything except for the glitter of material wealth and power. Even such highly handicapped persons are given a chance to start treading the path to salvation if only they will choose to truly listen.

The fourth line lists out another benefit – that by truly listening we can acquire the capacity to fathom the *asgāh,* literally deep ocean. The reference here is to the mysteries of this creation which for the uninitiated are as deep and as opaque as the oceans.

In other words, the Guru is saying that the most difficult of posers are not beyond the reach of one who has learnt to truly listen. Such a one will intuitively acquire insight into the greatest of mysteries.

The last two lines of the refrain, as seen earlier, say that the devotees are ever in a state of exaltation and that the removal of all our woes and evils will surely ensue from truly listening.

17

THE TRUE BELIEVER

Pauṛis 12 to 15

Having in the previous four *pauṛis* enlightened the devotee on the great merits of truly listening, the Guru now in these four *pauṛis*, from 12 to 15, takes us a step forward. If we have learned to listen then beyond that is the stage of having firm faith in the Lord's message given to us by the Guru. These *pauṛis* narrate the condition of high exaltation of those who travel beyond 'listening' to having faith.

The *Shabdarth* of the SGPC says that these *pauṛis* delineate for us the effects of living a life of firm faith by following the Guru's message. As the traveller of this world – the soul – acquires greater faith, the knowledge of the surroundings sharply improves. As understanding awakens the traveller is able to pick the right path and reaches his true destination. Not only himself, such a man of faith can also carry with him his family and associates. Such a man then becomes a *panch* (the exalted one) about whom we shall learn more in *Pauṛi* 16.

We shall thus, in these four *pauṛis,* read about the next stage of spiritual endeavour. In the *pauṛis* 8 to 11 we saw the Guru expound on the merits of achieving an open and receptive mind such as to enable us to really and truly hear the message, to truly imbibe its meaning and absorb oneself in the listening. Now in *pauṛis* 12 to 15 the Guru will tell us what to expect when having acquired the discipline of true listening, we begin the next stage and learn to let a true and unshakeable faith in the message of the Guru take hold of us. Having really 'heard', if we now attain full and unwavering faith in the message, then what ensues is described here. In this light let us look in detail at what the Guru is now telling us. He says in *pauṛi 12*:

Pauṛi 12

ਮੰਨੇ ਕੀ ਗਤਿ ਕਹੀ ਨ ਜਾਇ॥	*Mannay ki gat kahi na jāye.*
ਜੇ ਕੋ ਕਹੈ ਪਿਛੈ ਪਛੁਤਾਇ॥	*Je ko kahai pichhai pachhatāye.*
ਕਾਗਦਿ ਕਲਮ ਨ ਲਿਖਣਹਾਰੁ॥	*Kāgad kalam na likhaṇhār.*
ਮੰਨੇ ਕਾ ਬਹਿ ਕਰਨਿ ਵੀਚਾਰੁ॥	*Mannay ka beh karan vīchār.*
ਐਸਾ ਨਾਮੁ ਨਿਰੰਜਨੁ ਹੋਇ॥	*Aisa nām niranjan hoye.*
ਜੇ ਕੋ ਮੰਨਿ ਜਾਣੈ ਮਨਿ ਕੋਇ॥੧੨॥	*Je ko mann jāṇai mann koye.*

Brief glossary

ਮੰਨੇ	*Mannay*	Believer
ਗਤਿ	*Gat*	Condition
ਕਹੀ	*Kahai*	Describes, states
ਵੀਚਾਰੁ	*Vīchār*	Consideration, thought
ਨਿਰੰਜਨੁ	*Niranjan*	Without taint, pure, immaculate

Simply translated this *pauṛi* says that the spiritual condition of one who truly believes is beyond description and anyone who tries to explain will rue the effort. Paper and pen are insufficient to depict it and none is there to even be able to consider it. In the last two lines which is the refrain for these four *pauṛis,* the Guru says the great and immaculate name of the Lord can only be understood by one who has acquired complete faith. With this we can now look at it in more detail and also see what learned commentators have said.

The Guru in the first line says that it is impossible to express in words the condition of the one who truly believes. The word 'ਮੰਨੇ' – *mannay* – comes from the Sanskrit word *mannan* meaning reflection on, cogitation. One who has thus meditated on and reached a state of firm, unshakeable faith is the one the Guru is here talking about. Prof. Talib renders this word as 'state of faith' and translates the first line as 'inexpressible is the state of faith'. Dr. Sangat Singh renders *mannay* as referring to a 'man whose mind is satiated in God'. Bhai Vir Singh, Prof. Sahib Singh and Narain Singh have all rendered it in the sense of 'person who has achieved full and firm faith'. The meaning in either sense rings true but in the context of the next three *pauṛis* which also are on the theme of *mannay* the closer rendering is that of the person, one who has faith, rather than the state. The person who in the previous four *pauṛis* was given the message of true listening, having crossed that stage is now told of what to expect when he goes beyond the stage of true listening and acquires the firmness of unflinching faith which will carry him to the next stage of spiritual growth. Such a person is the one referred to by the Guru in this and the next three *pauṛis*.

The Guru is thus now telling us that if you become firm in faith, unshakeable in your belief in the Lord and His awesome majesty, free your mind from any taint of doubt you will achieve this state. Such a state is normal to expect if the message of true listening has really been imbibed. Such is the mystery and grandeur of the person who has reached this state that the Guru says, in the first line, that he finds himself at a loss on how to describe it. He goes further in the second line and says that if anyone were foolish enough to undertake the task of such description he would soon find the effort fruitless and the task impossible. So 'other-worldly' is this state that the one who attempts a description will rue the hopelessness of his effort.

In the third and fourth lines the Guru speaks of the *mannai*, meaning 'through the act of acquiring faith'. He further underlines the point and says that if our faith has reached that stage then there is no pen, no ink and no paper which could be used to spell out these mysteries. There is no consciousness really capable, he says in the fourth line, of even considering the greatness of the faithful, the true believer who has achieved the state of *mannay*, of complete faith.

The last two lines, the fifth and sixth, are the refrain common to these four *pauṛis*, no. 12 and nos. 13, 14 and 15 that follow. The Guru says here that the *Niranjan* – the Immaculate One, the Lord, may only be realized by one who has attained the status of the true believer. This is also rendered by some commentators to mean that the state of full belief will ensue if we meditate with full concentration on the One Immaculate Lord. So the two ways of looking at this, as put forth by Prof. Talib and Dr. Sangat Singh respectively, are the converse of each other. Is it the state of *mannay* that accrues from meditating on the Immaculate as Dr. Sangat Singh says, or is it that the state of *mannay* is the pre-requisite, which will then be followed by God-realization? The latter seems the more appropriate interpretation. The Guru is telling us the benefits and the meaning of true belief. Such a state, he says, is impossible to describe or to put to pen or paper; but such a state will lead us, through further meditation, to achieving the universally desired state of salvation.

Prof. Sahib Singh also renders the sixth line to say that the true understanding of the Immaculate Lord will only come to one who in his mind brings the state of complete faith and absorption in the Lord.

Osho in his commentary, 'The True Name', translates *mannay* as 'state of contemplation' and the last lines of the refrain are translated by him as:

'The Name of the flawless one is such
That only contemplating can know it.'

He distinguishes between 'thinking' and 'contemplating' and argues that these are different degrees of the same process. In thinking, you remain on the surface but in contemplation you plunge into the very depth of the word. He further says 'contemplation' means the absence of mind, where the 'word' resonates inside you at all times without your speaking it. In Sikhism the concept is somewhat differently understood and the effort in Sikhism is to so learn to recite the *nām* that it becomes a constant refrain within the subconscious.

Bhai Vir Singh has well described the state of gradually acquiring the purity of soul and mind through constant recitation of the 'Name' and thus reaching the stage of truly listening and then of firm faith. He says we are like vessels filled with impure water. When we inject into ourselves the pure water of devotion and meditation, the impure water is gradually driven out and the water in the vessel gets clearer steadily and surely. Thus at no stage is the vessel empty or even half full. It is always full but the contents are getting purified until one day it is all completely clear. The analogy is to cleanse our inner selves from the taints of sin and evil through the fresh water of *nām*. It also explains an essential difference between the Sikh way and some of the traditional Eastern ways which call for emptying the mind first and bringing ourselves to a zero state whereafter we can hope to infuse the knowledge of God into that vacuum. The Sikh way importantly differs in that it calls not for renunciation or removing oneself from the world of men. Rather, it calls for full and vigorous participation in life; living the life of the householder, working hard and honestly to earn our living and then sharing what we have with those less fortunate or otherwise needy, and all the while fixing the mind on Him and in a spirit of total surrender to His will.

So we see that the Guru has now taken us one step ahead of 'listening' and is taking us to the next stage of total faith - *Mannai*, the state in which the believer, the *mannay* exists; a state which is essential for further spiritual growth if we are to know about our Immaculate Lord. But, says the Guru, this state is not amenable to description in words. It is a state of the mind to be experienced and relished and not for discussion or narration.

18

BEYOND THE REACH OF DEATH

Pauṛi 13

ਮੰਨੈ ਸੁਰਤਿ ਹੋਵੈ ਮਨਿ ਬੁਧਿ॥	*Mannai surat hovai mann budh.*
ਮੰਨੈ ਸਗਲ ਭਵਣ ਕੀ ਸੁਧਿ॥	*Mannai sagal bhavaṇ ki sudh.*
ਮੰਨੈ ਮੁਹਿ ਚੋਟਾ ਨਾ ਖਾਇ॥	*Mannai muh chotta na khāye.*
ਮੰਨੈ ਜਮ ਕੈ ਸਾਥਿ ਨ ਜਾਇ॥	*Mannai jamm kay sāth na jāye.*
ਐਸਾ ਨਾਮੁ ਨਿਰੰਜਨੁ ਹੋਇ॥	*Aisa nām niranjaṇ hoye.*
ਜੇ ਕੋ ਮੰਨਿ ਜਾਣੈ ਮਨਿ ਕੋਇ॥੧੩॥	*Je ko mann jāṇai mann koye.*

Brief glossary

ਮੰਨੈ	*Mannai*	If one acquires faith
ਸੁਰਤਿ	*Surat*	Condition of the mind
ਮਨਿ	*Mann*	In the mind
ਬੁਧਿ	*Budh*	Awakening, consciousness
ਭਵਣ	*Bhavaṇ*	Building, here the world
ਸੁਧਿ	*Sudh*	Awareness, knowledge
ਮੁਹਿ	*Muh*	On the face
ਚੋਟਾ	*Chotta*	Injury, hurt
ਜਮ	*Jamm*	The messenger of death, Lord of death Yama
ਮੰਨਿ	*Mann*	If one believes

Simply translated this *pauṛi* says that if we acquire faith our minds will be awakened. The mystery of the principles of the universe will become clear. The hurt of distance from the Lord will not be suffered. By acquiring faith we will not be subject to the god of Death. The last two lines say that the 'Name' of the Lord is Immaculate and this truth may be only realized by acquiring faith. We can now look in more detail at the message and also see what the learned ones have to tell us.

Continuing the lesson the Guru further in this *pauṛi*, says in the first line that through this path will one achieve *surat* (awakening of the mind, the intellect). In other words, the awareness and knowledge of the universe is achieved through this state. Through such faith will the intuitive knowledge of all abodes arise in the mind. The Guru here is obviously speaking not only of the physical shape and structure of matter, but is really referring to the occult principle that underlines the reality. This inward realm also becomes clear to the mind that has grounded itself firmly in faith. The working of this grand and immense system, the real time universe that we in our mortal bodies are experiencing at all times, becomes clear. Beyond that the true, the real causal effect of this apparent reality is revealed spontaneously to the one whose faith is firm and whose belief is true and complete.

In the third line the Guru says such a person will not suffer injury or hurt. From what injury is this protection available is understood differently by commentators. Prof. Sahib Singh in *The Sri Granth Sahib Darpan* renders this to mean that such a person will be saved the injury that comes from succumbing to the worldly diversions, that is, he will be saved from greed, lust, anger, etc. and their evil effects. Bhai Vir Singh renders it as: "(Such a person) does not suffer from the harm of doubts (about the Lord)". He also gives the alternate meaning that such a one does not have to suffer the blows of Yama and Death.

Prof. Talib, however, renders this line to mean that the true believer is saved from suffering and injury in the hereafter. Osho translates it as: "You cease to repent your words," which, however, does not seem as convincing an interpretation because the word used by the Guru is 'ਚੋਟਾ' *chotta* - injury or hurt. Considering the context, especially when the fourth line talks of the freedom from the fear of death, Prof. Talib's interpretation seems to be the more appropriate one. Of course there is also a third interpretation, by Dr. Sangat Singh in his *Japji*. He translates the third line as: "He does not suffer the punishment of transmigration."

This is not too far in meaning from Prof. Talib's rendering. Transmigration into a lower form of existence is after all one of the punishments a soul can suffer. In the Judaic belief system, which includes the Islamic and Christian view, the sinning soul is supposed to undergo torments involving various human forms of infliction of torture, without even the hope of transmigration and another chance to rectify mistakes. Physical hells are also referred to in Hinduism. For instance, the *Mahabharata* says the *Pāndavas,* upon the end of their sojourn on earth made their way in human form to the heavens. However, the four *Pāndavas* along with Draupadi fell by the wayside. It was only the eldest, Yudhishtira – said to be *Dharma* incarnate – who along with his companion, a dog, reached the gates of heaven.

Yudhishtira, invited with respect to enter, refused until his loyal dog was also allowed in. Touched by his sense of loyalty he was permitted his wish but by then the dog had turned into the Dharamrāj who had only been testing Yudhishtira. Entering, he saw that his brothers and devout wife were all incarcerated in hell. Duryodhana and his cohort were on the other hand enjoying the pleasures of heaven. Saddened, Yudhishtira refused the offer to enter heaven and chose to join his dear ones. Soon enough the scene changed and around Yudhishtira and his family there was heaven. It was explained to him then they all had to languish this brief period in hell because there were a few sins they had committed, such as the pride of Arjuna, gluttony of Bhima, the vanity of Nakul and Sahdev and the weakness of Draupadi for Arjuna even though she was the wife equally of all the five brothers. The *Kauravas* were on the other hand entitled to a short stay in heaven because of some good deeds they performed on earth. Thus we see that the *Purāṇas* do entertain the notion of physical hell and heaven.

In the case of Sikhism this earth is recognized by the Guru as the arena of action in which we have been given the freedom to act and choose right from wrong so as to earn the merit requisite for our real selves, the soul within. The net effect of all our actions is going to be the achievement of greater or lesser proximity to the Lord; and this will be judged in the Divine Presence, in accordance with the merits of our actions. So, earth is the *Karmabhūmi* and here it is that this mortal vessel of the soul, the body, will suffer anguish and pleasures as per the laws established by the Lord. The notion that the soul even after it leaves this body would still be subject to the same sort of physical effects, is difficult to comprehend. That the soul could be subjected to physical torture after leaving this body is not consistent with the postulate that the soul is a separated portion of the Lord and is immaterial. The concept is also not consistent with the Guru's description of the Lord as an all-seeing, loving Entity that watches over His creation with compassion and pleasure. While the body is ordained to be a creature of the senses, the soul is immaterial, a part of the Ineffable, the Immanent. What physical tortures could it then be made to suffer? The only torture logically for a soul is an enforced separation from the Almighty. And this is what the Guru has said in the concluding *slok* of the *Japji* which says *Karmi āpo āpṇi kay neṛay kay dūr* - as your actions have been so shall be your distance from, or proximity to the Lord.

The third line, as we have above discussed, is to be interpreted as saying that if you are a true believer your soul will be saved from suffering the hurt of being banished from the Lord's presence, or being distanced from Him. The one who has acquired true faith will not suffer this injury. Even if the other rendering that we have discussed above is assumed to be correct, which it really is not, it would still mean that the faithful soul will be saved from whatever torments a man may fear.

The fourth line refers to man's fear of death. Lord Yama is the Lord of Death in Hindu mythology. He and his agents, called *Yamdūts*, are given the task of gathering the souls of the dead and taking them for divine adjudication. Yama is also the God in-charge for imposing the punishments as per the merit earned by a soul during the sojourn on this earth. As we saw in the example of the *Pāndavas* journey from this earth, Yama is supposed in the Hindu belief to assign the soul to the bliss and the pleasures of heaven or to the torments of hell depending on the merit earned by the soul during its sojourn on earth; and in this capacity almost merges with Dharmaraj. Yama is thus a much feared deity in the Hindu pantheon. He not only signifies the end of our lives depriving us of something which the vast multitude of humans cherishes the most, but he also has the power to judge and to subject us to punishment after life. Now who amongst us does not fear being put to the test, however well prepared we may feel we are. Yama is thus doubly dreaded.

The Guru says that if we have acquired true faith we will not be taken to Yama. There are instances available within the Hindu mythology of certain highly achieved souls going on their own and sometimes in their own physical bodies to the abode of gods. Arjuna for instance spent a year in *Indralok*, the kingdom and capital city of Lord Indra. The *Pāndavas* also were making their way bodily to their heavenly abode in their last journey from earth. The Guru says that the true believer will be at a stage where, like those ancient heroes and great souls, he will be beyond the jurisdiction of Lord Yama. This dread which afflicts the ordinary person can then hold no terror for the believer.

In the last lines which is the refrain for these four *pauṛi* the Guru again says that the Name of the Lord is Immaculate and this truth may only be realized by one who is a true believer.

The refrain has also been slightly differently explained but to the same effect by Narain Singh in his *Japji* in Punjabi, published by Bhagat Puran Singh. Narain Singh says, "These lines mean that the Name has now become Immaculate and has emerged in (hearts of) the *Bhagats* and taken them also above and beyond the grip of Illusion, where the *Bhagat* is no longer effected by Māya, thus making it easy for him to become one with the Lord." He further says, on page 122 of his commentary, that it can also be explained in the context of the four ways of reciting the Name: "In the beginning when recitation is done the words are spoken aloud – this is called the *Baikhri Bāṇi*. In the next stage it is not vocalized but is uttered sotto voce – this is called the *Madhma*. In the third stage it is not even sub-vocalized but is recited in the mind. This is a stage of awakening and enlightenment – this is called *Pasayanti* where it is not uttered at all but shines inside as the light. The fourth and final stage is the *Pra bāṇi* which is indicative of the Formless One Himself. Similarly, by true listening and true belief the *Bhagat* progresses in his achievements. He finally recites without reciting – he is constantly doing *Ajapā jāp*. Thus one who recites the Name with his heart, without use of his tongue is the only one who will know the vastness and grandeur of the 'Immaculate One'.

19

NOTHING SHALL BAR YOUR PATH

Pauṛi 14

ਮੰਨੈ ਮਾਰਗਿ ਠਾਕ ਨ ਪਾਇ॥	*Mannai mārag tthāk na pāye.*
ਮੰਨੈ ਪਤਿ ਸਿਉ ਪਰਗਟੁ ਜਾਇ॥	*Mannai pat(i) sio pargatt jāye.*
ਮੰਨੈ ਮਗੁ ਨ ਚਲੈ ਪੰਥੁ॥	*Mannai magg na chalai panth.*
ਮੰਨੈ ਧਰਮ ਸੇਤੀ ਸਨਬੰਧੁ॥	*Mannai dharma seti sanbandh.*
ਐਸਾ ਨਾਮੁ ਨਿਰੰਜਨੁ ਹੋਇ॥	*Aisa nām niranjan hoye.*
ਜੇ ਕੋ ਮੰਨਿ ਜਾਣੈ ਮਨਿ ਕੋਇ॥ ੧੪॥	*Je ko mann jāṇai mann koye.*

Brief glossary

ਮੰਨੈ	*Mannai*	If one believes, the state of true belief
ਮਾਰਗਿ	*Mārag*	Path
ਠਾਕ	*Tthāk*	Obstruction
ਪਤਿ ਸਿਉ	*Pat(i) sio*	With respect, honourably
ਪਰਗਟੁ	*Pargatt*	Visible
ਮਗੁ	*Magg*	Path
ਪੰਥੁ	*Panth*	Way, a religious grouping
ਸੇਤੀ	*Seti*	With
ਸਨਬੰਧੁ	*Sanbandh*	Connection, link, relationship

Simply translated this *pauṛi* says that if we truly believe we will not find obstructions on the path to God. We will earn honour in the divine presence. We will not be diverted into paths of narrow religiosity and we will discover the true religion which is true spirituality beyond all religions. In the last two lines the Guru says that the Immaculate Name of God may only be realized by one who truly believes. Let us now see in more detail the meaning of the message and also see what learned commentators have to tell us.

The Guru further describes in this *pauṛi* the fortune that awaits the true believer. He says in the first line, that the true believer will traverse the path – *mārag* - to God-realization without any hindrance - *tthāk*. No obstruction will stand in the way of the true believer as he walks this wondrous path through his life on this earth. Conversely, we can safely conclude that the unfortunate non-believer will find many ways of getting distracted from the straight and narrow true path. Each worldly toy or pleasure will divert him, each hardship will shake his faith and in bitterness at his misfortune the non-believer will lose track. He will say that a God that doesn't fulfil his every wish or lets him be subjected to the slightest trouble or sorrow is not a God worth following. All these events will be road blocks in the path of many of us. Not so for the true believer. These events and issues are seen by him as of little long-term significance and as mere manifestations of Māya. His mind remains steadfastly fixed and firm in his faith and he moves surely and steadily towards the Lord.

In the second line the Guru says such a fortunate one will proceed from this world with honour and distinction. Having been steadfast and having not let any obstruction stand in his journey to God-realization the true believer departs from the world and reaches the abode of the Lord with his honour intact. He earns respect and approval in the entire process of this movement from this mortal world to the true believer's tryst with the Divine.

In the third line the Guru says that the true believer does not get diverted into narrow paths and by-ways. The term ਮਗੁ - *magg*, and ਪੰਥੁ - *panth*, mean literally the same thing – path. In fact, they have been used together to describe a path, elsewhere also in the

SGGS, at page 1116, for example in *Tukhāri Chhant,* where the fourth Nanak says:

"Mārag panth chalay gur satgur sangg sikha."
(Page 1116, *SGGS*)

And Guru Nanak in *Tukhāri Rāg* says:
"Mundh naiṇ bharedi, guṇ sāredi, kiu prabh mila pyāray.
Mārag panth na jāṇau vikhṛa, kiu pāyiai pir pāray."
(Page 1111, *SGGS*)

In both cases the two words *mārag panth* are used to convey 'path', as it does here in this *pauṛi* also. There is however a slight distinction here as we shall see below.

Men in their search for the True One get divided into groups and sects. Religious leaders crop up and make loud proclamation that theirs is the magical formula for achieving God-realization. It is all too easy for the confused man to be taken in. Not all such leaders are false and not all these paths misleading. Many are the true seers and prophets who genuinely lead the follower out of the maze of worldly distractions and onto the true path. There is, as we noted earlier, no one single religion or system that could claim to have sole and exclusive rights to the passage from this world to the True Realm. However, the vast majority of these are narrow-minded and bigoted, and their stress is usually more on criticizing the other than truly guiding their own follower. The stress in these groups is on ritual and meaningless secret *Mantras*. Exclusivity and denigration of opponents are their hallmark. These are the narrow by-ways which if a man follows will end up in desolate wilderness. Mere religiosity cannot by itself lead anywhere, and it is no true path unless it leads the follower to spiritual pursuits and elevation of the mind and purification of the soul. Such barren by-ways are followed by many of these various groupings of men who form into religious brotherhoods which are also called *panth*. While *magg* or *mārag*, and *panth* are used interchangeably yet here the Guru is talking of not only the narrow by-ways but also the small misguided groups who are the followers of such pretenders claiming to be religious leaders. The man of true faith does not get sucked into these. His remains the search for true spirituality, well beyond the rituals and empty religiosity of the many narrow, bigoted groups who mislead many sincere and well-meaning seekers. This is what the Guru is saying when he says the true believer will not meet with hindrances.

The Guru concludes this argument in the fourth line. He says the true believer, having escaped the pitfalls of the narrow by-ways and religious groupings, establishes firm connection with the true religion. This is the religion that transcends religiosity and rituals and taps directly into the universal – the one religion that brings enlightenment and helps break through the veil of illusion and see reality. Such religion is the broad path that rejects exclusivity, that stresses the oneness of all creatures and of obedience and acceptance of the Lord's word, His commands. There is no creature outside the sweep of such religion; even the non-believer is loved and respected and prayed for. This is the path that contains the essence of all faiths and pathways to God.

In the last two lines, those of the refrain, the Guru again says that the wondrous and Immaculate Name of the God may only be realized by the true believer.

In short, the Guru enlightens us further in this *pauṛi* on the wonderful fate that awaits the true believer. The Guru correctly recognises man's yearning to earn respect and honour and to be able to reach the Lord as one of His accepted ones. The Guru addresses the common hindrances that prevent a man from achieving success in this endeavour, and reassures us that these shall not stand in the way of the true believer.

The Guru of course knows how easily man is diverted by worldly pleasures and material possessions; how easily is man shaken by hardships from his faith; and how these issues cause a man to lose track of his true path. The Guru knows how frantically men try to acquire respect among his peers, how they crave worldly honour and power over their fellowmen. In this desperate search, men will often commit any sin they deem necessary at that moment. Men will, in the grip of such base passions, unhesitatingly grab the rights of others and have no scruples in dishonourably acquiring wealth and possessions. It is an irony that even such a man may often be, in the eyes of the spiritually ignorant, looked upon with respect and even envy. In real fact, such a man has but acquired mere dross and guided by his ego, he has traversed the path to his damnation, increasing his distance from the Lord and loading the soul with burdens which will take many rebirths to remove.

The Guru shows us that as against the misguided ones of this type there are the true believers. Armoured in their unflinching faith and aware of the oneness of this entire creation, they tread the path of righteousness. What comes to their lot by way of material wealth they know to be but a gift from the Lord. Their eyes fixed firmly on the Lord's message as brought to them by the Guru, they travel through this minefield of distraction in comfort and contentment. It is often a wonder that such men, living in submission to the Lord's command, will often have acquired as much honour in this world, effortlessly and honourably, as any materially hungry man could crave. However, whether this honour and material success comes is not their aim and never in their prayers do they seek such baubles. The Guru says that such men travel through this journey on this mortal world in peace and joy, smoothly and without getting lost in the dead-ends and the narrow by-lanes of religiosity and having so travelled, will appear before the Lord in a state of honour.

Such men, the Guru says, of true faith are in such a state of enlightenment that they immediately recognize the world of the spirit, and the various dogmas and isms all become meaningless to them. Such men do not desperately keep shifting their allegiance from sect to sect or from one religion to the other. They waste no effort or precious time in seeking different pathways to the Lord. Their total immersion in the True One carries them past the need for such antics. Such fortunate men are forever in the presence of the Lord in their hearts and live in the world of the spirit. Their relationship is to the true religion – which shows them the oneness of all creation, the existence of the One Power – by whatever name, title or label men may have chosen to describe Him. Such a true believer is enabled to transcend into the realm beyond the mundane and only such a believer can truly attain God-realization.

20

ONWARDS TO SALVATION

Pauṛi 15

ਮੰਨੈ ਪਾਵਹਿ ਮੋਖੁ ਦੁਆਰੁ॥	*Mannai pāveh mokh duār.*
ਮੰਨੈ ਪਰਵਾਰੈ ਸਾਧਾਰੁ॥	*Mannai parvārai sādhār.*
ਮੰਨੈ ਤਰੈ ਤਾਰੇ ਗੁਰੁ ਸਿਖ॥	*Mannai tarai täray gur sikh.*
ਮੰਨੈ ਨਾਨਕ ਭਵਹਿ ਨ ਭਿਖ॥	*Mannai Nanak bhaveh na bhikh.*
ਐਸਾ ਨਾਮੁ ਨਿਰੰਜਨੁ ਹੋਇ॥	*Aisa nām niranjan hoye.*
ਜੇ ਕੋ ਮੰਨਿ ਜਾਣੈ ਮਨਿ ਕੋਇ॥੧੫॥	*Je ko mann jaṇai mann koye.*

Brief glossary

ਪਾਵਹਿ	*Pāveh*	Finds, reaches
ਮੋਖੁ	*Mokh*	Salvation
ਪਰਵਾਰੈ	*Parvārai*	Along with the clan or family
ਸਾਧਾਰੁ	*Sādhār*	With support (The SGPC's *Shabdarth* says 'reform')
ਤਰੈ	*Tarai*	Swims
ਤਾਰੇ	*Tāray*	Helps others swim
ਗੁਰੁ ਸਿਖ	*Gur Sikh*	The Guru and his disciple
ਭਵਹਿ	*Bhaveh*	Roams, drifts around
ਭਿਖ	*Bhikh*	Alms

Simply translated this *pauṛi* says that if we have true faith we will find the door to salvation. Not only the true believer himself but his kin will turn to godliness by his support. Beyond that even those who follow such a one will be spiritually elevated. By truly believing we will not need to go seeking alms, neither worldly nor spiritually. The name of the Immaculate Lord is so beyond the mundane that only the true believer can know of Him. With this we can now see in detail what the message is and what the learned ones say.

In this, the final *pauṛi* of the four on the theme of the true believer, the Guru concludes by telling us, in the first line, that the true believer finds the door to salvation. All religions, all pathways are designed for the sole purpose of achieving for the soul liberation from the cycle of birth and death. Some have chosen to describe this purpose differently and thus this goal may in some religions be described as the attainment of eternally joyful life among heavenly surroundings such as a man will on this world find pleasurable. The Muslim faith prescribes that the righteous shall be rewarded with eternal life in *Jannat,* or paradise where all physical gratification shall be always available. The Christian belief again postulates for the righteous eternal existence in a heaven peopled with divine creatures called 'Angels'. In such a heaven there is no sorrow or illness. In both these cases the implicit proposition is that this state is eternal and there is no rebirth for such souls. Thus call it 'Jannat' or 'Paradise', or 'Heaven' or 'Valhalla' as the Scandinavians do, or the state called *Nirvāna* by the Buddhists, the desired state in any religious belief system is one which rids man of the troubles and travails that are an inevitable concomitant of this worldly existence.

In Sikhism, as also in Hinduism, the ultimate aim for the soul is called *Mukti* or *Moksha.* This in the common parlance has been called *Mokh* by the Guru. The door to this desired state, says the Guru in the first line, is accessible straightaway to the true believer. The Guru has in the earlier *pauṛi* told us that the path of ritual purification and complicated and difficult disciplines are not necessary and are by themselves futile. Only if a spirit of self-surrender, of total obedience and faith, governs our actions can we hope to reach the Lord. He has told us in *pauṛis* 8 to 11 of the vital stage of listening and imbibing the Lord's word as given to us through the Guru. He is then telling us in these next four *pauṛis*, 12 to 15, of the attainments that will follow true belief, of how the passage through this world is eased, of how respect and honour will automatically come our way. Here the Guru says in the first line of this *pauṛi* that not merely these gifts but the biggest gift of all – that of access to the door of salvation – is reserved for the true believer.

We might here pause to note that in Sikhism while *Moksha* is a desired destination, the true Sikh even while on this earth, is able to live in a state that is unique in this faith and is called *Jivan Mukta* - freed from all bonds while living. The *SGGS* on page 275 in the ninth *asttapadi* says: 'The one who lives by the Lord's word is *Jivan Mukta'*. Such a one is not shaken either by too much joy or by sorrow. He is ever in high spirits and never downcast. For him gold has no greater attraction than simple mud. Nectar and bitter poison are to him the same. He is not troubled by insults, nor elated by honour. Wealth and poverty are to him the same. King or pauper is alike for him. He treats what the Lord has given him as the proper gift. In other words, he orders his life strictly in accordance with the Lord's will. Such a one, says Nanak, is the *Jivan Mukta.* The same message can be found at other places in the *SGGS,* such as *Rāg Āsa Mahla* 4, page 449 where the 4th Nanak says, *jīvan mukat so ākhīyai marr jīvai marīya* – he is *jīvan mukat* who while alive kills the *haumai* within. Again the Guru says, in *Rāg Māru Mahla* 1, page 1009, *jīvan mukat so ākhīyai jis vicho haumai jāye* – he is *jīvan mukat* who has shed *haumai* from within himself

The Guru in the second line says that not only he himself but all in the family of the true believer will also attain this happy state. The true believer having acquired for himself a high spiritual state now becomes the support for those who are in his immediate proximity and will help in their spiritual upliftment also. It is common human experience that we are all, to some extent, influenced by our surroundings. Whatever our innate nature we will begin to acquire characteristics and habits of whatever we are constantly exposed to. It is also an unfortunate truth that the acquisition of bad habits occurs faster and more easily than good habits. Greedy, corrupt or selfish friends and family will soon make a person also similarly evil. Good, pious and righteous family and friends will, maybe more slowly and maybe to a lesser extent, make a person righteous and good. Therefore, when in a family there is a true believer there is bound to be his effect rubbing off on those who live constantly in his company. He then becomes the spiritual support for his family and will reform them also to the path of Godliness.

In the third line the Guru says that not only he himself and his proximate family will be elevated but also those who are his followers. The true believer having himself attained the door to salvation will also become the vessel, the ship in which those who follow his path will also reach that blessed state. Giving the analogy of swimming through rough waters the Guru says that the true believer through the strength of his faith makes the journey safely. Such will be his strength that he will be able to support even those who are not themselves such strong swimmers but have taken his help in the passage. The true believer having risen to the stage of a Guru is then able to elevate also his disciples. In a way this is an extrapolation of the second line. After all the close disciples of the true believer are in the same position of proximity as his family. The second and third lines read together mean that anyone who learns from the true believer and exposes himself to his elevating proximity will reap the same rewards as the true believer himself. In other words, such fortunate ones will themselves become true believers and thus eligible to the same rewards.

Here we need to understand that the family of the believer or even the disciples of such a soul do not reach to salvation through the intercession of this believer. The concept of an intermediary between the soul and the Lord does not exist in Sikhism. Each individual soul has to by itself follow the path prescribed for it by the Guru. The Guru is not an intercessor. He is rather a facilitator, a guide who explains to the seeker the guidelines laid down for reaching the Lord. The Lord's word is brought to the individual through the Guru – which in the case of Sikhism is the *Sri Guru Granth Sahib.* A Sikh on the path of God-realization has to follow the commandments as prescribed in the *SGGS*. The Sikh treading such a path will greatly benefit from the proximity to and the company of the true believer and the path will become clearer to him and he will also be helped in overcoming any obstacles or removing any doubts that may arise on such a difficult journey.

Notwithstanding the help available as above from the presence of the true believer, the seeker yet has to work hard. The discipline and the training of the mind, the overcoming of the ego and the distancing from the allurement of Māya, such as power and dominion over others, possession of great wealth and the wide variety of distractions available in this world for pandering to the senses, are within the realm of each individual's personal sphere of activity. There is no outside force that can bring about such discipline; the effort has to be strictly personal, it has to come from within. The mere presence of a true believer either as your spiritual guide or as a member of the near family whom you respect and whose example you will want to follow is a major boost in any such effort. It is in this light the Guru says that the members of a believer's family, and by implication, the disciples of such a guide will also achieve salvation along with him.

This needs to be a little more clearly understood lest it be taken to mean that the Guru has sanctioned non-action or wrong doing even indirectly. So complete and certain is the message in Sikhism and so well-defined the pathway that no confusion should be allowed to arise on this issue. No sinner or purveyor of power or selfish egotism can hope to achieve this blessed stage merely from the accident of his having been born in the family of a true believer, nor by enrolling himself as a follower of such a man. There are unfortunately many who call themselves Sikhs but become the followers of one *dera* or the other. They then boast of how holy the *bāba* or the leader of the *dera* is. They hope that their mere act of having declared themselves the adherents of a holy man or even occasionally hosting and serving such a man is sufficient endeavour, and they now need do nothing further. What is worse is the commonly noticed phenomenon of the family and the relatives of such religious leaders seeming to be claiming a hereditary right to holiness! This is an illusion. It is true that such men are fortunate in having been blessed with proximity to a true believer either through birth or through later volition. This mere fact can by itself ease their path greatly, but still they need to work on themselves to discipline their egos. Probably all they need to do is to follow the example set and the direction shown by such a family member or spiritual guide. These spiritually elevated men can lead us, guide us but we need to always remember that in Sikhism they cannot be intercessors between us and the Lord. That concept belongs to some other path, Christianity, for example, where in some denominations of the religion God's representatives on earth are supposed to be able to intercede for the sinner. In Sikhism the journey is ours alone, the obstacles are for us to overcome and the self-discipline is ours to attain. It is the individual who has to decide that he must surrender his ego, that he must constantly recite the Lord's name until it becomes an *Ajapa Jāp* - the recitation without reciting, without words.

In the fourth line the Guru says that the true believer does not go seeking alms. We need to pause here and consider what alms the Guru is referring to. Surely not merely the alms of worldly goods – for the true believer has reached much beyond such needs. The reference is more to spiritual begging. We may here note that it is enjoined upon the true Sikh to live by honest toil for his own sustenance and also to lay out part of his income to help the needy. Thus seeking of alms even in a worldly sense is totally against the tenets of Sikhism. The community takes justifiable pride in the fact that rarely would one see a Sikh beggar on the streets. Also, even after facing the holocaust-like trauma of the partition of India, and losing all they possessed to rioters and looters, the Sikhs steadfastly stuck to their ethos and through sheer hard and honest toil were soon prosperous in their new homes in independent India. The seeking of alms is thus strictly against Sikhism in this world. But beyond that the Guru's message here is also to the alms for the inner self.

The Guru says that true believers are firm in their faith and follow the voice of the Lord that resides within all of us. They know the true religion, which is beyond all religiosity, and thus never have need of going from one religious leader to the next. They are satisfied and have not the need to keep shifting religions or sects in their search for the right path. They are steadfastly progressing on the one true path of spirituality – beyond all religions and yet incorporating all true religions. The need to seek for something else, the need to beg others for spiritual guidance does not ever arise.

The last two lines are the refrain which we discussed in the previous *pauṛi*. It says that the name of the Immaculate Lord is so beyond the mundane that only a true believer can achieve God-realization.

21

THE ENLIGHTENED ONES

Pauṛi 16

ਪੰਚ ਪਰਵਾਣ ਪੰਚ ਪਰਧਾਨੁ ॥	*Panch parwāṇ panch pardhān.*
ਪੰਚੇ ਪਾਵਹਿ ਦਰਗਹਿ ਮਾਨੁ ॥	*Panchay pāveh dargay mān.*
ਪੰਚੇ ਸੋਹਹਿ ਦਰਿ ਰਾਜਾਨੁ ॥	*Panchay soheh dar(i) rājān.*
ਪੰਚਾ ਕਾ ਗੁਰੁ ਏਕੁ ਧਿਆਨੁ ॥	*Pancha ka gur ek dhyān.*
ਜੇ ਕੋ ਕਹੈ ਕਰੈ ਵੀਚਾਰੁ ॥	*Je ko kahai karai vīchār.*
ਕਰਤੇ ਕੈ ਕਰਣੈ ਨਾਹੀ ਸੁਮਾਰੁ ॥	*Kartay kai karṇai nāhi sumār.*
ਧੌਲੁ ਧਰਮੁ ਦਇਆ ਕਾ ਪੂਤੁ ॥	*Dhaul dharam daya ka pūt.*
ਸੰਤੋਖੁ ਥਾਪਿ ਰਖਿਆ ਜਿਨਿ ਸੂਤਿ ॥	*Santokh thhāp rakhiya jin sūt.*
ਜੇ ਕੋ ਬੁਝੈ ਹੋਵੈ ਸਚਿਆਰੁ ॥	*Je ko bujhai hovai sachiār.*
ਧਵਲੈ ਉਪਰਿ ਕੇਤਾ ਭਾਰੁ ॥	*Dhawlai uppar keta bhār.*
ਧਰਤੀ ਹੋਰੁ ਪਰੈ ਹੋਰੁ ਹੋਰੁ ॥	*Dharti hor parai hor hor.*
ਤਿਸ ਤੇ ਭਾਰੁ ਤਲੈ ਕਵਣੁ ਜੋਰੁ ॥	*Tis tay bhār talai kawaṇ jor.*
ਜੀਅ ਜਾਤਿ ਰੰਗਾ ਕੇ ਨਾਵ ॥	*Jīv jāt ranga kay nāv.*
ਸਭਨਾ ਲਿਖਿਆ ਵੁੜੀ ਕਲਾਮ ॥	*Sabhna likhiya vuṛi kalām.*
ਏਹੁ ਲੇਖਾ ਲਿਖਿ ਜਾਣੈ ਕੋਇ ॥	*Eh lekha likh jāṇai koye.*
ਲੇਖਾ ਲਿਖਿਆ ਕੇਤਾ ਹੋਇ ॥	*Lekha likhiya keta hoye.*
ਕੇਤਾ ਤਾਣੁ ਸੁਆਲਿਹੁ ਰੂਪੁ ॥	*Keta tāṇ suwāliyo rūp.*
ਕੇਤੀ ਦਾਤਿ ਜਾਣੈ ਕੌਣੁ ਕੂਤੁ ॥	*Keti dāt jāṇai kauṇ kūt.*
ਕੀਤਾ ਪਸਾਉ ਏਕੋ ਕਵਾਉ ॥	*Kīta pasāo eko kavāo.*
ਤਿਸ ਤੇ ਹੋਏ ਲਖ ਦਰੀਆਉ ॥	*Tis te hoye lakh darīyāo.*
ਕੁਦਰਤਿ ਕਵਣ ਕਹਾ ਵੀਚਾਰੁ ॥	*Kudrat kawaṇ kaha vīchār.*
ਵਾਰਿਆ ਨ ਜਾਵਾ ਏਕ ਵਾਰ ॥	*Vāriya na jāva ek vār.*

ਜੋ ਤੁਧੁ ਭਾਵੈ ਸਾਈ ਭਲੀ ਕਾਰ॥	*Ju tudh bhāvai sāyi bhali kār.*
ਤੂ ਸਦਾ ਸਲਾਮਤਿ ਨਿਰੰਕਾਰ॥ ੧੬॥	*Tu sada salāmat nirankār.*

Brief glossary

ਪੰਚ	*Panch*	The exalted ones, the elect
ਪਰਵਾਣ	*Parwāṇ*	Accepted
ਪਰਧਾਨੁ	*Pardhān*	Leaders, prominent ones
ਸੋਹਹਿ	*Soheh*	Looks befitting, shines
ਰਾਜਾਨੁ	*Rājān*	Kings
ਦਰਿ	*Darr*	Gate, portals, abode
ਕਰਤੇ ਕੈ ਕਰਣੈ	*Kartay kai karṇai*	The creation of the Lord
ਸੁਮਾਰੁ	*Sumār*	Measure, count
ਧੌਲੁ	*Dhaul*	The bull
ਦਇਆ ਕਾ ਪੂਤੁ	*Daya ka poot*	Offspring of compassion
ਸੰਤੋਖੁ	*Santokh*	Contentment
ਥਾਪਿ ਰਖਿਆ	*Thāp rakhiya*	Has established
ਸੂਤਿ	*Sūt*	The joining thread, Sanskrit *sūtra*
ਜੀਅ ਜਾਤਿ	*Jīv jāt*	Creatures
ਵੁੜੀ	*Vuṛi*	Flowing, moving
ਸੁਆਲਿਹੁ ਰੁਪੁ	*Suwāliyo rūp*	Beautiful forms
ਕੂੜੁ	*Kūt*	Assessment (of a standing field of grain)
ਪਸਾਉ	*Pasāo*	Spread
ਸਦਾ ਸਲਾਮਤਿ	*Sada salāmat*	Eternal, immutable
ਕੁਦਰਤਿ	*Kudrat*	An Arabic word meaning nature. Here, Lord's might
ਨਿਰੰਕਾਰ	*Nirankār*	Formless One

In these four *pauṛis*, from sixteen to nineteen, the Guru has expounded on the Lord's grandeur and the devotee's relationship with Him. The refrain in these *pauṛis* is that so vastly beyond us is the Lord and so unworthy are we that we cannot even offer ourselves as sacrifice to Him even once.

Simply translated, the sixteenth *pauṛi* says that the *Panch* - the Elect- shall be accepted as pre-eminent among mankind. They will also find honour before the Lord, and will be resplendent in that court. Their minds are ever fixed on the Lord. If one were to attempt description he will soon find that the Lord's limits cannot be fathomed. The mythical *Dhaul*, Bull, is actually *Dharam* – the operating system of the universe as laid down by the Lord, and hence begotten of His Grace. The thread that holds it all together is *santokh* – contentment. If we believe that the mythical 'Bull' actually exists then how much is the burden it is carrying? The worlds are infinite, what could support them all? The Guru then says, in line 13, that there are beings of myriad types and for each is his fate written down by His flowing pen. The depth of this mystery none can plumb. How great is His might, how resplendent His form, and how great His gifts none can hope to estimate. With one 'Word' was it all created and from there gushed forth unnumbered streams (of varieties of beings). In the last four lines of the refrain the Guru says he does not have the ability to compute and express the vastness of this creation, and he is not fit even to be a sacrifice even once to the Lord. We can now look at this *pauṛi* in more detail and also see what the learned ones have written about it.

In this *pauṛi* the Guru speaks to us of the *Panch*. The word also translates as 'five'. However, it is much more commonly interpreted in the sense of 'the exalted ones'. When the village's elders are elected or chosen otherwise by virtue of their superior qualities, they are even today called *Panch* and the chief among them is called *Sarpanch*. The name and title is ancient. In the earliest organised habitations in India the elders were called *Panch* and they had the power of judgement over the common folk. The Guru is using the term in that sense here.

As we saw in the *pauṛis* 8 to 11, the Guru told us of the attainments we can expect to reach were we to learn to truly listen. He then went a step beyond in *pauṛis* 12 to 15 and told us what could be expected if we not only listened but also acquired true and unshakeable faith in the One Lord. Now here the Guru tells us of the end-product of following the disciplines prescribed in the *pauṛis* 8 to 15. The ones who have learnt to truly hear and to fix their faith firmly will now reach the stage of *Panch* – the elect, the elite, the chosen ones. The Guru proceeds to tell us here of these *Panch*, the exalted ones.

The Guru says in the first line, they are the elect. As a result of the discipline they acquired through true listening and true believing, they are now the chosen, the enlightened ones. This appellation used by the Guru is to be viewed in the context of humanity at large or even all creation which is in varying stages of their journey to the final goal – union with the True One. In this vast mass there are the lowest of beasts, there are the higher, more evolved animals and above all of them the Lord has placed mankind, the apex of this great pyramid. Even within mankind, we have the large majority who have got ensnared by the glitter of Māya and have gone chasing after the illusory joys of power, wealth or mere sensory gratification. There are but only a few fortunate ones, blessed by the Lord Himself, who having put in the effort and discipline taught by the Guru and having learnt to control their mind are able to gain the true and everlasting pleasure of living in tune with the Lord's will. So we can see that there are very few indeed who can reach this lofty status and how large is the mass from amongst whom they have been chosen. In another belief system – the Christian – these would be called saints.

The Guru says that these *Panches* shall be *parwāṇ*, the accepted; they shall be *pardhān*, pre-eminent among mankind. Not only among men, says the Guru in the second line, but they shall also receive honour in the Divine Presence. The word *dargāh* is used for any abode where a holy person lives or had lived in the past. It also describes the doors – the gates – to a great mansion. Here it is used to refer to the Lord's court, metaphorically the greatest of all mansions. The Guru says that in this 'Divine Court' these chosen ones will find a place of honour and be accorded great respect. They will shine there in all splendour.

In the third line the Guru says that not only are they exalted in the 'Divine Court' but, says Prof. Sahib Singh, they also bring lustre to the courts of earthly kings. This is slightly differently seen by Bhai Vir Singh, who renders it as: "They shall be resplendent like kings even in the Divine Court." This is also quite an appealing interpretation. In either sense the Guru is telling us that these chosen ones have succeeded in making wholly successful their lives on this earth and found honour and respect not only among the world of men but have also ensured that their after-life is full of honour. A person who has done well is in common parlance often described as 'having made a success of both worlds'. Reference here is to this line of thought, though really one could say that once one has achieved the ultimate honour of reaching the Lord's presence and finding His love and approval, of what significance is the mere worldly honour of the courts of kings. Yet the point is made by the Guru to highlight the completeness of the honour due to a *Panch*.

The fourth line has been interpreted variously by learned commentators. Iqbal Singh in his *The Essence of Truth: Japji and Other Sikh Scriptures* refers to Mahakavi Santokh Singh who translated it as: "The concentrated meditation on God after controlling the five sense organs is the true preceptor."

Thus, this great and learned poet has taken the word *Panch* to refer to the five senses. Osho in *The True Name*, Vol. I, also renders it as: "Attention is the Guru of the five."

Explaining this further, Osho interprets it in his own way and says: "Nanak says the one is divided into five because of the five senses. If you seek the one within these five you shall attain, you become the *Sidhha*, the emancipated one."

Most other commentators have used the term *Panch* in the same sense as in the first three lines. Prof. Sahib Singh in his *Sri*

Guru Granth Sahib Darpan translates and explains it as meaning: "These chosen one's minds are focussed on the Guru alone." Dr. Sangat Singh uses it in the same sense. Dr. Gopal Singh renders it as: "They fix their minds on the one Master only." Prof. Talib also gives this as a possible meaning but renders it as: "By meditation on God do they find illumination." It will thus be seen that the more appropriate interpretation is that these *Panch*, the 'Chosen Ones' have their minds fixed wholly on the Lord. In other words, we can say that the Chosen Ones forever meditate on the Guru – the One Lord. Or slightly differently, that constant meditation on the name is the only Guru that the Chosen Ones have.

The Guru then in the fifth and sixth lines touches on another thought which is a recurring theme in the entire *Gurbāṇi*; that the Lord is beyond description. The Guru says here that if anyone were to attempt a description of the vast creation of the Lord he will soon discover that His deeds are beyond computation. Prof. Talib has rendered this line as: "One attempting to express God's creation and contemplating it shall above count and computation find it."

The context here is that many ancient seers had written holy texts musing about how the world was created and when; how vast it is and why was it created. Following from such speculation was one commonly held belief that the entire universe, or this world, rests on a bull which the Guru refers to in the next lines and which we shall discuss there. Here we may note is another thread being woven by the Guru into the tapestry. Having told us that the chosen ones possess great powers and hold in the spiritual sense a highly exalted position, the Guru puts in a cautionary word here. He says notwithstanding their greatness even the chosen ones, if they, like the ancient rishis, were to start to sit back and speculate on the Creator and His creation itself then their effort will soon prove to be worse than futile. He says that never is it possible to describe or enumerate the mystery of this vast creation. It is beyond man's capacity to compute.

In lines 7 to 9, the Guru talks about the myth commonly prevailing in Hindu mythology, regarding the celestial bull which holds up the Lord's creation, which we have referred to above. Some of the ancients who took the wrong path of seeking to put numbers and dates on creation then had to make further suppositions to explain what was holding the entire vast world in position. They, for this purpose, postulated a mythical bull of cosmic proportions which was said to carry this vast load and keep it stable. We can compare this to the Atlas myth in Greek mythology where it was said that Atlas, the Titan had been punished with holding up for eternity this Earth on his shoulders. These myths also incidentally became convenient explanations for natural phenomenon like earthquakes which were attributed to the bull, or Atlas, shifting the load to ease their aching muscles.

The Guru answers this myth in the seventh and eighth lines with an explanation in total accordance with his world-view. He admits there is a bull, but this bull is *Dharam* and it is begotten of compassion. *Dharam* is literally translated as either religion or righteousness, but here it is to be understood in the sense of 'The Order as ordained by the Lord'. The term is used in this sense to describe the innate nature of a thing. The word *Dharma* has very often been used in this context. Thus, we say the *Dharma* of fire is to burn, that of water is to quench, that of the sun is to give light and heat. The Lord has so ordained that to each of His creation is given an innate characteristic. The characteristic of the over-arching *Dharma* is to uphold creation, the natural order. The Lord having brought this creation into existence has then ordained the manner in which it shall function. The Lord's will, the Divine Order is then the bull which holds up this world.

And how was this 'Bull' placed in position? The Guru says it was born of *Daya*. This term is used to mean 'mercy' or 'compassion'. The Lord wanted His creation to function in an orderly and predictable fashion because He has love for it. As we discussed in the third *pauṛi*, and as the Guru will tell us in *pauṛi* 37: *Vekhai vigsai kar vichār* – the Lord sees His creation and He is pleased with it. This affection and love caused the *Dharma* to be put in place to function as the upholder of creation. The Guru says that this vast and diverse creation has the *sūt* – Sanskrit *sutra*, the common thread that holds the beads of a necklace together – in the form of contentment. Narain Singh in his *Japji Sahib*, p. 135, explains it well. He says that the various powers put in place by the Lord to keep the natural order going all work in a state of contentment, never seeking to exceed the authority the Lord has vested in them. Thus is the complexity of this vast creation managed in an orderly fashion and thus is the natural order of the universe upheld. The Guru here says in the ninth line that if we can truly comprehend this truth, we can acquire divinity. True comprehension can come only to the one who has surrendered his will to the Lord, the one who has learnt to truly listen, the one who has acquired true faith. Such a one must also then realize that the only upholder of this creation is the Lord's word, the *Dharma* He has put in place to keep the system functioning in harmony. Many other learned commentators have also described it broadly on the same lines.

In the tenth to twelfth lines the Guru returns to the myth of the 'Bull'. He says that if there indeed is such a bull then how much is the load it is carrying. There is not one but an endless succession of worlds. There is a world beyond the next, the universe is infinite as is the Lord who created it and who permeates it. If one world, ours, is sustained by a bull then is it also carrying all these other worlds? Which bull could be holding up all of these uncountable earths? Giani Sant Singh Maskin in his beautifully expressed audio commentary on the *Japji Sahib* says that even if such a bull were really to exist then the question would remain as to what is the support beneath the bull. Giani ji, however, renders the ninth line a little differently and says that if one were to understand and were to claim that he has acquired the knowledge of this mystery then – as in the next two lines – let him also explain this mystery. We will here note that the Guru is talking of a multiverse, an infinitely layered reality, a concept only recently becoming acceptable among scientifically-oriented men, and especially popular among writers of imaginative fiction. In the fifteenth and sixteenth century, when the debate was still centering on whether the sun or the earth was the centre of the system, here was a seer looking at the great reality. This, he said, is an infinite system. Ours is not the only universe, or this the only world where sapient beings exist. There is no bull that could sustain this mass. The sustenance and upholding of such a system is only *Dharma* – the underlying principle through which the Lord has ensured that things move as He intended.

We need to pause here to again take a look at this important concept of what is termed as *Dharma*. It is used to describe many concepts. It is commonly translated as religion and so we have the expression Hindu *Dharma*, *Īsāyi* (Christian) *Dharma* and so on. The term also denotes duty, something that is right and correct. In this sense we have the concepts of *Pativrata Dharma* – the correct code of conduct for the ideal wife; *Kshatriya Dharma* – the code prescribed in ancient times for the *Kshatriya* or warrior class. As we saw earlier the third concept is 'the innate nature of a thing' where we noted that the innate nature of fire is to burn and of water is to quench. The term is here not used in any of these limited contexts. The Guru here is talking of the *Dharma* of all creation – the underlying principle or the scheme of things prescribed through which the Lord Creator ensures – without ever having to intervene – that things move as He intended, as He ordained. Thus, the sun keeps pouring out life-giving energy which we mortals on this world use for sustenance; the worlds rotate and revolve and move through space and time as He ordained and never do they go randomly wandering; the stars keep burning and dying or going Nova or are born again as new stars; matter transforms into energy and matter is formed again.

Each of the intricate aspects of the functioning of this wondrous creation is pre-regulated, as is the vast massiveness of the created worlds. This *Dharma* is that bull holding up the world. And it is a manifestation of the Lord's compassion and love for His creation, in other words this bull (*dhaul*) is born of compassion (*daya*). Holding it all together is *santokh* (contentment) which is the thread that runs through all these various powers and keeps all things in their eternal order. Here, contentment is to be read as the quality of not wanting to change – of being happy with what is. Were even one of the components to go rogue and give up its *Dharma,* it would obviously throw into chaos this finely balanced and extremely complex structure.

In the thirteenth and fourteenth lines the Guru again refers to the vastness and complexity of the creation. He says that there are creations of various types and groups – of varying hues and natures. The Guru's reference is obviously to the rich variety of beings visible on this earth alone. Remember the Guru says there is an unending succession of worlds obviously each with its own set of creatures. We need but look at only this one world of ours to notice how vast and complex is the nature and the number of created beings. The Guru then tells us that for all of these unnumbered creatures their lot has been written down by the flowing pen of destiny.

Compare the thought with the couplet penned by the mystic Omar Khayyam in his 51st *Rubāyi* which Fitzgerald has translated as:

The Moving Finger writes; and, having writ,
Moves on: nor all your Piety nor wit
Shall lure it back to cancel half a line,
Nor all your Tears wash out a word of it.

The concept refers to the inevitability of our lot as prescribed by an overwhelming Immutable Power. The Guru says here that all the created beings have their lives governed by the Lord's inexorable will.

In the fifteenth and sixteenth lines the Guru clarifies for our benefit that the details of this great mystery none can hope to comprehend. If anyone were to seek to make an attempt to delineate such an account he will soon discover how impossibly beyond account are the details of this great and ineffable mystery. There is thus no one else, but the Lord Himself, who can aspire to write such an account. Prof. Talib, however, renders the concept slightly differently. He says:

"All the wise ones have attempted accompt of these at one stretch –

Yet who may render the true account of all these?"

The meaning here does not get really altered with this interpretation also. There is no doubt that it is only the Lord Himself, having brought into existence this vast creation who knows the details thereof.

In the next two lines, the seventeenth and eighteenth, the Guru says that the Lord's power is beyond reckoning. He poses the question how great is the *tāṇ* (might), and how resplendent His *rūp* (form); how immeasurably great are His gifts to His creation. He answers that there is none who could possibly make an estimate of these. *Kūt* 'ਕੂਤ' is a term describing an assessment made of the value of a crop while it is still standing in the field. This device is used between traders and farmers to settle payments. The Guru says that this *Kūt* is just impossible when it comes to measuring the Lord's greatness. Giani Sant Singh Maskin uses the word *Kūt* as *kuwwat* which in vernacular would normally be written and pronounced similarly. The word means power or capacity. So, Giani ji says: "Who has the power to make an account or to understand the greatness of the Lord?" The generally accepted sense of *kūt* is 'estimate', and that is the sense in which practically every other commentator uses it. As we may see, the sense of these lines does not much change in either rendering.

In the nineteenth and twentieth lines the Guru further elaborates on the previous two lines. The Lord whose power is beyond description and whose beauty is resplendent beyond measure, and who has given to His creation gifts that cannot be counted is also the Lord who with *eko kuāo* (one word) has brought this vast creation into existence. From that existence, that creation mandated by one word of the Lord, have emerged the hundreds of thousands of streams. Stream here refers to the types and varieties of beings that exist. His word brought it all into existence and then there emerged the vast variety of creatures.

Notice here the remarkable similarity to the creation process as is believed in practically all the systems of religions, all over the world. The ancient Greeks spoke of the *Logos*, the 'word made incarnate'. The Bible speaks similarly of the Lord uttering the one command: 'Let there be Light' and the creation coming into being instantaneously. Before that command was uttered: 'the earth was without form, and void …', as it says in *Genesis*, Chapter 1, (paras 2 and 3). The Hindu, and most Eastern faiths, similarly believe that the mystical 'word' is the mode through which the Lord created the universe. *Om*, or *Aum*, is the sound which according to the Hindu religion is the sound of creation. All the great seers have had the same experience of the reality. The Guru's message here also says that it is the 'one word' which caused the entire creation. The multiplicity of living things is also in accordance with the Lord's will and an ordained follow-up of the creation process. The mystical belief is that this divine word, called *Om* or *Onkār* in most Eastern religious resonates even today through all creation and will so continue to resonate for all eternity. It is the *anhad nād*, the divine sound. It is a practice in the Hindu meditation exercises to try and achieve resonance with this sound. It is really another way of saying that control of the mind and disciplining one's thoughts to be truly fixed on the Lord will bring salvation and oneness with the universe.

In the last four lines, the twenty-first to twenty-fourth, which are the refrain in this set of four *pauṛis*, the Guru expresses his helplessness when it comes to describing the Lord's grandeur. He says, "Where do I have the ability to compute and express the vast extent and the great mysteries of this Creation." He says he is not even fit to be a sacrifice even once to that Mighty One. These lines will recur in the next three *pauṛis.*

In olden times sacrifice to the gods was a popular and much prescribed method of worship. The greater the god, more the sacrifices to Him. The Guru of course deprecated all such ritualistic approaches. He therefore uses this metaphorically to make his audience understand the idea in terms they were familiar with. The idea is to highlight the huge disparity between the Lord and himself. In total humility he says that in comparison to the greatness of the One Lord his own person is utterly worthless – so much so that it is not even worth offering as a sacrifice even once. Repeating the message of surrender of the self, the Guru says in the twenty-second line that whatever pleases the Lord is right and befitting, because the Lord is Immutable, Ever-Perfect; He is the *Nirankār* (Formless One). These are the words of one who is in a true state of surrender and no longer has a wish for anything except what the Lord is pleased to render to His devotee.

22

SEEKING HIS BENEDICTION

Pauṛi 17

ਅਸੰਖ ਜਪ ਅਸੰਖ ਭਾਉ॥	*Asankh jap asankh bhāo.*
ਅਸੰਖ ਪੂਜਾ ਅਸੰਖ ਤਪ ਤਾਉ॥	*Asankh pūja asankh tapp tāo.*
ਅਸੰਖ ਗਰੰਥ ਮੁਖਿ ਵੇਦ ਪਾਠ॥	*Asankh granth mukh ved pātth*
ਅਸੰਖ ਜੋਗ ਮਨਿ ਰਹਹਿ ਉਦਾਸ॥	*Asankh jog mann rahay udās.*
ਅਸੰਖ ਭਗਤ ਗੁਣ ਗਿਆਨ ਵੀਚਾਰ॥	*Asankh bhagat guṇ gyān vīchār.*
ਅਸੰਖ ਸਤੀ ਅਸੰਖ ਦਾਤਾਰ॥	*Asankh sati asankh dātār.*
ਅਸੰਖ ਸੂਰ ਮੁਹ ਭਖ ਸਾਰ॥	*Asankh sūr muh bhakh sār.*
ਅਸੰਖ ਮੋਨਿ ਲਿਵ ਲਾਇ ਤਾਰ॥	*Asankh maun liv lāye tār.*
ਕੁਦਰਤਿ ਕਵਣ ਕਹਾ ਵੀਚਾਰੁ॥	*Kudrat kawaṇ kaha vīchār.*
ਵਾਰਿਆ ਨ ਜਾਵਾ ਏਕ ਵਾਰ॥	*Vāriya na jāva ek vār.*
ਜੋ ਤੁਧੁ ਭਾਵੈ ਸਾਈ ਭਲੀ ਕਾਰ॥	*Jo tudh bhāvai sāyi bhali kār.*
ਤੂ ਸਦਾ ਸਲਾਮਤਿ ਨਿਰੰਕਾਰ॥੧੭॥	*Tu sada salāmat nirankār.*

Brief glossary

ਅਸੰਖ	*Asankh*	Countless
ਭਾਉ	*Bhāo.*	Love
ਤਪ ਤਾਉ	*Tapp tāo.*	Meditation
ਗਰੰਥ	*Granth*	Holy books, scriptures
ਮੁਖਿ ਵੇਦ ਪਾਠ	*Mukh ved pātth*	Recite prayers from memory
ਗੁਣ ਗਿਆਨ ਵੀਚਾਰ	*Guṇ gyān vīchār.*	Think on the Lord's grandeur
ਰਹਹਿ ਉਦਾਸ	*Rahay udās*	Remain detached
ਸੂਰ	*Sūr*	Warriors
ਮੋਨਿ	*Maun*	Maintaining silence or quietude

ਭਖ ਸਾਰ	*Bhakh sār*	Eating iron (standing up to attacks)
ਲਿਵ ਲਾਇ ਤਾਰ	*Liv lāye tār*	Contemplation (fixing mind on the Lord)

Simply translated this *pauṛi* says that countless are the prayers being chanted to the Lord, uncountable those who live in devotion to Him. Countless are the scriptures, as also the learned ones reciting these. Countless are the *Yogis* living in detachment. Countless are the devotees reflecting on His virtues, countless righteous ones and as many great philanthropists. Countless the warriors fighting and willing to suffer injury for what is right. There are countless who maintain silence to focus their minds on the Lord. The Guru says he does not have the capacity to compute and express the vastness of this creation, and he is not fit to be a sacrifice even once to the Lord.

In this *pauṛi*, and the next two, the Guru describes the great variety of creatures that exist and the activity that ceaselessly goes on in the Lord's creation. Here in the first and second lines he says, countless are the prayers being chanted to the Lord; uncountable are those who live in devotion to the Lord. There is no one way in which the Lord is to be worshipped or to be shown devotion. In an infinite universe countless will be the creatures. Each will, in accordance with his own nature and his own capacity, worship Him in His own way. As long as it pleases the Lord and comes from the heart, none of the forms or systems of worship is in any way incorrect. Similarly, the expression of the love and awe for the creator can vary from place to place and from person to person. In whatever shape it emerges – as long as it has the Lord as its sole object – it is acceptable. Countless are thus the worshippers and the devotees and countless are the ways in which devotion is shown and worship is carried out.

In the third and fourth lines the Guru says that countless are the scriptures and countless the number of learned ones who are reciting the scriptures. Countless are the *yogis* living in detachment from the world. The Guru is in this *pauṛi* listing out all the good and deserving creatures in this universe. All the worshippers and those who love Him, all those sitting in meditation and contemplating Him have been listed in the first two lines. Those who recite the scriptures and the yogis undergoing the prescribed practices for achieving union with Him are in these two lines now listed. And the Guru tells us again that their numbers are countless. Lest anyone seek to assume any exclusivity or think he is special because he can recite the scriptures or has mastered the *yogic* practices or sits in deep meditation, the Guru reminds us that in this endless creation, there are countless ones who do the same. Lest we dream our form of worship or our holy scriptures unique or special, the Guru reminds us that not one but countless are the scriptures and countless the ways in which He is worshipped. All are equally acceptable to Him as long as the criterion of surrender and love is observed.

The term *jog* (ਜੋਗ) is the term popularly used for *Yoga,* which literally means 'union'. The *yogic* practices are designed to train the mind to achieve oneness with God. The term here is translated both to describe the yogi himself or the discipline he follows, the practices of *Yoga.* The term *udās* (ਉਦਾਸ) literally means disinterested or disenchanted. Here it is meant to denote detachment from this world so that the detached mind attaches itself instead to the Lord. It may be interesting to note that Guru Nanak's eldest son Baba Srichand founded a sect of ascetics known as *Udāsis.* It still exists today and its members live a life of total detachment from the world and practice severe self-discipline. *Yoga,* as it trains the mind towards union with the Lord, also brings with it a certain level of detachment from the world. The Guru says countless are such *yogis*, and such practices of *Yoga*, and countless are those ascetics who love with minds detached from this material world.

In the fifth and sixth lines the Guru refers to another group of those on the right path. These are the *Bhagats* – devotees who live only to reflect on His great virtues and divine knowledge.

The term *sati* (ਸਤੀ) in the sixth line has been differently translated. The SGPCs *Shabdarth* renders it as 'philanthropists' or 'those who give'. Prof. Sahib Singh in the *Sri Guru Granth Sahib Darpan*, p. 80, translates it as 'Lovers of Truth'. This is also the sense in which Narain Singh in his *Japji Sahib* takes it. Iqbal Singh in *Japji and other Sikh Scriptures* translated it as 'Righteous'. *Sat(i)* is the popular form of Sanskrit *satya* – true or real. Those who strictly observe and uphold truth would be the *Satis*. In the same line the Guru has referred to *dātār* (ਦਾਤਾਰ) which clearly means those who give, or donors.

Thus, *Sati* here could not be denoting givers, donors, or philanthropists. It should more appropriately be understood as being used in the sense of 'the righteous'. The Guru is saying that there are *asankh* (countless) who could be styled thus. There are also countless *dātār* (large-hearted givers, donors). They could be those who give of their wealth or of their knowledge or even higher, those who give of their hard earned spiritual merit.

In the seventh and eighth lines the Guru lists another category of those who are counted among the good. These are the *sūr* – those true warriors who bravely suffer sword blows on their faces but flinch not. Obviously, the Guru cannot be speaking here of those who are by nature aggressive and fight and struggle just for the sheer love of fighting and while doing so gladly suffer injury, however bravely they may do so. Those fighting the unjust battle cannot be worthy of honour. The *Gurbāṇi* tells us:

'Sūra so pehchānīyai jo larai dīn kay heit,
purja purja katt marai kabhon na chhādday kheit.'
(Bhagat Kabir, *Rāg Māru*, page 1105, *SGGS*)

Only he who fights to uphold the *Dharma* can be recognized as a true warrior. The brave ones who do not flinch from the blows of iron swords and are worthy of respect are the ones whose fight is just. Struggling for what is right, they cheerfully suffer personal injury but do not turn tail. Such are the ones the Guru is referring to here. And he says that there are countless such heroes.

There are at the same time countless those who have taken to silence and fixed their minds steadfastly on the One Lord. *Maun* (ਮੋਨਿ) is a Sanskrit term meaning silence. There is a class of devotees who approach their worship in this form. It is a belief among mystics that too much talking wastes precious psychic energy. Even popularly, it is recognized that the one who talks too much is foolish and is bound to make mistakes. 'Silence is golden' is in fact a popular saying. *Maun* or abstaining from talking is thus deemed a first step to retaining your energies and then redirecting them to spiritual pursuits. Followers of this path are countless, says the Guru. They maintain silence and learn to concentrate their minds constantly on the Lord. It may here be worthwhile to note that the path of *Maun* requiring detachment from active life and a quietist non-participative approach to this life is not an accepted path in Sikhism. In fact, the *Gurbāṇi* says, "*Jab lagg dunīya rahīyai Nanak kichh sunīyai kichh kahīyai,*" (*Rāg Dhanāsri Mahla* 1, p. 661, *SGGS*). This means that while we are alive on this earth we must speak and we must listen. However, since these ones keeping *maun* are doing so for seeking God, they have here been listed among the good persons.

In the last four lines the Guru again takes up the refrain that we had discussed in the previous *pauṛi*. He says that the Lord, the Immaculate and the Formless One, is so far beyond man's limited ken that we are not worthy of even offering ourselves as a sacrifice to Him even once.

The Guru has listed here from among His creatures the ones that follow the path of righteousness and while differing in many ways, one from the other, in their approach to the Lord and thus often following totally different paths, are all equally His creatures. And, says the Guru, their numbers are legion. Countless are they. We may note that the word *maun* used here is also interpreted by Bhai Vir Singh in his commentary as *Muni.* In this sense the translation would be, 'countless are the *munis* – the devotees who have achieved great knowledge of the Divine'. One would hesitate to differ with a mystic poet of Bhai Sahib's eminence but considering that almost uniformly the other commentators have used *maun* as meaning silence that is the sense in which the above interpretation has been attempted.

23

EVEN THEN HIS CHILDREN

Pauṛi 18

ਅਸੰਖ ਮੂਰਖ ਅੰਧ ਘੋਰ॥	*Asankh mūrakh andh ghor.*
ਅਸੰਖ ਚੋਰ ਹਰਾਮਖੋਰ॥	*Asankh chor harāmkhor.*
ਅਸੰਖ ਅਮਰ ਕਰਿ ਜਾਹਿ ਜੋਰ॥	*Asankh amar kar jāhe jor.*
ਅਸੰਖ ਗਲਵਢ ਹਤਿਆ ਕਮਾਹਿ॥	*Asankh galwaddh hatiya kamāhe.*
ਅਸੰਖ ਪਾਪੀ ਪਾਪੁ ਕਰ ਜਾਹਿ॥	*Asankh pāpi pāp kar jāhe.*
ਅਸੰਖ ਕੂੜਿਆਰ ਕੂੜੇ ਫਿਰਾਹਿ॥	*Asankh kūṛiyār kūṛay phirāhe.*
ਅਸੰਖ ਮਲੇਛ ਮਲੁ ਭਖਿ ਖਾਹਿ॥	*Asankh malechh mal bhakh khāhe.*
ਅਸੰਖ ਨਿੰਦਕ ਸਿਰਿ ਕਰਹਿ ਭਾਰੁ॥	*Asankh nindak sir karay bhār.*
ਨਾਨਕੁ ਨੀਚੁ ਕਹੈ ਵੀਚਾਰੁ॥	*Nanak nīch kahai vīchār.*
ਵਾਰਿਆ ਨ ਜਾਵਾ ਏਕ ਵਾਰ॥	*Vāriya na jāva ek vār.*
ਜੋ ਤੁਧੁ ਭਾਵੈ ਸਾਈ ਭਲੀ ਕਾਰ॥	*Jo tudh bhāvai sāyi bhali kār.*
ਤੂ ਸਦਾ ਸਲਾਮਤਿ ਨਿਰੰਕਾਰ॥ ੧੮॥	*Tu sada salāmat nirankār.*

Brief glossary

ਮੂਰਖ ਅੰਧ ਘੋਰ	*Mūrakh andh ghor*	Extreme idiots
ਹਰਾਮਖੋਰ	*Harāmkhor*	Those who live on unearned wealth
ਅਮਰ	*Amar*	Rule sovereignty (here despots and tyrants)
ਕਰਿ ਜਾਹਿ ਜੋਰ	*Kar jāhe jor*	Use brute force
ਗਲਵਢ	*Galwaddh*	Cut throat, murderer
ਕੂੜਿਆਰ	*Kūṛiyār*	Purveyors of falsehood
ਕੂੜੇ ਫਿਰਾਹਿ	*Kūṛay phirāhe*	Live in falsehood

ਮਲੇਛ	*Malechh*	Impious, living in filth, here low-minded
ਮਲੁ ਭਖਿ ਖਾਹਿ	*Mal bhakh khāhe*	Gorge on filth
ਨੀਚੁ	*Nīch*	Lowly ones

Simply translated this *pauṛi* says that countless are the highly ignorant fools. Countless are the thieves and the ingrates. There are countless ruling through brute force and countless are the cut-throats. The count of sinners is endless too. Countless are there who blindly accumulate worldly goods, and are caught in false illusions and falsehood. Countless are the lowly who subsist on filth, and countless those who incur the load of denigrating others. In the last four lines the Guru says he does not have the capacity to compute and express the vastness of this creation; and he is not fit for sacrifice even once to the Lord. We can now look at the *pauṛi* in more detail and also see what some learned ones have said.

In the previous *pauṛi* the Guru had spoken of all those who were high-minded, pious, engaged in meditation or engaged otherwise in activities that are spiritually elevated and therefore in accordance with what the Guru has prescribed; and thus pleasing to the Lord and in accordance with the Lord's way. Here, in this *pauṛi*, the Guru now lists out those who are engaged in activities less desirable and following paths far from what could take them towards the Lord.

The SGPC's *Shabdarth* says about this *pauṛi* that it has to be read together with the previous because the Guru is saying that where there are so many *Granths* (scriptures) being read and worship and *yogic* practices going on, there should have been only enlightenment all round; yet there are countless who are ignorant. Where there are so many with detached and disciplined minds, so many who give without hesitation then the atmosphere should be free from avarice, yet in reality we see the sad truth that there are so many who covet and love to live on unearned or ill-gotten wealth. Where there are so many brave ones ready to fight for just causes there should be no high-handedness, yet so many despots rule with tyranny. Similarly, the other points made in *pauṛi* 17 are according to the *Shabdarth* given counter-point in this *pauṛi*. This is because men have forgotten now to live in accordance with the Lord's will, but are rather mistakenly choosing some limited practices and rituals, the *Shabdarth* says.

Giani Sant Singh Maskin in his audio commentary says that the Guru has used these two *pauṛis* to describe the two streams that co-exist in this world, the stream of goodness and the stream of evil, because he wants to highlight for us that in both these categories all those who exist are the Lord's creatures regardless. This is certainly the more appealing interpretation. The aim of the Guru obviously was to stop us from hating anyone even if they are indulging in evil. The Guru has driven home this point in the last four lines. Whereas in the other three *pauṛis* the opening line of the four-line refrain is *kudrat kavaṇ kaha vīchār,* in this *pauṛi* very deliberately and for a significant purpose he substitutes, *Nanak nīch kahai vīchār*. The Guru has in a remarkable exhibition of humility listed himself also as a *nīch* (lowly one). The Guru is telling us not to start feeling superior or wanting to shun the ones listed in this *pauṛi*, because however misguided they be they are the Lord's creatures too, part of the mysterious divine purpose.

The Guru says in the first and second lines that the number of those who are *mūrakh* (witless) and live in the greatest depths of ignorance is countless. The thieves and the ingrates are countless too. There are innumerable fools of utter purblindness. As many are those, says the Guru, who live in thievery and indulge in acquiring wealth through unrighteous ways. Bhai Vir Singh in his commentary, p. 25, says that a *mūrakh* (ਮੂਰਖ), a fool, is one who could be taught to improve. The term 'ਮੂਰਖ ਅੰਧ ਘੋਰ' - *mūrakh andh ghor* - describes the fool so deeply sunk in ignorance that he is beyond redemption. This is the category of fool who is blind to all reason, yet so sure of himself that he becomes worse the more you reason with him. The thief (*chor*) is the one, obviously, who steals or pilfers what belongs to others. The 'ਹਰਾਮਖੋਰ' - *harāmkhor* - is the one who lives on what is not legitimately his. Whatever we consume must be what we have earned through our own efforts or what rightfully belongs to us. Consuming anything else is being a *harāmkhor*. The term *harām* is given much importance in any system of morally correct ethical values. Every religion incorporates this concept. In Islam it has high importance and is a determinant of whether the Muslim will achieve *Jannat* (Paradise) or *Jahannum* (Hell). The Guru has also listed this category prominently among the wrongdoers.

In the third and fourth lines the Guru speaks of those who rule over others through use of brute force, the despots and the tyrants. Innumerable is their number. As countless are *galwaddh* (the cut-throats), who have made killing their profession their way of life. The rulers in this world who function through sheer might are visible to all of us even today. We all see the principle of 'might is right' operating rampant. Respect for others' rights, others' feelings, others' property is all too often given the go by. Countless, says the Guru, are such purvayors of the power of terror and those who shamelessly take and without qualms consume what is not theirs.

In the fifth and sixth lines the Guru says innumerable are the *pāpi* (the sinners) who all their lives commit nothing but sins. Goodness is just not there in their nature or sometimes it is so suppressed by the evil in them that it never has a chance to control their actions. There are countless *kūṛiyār* (those deeply caught up in falsehood) living helplessly in an everlasting circle of falsehood. 'ਕੂੜ' - *kūṛ* - is a term used by the Guru more than once for falsehood, for illusion, for the veil that separates man from his Creator. The purpose of following the practices of Sikhism – as of any other true religion – is to somehow break through this veil. The term also connotes the dross we accumulate as we blindly go after pelf and power, after worldly possessions forgetting our true path. There are countless followers of this superficially attractive path trapped in this vicious circle.

In the seventh and eighth lines the Guru talks of another group of the unfortunate ones. He says countless are the 'ਮਲੇਛ' – *malechh* - the impure ones, who sustain themselves on filth. Countless also are the *nindak* (the denigrators) who accumulate the load of speaking ill of others. *Malechh*, in the Hindu caste system, was meant to describe a non-Hindu, i.e., someone outside the pale and not belonging to any of the *Varṇas* (castes). Among the four castes there arose an informal hierarchy with the Brahmin, the Kshatriya, the Vaishya and the Shudra being deemed to have importance in the descending order as above. The original connotation may only have been meant to describe each group according to the tasks it performed, each vital in its own way – the Brahmin as the teacher and philosopher, the Kshatriya as the warrior, the Vaishya as the tradesman and the middle class, and the Shudra as the performer of physical tasks. Over time the Shudra came unfortunately to be shunned as the lowest. The other castes would not consort with the Shudra, something that eventually sapped the Hindu civil society. Remnants of this pernicious practice continue to plague the modern Hindu, laws to the contrary notwithstanding. The *Malechh* in this hierarchy was deemed even lower than the Shudra. It came to acquire a highly pejorative connotation and was gradually used for the basest of the base, the totally uncivilized. It is in this context the Guru uses it here. It should be noted here that the Guru did not even remotely sanction the hierarchies of the *Varṇa* system which in his times also were ruling Hindu society. In fact his message is quite to the contrary, as unequivocally enunciated in the *Gurbāṇi*. For the Guru all humans are equal and only the righteousness of their actions and the purity of their minds establishes their rank in the ayes of the Lord. Since the Guru was addressing a particular audience in the context of a particular milieu the then prevailing terms have been used in the commonly understood way.

The Guru further says in the eighth line that countless are those who indulge in slander, who denigrate others. Doing 'ਨਿੰਦਿਆ' – *nindiya* - speaking ill of others or slandering them is another ill-deed the Guru will be found deprecating throughout his discourse, and so he lists it also in this *pauṛi*. As can repeatedly be seen in the *SGGS* the Guru held in lowest esteem those who slandered others. The prescription against this occurs more than once in the *Gurbāṇi* as a quick reference to the *Mahan Kosh* of Bhai Sahib Kahan Singh will readily show. The Guru says here that such slanderers are acquiring a load of calumny which will burden them in the hereafter.

Finally, in the next line, the ninth, the Guru having described these various malefactors, sinners and wrong-doers then owns them up and in awesome humility lists himself along with them in the same category. He says that the lowly Nanak, having contemplated, says that the Lord is Eternal, Immaculate, the Formless One and that Nanak is unworthy of being offered even once as a sacrifice to Him. Thus, we will notice that while the last three lines of the four-line refrain are retained intact, only the first line, wherein the other three *pauṛis,* the sixteenth, seventeenth and nineteenth, the line *kudrat kavaṇ kaha vīchār* occurs, here it has become '*Nanak nīch kahai vīchār'*. It will be noted that in any major religious belief system it is the usual style of the Prophet, or the great seer, to give his followers his message from a position of authority, the message almost always comes couched as an edict as from a higher to the lowly and the ignorant. The Guru's approach is unique here. Having repeatedly told us that the ego is our enemy and that we need to control it the Guru here shows how completely he himself has achieved this control. He says if there are countless despicable ones then he is willing to be considered a part of them also. All creatures, whether they have great qualities of good or are evil-doers are all equally the Lord's creation, and whatever pleases the Lord, whatever He wills is good. The Guru has no hesitation in being listed among the bad ones also. He has also in parting told us that not to feel superior or smug after reading this list of evil-doers. Do not assume that you are above such reprobates. Accept them also as equally serving the Lord's purpose.

The last three lines, the tenth to twelfth, are the same as in the previous *pauṛi* where we have discussed them. The Guru is saying that so vastly beyond our worth is the Lord that we are not worth even being offered as sacrifice to Him even once.

24

WORDS CANNOT DESCRIBE HIM

Pauṛi 19

ਅਸੰਖ ਨਾਵ ਅਸੰਖ ਥਾਵ॥	*Asankh nāv asankh thhāv.*
ਅਗੰਮ ਅਗੰਮ ਅਸੰਖ ਲੋਅ॥	*Agam agam asankh low.*
ਅਸੰਖ ਕਹਹਿ ਸਿਰਿ ਭਾਰੁ ਹੋਇ॥	*Asankh kahay sirr bhār hoye.*
ਅਖਰੀ ਨਾਮੁ ਅਖਰੀ ਸਾਲਾਹ॥	*Akhari nām akhri sālāh.*
ਅਖਰੀ ਗਿਆਨੁ ਗੀਤ ਗੁਣ ਗਾਹ॥	*Akhari gyān geet guṇ gāh. (5)*
ਅਖਰੀ ਲਿਖਣੁ ਬੋਲਣੁ ਬਾਣਿ॥	*Akhari likhaṇ bolaṇ bāṇ.*
ਅਖਰਾ ਸਿਰਿ ਸੰਜੋਗੁ ਵਖਾਣਿ॥	*Akhra sirr sanjog vakhāṇ.*
ਜਿਨਿ ਏਹਿ ਲਿਖੇ ਤਿਸੁ ਸਿਰਿ ਨਾਹਿ॥	*Jin eh likhay tis sir(i) nāh(i).*
ਜਿਵ ਫੁਰਮਾਏ ਤਿਵ ਤਿਵ ਪਾਹਿ॥	*Jiv phurmāye tiv tiv pāh(i).*
ਜੇਤਾ ਕੀਤਾ ਤੇਤਾ ਨਾਉ॥	*Jeta kīta teta nāo. (10)*
ਵਿਣੁ ਨਾਵੈ ਨਾਹੀ ਕੋ ਥਾਉ॥	*Viṇ nāvai nāhi ko thhāo.*
ਕੁਦਰਤਿ ਕਵਣ ਕਹਾ ਵੀਚਾਰੁ॥	*Kudrat kavaṇ kaha vīchār.*
ਵਾਰਿਆ ਨ ਜਾਵਾ ਏਕ ਵਾਰ॥	*Vāriya na jāva ek vār.*
ਜੋ ਤੁਧੁ ਭਾਵੈ ਸਾਈ ਭਲੀ ਕਾਰ॥	*Jo tudhh bhāvai sāyi bhali kār.*
ਤੂ ਸਦਾ ਸਲਾਮਤਿ ਨਿਰੰਕਾਰ॥੧੯॥	*Tu sada salāmat nirankār.*

Brief glossary

ਨਾਵ	*Nāv*	Names
ਥਾਵ	*Thhāv*	Places
ਅਗੰਮ	*Agam*	Beyond reach, inaccessible
ਲੋਅ	*Low*	Worlds, regions, realms
ਅਸੰਖ ਕਹਹਿ	*Asankh kahay*	If you say countless
ਸਾਲਾਹ	*Sālāh*	Praise

ਸੰਜੋਗੁ ਵਖਾਣਿ	*Sanjog vakhāṇ*	Describe the fates (*sanjog* – destiny)
ਏਹਿ ਲਿਖੇ	*Eh likhay*	The One who wrote them
ਤਿਸੁ ਸਿਰਿ ਨਾਹਿ	*Tis sirr nāhin*	Not on his head, He is not ruled by these
ਫੁਰਮਾਏ	*Phurmāye*	Ordains, decrees
ਜੇਤਾ	*Jeta*	As much
ਤੇਤਾ	*Teta*	That much

Simply translated, this *pauṛi* says countless are His names and countless the spaces created by Him. Countless are the worlds, one beyond the other. Using words to describe them as countless is also wrong and saying so casts a burden on us. Yet are words necessary to recite His name and sing His praises. Knowledge about Him also comes through words and we need them to laud Him. The scriptures also need words to be written, and words are necessary to prescribe the fate of all. Yet, He who writes these fateful words is not Himself subject to fate. We all get what He ordains. All that is created is His manifestation, there being nothing existing beyond Him. No place exists where His Name is not present. In the last lines the Guru says he does not have the capacity to compute and express the vastness of this creation, and he is not fit even to be a sacrifice even once to the Lord. We can now see the message at more length and also see what learned commentators have said on this *pauṛi*.

Having in the previous two *pauṛis* described the entire extent and categories of creatures both the holy, the good as well as the evil, the sinner, the Guru now speaks of the vast creation in the midst of which these good or evil creatures exist.

He says in the first line that countless are the names and countless the spaces created by Him. Almost all commentators have rendered the first line as: "Countless are the names of His Creations and countless their places." The translation by Prof. Sahib Singh renders it as referring to creations, while Prof. Talib and Narain Singh say this refers to the names of God. What the Guru is saying is that there is a multiplicity of names such that these are countless. Since in all religions the names by which God is known are indeed many, this line could be taken that way. However, in no religion are such names deemed to be infinite. On the other hand, in Sikhism infinity of worlds is a concept the Guru has already given us. Apparently, here the reference is to the types of beings or creatures. So, the first line should more appropriately be taken to mean that countless are the creations each with its own name, and countless are the places created – the realms into which creation has been divided.

In the second and third lines, the Guru says innumerable are the worlds, one beyond the other, so much beyond mankind's ken are these that in describing them as *asankh* (countless) is incorrect because that implies that we are trying to number them. Another interpretation, as given by Bhai Vir Singh, is that there are countless those who claim to be able to describe Him, but in so claiming they are acquiring a great burden of sin because there is no description really possible. Alternatively, as Narain Singh puts it, even if a thing is countless it could have some limits. By labelling it even as *asankh*, the concept runs the danger of being incompletely understood. To put a label, even of *asankh*, on this creation would thus be an inaccuracy which would incur a great burden of sin. In short, the variety and extent of His creation is beyond any description because it is incomprehensibly beyond human understanding. For anyone to even claim to use words to describe this wondrous creation is to claim an ability to comprehend the incomprehensible. The only correct thought is to admit that we do not know even the outlines of this great mystery.

In the third to sixth lines, the Guru takes us further into this concept. Having said that it is hopeless to use words or figures to attempt a description the Guru here says that not always are words pointless or useless. For it is through words only that we mortal men, limited as we are to using language and words to express our thoughts and our feelings, can recite His name and sing His praises. Thus, while unable to explain the great mystery, the words we know are the only vehicle we have to try and reach the Lord. The Sikh faith is called *Nām Mārag*, the way of the name. Reciting His name while keeping the mind under control is a major prescription for the Sikh. How else could we do that except through words? So the Guru says we can take His name through words only, and only then can we sing His praises.

We have to carefully understand that when attempting to express the Creator in human terms, if a man were to assume that he has really comprehended even a tiny fraction of the Divine mystery then does the element of *haumai* enter into it. On the other hand, when pondering in awe about these wonders one attempts paeans of praise and expresses his joy, his awe and also his mystification, his ignorance in humble surrender the element of *haumai* does not cast its shadow and no element of sin attaches to the use of words about the Lord for this purpose. It is in this context that the Guru now goes on to say that only through words is the name of God recited, only through words are praises sung. Through words can the knowledge about God be acquired or His greatness discussed; only words can be used in singing psalms to His splendour, about His attributes. The writing of the scriptures – the 'ਬਾਣੀ' - *bāṇi* – is also possible only through words and so will their recital need language, words.

The Lord has also through words only prescribed for each person his lot and inscribed it on his forehead. It is the Sikh, and most Eastern religious, belief system that one's forehead carries inscribed on it the fate that is for each individual prescribed. It is this sign, invisible to the human eye but clear to acvieved souls and the more divine creatures of the Lord, that determines the place and status the soul will command beyond this world. This is the rendering which Iqbal Singh has used quoting Tarlochan Singh, Bhai Jodh Singh and others. Prof. Sahib Singh, Prof. Talib and the *Shabdarth* translate *Akhra sirr sanjog vakhāṇ* as meaning that through use of words is the relationship of man and God described. *Sanjog* is indisputably rendered as destiny. *Akhra sirr* is used to mean 'through words'. In other words, *sirr* is not here used as denoting 'forehead'. It is rather combined with *Akhra* and read together the phrase would mean 'through use of words'. This seems the more appropriate interpretation. The seventh line then would mean: 'through use of words only is man's destiny – his relationship with God – described'.

The Guru says in the eighth and ninth lines that the Lord who has prescribed this destiny for man is Himself not subject to it. There is no such writing on His forehead. In other words, the Lord is the Bestower of destiny, and is obviously not subject to it. He Himself is the master of all and there is none who, for the Lord can determine His fate. Nor is it within human ken to determine our own fate. The Divine Order is ordained for us by the Lord but He Himself is not bound by it; but as He ordains so shall we obtain.

In the tenth and eleventh lines the Guru says that all that is created is His manifestation – all creation is He Himself manifest. Thus, nothing exists which is beyond Him. The Lord is Immanent in His creation. In this sense, the Guru says whatever exists is His name, and there is not a place which is not His name.

In the last four lines of the refrain, the Guru again says that it is beyond human capacity to contemplate and express His nature. He says he is unworthy even once to be made a sacrifice to Him. Thus, from such a lowly and humble position how could he possibly speak or comment on this great mystery. He says whatever the Lord wills is good, because the Formless One is Immaculate and Eternal. The message of complete surrender is thus once again repeated.

25

HIS NAME CLEANSES ALL

Pauṛi 20

ਭਰੀਐ ਹਥੁ ਪੈਰੁ ਤਨੁ ਦੇਹ॥	*Bharīyai hathh paer tann deh.*
ਪਾਣੀ ਧੋਤੈ ਉਤਰਸੁ ਖੇਹ॥	*Pāṇi dhhotai utrus kheh.*
ਮੂਤ ਪਲੀਤੀ ਕਪੜੁ ਹੋਇ॥	*Mūt palīti kapaṛ hoye.*
ਦੇ ਸਾਬੂਣੁ ਲਈਐ ਓਹੁ ਧੋਇ॥	*De sabūṇ laīyai oh dhoye.*
ਭਰੀਐ ਮਤਿ ਪਾਪਾ ਕੈ ਸੰਗਿ॥	*Bharīyai mat(i) pāpa kai sung.*
ਓਹੁ ਧੋਪੈ ਨਾਵੈ ਕੈ ਰੰਗਿ॥	*Oh dhopai nāvai kai rung.*
ਪੁੰਨੀ ਪਾਪੀ ਆਖਣੁ ਨਾਹਿ॥	*Punni pāpi ākhaṇ nāhe.*
ਕਰਿ ਕਰਿ ਕਰਣਾ ਲਿਖਿ ਲੈ ਜਾਹੁ॥	*Kar kar karṇa likh lai jāh(u).*
ਆਪੇ ਬੀਜਿ ਆਪੇ ਹੀ ਖਾਹੁ॥	*Āpay bīj āpay hi khāh(u).*
ਨਾਨਕ ਹੁਕਮੀ ਆਵਹੁ ਜਾਹੁ॥੨੦॥	*Nanak hukmi āwo jāh(u).*

Brief glossary

ਭਰੀਐ	*Bharīyai*	If we fill
ਧੋਤੈ	*Dhhotai*	By washing
ਪਲੀਤੀ	*Palīti*	Smeared with filth
ਮਤਿ	*Mat(i)*	The mind, the intellect
ਨਾਵੈ ਕੈ ਰੰਗਿ	*Nāvai kai rung*	By the love of His name
ਪੁੰਨੀ ਪਾਪੀ	*Punni pāpi*	Pious deeds and evil
ਆਖਣੁ ਨਾਹਿ	*Ākhan nāhe*	Are not mere words
ਕਰਿ ਕਰਿ ਕਰਣਾ	*Kar kar karṇa*	Doing deeds, action
ਲਿਖਿ	*Likh*	Will be written
ਲੈ ਜਾਹੁ	*Lai jah(u)*	Will take along
ਆਵਹੁ ਜਾਹੁ	*Āwo jah(u)*	Will undergo reincarnation

Simply translated this *pauṛi* means if we soil our hands and bodies, water can wash it off. If our clothes are begrimed soap will suffice. If our minds get soiled [by our bad actions and sins] the only cleansing agent is *Nām*, the devoted recitation of His name. The terms *punn* (good deeds) and *pāp* (sins) are not empty phrases, our actions will have inevitable consequences for our souls. We will have to ourselves reap the fruit, good or bad, of our actions. We can now look at the message in more detail and also see what commentators have to tell us.

In this *paur.i* the Guru has further expounded on the message put forth in the first and second *paur.is*. We saw in the first *paur.i* the Guru said, "*Hukam rajāyi chaln.a Nanak likhiya nāl*". In the second *paur.i* he added, "*Hukmi uttam nīch hukam(i) likh dukh sukh pāiay*". The entire universe is functioning according to the Order imposed by the will of the Lord. This, the Guru has called *Hukam*. Part of this Order is that the actions which we perform will inevitably get their fruit accordingly. The Guru in the previous few *paur.is* has concentrated on the oneness of all creation. The Lord is Immanent and thus each human carries within himself the divine spark, the potential for regaining oneness with the Lord. This, however, does not mean that all men are always at the same stage of spiritual development. It also does not mean that because we carry the divine spark we are exempt from our spiritual duty to uplift ourselves. Each man, notwithstanding that divine spark, differs from the other in the level of his spiritual development. Over the many re-births along the chain of created beings man has in each case, depending on his own actions, acquired higher or lower merit. Actions leave their inevitable mark on the soul; bad actions slide us down the ladder and good actions uplift the soul on the path towards the Lord. The actions of the man are the determinants of his fate in this sense. As the *Gurbān.i* says on page 470, *SGGS*:

'Manda changa āpṇa āpay hi kīta pāvṇa'

(*Asa di Vār*, *Mahla* 1)

Again:
'Daday dos na deu kise dos karamma āpṇaya
Jo mai kiya so mai paiya dos n dījay avar jana.'
(*Asa di Vār*, *Mahla* 1, page 433, *SGGS*)

This broadly translates as: "The good and the bad of our actions will on our own heads be visited." And again, "Lay not the blame at another's door; the fault lies in our own actions. Whatever I did, so was I rewarded." This theme runs continuously throughout *SGGS*. Hence is Sikhism not a religion for the quietist; nay it requires of us constant action with scrupulous attention to the propriety of what we do. The Guru now says here that if the soul gets besmeared with the filth of bad actions; cleanse it with the *Nām*, the Lord's name. To drive home this lesson the Guru gives in the first and second lines the analogy from everyday life. He says that were our hands and our bodies to get soiled with dirt it is easy to wash them clean with water.

Carrying the analogy further in the third and fourth lines he says if our apparel gets soiled, if our clothes become grimy and filthy we can still accomplish the cleansing by additionally using some soap.

In the fifth and sixth lines the Guru comes to the point of the lesson he intends to impart in this *paur.i*. Having given the analogy of cleaning our bodies or our clothes he now raises the issue of how to cleanse our real selves of the filth we, our *mat(i)* our intellect, our mind, may have accumulated. He says the cleansing agent here is the *Nām*, the loving recitation of His name.

In the seventh and eighth lines the Guru warns us not to think of *Punni* and *Pāpi* (good or evil deeds) merely as words. It is for certain that whatever actions we perform will indelibly be written on our souls and the consequences thereof we will carry with us into the future, into new incarnations. Your good deeds, your piety, your living in accordance with the Lord's way, as spelt out by the Guru, will assuredly earn you merit. Equally, you will accumulate the onerous load of your evil deeds. The pain and suffering that you inflict on others, the unjust acquisition of wealth and amassing of meaningless mounds of material goods, your snatching what is not rightfully yours will add up an inevitable burden of sin.

In the last two lines, the ninth and tenth, the Guru says we will ourselves reap the crop of the seeds we strew. Bound by the record of our good or evil we will face the scrutiny of the Lord's justice and will remain accordingly in the circle of rebirths commensurate with what we may have accumulated. The stress here is strongly on our actions being the determinants of our destiny.

We see here how much importance the Guru lays on our actions. How we conduct ourselves in the world of men is shown to carry consequences into the after-life, and it will determine our place and our fate in the play of transmigration of souls that the Lord has decreed. We saw this theme touched upon earlier also, in *paur̤i* 4, line 6, the penultimate line, *Karmi āvai kapr̤a nadri mokh duār.*

It is through our actions that we will earn the right to the material body, the apparel which this soul wears on this earth from birth to birth.

Inherent throughout this *paur̤i* no. 20 is the thought mentioned in the second half of the above line. While our actions are vitally important, we must remember that at any time at all, when the Lord so chooses He may grant us His transcendent grace and pluck us, whether we are worthy or not, out of this circle of rebirths and take us, our souls, into eternity with Him. While always praying for such a boon it is, in the meanwhile, vital that our conduct remains in tune with God's will. It has to be our effort that through exemplary conduct governed by love for the Lord's creation and through surrender to His will we acquire enough merit so as to earn higher and better stations in our rebirth. If we do that we should set in motion a virtuous circle where we acquire better and higher place in each successive birth, which will then give us the opportunity and the motivation to follow even more strictly the rightful path, further speeding up the acquisition of more spiritual merit, a truly benign cycle will thus get established.

26

THE HIDDEN TĪRATH WITHIN

Pauṛi 21

ਤੀਰਥੁ ਤਪੁ ਦਇਆ ਦਤੁ ਦਾਨੁ॥	*Tīrath tap(u) daya dat(u) dān.*
ਜੇ ਕੋ ਪਾਵੈ ਤਿਲ ਕਾ ਮਾਨੁ॥	*Je ko pāvai til ka mān.*
ਸੁਣਿਆ ਮੰਨਿਆ ਮਨਿ ਕੀਤਾ ਭਾਉ॥	*Suṇiya maniya man(i) kīta bhāo.*
ਅੰਤਰਗਤਿ ਤੀਰਥਿ ਮਲਿ ਨਾਉ॥	*Antargat tīrath mul(i) nāo.*
ਸਭਿ ਗੁਣ ਤੇਰੇ ਮੈ ਨਾਹੀ ਕੋਇ॥	*Sabh guṇ teray mai nāhi koye.*
ਵਿਣੁ ਗੁਣ ਕੀਤੇ ਭਗਤਿ ਨ ਹੋਇ॥	*Viṇ guṇ kītay bhagat(i) na hoye.*
ਸੁਅਸਤਿ ਆਥਿ ਬਾਣੀ ਬਰਮਾਉ॥	*Suast āth bāṇi barmāo.*
ਸਤਿ ਸੁਹਾਣੁ ਸਦਾ ਮਨਿ ਚਾਉ॥	*Sat(i) suhāṇ sada mann chāo.*
ਕਵਣੁ ਸੁ ਵੇਲਾ ਵਖਤੁ ਕਵਣੁ ਕਵਣ ਥਿਤਿ ਕਵਣੁ ਵਾਰੁ॥	*Kavaṇ so vela vakhat kavaṇ, kavaṇ thit(i) kavaṇ vār.*
ਕਵਣਿ ਸਿ ਰੁਤੀ ਮਾਹੁ ਕਵਣੁ ਜਿਤੁ ਹੋਆ ਆਕਾਰੁ॥	*Kavaṇ se ruti mah kavaṇ jit hova ākār.*
ਵੇਲ ਨ ਪਾਈਆ ਪੰਡਤੀ ਜਿ ਹੋਵੈ ਲੇਖੁ ਪੁਰਾਣੁ॥	*Vel na pāyīa pandti je hovai lekh purāṇ.*
ਵਖਤੁ ਨ ਪਾਇਓ ਕਾਦੀਆ ਜਿ ਲਿਖਨਿ ਲੇਖੁ ਕੁਰਾਣੁ॥	*Vakht na pāyio kādīya je likhan lekh Korāṇ.*
ਥਿਤਿ ਵਾਰੁ ਨਾ ਜੋਗੀ ਜਾਣੈ ਰੁਤਿ ਮਾਹੁ ਨਾ ਕੋਈ॥	*Thit(i) vār na jogi jāṇai rut(i) māh na koyi.*
ਜਾ ਕਰਤਾ ਸਿਰਠੀ ਕਉ ਸਾਜੇ ਆਪੇ ਜਾਣੈ ਸੋਈ॥	*Ja karta sirtthi kau sājay āpay jāṇai soyi.*
ਕਿਵ ਕਰਿ ਆਖਾ ਕਿਵ ਸਾਲਾਹੀ ਕਿਉ ਵਰਨੀ ਕਿਵ ਜਾਣਾ॥	*Kiv kar ākha kiv sālāhi kiv vārni kiv jāṇā.*
ਨਾਨਕ ਆਖਣਿ ਸਭੁ ਕੋ ਆਖੈ ਇਕ ਦੂ	*Nanak ākhaṇ sabh ko ākhai ik du*

ਇਕੁ ਸਿਆਣਾ॥	*ik syāṇa.*
ਵਡਾ ਸਾਹਿਬੁ ਵਡੀ ਨਾਈ ਕੀਤਾ ਜਾ ਕਾ ਹੋਵੈ॥	*Vadda sahib vaddi nāyi kīta jāka hovai.*
ਨਾਨਕ ਜੇ ਕੋ ਆਪੌ ਜਾਣੈ ਅਗੈ ਗਇਆ ਨ ਸੋਹੈ॥੨੧॥	*Nanak je ko āpau jāṇai aggai gaya na sohai.*

Brief glossary

ਤਪੁ	*Tap(u)*	Austerities, penance
ਤਿਲ ਕਾ ਮਾਨੁ	*Til ka mān*	Honour equal to a sesame seed
ਦਤੁ	*Dat(u)*	Given, donated
ਦਾਨੁ	*Dān*	Donations, alms
ਮਨਿ ਕੀਤਾ ਭਾਉ	*Mann kīta bhāo.*	Has acquired love
ਅੰਤਰਗਤਿ	*Antargat*	Internally, inwards
ਮਲਿ	*Mul(i)*	Wash thoroughly
ਵਿਣ ਗੁਣ ਕੀਤੇ	*Vin guṇ kītay*	If you do not give me the virtue
ਸੁਅਸਤਿ	*Suast*	Salutation, literally 'may all be well with you.'
ਆਥਿ	*Āth*	Worldly riches
ਬਰਮਾਉ	*Barmāo*	Lord Brahma
ਸਤਿ ਸੁਹਾਣ	*Sat(i) suhāṇ*	The Eternal is beautiful
ਵੇਲਾ	*Vela*	Time
ਵਾਰੁ	*Vār*	Day of the week
ਹੋਆ	*Hova*	Was created
ਆਕਾਰੁ	*Ākār*	Creation
ਜਿ ਹੋਵੈ ਲੇਖੁ ਪੁਰਾਣੁ	*Je hovai lekh purāṇ*	It would be recorded in the *Purāṇs*
ਸਿਰਠੀ	*Sirtthi*	The world
ਨਾਈ	*Nāyi*	Greatness, justice, name
ਨ ਸੋਹੈ	*Na sohai*	Is not honoured

Simply translated this *pauṛi* says that going on pilgrimages may earn some merit but that is ephemeral and insignificant. Instead, we must meditate on the Lord, listen to His word, imbibe it and have firm faith. Have in the heart deep love for Him, and you will find the *Tīrath* inside you to wash all grime away. All merits are for the Lord to grant and without these we cannot even meditate. Salutations, the Guru says, to the Lord, from whom we seek the boon of His *Bāṇi*, His word. What was the time when creation took place, what date or phase of the moon was it? The Guru says none can fathom it, neither *pandit* nor *kāẓi* – the learned ones of the Hindus and the Muslims – or they would have mentioned it in their scriptures. The *jogis* can also not tell; in fact no one can. Only the Creator Himself knows that reality. How can we describe Him? Many, each wiser than the other, have attempted the description but cannot succeed. The Lord is great and all that happens is His doing. Anyone who is vain enough to claim to have fathomed Him will not receive honour before the Lord. We can now look at it in more detail and also see what learned commentators have said.

The Guru in this *pauṛi* takes his message to us further. In the first and second lines he tells us that going on pilgrimages, to *Tīrath* (the holy places), practicing great austerities for self-discipline and giving large-heartedly to the needy and the deserving are in their limited context all good deeds which will earn some merit. This merit is, however, ephemeral and its real worth is but that of a *til* - sesame seed, meaning something insignificant). The Guru is again reiterating the scant regard he has for such rituals and austerities. Earlier, in the sixth *pauṛi*, we saw the Guru tell us that pilgrimages and ritual baths have meaning only when they are pleasing to Him; or in other words the real pilgrimage is that action which pleases Him. Here he touches upon it again to the same effect but from a slightly different angle. He says the real honour comes from the Lord and the hard austerities and pilgrimages are in contrast merely an insignificant raising of the spiritual merit.

In the third and fourth lines he explains what a man must do. He says true merit is to be earned only through *suṇiya*, *maniya*, and *man(i) kīta bhāo*. Earlier we saw that the Guru had devoted a whole four *pauṛis* each to the concept of *suṇīye* and *manīye*. From *pauṛi* 8 to 11, he told us the great significance of *suṇiye*– of truly hearing and imbibing God's message as given to us by the Guru. Then from *pauṛi* 12 to 15 he expatiated on the even higher merit of the next step *manīye* – acquiring full and unshakeable faith in the Lord's word. Passing those two stages the devotee would become *panch* – the elite, the chosen – as the Guru told us in *pauṛi* 16. Here the same message is reiterated. The Guru asks to forget about going to pilgrimages or undergoing hard austerities. Instead, he asks us to meditate on the Lord, listen to His word, imbibe it fully, acquire full faith in Him and His word. Having done that, generate in your heart deep love for Him. If you do this then the *Tīrath* will exist inside you. Without moving an inch you can visit this internal *Tīrath* and wash the soil and the grime of your sins from your mind, your intellect, your inner-self. The Guru says wash repeatedly and as thoroughly as you need until no trace is left of the load of filth of sins you have over the course of various lives accumulated. In other words, not rituals but hearing truly the Lord's teaching, developing faith in Him and acquiring deep love and devotion for Him are the true paths to His presence.

In the fifth and sixth lines the Guru has for us a slight cautionary note. He tells us that even the acquiring of the merits whereby the innate *Tīrath* becomes available to us is not entirely in our hands. The Guru says that all virtues, all good qualities are the Lord's to grant, and not ours to acquire. The Guru says he is aware that without these qualities, these virtues, he cannot enter the state of *Bhakti*, of devotion to the Lord. This is quite in accordance with the Guru's message of total surrender. Do not presume that your own efforts will give you the necessary merit – because down that path lies *haumai*. If I think I can on my own earn the merit and enter into a state of true devotion to Him then I am assuming that He is not a necessary part of the exercise. The sense of the 'self' this denotes is, in Sikhism, the anti-thesis of the true path, that of total surrender, of seeing Him as the Sole Cause.

In the seventh and eighth lines the Guru completes this message. He says to the Lord that since all virtues, all merits are Yours to grant and are not mine to acquire – and since without these qualities I cannot enter the state of *Bhakti* – therefore, O Lord grant to me the boon that I may recite Your name. The word used is *suast.* It is a phrase used customarily by the alms-seeking brahmins when given something by the householder. The word is used to indicate 'salutation'. Here the Guru can be said to be using the analogy of himself being the seeker of alms and the Lord being the householder donor. The alms he seeks is His *bāṇi*. The Guru has used the same analogy in:

"Ik dakhṇa hau tai pai māngo, deh āpṇa nām."
(*Rāg Prabhati*, *Mahla* 1, page 1329, *SGGS*)

(The only alms I seek from You is that You give me
the gift of reciting Your name.)

The Guru further, in line 8, addresses the Lord as *Sat(i) Suhāṇ* – Eternal, True and supremely Beautiful, and ever in bliss. The Guru is immersed in awe and wonder at the Divine Beauty. *Suhān* or *Saundarya*, which is how Bhai Vir Singh has translated it, means beauty supreme and that is what the Guru sees when he remarks on the grandeur of the Lord's creation. A question then arises in his mind about this wondrous creation, which he answers in the next few lines.

Before looking further we may note that even the learned ones seem to have found the seventh and eighth lines not easy to construe and have differently interpreted these. The term *Bāṇi Barmāo* has been translated by Narain Singh as the language of Brahma to which the Guru is offering salutations. Iqbal Singh renders these lines as:

"Salutations to Him, creator of Māya,
whose form is the Holy Word
True, beautiful, there is
perpetual rapture in His heart."

Macauliffe had rendered it quite differently as:
"From the Self-existent proceeded Māya, whence issued
a word which produced Brahma and the rest."

Macauliffe, though, does in the footnotes also refer to the other rendering, that of *suast*, meaning 'Blessing on Thee', which he says is said to have been the first salutation that Brahma addressed to the Lord. On the other hand, Bhai Vir Singh has rendered it as: "Accept my salutations and grant me godly virtues, Thou who are Truth, all resplendent and who Divine Consciousness and All Bliss."

Dr. Gopal Singh renders this as: "O Primal Word, Māya, Brahma, Hail to Thee. Thou that are Truth, Ever-Joy, Beauty." Prof. Talib translates it as: "Salutations to Him, Creator of Māya, Whose form is the holy Word; Eternal, holy, supreme Beauty, ever Blissful." Dr. Gopal Singh also says that according to Vivekananda, *Svasti* is a blessing meaning 'God be unto you'. Similarly, he says the word *Āth* here means *Māya.*

The reader can form his own view from this wide variety of interpretations. But, here, the more appealing, and the most consistent with the message of the *SGGS*, is the interpretation adopted by Bhai Vir Singh, that the Guru is giving salutations to the Lord and seeking the boon of those virtues that will enable him to do the right *Bhagti* and be immersed in His *Bāṇi.*

In the ninth and tenth lines the Guru has enunciated the natural curiosity that inevitably arises in all of us at the awesome grandeur of the Lord's creation. He asks when this wondrous thing was created. What was that hour, what time was it, what was the date and what day of the week was it. What was then the season, what month was it when this creation came into being. The terms *Vela* and *Vakhat* refer to the time of the day and the hour. *Thit(i)* comes from the Sanskrit *Tithi* and is a term used to describe time and events according to the lunar system of reckoning as commonly used in India, and usually the phases of the moon describe the day. Thus, *dūj* or *teej* describe the second or third day of the new moon, *ekādashi* describes the eleventh and so on. *Vār* is the reckoning of time by the solar system. In this we have the days of the week. The Guru is here raising the question whether anyone can explain the time of the creation according to any of these systems.

In the eleventh and twelfth lines he answers this rhetorical query and says the time of this creation has not been fathomed by anyone. The *Pandits*, whose work it is to create records of birth, know it not. These learned *Pandits* have created records of all known things and have written the *Purāṇas*, Holy Scriptures, to describe all knowledge. Had any of them learnt anything of this great secret surely there would have been a record in some *Purāṇa* or other ancient scripture. Similarly, the *Kāẓi* knows it not or else it would have been so mentioned in some *Korānic* record.

Here there is an interesting side-note that Prof. Sahib Singh refers to in the *Sri Guru Granth Sahib Darpan*, page 93. The twelfth line which says *Vakhat na pāiyo kādīya je likhan lekh Korān,* was conveniently twisted by the 'Qadiānis', also called Ahmediya Muslims, who ironically are no longer even allowed to call themselves Muslims in Pakistan. Their head-quarters are in Qadian, a small town in the Indian Punjab – hence the name 'Qadianis'. The term *Vakhat* (ਵਖਤੁ) happens to be the popular pronunciation in Punjabi for the word *Waqt* (time). However, as written it also sounds like another Punjabi word which translates as 'travail, or serious problem'. Surrounded as Qadian is by Sikh majority areas, the Qadianis were under peril especially during the riots that accompanied the partition of the country in 1947, with Qadian falling on the Indian side by a few miles. So the meaning was sought to be given to this line to say that it meant an injunction by Guru Nanak to his Sikhs to cause no trouble to those in Qadian who write the *Korān*, i.e., the Ahmediya Muslims! How easy it is to twist the necessarily cryptic language used in the poetry of the *SGGS*. How easy it is also to misinterpret!

In the thirteenth and fourteenth lines, having referred to the *Pandits* and the *Kāzis,* the religious representatives of the two main prevailing religions – Hindu and Muslim – to which his audience belonged, the Guru in these lines now turns to the *Jogis*. These were at that time a very popular and numerous group of holy men divided into a number of sects or *panths*. The Guru, as we will later also in the *Japji* see, will address the *Jogis* more than once. They also make an appearance more than once in the *SGGS*, and the Guru uses them and their practices to drive home the message of true spirituality that is the bedrock of Sikhism. The Guru here says that the day and date of creation is not known to the *Jogi* also, and adds that there is none who knows the month or the season when that event occurred. There is, however, one who does indeed know, and that one is the Creator Himself. The mysteries of the Lord, of His creation are not within any mortal's ken, nor are they known even to the holiest and the most learned. Only He Himself can know when and how it was. The Guru's message of surrender and submission shines through these lines also. He is telling us that there is no earthly wisdom in any entity howsoever wise or mighty which could reveal the ultimate mysteries to us. Seeking for knowledge to try and discover these mysteries is only an exercise in *haumai*. Accept that there are matters truly and completely beyond human ken.

In the fifteenth and sixteenth lines, the Guru says that since so impenetrable is the mystery of the Lord, so much beyond human knowledge or capacity is the Lord and His creation, how then am I to describe Him. It is wisdom, he says, to recognise the Lord's immeasurable power and admit that no words exist which could be used to describe Him. It is impossible, in this state of ignorance, to even find ways to sing praises to Him. Describing Him is impossible; knowing Him is impossible. In spite of this definite truth, says the Guru, there are numerous wise ones, each claiming greater wisdom than the next and making claims that they have understood the Lord and know Him.

In the last lines, the seventeenth and eighteenth, the Guru enters a word of warning for such wise ones. He says the Lord is the greatest and so is His ਨਾਈ - *nāyi*, which Prof. Sahib Singh translates as *Vaddiāyi* (greatness, grandeur). It is also, by some, rendered as His justice, or His name, though in this context greatness seems the more appropriate meaning. In either sense what the Guru is telling us is that the Lord is above all. All that happens is by His will. Thus, anyone who is vain enough to make a claim to have fathomed Him will not receive honour before the Lord. Here again the underlying message is that anyone rash enough to claim knowledge of the unknowable is acting from ego and pride – from *haumai*. These, the Guru repeatedly tells us, are very serious demerits and will be held against us when our accounts finally come up for settlement in the Lord's presence.

To summarise, the Guru has said that those whose minds are fixed on the *Nām*, who have complete faith and love for Him, their minds will be purified. This devotion is also a gift from God and not an acquisition through personal effort. This upliftment of the soul does not make the devotee capable of describing the divine mystery. No *Pandit*, no *Kāẓi*, no *Jogi,* none can breach that secret. So great is the Lord that only He Himself knows about His mysteries.

27

THE LORD HAS NO BOUNDS

Pauṛi 22

ਪਾਤਾਲਾ ਪਾਤਾਲ ਲਖ ਆਗਾਸਾ ਆਗਾਸ॥	*Pātāla pātāl lakh āgāsa āgās.*
ਓੜਕ ਓੜਕ ਭਾਲਿ ਥਕੇ ਵੇਦ ਕਹਨਿ ਇਕ ਵਾਤ॥	*Oṛak oṛak bhāl thakay ved kahan Ik vāt.*
ਸਹਸ ਅਠਾਰਹ ਕਹਨਿ ਕਤੇਬਾ ਅਸੁਲੂ ਇਕੁ ਧਾਤੁ॥	*Sahas atthārāh kahan kateba asloo Ik dhāt.*
ਲੇਖਾ ਹੋਇ ਤ ਲਿਖੀਐ ਲੇਖੈ ਹੋਇ ਵਿਣਾਸੁ॥	*Lekha hoye ta likhīyai lekhai hoye viṇās.*
ਨਾਨਕ ਵਡਾ ਆਖੀਐ ਆਪੇ ਜਾਣੈ ਆਪੁ॥੨੨॥	*Nanak vadda ākhiyai āpay jāṇai āp.*

Brief glossary

ਪਾਤਾਲ	*Pātāl*	Nether worlds
ਆਗਾਸ	*Āgās*	Sky, heavens
ਭਾਲਿ	*Bhāl*	Search
ਵੇਦ	*Ved*	Knowledge, the four *Vedas*
ਇਕ ਵਾਤ	*Ik vāt*	In one voice, in one word
ਸਹਸ ਅਠਾਰਹ	*Sahas atthārāh*	Eighteen thousand
ਕਤੇਬਾ	*Kateba*	Books (here the scriptures, holy books)
ਅਸੁਲੂ ਇਕ ਧਾਤੁ	*Asloo ik dhāt*	Real is one Essence
ਲੇਖਾ ਹੋਇ	*Lekha Hoye*	If it could be measured or recounted

ਵਿਣਾਸੁ	*Viṇās*	Annihilation
ਲਖ	*Lakh*	Hundred thousand, here innumerable

Simply translated this *pauṛi* tells us that the count of the nether regions and of the heavens above is unlimited. Efforts to measure this vast mystery are fruitless and the *Vedas* tell us the same. Even the holy books of the Semitic religions say there are 18000 created worlds but they also agree that there is but one underlying Essence. The Lord is beyond description and whoyever attempts to measure Him will soon run out of numbers and for describing Him words will not suffice. The Supreme One Himself only knows His own measure.

In this *pauṛi* the Guru is carrying further the point he stressed in the previous *pauṛi* and by giving further examples he wants us to forget about measuring, counting or writing about the description of the Lord. He wants us to thoroughly imbibe the message that the Lord is beyond comprehension and our only appropriate relationship with Him is one of complete surrender and of love and awe.

The Guru says in the first line that the count of the nether regions and of the heavens above is unlimited and not in man's capacity to measure. There is a remarkable congruity among the many people of areas otherwise fairly far apart, regarding the concept of creation in so much as it is taken to be consisting of three broad parts, the heavens above where dwell the favoured ones, the middle earth where we dwell, and the world below, the nether regions, where dwell terrors and monsters. Thus, the Greeks and the Romans had their Olympus where Zeus, or Jupiter, reigned over the gods. Then there was its counterpart, the nether worlds where Hades or Pluto ruled over the shades of the dead. In between was this, our world of mortal men. Similar is the Hindu mythology with *Swarag* above, which is said to be peopled by gods, saints and other demi-gods, and a *Pātāl* where rule the Snake gods and sundry other less desirable beings. In between is the world of men. The Guru says that if these do indeed exist then there is not just one of each. There is, he tells us, a *Patāl* beyond each *Pātāl*, and there are 'lakhs' of upper worlds or heavens. Though 'lakh' means literally, in the Hindu system of counting, a hundred thousand but here it is not intended by the Guru to put any definite number to the heavens. In the context here the term 'lakh' is used to indicate that there are innumerable such heavens.

In the second line the Guru says that efforts have endlessly been made, and then given up in hopelessness, to try and measure this vast mystery and to explain it. Finally, those who made this foolhardy attempt all gave up, in helpless fatigue, their futile efforts. So do the *Vedas* unanimously say. Another construction put in this line is that the *Vedas* have delved deep into this search but in the end have in one voice expressed helplessness. In fact the *Mandduk̤ya Upnishad* III-26 does say: *Neti, Neti* – not this, not this. In other words, no description was possible and the only way to express Him is by saying that He is not subject to description. This *Neti, Neti* is but an expression of man's helplessness in the presence of the Infinite. The SGPC's *Shabdarth* makes a slightly different point and renders this line to say that the *Vedas* say in unison that the efforts to locate His limits have been useless and the searchers have given up in exhaustion.

In the third line the same concept is stressed by giving examples from other religions. The words *Sahas Atthārāh* have been construed in various ways. Thus, Dr. Sangat Singh says: "Thousands of saints, eighteen *Purāṇas* and the Semitic texts viz, *Torah, Zabur* (Psalms), *Injīl* (Gospel) and *Korān* all unanimously say that the source, the Principle of all creation is one God." Prof. Talib sees it differently. He says, "Muslim scriptures declare the number of species eighteen thousand. Vain is such count. Nothing is real but the One Essence." Iqbal Singh renders it yet another way. He translates it as: "Eighteen thousand worlds, say the Semitic Scriptures. But there is only one Reality, that this creation is infinite."

This difference in approach arises from the fact that, as essential and inevitable in the poetic form, the Guru has expressed himself in one word where the thought behind is cosmically vast. The term *Sahas Atthārāh* lends itself to various meanings. Eighteen – *Atthārāh* – happens to be the usually accepted number of the major Hindu *Purāṇas*; *Sahas* means thousand. *Kateba* means books or scriptures. Further, the Semitic religions are all governed by their Holy Book, and the Jews, Christians and Muslims are defined together as the people of the 'Book'. In this light, Prof. Sahib Singh attempts the interpretation as: "The four books (of the Muslims and the Christian etc.) say that there are eighteen thousand worlds but their one base is the Lord". Narain Singh also follows this interpretation, as does the *Shabdarth* of the SGPC. There is another rendering, that by H.S. Doabia who translates it thus: "The saints, the eighteen *Purāṇas* and the four religious books of Jews, Christians and Muslims conclude that God is limitless."

Bhai Vir Singh, the noted scholar and mystic, sees it as: "Thousands of *Rishis Munis* and *Ālams*, eighteen *Purāṇas*, Four *Vedas* say the same truth —". He has rendered *Ālam* here as meaning the learned ones. Bhai Vir Singh also mentions the other interpretation in his commentary, *Santhya Sri Guru Granth Sahib*, page 110. Referring to the Muslim belief system, he says that the *Munājāt*, page 1, says **'ਕੀਏ ਕੁਨ ਸੇ ਆਲਮ ਅਠਾਰਾ ਹਜ਼ਾਰ'** - *Kiye kun se Ālam Atthārāh hazār* - meaning that with His word were created the eighteen thousand worlds.

Giani Maskin, however, takes it to refer to the concept of *Atthārāh hazār Ālam*, again interpreting *Ālam* not as worlds but as the 'learned teachers', the word lending itself to both meanings – learned one or world. He says the eighteen thousand learned ones and the books of the Semitic religions also all say that the basic essence is but 'one'."

In his translation Macauliffe renders it as: "The thousands of *Purāṇas* and Muhammadan books tell that in reality there is but one principle." He adds that there are only eighteen *Purāṇas*, while the expression in the text means a thousand times eighteen or an indefinite number. He adds that, "The word *Sahans* is also understood by *gyānis* to refer to *rikhis* and learned men in indefinite numbers." In the Sikh system of belief there is of course no such limit or number put on the worlds created. There are in this belief system infinite universes or worlds and these exist endlessly one after the other beyond human capacity to count. In each and all is immanent the Lord Himself. Whether the reference to the phrase 'eighteen thousand' here is to the Muslim concept of eighteen thousand worlds – *ālam* - or to the Hindu *Purāṇas* numbering eighteen is, in the light of the above variety of possible meanings, differently seen by the learned commentators.

The essence of the message is that the Lord is the underlying cause of all creation, and either rendering would lead to this conclusion. It, however, appears logical that having in the previous line referred to the *Vedas* the Guru here is now referring to the Semitic or specifically the Muslim thought. The more appropriate rendering here should be that even though the 'Books', referring to the Semitic scriptures, the *Torah*, the *Bible*, the *Zabur* and the *Korān*, say that there are eighteen thousand created worlds yet they also agree that there is but one underlying Essence. The word *Asaloo* (ਅਸੁਲੁ) is of Arabic origin, meaning 'the basic foundation'. The word *Dhāt* (ਧਾਤ) means literally metal but is also used to describe the 'essence of a thing'.

In the fourth line the Guru, reiterating the important and recurring theme of the *Japji*, says that since the Lord is so much beyond description then obviously it is not possible to give an account of Him. If we attempt to measure Him we will run out of numbers, if we start to describe Him there will soon be no words left to us. The *Shabdarth* translates it as: "The one attempting the account will come to his end but the account will not ever be completed." Prof. Talib puts it as: "His infinity no one may measure or state, Men's lives are swallowed up in the effort."

Iqbal Singh renders it as: "If it could be written it would have been. Men's lives are swallowed in that fruitless effort."

Doabia renders it as: "If there be any account of God, then alone the mortal can write the same …." In short, the Guru is telling us to not enter into the fruitless pursuit of attempting to measure or describe Him. Any such task will be beyond accomplishment.

In the fifth and last line the Guru sums it up. He says the Supreme One Himself can only know how great He is. Prof. Sahib Singh translates it as: "The Lord whom the entire world is calling great, only He Himself knows His own greatness." The phrase *Nanak vadda ākhiyai* is interpreted as "Sayeth Nanak know that He is supreme," by Prof. Talib. Macauliffe renders it as: "If God can be described by writing, then describe Him; but such description is impossible." Dr. Sangat Singh puts it as: "O, say only 'God is great'," while Iqbal Singh puts it as: "O Nanak, call Him great." There is thus unanimity at least on this line. The short point brought out in this *pauṛi* simply is that the Lord is supreme, beyond anyone's ability to describe. He Himself only knows His own measure. The conclusion for us is that let no one waste time in fruitless attempts to describe Him. Just surrender yourself whole-heartedly to Him and live your life in awe of Him and in great and loving devotion to Him.

28

THE STREAM AND THE OCEAN

Pauṛi 23

ਸਾਲਾਹੀ ਸਾਲਾਹਿ ਏਤੀ ਸੁਰਤਿ ਨ ਪਾਈਆ।	*Sālāhi sālāh eti surt(i) na pāyīa.*
ਨਦੀਆ ਅਤੈ ਵਾਹ ਪਵਹਿ ਸਮੁੰਦਿ ਨ ਜਾਣੀਅਹਿ॥	*Nadīya atai vāh paveh samund na jāṇīye.*
ਸਮੁੰਦ ਸਾਹ ਸੁਲਤਾਨ ਗਿਰਹਾ ਸੇਤੀ ਮਾਲੁ ਧਨੁ॥	*Samund sāh sultān girha seti māl dhan.*
ਕੀੜੀ ਤੁਲਿ ਨ ਹੋਵਨੀ ਜੇ ਤਿਸੁ ਮਨਹੁ ਨ ਵੀਸਰਹਿ॥੨੩॥	*Kīṛi tul na hovni je tis manhu na vīsray.*

Brief glossary

ਸਾਲਾਹਿ	*Sālāh*	Praises
ਏਤੀ ਸੁਰਤਿ	*Eti surt(i)*	Knowledge of Him
ਨਦੀਆ	*Nadīya*	Rivers
ਵਾਹ	*Vāh*	Rivulets, streams
ਸਮੁੰਦਿ	*Samund*	Oceans
ਨ ਜਾਣੀਅਹਿ	*Na jāṇīye.*	Not known, are not known
ਸਾਹ ਸੁਲਤਾਨ	*Sāh sultān*	King of kings
ਗਿਰਹਾ	*Girha*	Mountains; in Persian, purse or pocket
ਕੀੜੀ ਤੁਲਿ	*Kīṛi tul*	Equal to an ant
ਵੀਸਰਹਿ	*Vīsray*	Forgets

Simply translated this *pauṛi* says that ceaselessly singing praises of the Lord does not mean that His greatness can be comprehended.

Just as streams and rivulets lose identity when they reach the ocean, so is the devotee absorbed and cannot measure the Lord after reaching Him. Emperors of great wealth and great territories are not the equal of an ant if in the latter's heart God is not forgotten. Let us now see it in more detail and also see what learned commentators have to say.

The Guru again touches upon the recurring theme of singing the praises of the Lord. In the first line he says ceaselessly singing praises of Him does not mean that His greatness can be comprehended. The word 'ਸਾਲਾਹੀ' – *Sālāhi* - has been translated as "the Lord who deserves laudation", by Prof. Sahib Singh as also by Narain Singh. Bhai Vir Singh renders it as "those who praise". The word has also been rendered by Dr. Sangat Singh as 'praises' or those who sing praises. Iqbal Singh also calls it as 'worshippers', and Doabia translates it as 'praisers'. Prof. Talib has left it open and has rendered it neutrally without specifically translating the word *Sālāhi.* He says for this line: "All God's laudation, repeated over and over again comprehends not His greatness." Giani Sant Singh Maskin in his audio commentary explains this *pauṛi* also in this sense. This certainly rings the truer rendering since the Guru is pressing home the lesson of man's incapacity to understand Him. In short, the Guru is telling us that while the Sikh is required to meditate on His name and to sing praises to Him, do not presume that this will automatically result in any comprehensive understanding of the Lord.

In the second line the Guru repeats that the Lord is unknowable. Giani Maskin gives a very appealing explanation of this; that the Guru is telling us that though it may be useless to expect to resolve the mystery of the Lord and His creation through singing of the Lord's praises, yet deem not the effort fruitless. The Guru gives here an analogy of the waters of this earth that flow through *nadīya* – streams - and *vāh* – rivulets, as also in the form of great rivers into the oceans. He says once these enter the ocean there is no distinction left between the ocean's water and the waters from these various sources. All become one with the ocean. Similar is the state of the devotee who, seeking to know God, sits in meditation singing praises of him. If one fortunate day he does succeed in reaching Him then the devotee will at that time be as one with Him, and he will no longer be of this world so as to be able to tell us of the experience. As the Guru has said, such a one will not be able to find the words. But once the devotee is one with the Lord, his position is the same as of a river entering the ocean. The devotee cannot, even after he succeeds in reaching God-realization, hope to say: 'This is what He is.' Just as streams and rivulets when they reach the vast ocean cannot retain the separateness of their identity and cannot hope to know the identity, the size and the extent of the ocean into which they have merged, the devotee, even when successful, cannot know the measure of the Lord.

In the third and fourth lines the Guru speaks further of those who steadfastly fix their minds on the Lord. The worth of those who are thus blessed is now contrasted to the possessors of wealth in this world. The Guru says if we compare a mighty emperor master of an empire vast as the *samund* (ocean), and possessed of wealth equal to the mountains on this earth, yet is his worth less than that of an otherwise insignificant ant in whose mind the Lord resides. The word *girha* has been taken as the plural of *giri* or mountain. There is another meaning to the word in Persian, which is knot, or pocket or purse. Even in this sense the meaning does not change and we could say that emperors ruling over empires vast as oceans and possessing in their treasuries great money and property are not worth an ant's value if in the ant's mind God is not forsaken. Bhai Vir Singh has also taken the word *Kīṛi* in the sense of a very poor and humble person which of course does not materially alter the overall sense of the message, which is that the humblest one, if he is immersed in the Lord, is greater than the possessor of the greatest material wealth.

To summarise, the Guru has here in this brief four-line *pauṛi* told us that though singing of praises will not open the mysteries of the Lord, yet is the exercise not devoid of purpose. Those truly devoted, retaining the Lord in their minds, are worth greatly more than the great emperors however wealthy or mighty. The importance of meditating on the Lord is here repeated, for the Guru has already prescribed this as our main device for reaching Him, when in *Pauṛi* 4 he told us: *Amrit vela sach nāu vaddiāyi vīchār* - rise at the ambrosial hour and meditate on His greatness.

29

BEYOND ALL RECKONING

Pauṛi 24

ਅੰਤੁ ਨ ਸਿਫਤੀ ਕਹਣਿ ਨ ਅੰਤੁ॥	*Unt na sifti kahaṇ na unt.*
ਅੰਤ ਨ ਕਰਣੈ ਦੇਣਿ ਨ ਅੰਤੁ॥	*Unt na karṇai deiṇ na unt.*
ਅੰਤੁ ਨ ਵੇਖਣਿ ਸੁਣਣਿ ਨ ਅੰਤੁ॥	*Unt na vekhaṇ suṇaṇ na unt.*
ਅੰਤੁ ਨ ਜਾਪੈ ਕਿਆ ਮਨਿ ਮੰਤੁ॥	*Unt na jāpai kiya man(i) munt.*
ਅੰਤੁ ਨ ਜਾਪੈ ਕੀਤਾ ਆਕਾਰੁ॥	*Unt na jāpai kīta ākār.*
ਅੰਤੁ ਨ ਜਾਪੈ ਪਾਰਾਵਾਰੁ॥	*Unt na jāpai parāvār.*
ਅੰਤੁ ਕਾਰਣਿ ਕੇਤੇ ਬਿਲਲਾਹਿ॥	*Unt kāraṇ ketay billāhe.*
ਤਾ ਕੇ ਅੰਤ ਨ ਪਾਏ ਜਾਹਿ॥	*Ta kay unt na pāye jāhe.*
ਏਹੁ ਅੰਤੁ ਨ ਜਾਣੈ ਕੋਇ॥	*Eh unt na jāṇai koye.*
ਬਹੁਤਾ ਕਹੀਐ ਬਹੁਤਾ ਹੋਇ॥	*Bahuta kahīyai bahuta hoye.*
ਵਡਾ ਸਾਹਿਬੁ ਊਚਾ ਥਾਉ॥	*Vadda sahib ūcha thāo.*
ਊਚੇ ਉਪਰਿ ਊਚਾ ਨਾਉ॥	*Ūchay ūpar ūcha nāo.*
ਏਵਡੁ ਊਚਾ ਹੋਵੈ ਕੋਇ॥	*Evadd ūcha hovai koye.*
ਤਿਸੁ ਊਚੇ ਕਉ ਜਾਣੈ ਸੋਇ॥	*Tis ūche ko jāṇai soye.*
ਜੇਵਡੁ ਆਪਿ ਜਾਣੈ ਆਪਿ ਆਪਿ॥	*Jevadd āp jāṇai āp āp.*
ਨਾਨਕ ਨਦਰੀ ਕਰਮੀ ਦਾਤਿ॥੨੪॥	*Nanak nadri karmi dāt.*

Brief glossary

ਅੰਤੁ	*Unt*	Limits
ਸਿਫਤੀ	*Sifti*	Good qualities
ਕਰਣੈ	*Karṇai*	Action, doings
ਦੇਣਿ	*Deiṇ*	Giving
ਮਨ ਮੰਤੁ	*Mann munt*	Purpose in the mind

ਆਕਾਰੁ	*Ākār*	Creation
ਪਾਰਾਵਾਰੁ	*Pārāvār*	Boundaries this end and the opposite
ਬਿਲਲਾਹਿ	*Billāhe*	Waiting, helplessly yearning
ਥਾਉ	*Thāo*	Place
ਨਦਰੀ	*Nadri*	Glance of grace, or the Lord who gives the glance of grace
ਕਰਮੀ	*Karmi*	Grace, or through the Lord's grace
ਦਾਤਿ	*Dāt*	Gifts

Simply translated this *pauṛi* says that the grand attributes of the Lord are not subject to any count or measure. Not by seeing nor hearing can His limits or the limits of what He intends be measured. It is impossible to determine the shape or size of this vast creation. Many restlessly search for these limits but fail to find them. This happens because these limits are really unknowable. He is higher than the highest we can think of. The Lord is great and His station most exalted. His name is higher than the highest. Only someone equally high could measure Him [but obviously none such exists]. The Lord alone is capable of knowing His own limits. The gift of His name can come only as a measure of His benediction. Let us now see in more detail what the message is and what the learned ones have to tell us.

The Guru in this *pauṛi* expounds further on the impossibility of fathoming God. In the first and second lines he says that the grand qualities and attributes of the Lord are not subject to any count or measure. They are immeasurably beyond any human capacity to comprehend. There is then obviously no limit on the description thereof; in other words, no finite being could attempt the description. The Lord's actions or doings are also beyond count. So are the bounties He has bestowed on us. It is the Guru's prescription that we must constantly sing praises of the Lord. Were we to attempt praise of a human or a mortal thing we could complete the task in a dozen words. Someone very exalted may need a few extra. Not so with the Lord. We will run out of words and capacity but His qualities would remain yet to count. His doings similarly are infinite. The Creator who brings into existence an infinite universe can obviously not be subject to a count of what all He has done. Further while creating, the Lord has also bestowed on his creation gifts, which are beyond any count. As the Guru told us in the third *pauṛi*, *Denda day lainday thakk pāhe* - the Lord keeps bestowing such that we who receive these gifts will tire of receiving but not He of giving.

In the third and fourth lines there is more on the same theme. The Guru says that not by seeing nor by hearing can His limits be determined. The human curiosity which drives us to probe and also to seek to know more is here addressed. Humans mainly use their eyes and their ears to determine the nature of what is before them. The capacity of the eye to see and of the ear to hear is limited in us mortals. None such exist who using these sense organs could reach those infinite boundaries. It is equally impossible to know what is in His mind. *Mann munt* means the plan in the mind or the idea behind what actions He has performed. These, the Guru says, are also beyond human ken. The third line has also been rendered differently both by Prof. Talib and by Iqbal Singh who take it to mean that there are no limits to what the Lord hears or what He sees. This, however, does not quite fit into the context. The Guru is describing man's incapacity when faced with the Infinite. The sight or hearing mentioned here has to relate to that basic concept or thought. Thus, the interpretation above which is also used by Prof. Sahib Singh and Narain Singh, and many other commentators, seems the more appealing. The Guru's reference here in this, the third, line is more possibly to human limitations.

In the fifth and sixth lines the Guru refers to the visible creation and says it is impossible to determine the shape or size of it, nor is it possible to say where one end starts or where is the other end. The term *Pārāvār* means 'this end and the other end'. Anything mortal or of this world is easy to thus describe – its *Paravār* will be always known. Not so for the Lord's creation however.

In the seventh and eighth lines the Guru refers to the ancient and long list of learned ones who have yearned somehow to ascertain His limits, but says that there is none who has succeeded so far. The term *Billāhe* denotes someone moaning in agony to acquire something; having a great yearning which if unfulfilled brings great pain. The learned ones, the *Rishis* and *Munis*, the great scholars of mystic knowledge have from times immemorial sought for some way or device to measure Him or even His creation. Obviously, they have failed painfully because the Infinite just has no limits.

In the ninth and tenth lines, the Guru sums it up and says that all their efforts have failed because there really exists no limits. He says none has ever acquired this knowledge and the fact is that the more we attempt to describe and measure Him the more of Him we shall see beyond those descriptions, like a traveller seeing a mountain ahead thinks he will soon reach the highest point, only to discover on reaching that ridge that there is a whole chain of ever higher mountain ahead which were hidden by the first range and become now visible as he attains some height. In the same way the seeker will see greater heights, and insight, of the Lord's wonders as he scales the path towards Him through recital of His name as the Guru has laid down for us.

The above thought is elaborated further in the eleventh to fourteenth lines. The Guru says the Lord is supreme and His station is exalted, the seat where He resides is exalted. His name is the most exalted, higher than the highest. Thus, if someone were to achieve that much height only then can he hope to know the limits of the Lord. Now this obviously is an impossible proposition. By definition the Lord is unique. He is that power which has through His Will brought into existence this vast creation which is without limits. He resides in it and is immanent in every atom, every part of His creation. Who then from within this creation could ever expect to rise to the level where he could be the equal of the Lord? If that impossibility were to occur then the uniqueness of the Lord would no longer be. Such an event just cannot in the scheme of His creation occur. The Guru is indirectly again stressing the same message, that the Lord is unknowable.

In the last two lines, the fifteenth and sixteenth, the Guru makes this indirect message eminently clear and direct. He says that the Lord alone is capable of knowing how vast His own limits are. This last line, *Nanak nadri karmi dāt* has found different interpretations. Prof. Talib says, "Saith Nanak: Devotion to Him is blessing coming through His glance of grace."

Dr. Sangat Singh, on the other hand, says, "His acceptance follows the benediction of one's deeds by His grace."

Iqbal Singh attempts it another way: "Nanak, God the merciful by His grace bestows His gifts." Prof Sahib Singh says, "Every gift comes from the benediction of the Lord who bestows on us this glance of grace." Narain Singh puts it as: "The gift of His name comes from His grace."

The different approaches come from the different ways the two words *Nadri* and *Karmi* can be interpreted. The word *Nadri* means sight or glance; *Nadri* can then mean 'the one with the glance (of grace)' or 'through or by the glance (of grace)'. Similarly, *Karmi* means benediction or blessing and *Karmi* can also mean 'the one who gives the blessing' or 'through the blessing'. Further, the word *Dāt* means gift. But the question here is which gift. These differing interpretations obviously will lead to different rendering by the learned ones.

Narain Singh has here the more appealing explanation. He says that in this *pauṛi* the Guru is telling us that the correct way of life for mankind is to sing His praises and hope one day to become one with Him. It is an error to seek to measure Him because he is beyond the capacity of man's senses. Through none of the devices available, neither to humans nor by use of the senses can His limits be determined, as the Guru has explained by giving one example after the other in this *pauṛi*. The only way to know Him is to go beyond the limits of the human senses and to achieve oneness with Him. This, the Guru says, is possible only through reciting His name and singing His praises. Reciting His name is also possible only if the Lord so bestows on us this gift. The biggest gift for any seeker to ask from the Lord is the gift of His name. This will come to us only as a blessing, a benediction from the One through His glance of grace.

The gift – *Dāt* – spoken of here is thus the gift of His name, the only gift that can at all make it possible to know Him. All the other parameters mentioned in this *pauṛi*, sight or hearing or intellect or even devotion, can never be expected to give you the measure of Him. This is also close to the rendering by Prof. Talib. The alternate view that the gifts spoken of here mean all and every gift, material or otherwise, that we humans receive all come from His blessing, does not greatly alter the sense. Bhai Vir Singh's explanation also is interesting here. It says, "… to experience him you have to rise above the mind, and thought and words. Recitation of His Name raises you higher than your mind can, and only when you reach that stage will you realize Him …" Here again we see that the gift spoken of is the gift of His name which also can come only as a measure of His grace, as a benediction. This could be taken as what the Guru intended to tell us in these lines.

30

THE HIGHEST OF THE HIGH

Pauṛi 25

ਬਹੁਤਾ ਕਰਮੁ ਲਿਖਿਆ ਨਾ ਜਾਇ॥	*Bahuta karam likhiya na jāye.*
ਵਡਾ ਦਾਤਾ ਤਿਲੁ ਨ ਤਮਾਇ॥	*Vadda dāta til na tamāye.*
ਕੇਤੇ ਮੰਗਹਿ ਜੋਧ ਅਪਾਰ॥	*Ketay mangay jodh apār.*
ਕੇਤਿਆ ਗਣਤ ਨਹੀ ਵੀਚਾਰੁ॥	*Ketia gaṇat nahi vīchār.*
ਕੇਤੇ ਖਪਿ ਤੁਟਹਿ ਵੇਕਾਰ॥	*Ketay khap tutteh vekār.*
ਕੇਤੇ ਲੈ ਲੈ ਮੁਕਰੁ ਪਾਹਿ॥	*Ketay lai lai mukar pāhe.*
ਕੇਤੇ ਮੂਰਖ ਖਾਹੀ ਖਾਹਿ॥	*Ketay mūrakh khāhi khāhe.*
ਕੇਤਿਆ ਦੂਖ ਭੂਖ ਸਦ ਮਾਰ॥	*Ketia dūkh bhūkh sad mār.*
ਏਹਿ ਭਿ ਦਾਤਿ ਤੇਰੀ ਦਾਤਾਰ॥	*Eh bhi dāt teri dātār.*
ਬੰਦਿ ਖਲਾਸੀ ਭਾਣੈ ਹੋਇ॥	*Bund khalāsi bhānai hoye.*
ਹੋਰੁ ਆਖਿ ਨ ਸਕੈ ਕੋਇ॥	*Hor ākh na sakai koye.*
ਜੇ ਕੋ ਖਾਇਕੁ ਆਖਣਿ ਪਾਇ॥	*Je ko khāyak ākhaṇ pāye.*
ਓਹੁ ਜਾਣੈ ਜੇਤੀਆ ਮੁਹਿ ਖਾਇ॥	*Oh jāṇai jetīya muh khāye.*
ਆਪੇ ਜਾਣੈ ਆਪੇ ਦੇਇ॥	*Āpay jāṇai āpay day.*
ਆਖਹਿ ਸਿ ਭਿ ਕੇਈ ਕੇਇ॥	*Ākhay se bhi keyi kay.*
ਜਿਸ ਨੋ ਬਖਸੇ ਸਿਫਤਿ ਸਾਲਾਹ॥	*Jis no bakhse sift sālāh.*
ਨਾਨਕ ਪਾਤਿਸਾਹੀ ਪਾਤਿਸਾਹੁ॥੨੫॥	*Nanak pātsāhi pātsāh.*

Brief glossary

ਕਰਮੁ	*Karam*	Grace, blessing
ਨ ਤਮਾਇ	*Na tamāye*	Has no craving
ਜੋਧ	*Jodh*	Warriors
ਅਪਾਰ	*Apār*	Unknowable

ਗਣਤ	*Gaṇat*	Count, calculation
ਖਪਿ ਤੁਟਹਿ	*Khap tutteh*	Broken in exhaustion
ਵੇਕਾਰ	*Vekār*	In evil deeds
ਮੁਕਰੁ	*Mukar*	Deny, disown
ਖਾਹੀ ਖਾਹਿ	*Khāhi khāhay*	Keep (greedily, taking)
ਦੂਖ ਭੂਖ	*Dūkh bhūkh*	Woes and penury
ਸਦ ਮਾਰ	*Sad mār*	Always suffer from
ਖਾਇਕੁ	*Khāyak*	Fool
ਸਿ ਭਿ	*Se bhi*	Even those
ਕੇਈ ਕੇਇ	*Keyi kay*	Few, rare ones, many

Simply translated this *pauṛi* tells us that the Lord is the highest giver of gifts and expects nothing in return. Many seek from Him valour; there is no count of how many beg at His door. Many take His gifts and use them for wrong purposes. Many ingrates shamefully deny the bounty they have got. Many fools just keep gobbling up these gifts. Many are those who are mired in penury, but even this is a gift from the Lord. Liberation from the cycle of births comes only by His grace. There is none else who can even speak of it. If some fool were to try to explain the process of liberation in any other way he will suffer for it. The Lord knows our real worth and accordingly rewards us. The most important gift is of singing the Lord's praises; of true devotion to Him. The one who gets this great gift is the king of kings. Let us now see in more detail the message and also see what the learned ones have to say.

In the previous *pauṛi* we saw the Guru educate us that the real gift to seek from the Lord is the gift of His name. Here, in this *pauṛi*, the Guru enumerates the various types of gift seekers who importune the Lord; and will in conclusion again reiterate that the real gift is not worldly greatness but the gift of ever singing His praises.

In the first and second lines the Guru says that He is the *vadda dāta* or high donor. This is a theme the Guru has touched on more than once in the *Gurbāṇi* to tell us that all that exists is but a gift from the Lord and that His gifts keep endlessly coming until the recipient may get exhausted of receiving. Which is exactly what the Guru told us in *pauṛi* 3 of the *Japji Sahib*, where said *denda day lainday thakk pāhe*. The word *Karam,* in the first line, is the Persian 'blessing' and not the Sanskrit 'action'. The Guru says great is His benediction and it is not possible even to put it in words. The great Donor, the high Benefactor keeps giving without any expectation in return. Humans are likely to give their gifts only where they expect in return some benefit either by way of money or gratitude or some favours. In the human mind the link between the giving and the expected return is thus inextricable. The Guru, it is said here, is a giver, the highest of all givers whose gifts never cease. He differs sharply from us though in that there is no expectation behind those gifts. The giving here is a true benediction, free from all taint of any greed or expectation at all. *Tamah* is an Arabic word that means greed. There is not an iota of that here, the Guru says.

The Guru now lists some of those who seek favours from this great Donor. In lines 3 and 4, he says numerous are those who seek valour from Him. There are many similarly begging at His door, whose number is impossible to measure. The third line has been interpreted by Prof. Sahib Singh and also by Bhai Vir Singh as: "many are the peerless warriors who beg from him". Some have interpreted it also as "many are those who seek from him unmatched valour". The first of these seems the more appropriate rendering.

In the fifth line the Guru expounds on the seekers of gifts who don't even know what gift is in their own best interest. He says the number of those is large who having taken from the Lord use the gifts only for evil deeds, so thoroughly and intensely, that doing so they exhaust themselves. The lesson here is that we do not even always know what to ask from the Lord that could really benefit us, elevate us. The Lord is the Bestower without a limit.

While He has loaded us with His gifts, there are many who have not learnt how to use these gifts. So they misuse these great gifts and in following evil ways exhaust themselves, squandering the Lord's gifts for mere sensual gratification. We also need to note that the Lord does not decide to withhold his gifts just because they will be misused. The debauches who bring ruination upon their own selves are also the recipients of bounty from the same divine Giver. It is their own folly that converts this bounty into a means to their own damnation.

In the sixth and seventh lines the Guru speaks of another category. He says there are numerous those who shamelessly deny the rich bounty they have received. These are the ingrates, a category the Guru has held to be particularly despicable elsewhere also in the *Gurbāṇi*. We of course see all around us people who when blessed with success in any worldly endeavour, say in acquiring wealth or power, forget altogether from where it came. They presume that it is their own skill or capabilities, which brought them these gifts. The Real Source is forgotten or ignored and presuming oneself the doer, the pride in oneself only gets strengthened further. Forgetting the True Source in this fashion generates *haumai* – an exaggerated sense of selfness, which is the enemy of progress towards the Lord. The Guru in the seventh line says countless are the fools who keep gobbling up their gifts. The theme again is that these greedy ones do so because they are ingrates, without that redeeming sense of gratitude.

In the eighth and ninth lines the Guru now turns to those whose lives are mired in penury and trouble. In the previous two lines the reference was to the legions that waste the Lord's gifts in dissipation and also those whose main characteristic is ungratefulness. Thus, while there are so many who over-indulge themselves in enjoying the Lord's gifts, at the same time there are the many whose lot is suffering and severe neediness. The Guru is saying here that do not think that this group is bereft of the Lord's bounty. That bounty is universal, unconditional and the gift to each one of the Lord's creation. This penury and travail, the Guru says, is a gift too. The Guru has spoken of those whom plentiful and bounteous gifts lead only towards over-indulgence, egotism and ungratefulness. Better then the gift which will turn man's mind towards God. These troubles and penury are in their own way a gift. No one would surely want to seek an over-indulgence in these! However, these seemingly harsh gifts will often turn the mind away from the world of men to the world of spirituality. Great is the devotee who, even when happiest and most successful, keeps his mind fixed on the Lord and does not fall into the trap of believing that it is all due to his own strength or capacity. He sees in his heart that it is a gift from the Lord, and is filled with gratitude for the gift. Most, however, will not have that good sense. God will be forgotten and pride and vanity will rule. There will be very few who can easily forget the Lord when trouble strikes. The mind then whole-heartedly fixes itself on Him. Thus is penury and trouble a gift.

The essence of the message here is that when we try to use our own will and seek from the Lord the fulfilment of our own desires, we almost always go astray. The warrior seeking valour may even get his wish and it may lead to some momentary glory for him. But that is not the path the Guru is laying for us. The seekers after wealth, money, property or power will in their prayers seek more of the same. They may get their wish but in the end it will only mean ephemeral sensory satisfaction, a passing pleasure in being able to eat either better or spend more, a transient satisfaction in dominance over others. All such prayers lead us off the right path, because they arise from our own limited capacities and we can never see the end results. Sometimes the gift of penury may be our biggest blessing. Troubles may be the Lord's way of turning us on to the right path. In any case, better these than the debauchery of the dissipated ones, the ungratefulness of those who while bountifully provided, are neglectful of the purpose of this life and who seek never to follow the difficult but very productive path the Guru has prescribed. While nobody is likely to pray for travails and poverty, yet often will these gifts come to us for our own good and thus are they blessings indeed. The line *Eh bhi dāt teri dātār* says this precisely, that when these troubles come they are a gift from God. In fact, these lines are a good description of the true devotee's approach to his life. In whatever condition the Lord chooses to keep his devotee, whatever he chooses to bestow is to be accepted willingly as a gift from the Lord. Thus is born contentment – *Santokh* - which is an ideal the Guru repeatedly recommends.

In the tenth and eleventh lines the Guru says that the liberation from the cycle of birth and re-birth comes only through the Lord's grace; there is none else who can even speak of it. This liberation is the ultimate aim of the seeker in Sikhism, as indeed it is in all Eastern religions. Liberation means escape from this cycle; it means the re-union of the individual soul with the Lord, after which all earthly travails cease. How does this come? Only through the Grace of the Lord, when He chooses to bestow it, and in what fashion He decides to do so. It is the seeker's duty to work hard to prepare himself to be worthy, and the prescribed key here is total self-surrender. However high and spiritually elevated a person may become yet is it not in his own hands to stand up and claim that he is now worthy of and ready for salvation. None can say when this happy moment will occur. Only the Lord knows, only He decides whom He has so chosen. The Lord will, at His own pleasure, turn the glance of benediction, of grace on his devotee; and when that happens, instantaneously will the soul be liberated from its bondage to time and space; and from death, and birth and re-births. To quote Prof. Talib, "The attainment of liberation is a primal mystery which by no effort may be forced. Nor can man know how this blessing descends."

In the twelfth and thirteenth lines the Guru expounds further on the foolishness of trying to explain the process of liberation of the soul in any other way. He says if some fool were to dabble in it he shall soon know how he is punished. *Munh* means face and this line literally means 'he will know how many blows he will suffer on his face'. The Guru is saying that such efforts are quite obviously an exercise in *haumai*, and we must not try to even claim to know how the Divine Mind works, or how the Lord's order will work in this highest mystery of all. The punishment for such hubris will be the displeasure of the Lord, resulting in distance from Him which is the most severe punishment possible for a devotee. Prof. Sahib Singh has explained it slightly differently. He says if some fool attempts to determine some other method then he only knows how much suffering this foolishness will bring him. He renders the previous two lines to mean that the liberation from the bonds of Māya can come only by living in accordance with His will. No way other than living by His will can be said to be efficacious.

The word *khāyak* in the thirteenth line is rendered as 'fool'. Bhai Vir Singh in his commentary translates it as 'fool' but adds that the line could also be attempted as *Je ko khāye ku ākhaṇ pāye,* thus separating the word *khāyak* (ਖਾਇਕੁ) into *khāye ku* (ਖਾਇ ਕੁ). This would translate as 'having eaten', rendering the line to indicate as if someone were to 'eat and then speak of it'. However, the word has also been used by the Guru in *Vār Sri Rāg Mahla* 1 at page 83, SGGS, where he says, *Dīdār pūray pāyesa thāo nāhin khāyeka.* The term 'ਖਾਇਕੁ' - *khāyak* is again used pejoratively here as referring to those who make tall claims without substance. Prof. Sahib Singh also translates it as: "persons lacking in solidity". The more appealing therefore is 'fools', or as Prof. Talib says 'reprobate'.

In the fourteenth and fifteenth lines the Guru says that the Lord alone knows the real worth of the individual and only He can determine who deserves what and He accordingly rewards each one of us. However, there are few who express gratitude for what they receive. These lines have again been variously understood. Prof. Sahib Singh translates it as, "Not every one is ungrateful and many are there who say that the Immortal One himself knows the needs of men and gifts them accordingly." The first of these two lines is almost uniformly agreed upon in its interpretation; that the Lord alone knows the needs of His created beings and he accordingly gives to each what they deserve. The fifteenth line is seen differently. The words *Se bhi keyi kay* (ਕੇਈ ਕੇਇ) in this view are seen as 'ਕੇਈ ਕੇਇ' - *keyi kay* - meaning a few only, the rare ones. Prof. Sahib Singh calls it 'many people'. Similarly, 'ਸਿ ਭਿ' - *se bhi* - can mean 'even this' or 'even those'. In the context of the *Bāṇi*, the more appropriate translation would be that 'few are those who acknowledge this truth'. This is also the interpretation most commentators, other than Prof. Sahib Singh, have adopted. The enlightened ones in this world are few indeed, and many are those who think they are themselves the cause of what happens. The common fallacy we all suffer from is the illusion that our fate is in our own hands. We strive mightily and look for commensurate results immediately. Of course the knowledge is often then knocked into us the hard way by the buffeting we receive at the hands of events, but most of us stubbornly keep denying the reality. There are few indeed who have the good sense to accept that what we receive is what our actions, our *karma* over the ages and re-birth, has made us entitled to. The Lord alone knows the sum total of those actions, that *karma*, and the Lord alone can determine what we deserve. Few indeed are those whose eyes are opened sufficiently to see this. The sense of these lines is that the Guru wants us to be ever conscious of this and to always render gratitude to the Lord for whatever He chooses to give us. For what He gives us will always be befitting, and in accordance with our real worth. It is also a gift of love from the all-compassionate Lord and is meant to guide us on the right path towards Him.

In the last two lines, the sixteenth and seventeenth, the Guru brings us to the focus of this *pauṛi*. What gift is the most valuable of all, what is it that we should wish for above all. It is an unfortunate reality that most of us do not realize that the Lord, our Creator, knows more than anyone what is best for us. In a state of complete self-surrender the question of seeking anything other than His blessings will just not arise. However, human as we are, and easily beguiled by the glitter of Māya in the midst of which we are placed, we tend to adopt wrong ways, and our prayers almost always turn to seeking more material possessions and worldly success. The Guru has in this *pauṛi* itself given the example of those seeking unmatched valour. Such warriors, if they then turn their attention to using that Might to personal advantage, will have lost their way. If, on the other hand, in a spirit of surrender, they use that prowess for the Lord's purpose – to help the oppressed, to right the wrongs – then the blessing will bring them closer to the Lord. What happens to all of us almost uniformly is that personal wealth, power, good health, comfort and success in worldly pursuits become almost the only things we pray for. The right prayer for us must be to seek the gift of His name. The material gifts we seek will only engender more *haumai* through greed for even more. Accept that He knows what is best for us and let Him decide what material gifts He may choose to give us. Then accept these happily and without demur. If there is any one thing we must insist upon in our prayers it is the gift of singing His praises. For, in these last lines the Guru says the one on whom the Lord has conferred the benediction of singing His praises, which is to say the gift of true devotion to Him, becomes like a king of kings. The ability to devote oneself to Him and to sing His praises is also but a gift from the Lord. Seek always in your prayers this greatest of all gifts. Not material wealth or power will make you great but it is this great gift that will elevate you above all men, in this world and, more importantly, will it bring you true honour in the Divine Presence.

31

PRICELESS IS HIS NAME

Pauṛi 26

ਅਮੁਲ ਗੁਣ ਅਮੁਲ ਵਾਪਾਰ ।।	*Amul guṇ amul vāpār.*
ਅਮੁਲ ਵਾਪਾਰੀਏ ਅਮੁਲ ਭੰਡਾਰ ।।	*Amul vāpārīye amul bhanddār.*
ਅਮੁਲ ਆਵਹਿ ਅਮੁਲ ਲੈ ਜਾਹਿ ।।	*Amul āveh amul lai jāhe.*
ਅਮੁਲ ਭਾਇ ਅਮੁਲਾ ਸਮਾਹਿ ।।	*Amul bhaye amula samāhe.*
ਅਮੁਲੁ ਧਰਮੁ ਅਮੁਲੁ ਦੀਬਾਣੁ ।।	*Amul dharam amul dībāṇ.*
ਅਮੁਲੁ ਤੁਲੁ ਅਮੁਲੁ ਪਰਵਾਣੁ ।।	*Amul tul amul parvāṇ.*
ਅਮੁਲੁ ਬਖਸੀਸ ਅਮੁਲੁ ਨੀਸਾਣੁ ।।	*Amul bakhsīs amul nīsāṇ.*
ਅਮੁਲੁ ਕਰਮੁ ਅਮੁਲੁ ਫੁਰਮਾਣੁ ।।	*Amul karam amul phurmāṇ.*
ਅਮੁਲੋ ਅਮੁਲੁ ਆਖਿਆ ਨ ਜਾਇ ।।	*Amulo amul ākhiya na jāye.*
ਆਖਿ ਆਖਿ ਰਹੇ ਲਿਵ ਲਾਇ ।।	*Ākh ākh rahay liv lāye.*
ਆਖਹਿ ਵੇਦ ਪਾਠ ਪੁਰਾਣ ।।	*Ākheh ved pātth purāṇ.*
ਆਖਹਿ ਪੜੇ ਕਰਹਿ ਵਖਿਆਣ ।।	*Ākheh paṛeh karay vakhiyāṇ.*
ਆਖਹਿ ਬਰਮੇ ਆਖਹਿ ਇੰਦ ।।	*Ākheh barmay ākheh ind.*
ਆਖਹਿ ਗੋਪੀ ਤੈ ਗੋਵਿੰਦ ।।	*Ākheh gopi tai govind.*
ਆਖਹਿ ਈਸਰ ਆਖਹਿ ਸਿਧ ।।	*Ākheh īssar ākheh sidh.*
ਆਖਹਿ ਕੇਤੇ ਕੀਤੇ ਬੁਧ ।।	*Ākheh ketay kītay budh.*
ਆਖਹਿ ਦਾਨਵ ਆਖਹਿ ਦੇਵ ।।	*Ākheh dānav ākheh dev.*
ਆਖਹਿ ਸੁਰਿ ਨਰ ਮੁਨਿ ਜਨ ਸੇਵ ।।	*Ākheh sur nar mun jan sev.*
ਕੇਤੇ ਆਖਹਿ ਆਖਣਿ ਪਾਹਿ ।।	*Ketay ākheh ākhaṇ pāhe.*
ਕੇਤੇ ਕਹਿ ਕਹਿ ਉਠਿ ਉਠਿ ਜਾਹਿ ।।	*Ketay kah kah utth utth jāhe.*
ਏਤੇ ਕੀਤੇ ਹੋਰਿ ਕਰੇਹਿ ।।	*Etay kītay hor kareh.*
ਤਾ ਆਖਿ ਨ ਸਕਹਿ ਕੇਈ ਕੇਇ ।।	*Ta ākh na sakeh keyi kay.*
ਜੇਵਡੁ ਭਾਵੈ ਤੇਵਡੁ ਹੋਇ ।।	*Jevadd bhāvai tevadd hoye.*

ਨਾਨਕ ਜਾਣੈ ਸਾਚਾ ਸੋਇ॥	*Nanak jāṇai sacha soye.*
ਜੇ ਕੋ ਆਖੈ ਬੋਲੁਵਿਗਾੜੁ॥	*Je ko ākhay bolvigāṛ. (25)*
ਤਾ ਲਿਖੀਐ ਸਿਰਿ ਗਾਵਾਰਾ ਗਾਵਾਰੁ॥੨੬॥	*Ta likīyai sir gāvāra gāvār.*

Brief glossary

ਅਮੁਲੁ	*Amul*	Priceless, invaluable
ਗੁਣ	*Guṇ*	Qualities, characteristics
ਵਾਪਾਰ	*Vāpār*	Trade, commerce
ਦੀਬਾਣੁ	*Dībāṇ*	Court
ਤੁਲੁ	*Tul*	Scales, balance
ਪਰਵਾਣੁ	*Parvāṇ.*	Weights, meanness
ਕਰਮੁ	*Karam*	Blessing (Also in Sanskrit – action)
ਨੀਸਾਣੁ	*Nīsāṇ*	Sign, mark
ਫੁਰਮਾਣੁ	*Phurmāṇ*	Order, dictate, ordinance
ਲਿਵ ਲਾਇ	*Liv lāye*	In ecstatic communion
ਵਖਿਆਣ	*Vakhiyāṇ*	Commentary
ਬੁਧ	*Budh*	The enlightened (not Gautam Budhha here)
ਦਾਨਵ	*Dānav*	Demons
ਦੇਵ	*Dev*	The gods
ਸੁਰਿ	*Sur*	Demi-gods
ਸੁਰਿ ਨਰ	*Sur Nar*	Men with godly qualities
ਮੁਨਿ ਜਨ	*Munn Jan*	Holy persons
ਸੇਵ	*Sev*	Those who serve
ਬੋਲਵਿਗਾੜ	*Bolvigāṛ*	One who twists words, here empty gobbler

Simply translated this *pauṛi* says that priceless are the qualities of the Lord and invaluable the trading in these, referring to those who seek God and teach and exchange knowledge of it with like-minded others who are invaluable too, as is the store of their knowledge. Invaluable are those who buy this and those who carry it away, who are in adoration of Him and are rapt in Him. Invaluable are the *dharam* and the assemblies where it is traded. Invaluable are the weights and measures for measuring this precious commodity, and priceless the benediction through which we gain it. The Lord is invaluable beyond the power to describe, and those who attempt it become totally absorbed in Him. And can no longer describe Him. Yet are the *Vedas* and *Purāṇas* describing Him and the learned discoursing about Him. Even Brahma, Indra*, Gopis* and *Govinds* speak of Him. *Īssar* and the *Sidhs* speak, as do enlightened ones. *Dānavs* and *Devtas* speak as also the *Surnar* (men of godly qualities), the *Munis* and the servants of the Lord. Many try to describe Him but their attempts are futile and they go unsuccessful from this world. Even if the Lord created as many more creatures yet would they fail to describe Him. The Lord can be as great as He may choose, so He only knows His own limits. If anyone arrogates to himself such power he will be known as the most errant fool. Let us now look at it in more detail and also see what the learned ones have said on the subject.

From *pauṛi* 22 to this, the twenty-sixth *pauṛi*, the Guru has told us repeatedly of the awesome greatness of the Lord. In the twenty-second and twenty-third *pauṛi* we were told of the vastness of His creation, and then in the twenty-fourth *pauṛi* the things that exist in this immeasurably vast universe were enumerated. The many earthly gifts men seek were referred to in the twenty-fifth *pauṛi*; also mentioned was how men are seeking constantly from the Lord and how eternal is this grant of gifts even though we foolish men don't always express proper gratitude. Now in the twenty-sixth *pauṛi* the Guru goes a step beyond the material things and touches upon the high moral values. The thrust of the lessons in all these *pauṛis* is to generate in our minds awe, love and devotion for the Lord and to turn us towards the reciting of His name which alone is the path to salvation. Having attended to all these aspects the Guru will in the next *pauṛi*, the twenty-seventh, give us an overview of the Divine Court.

In this *pauṛi*, in the first and second lines, the Guru speaks of the Lord and says 'priceless are His qualities'. No human mind can put a value on these. There are, however, many who seek after Him and try to learn of these qualities. They exchange this knowledge; they talk of it; they learn and they teach. This is the *vāpār* – the trading the Guru refers to here. He says not only are the Lord's qualities invaluable, but also is invaluable this trading that occurs among the devotees. As invaluable is this trade, says the Guru. Not only the trade but also the fortunate ones who do this trade are beyond value. The *bhanddār* (treasure) of these godly qualities is also beyond value. The word 'traders' used here is likely to be a little hard to understand. Trade usually carries a sense of profit taking and of greed and material advantages. What is this trade and traders the Guru has in view? Obviously here this refers to those who speak the name of the Lord, who write about it and take the message to as many as they can. They are the dealers, the traders in this holy commerce. The Guru says that since their choice of the commodity is beyond price, they themselves attain the same value. The stores of this commodity, the singing of praises and exalting the Lord's name, is also then equally valuable.

The commodity spoken of in these two lines is abstract and there cannot be a normal market where such sale or purchase could be carried out. This commodity is then obtainable only in the courts of holiness where the *dharam* is to trade in these goods. These are the places, the houses of God, the meeting places of the devotees where seekers congregate.

In the third to fifth lines this thought is further expounded by the Guru. He says invaluable are those who come to purchase this commodity and priceless those who carry some of it away with them. Invaluable is the *dharam* and priceless the court. Bhai Vir Singh has interpreted it to say that these courts are the assemblies where true Sikhs congregate and where the exchange and trading of these goods then takes place. Both these, the *dharam* and the courts, are priceless. Other commentators have taken a more direct interpretation to render this fifth line, that invaluable is His justice and invaluable His court where it is dispensed. Since the Guru is here teaching us to train ourselves to seek the Lord, the reference has to be to humans who are engaged in this most proper endeavour and therefore Bhai Vir Singh's rendering would appear more convincing.

In the sixth to eighth lines the Guru further says that invaluable are the weights and the measures by which this precious commodity is measured and disbursed. Since the commodity we are talking about is not of this world and since it is not even ours to take at will, the Guru says priceless is the *bakhsīs* – the benediction through which we gain access to it. It is the belief that on our foreheads is embossed the mark of this approval, visible only to the mystic eye. Only when His glance of grace turns on us, and when He gives us His benediction that this priceless commodity becomes accessible to us. Further, he says invaluable is *karam* (His grace), and invaluable the *phurmāṇ* (His ordinance). The grace referred to here is obviously the grace by which the mark of the Lord's benediction is embossed on our foreheads. The ordinance is the order by which the system of this universe operates under the will of the Lord.

In the ninth and tenth lines, the Guru says He is invaluable beyond all power to describe. Those who have attempted to speak of it have tried unsuccessfully and their efforts end up in their becoming totally absorbed in Him and with that their attempts at description too come to an end. It actually is quite a 'Catch 22' situation when it comes to speaking of the Lord. We who are in this world cannot express in words anything about Him who is Infinite and much beyond this world. To know about Him we have to constantly recite His name, sing His praises and try to develop unshakeable faith in Him. When the rare few do succeed in this endeavour they will rise to the level where they will become one with Him. Now they are no longer of this world and their effort to explain Him to us becomes the *gūngay ki mitthīāyi* (the man without speech seeking to describe the sweetness of what he has greatly enjoyed). The attempt at description thus just cannot succeed.

In the eleventh and twelfth lines, the Guru says, even though it is impossible to describe Him yet there are many who talk of Him. He says, the *Vedas* talk of Him. In spite of the impossibility of measuring Him, evaluating Him or describing His qualities, the effort yet goes on. Not only the *Vedas* – the ancient holy texts – but all religious prayers, the 'ਪਾਠ' – *pātth* -, and all *Purān. as* speak about Him. Not only do these scriptures speak of Him but many learned ones give *Vakhiyān.* (commentaries). In this manner the holy scriptures seek to try and explain Him; those learned ones who have studied these and expostulated on these are also speaking of Him, in spite of the impossibility of really describing Him.

In the thirteenth and fourteenth lines, the Guru says not only the scriptures but His divine creatures also are engaged in the same activity and also speak of Him. Thus are Brahma, through whom the Lord gets the process of creation carried out, and Indra, who is the king of the various gods created by Him, speaking of Him. *Gopis* and *Govinds* speak of Him. *Govind* is a name used by the devotees for the Lord, but it is used also for Lord Krishna, an incarnation, or *avatār* of Lord Vishnu, in the Hindu belief system, who is part of the holy trinity and who is charged by the Lord Himself with preserving the system of the world, the universe. In the Krishna *avatār*, *Govind* indulged in the mystical *rās līla* (play of love with the *Gopis*; literally the cowherd girls, the milkmaids). The *Gopi* has come to symbolize true devotion and the *Gopi* and *Govind* relationship signifies the divine relationship between the mortal and the Lord. The Guru says that the *Gopis* and *Govind* also speak of Him.

In the fifteenth and sixteenth lines, the Guru lists some more divine beings who are talking of Him. He says Īssar and the *Sidhs* do so. Īssar is a name used for Lord Shiva, the third member of the trinity of Brahma, Vishnu, Mahesh (Shiva). Shiva is the member whose charge it is to bring about the dissolution of the world when the Lord so wishes. *Sidh* is used to describe an adept who has through esoteric practices achieved power over nature. Beyond them, says the Guru, are the many *Budh* (enlightened ones) created by Him. The word *Budh* is used also for Gautama Budhha, the prince after whom Budhhism is named. Commentators have taken either meaning. Prof. Sahib Singh, Narain Singh and Dr. Sangat Singh take the reference here as to Gautam, the Budhha. Prof. Talib, Iqbal Singh and Bhai Vir Singh have used it as 'the enlightened'. Both renderings would seem to apply here. Since the Guru is talking of the Brahmas, Vishnus, Īssars, Indras, *Govind* and *Gopis* he could be listing the Budhha among them in the same context. Gautam, known as Prince Siddharth in his early years, was born in 624 BCE to King Sudhodhan and Māyadevi of Kapilvastu. He was married to Princess Gopa and had a son who was named Rahul. At the age of 28, he took *sanyās*, renouncing the world, and through long austerities achieved enlightenment at Gaya and was thereafter known as the Budhha. He passed from this world at the age of 80. Budhhism is the religion followed by his numerous followers, concentrated today mainly in East Asian countries. However, the Hindus have, true to the Hindu practice, incorporated him and he is also an *avatār* of Vishnu in Hinduism. However, the rendering as 'the learned' seems here the more appealing. The Guru is saying that the many *Budh* – the learned ones, enlightened ones, also speak of Him.

In the seventeenth and eighteenth lines, the Guru lists the *Devtas* and their opponents, the *Asuras*. It may be of interest to see how the *Dānavs* and *Devas* are viewed in mythology and how they came into being. The *Encyclopedia Britannica* (15th edition) has the following to say about the *Deva*:

"*Deva* (San-skrit: 'divine'), Iranian *Daeva*, in *Vedic* India, one of the many divine powers, roughly divided on the basis of their identification with the forces of nature into sky, air and earth divinities (e.g., Vāruṇa, Indra, Soma). In the later monotheistic systems, the *Devas* became subordinate to the one Supreme Being. During the Vedic period, the gods were divided into two classes – the *Devas* and the *Asuras* (in Iranian, *Daevas* and *Asuras*). In India the *Devas* came to be more powerful than the *Asuras*, and the latter word took on the meaning of demon. In Iran the reverse took place, and the *Daevas* were denounced as demons by Zoroaster. They still survive as such in the *Divs* of Persian folklore, especially through Ferdowsi's epic *Shah-nameh* (1010; *Book of Kings*)."

The common belief in Hindu mythology is that the *Dānavs* and the *Daityas*, both classified as *Asuras*, were the progeny of the great sage Kashyap and their mothers were *Dānu* and *Diti,* two daughters of *Prajāpati* Daksh. The *Daityas* were titanic in stature while the *Dānavs* were of normal proportions. Both are the epitome of the baser instincts of mankind. *Devtas* are, on the other hand, in Hindu mythology, a class of divine beings believed to stand for goodness, and therefore are accorded worship. The *Asuras* are, as we have seen above, their counterparts believed mainly to be standing for evil. The Guru says that both these categories sing of Him. The *Dānavs* were the progeny of the great sage Kashyap and thus divine in their own right. They too sing of the Lord, because they are after all the Lord's creation. That they are the manifestation of the aggressive and brutal aspects of man's nature is part of the mystery of creation. Their purpose in this universe is known best to the Lord Himself. They are not, for all the baseness attributed to them, any the less the Lord's own. The Guru says that the *Dānavs* sing of Him too as do the *Devas*. Thus in the same line are spoken of the power-seeking *Dānavs* and their eternal opponents, the *Devas* whose lord is Indra. The Guru says that both equally express His greatness. Not only these semi-divine and super-human creatures are listed but the Guru also adds to this list the humans with godly qualities. He says the *Sur-nar* sing of Him. This word literally means 'devta-man'. *Devta* is the term for the semi-divine dwellers of the Upper Regions. This term is rendered by learned commentators either as *devtas* and men both sing of Him' or, probably more correctly, as 'the men with qualities like devtas sing of Him', which refers to the pious, the saintly, the ones who have controlled their baser natures. Similarly, *Mun-jan* in line 18 is a composite word meaning men who have become *Munis*. These *Munis* were the hermits who withdrew from the world of men and often retired to distant and lonely hermitages devoting themselves to severe self-discipline to acquire control over their minds, and acquiring mystical powers and spiritual merit. These ascetics and hermits were highly regarded. The Guru says these holy persons also talk, or sing, of Him. The last word in the eighteenth line, 'ਸੇਵ' – *sev* - is generally translated as servant or votary. Bhai Vir Singh in his commentary on the *Japji Sahib* has translated it as a follower of Jainism. He says it is an abbreviation from 'ਸਵੇਤਾਂਬਰੀ' (*svetambari*), meaning literally white-clothed, one of the sects of the Jains, distinguished by the completely white attire they always sport. However, the more common rendering, i.e., servant, votary or devotee seems here the more appropriate. The sense here is clear beyond any doubt. The Guru is saying that the followers and adherents of the various systems, sects, religions, as also persons and creatures of all types, lowly or high, demonic or saintly, all are speaking about Him.

In the nineteenth and twentieth lines, the Guru says that all these creatures attempt to describe Him, through talking of Him or singing His praises. There are so many making this attempt but in the end they do not succeed and go from this world still making the attempt but having found no way to really describe Him. It is noteworthy that among this list of the ones who are making this futile attempt the Guru lists all the great ones, human or divine. He lists the most learned and spiritually exalted among the humans. He lists the gods and he even lists the holy trinity of Brahma, Vishnu and Mahesh *(*Shiva*)*. The

Guru's world view here is clearly visualizing a Creator who is unique all by Himself, and who has no equal. The world operates as per His command as prescribed by Him through His will and as per His scheme of things. All commonly understood powers come within the ambit of this. The Holy Trinity is seen as the prime operative for the practical operation of the Lord's will. They do the creating and the preserving but the entire process is governed by the Lord Himself and they operate within, and as per, the limits He has set. Thus, Brahma cannot be the destroyer, nor can Shiva become the preserver. The lesser beings, gods like Indra included, are subordinate to this trinity and in this fashion does the universe function. None of these can hope to know the size, the shape and the description of the Creator who brought it all into being, and who sets the rules, the limits for it to operate.

In the twenty-first and twenty-second lines, the Guru goes a step further to make this point. Since the universe, this creation, is infinite the created beings spoken of in the previous lines are also equally beyond any count. The Guru says that all these together cannot succeed in knowing Him. Not only these but if the Lord were to create as many more similar creatures, even then will all of them not be able to speak of Him, or in other words He shall remain as inscrutable no matter how many persons or powers make the effort to decipher Him.

In lines twenty-third and twenty-fourth, the Guru gives another explanation of why such attempts are bound to fail. The determining of an entity's measure is possible when it has dimensions that are fixed. Here, the Guru says, we are talking of Him who has no fixed determinants. The Lord is as great as He wishes to be. Who outside of Him exists who could define Him by numbers or figures? The Guru says the only one who can then do proper justice and honour to the description is the Lord Himself. The word used here is 'ਸਾਚਾ' – *sācha* - or the True One. This is in the context of the Lord as the only, the Ultimate

Reality. All else is but a reflection of Him and has no existence independent of Him.

In the last two lines, the twenty-fifth and twenty-sixth, the Guru sums up to say that the above is the Ultimate Reality and if any human seeks to arrogate to himself the power of such description then he will but be known as 'ਗਾਵਾਰਾ ਗਾਵਾਰੁ' - *gāvāra gāvār* - or the most arrant of fools. While we know that invaluable are the qualities of the Lord and that a vast multitude of great ones, human and divine, are attempting to describe Him, we can be sure that none can succeed in really describing Him. The Lord is not a fixed measurable entity but rather has as much greatness as it may please Him to attain; and He is ever beyond comprehension.

32

THE COURT DIVINE

Pauṛi 27

ਸੋ ਦਰੁ ਕੇਹਾ ਸੋ ਘਰੁ ਕੇਹਾ ਜਿਤੁ ਬਹਿ ਸਰਬ ਸਮਾਲੇ॥
So dar keha so ghar keha jit beh sarab samālay.

ਵਾਜੇ ਨਾਦ ਅਨੇਕ ਅਸੰਖਾ ਕੇਤੇ ਵਾਵਣਹਾਰੇ॥
Vājay nād anek asankha ketay vāvaṇhāray.

ਕੇਤੇ ਰਾਗ ਪਰੀ ਸਿਉ ਕਹੀਅਨਿ ਕੇਤੇ ਗਾਵਣਹਾਰੇ॥
Ketay rāg pari siu kahīan ketay gāvaṇhāray.

ਗਾਵਹਿ ਤੁਹਨੋ ਪਉਣੁ ਪਾਣੀ ਬੈਸੰਤਰੁ ਗਾਵੈ ਰਾਜਾ ਧਰਮੁ ਦੁਆਰੇ॥
Gāveh tuhno pauṇ pāṇi baisantar gāvai rāja dharam duāray.

ਗਾਵਹਿ ਚਿਤੁ ਗੁਪਤੁ ਲਿਖਿ ਜਾਣਹਿ ਲਿਖਿ ਲਿਖਿ ਧਰਮੁ ਵੀਚਾਰੇ॥
Gāveh Chit Gupt likh jaṇeh likh likh dharam vīchāray.

ਗਾਵਹਿ ਈਸਰੁ ਬਰਮਾ ਦੇਵੀ ਸੋਹਨਿ ਸਦਾ ਸਵਾਰੇ॥
Gāveh Īssar Barma Devi sohan sada sawāray.

ਗਾਵਹਿ ਇੰਦ ਇਦਾਸਣਿ ਬੈਠੇ ਦੇਵਤਿਆ ਦਰਿ ਨਾਲੇ॥
Gāveh Ind indāsaṇ baitthay devtia dar nālay.

ਗਾਵਹਿ ਸਿਧ ਸਮਾਧੀ ਅੰਦਰਿ ਗਾਵਨਿ ਸਾਧ ਵਿਚਾਰੇ॥
Gāveh sidh samādhi andar gāvan sādh vichāray.

ਗਾਵਨਿ ਜਤੀ ਸਤੀ ਸੰਤੋਖੀ ਗਾਵਹਿ ਵੀਰ ਕਰਾਰੇ॥
Gāvan jati sati santokhi gāveh vīr karāray.

ਗਾਵਨਿ ਪੰਡਿਤ ਪੜਨਿ ਰਖੀਸਰ ਜੁਗੁ ਜੁਗੁ ਵੇਦਾ ਨਾਲੇ॥
Gāvan pandit paṛan rakhīsar jug jug veda nālay.

ਗਾਵਹਿ ਮੋਹਣੀਆ ਮਨੁ ਮੋਹਨਿ ਸੁਰਗਾ ਮਛ ਪਇਆਲੇ॥
Gāveh mohṇīya man(u) mohan surga machh payiālay.

ਗਾਵਨਿ ਰਤਨ ਉਪਾਏ ਤੇਰੇ ਅਠਸਠਿ ਤੀਰਥ ਨਾਲੇ॥	*Gāvan ratan upāye tere atthsathh tīrath nālay.*
ਗਾਵਹਿ ਜੋਧ ਮਹਾਬਲ ਸੂਰਾ ਗਾਵਹਿ ਖਾਣੀ ਚਾਰੇ॥	*Gāveh jodh mahābal sūra gāveh khāṇi chāray.*
ਗਾਵਹਿ ਖੰਡ ਮੰਡਲ ਵਰਭੰਡਾ ਕਰਿ ਕਰਿ ਰਖੇ ਧਾਰੇ॥	*Gāveh khandd manddal varbhandda kar kar rakhay dhāray.*
ਸੇਈ ਤੁਧੁਨੋ ਗਾਵਹਿ ਜੋ ਤੁਧੁ ਭਾਵਨਿ ਰਤੇ ਤੇਰੇ ਭਗਤ ਰਸਾਲੇ॥	*Seyi tudhno gāveh jo tudh bhāvan ratay teray bhagat rasālay. (15)*
ਹੋਰੀ ਕੇਤੇ ਗਾਵਨਿ ਸੇ ਮੈ ਚਿਤਿ ਨ ਆਵਨਿ ਨਾਨਕੁ ਕਿਆ ਵੀਚਾਰੇ॥	*Hor ketay gāvan se mai chit na āvan Nanak kia vīchāray.*
ਸੋਈ ਸੋਈ ਸਦਾ ਸਚੁ ਸਾਹਿਬੁ ਸਾਚਾ ਸਾਚੀ ਨਾਈ॥	*Soyi soyi sada sach sahib sācha sāchi nāyi.*
ਹੈ ਭੀ ਹੋਸੀ ਜਾਇ ਨ ਜਾਸੀ ਰਚਨਾ ਜਿਨਿ ਰਚਾਈ॥	*Hai bhi hosi jāye na jāsi rachna jin rachāyi.*
ਰੰਗੀ ਰੰਗੀ ਭਾਤੀ ਕਰਿ ਕਰਿ ਜਿਨਸੀ ਮਾਇਆ ਜਿਨਿ ਉਪਾਈ॥	*Rangi rangi bhāti kar kar jinsi māya jin upāyi.*
ਕਰਿ ਕਰਿ ਵੇਖੈ ਕੀਤਾ ਆਪਣਾ ਜਿਵ ਤਿਸ ਦੀ ਵਡਿਆਈ॥	*Kar kar vekhai kīta āpṇa jiv tis di vaddīāyi. (20)*
ਜੋ ਤਿਸੁ ਭਾਵੈ ਸੋਈ ਕਰਸੀ ਹੁਕਮੁ ਨ ਕਰਣਾ ਜਾਈ॥	*Jo tis bhāvai soyi karsi hukam na karṇa jāyi.*
ਸੋ ਪਾਤਿਸਾਹੁ ਸਾਹਾ ਪਾਤਿਸਾਹਿਬੁ ਨਾਨਕ ਰਹਣੁ ਰਜਾਈ॥੨੭॥	*So pātsāh saha pātsāhib Nanak rahaṇ rajāyi.*

Brief glossary

ਦਰੁ	*Dar*	Gate, abode
ਸਮਾਲੇ	*Samālay*	Taking care
ਰਾਗ ਪਰੀ	*Rāg pari*	*Rāgas* and their *rāginis*
ਵਾਵਣਹਾਰੇ	*Vāvaṇhāray.*	Players of music
ਪੰਡਿਤ	*Pandit*	Learned, knowledgeable
ਬੈਸੰਤਰੁ	*Baisantar*	Fire
ਚਿਤੁ ਗੁਪਤੁ	*Chit gupt*	Recording angel
ਦੇਵੀ	*Devi*	Consort of *Shiva*, the female divine principle
ਇਦਾਸਣਿ	*Indāsan*	*Indra's* throne

ਰਖੀਸਰ	*Rakhīsar*	Great *rishi* (literally, god of *rishis)*
ਮੋਹਣੀਆ	*Mohṇīya*	*Apsaras* (celestial beauties, attendants of Indra's court)
ਸੁਰਗਾ	*Surga*	In the heaven
ਮਛ	*Machh*	Earth, the middle regions
ਪਇਆਲੇ	*Payiālay*	Nether worlds
ਰਤਨ ਉਪਾਏ	*Rattan upāye*	Jewels created
ਖਾਣੀ ਚਾਰੇ	*Khāṇi chāray*	The four sources of life
ਖੰਡ ਮੰਡਲ	*Khandd manddal*	Continents and worlds
ਵਰਭੰਡਾ	*Varbhandda*	The universe
ਧਾਰੇ	*Dhāray*	Supported, sustained
ਭਗਤ ਰਸਾਲੇ	*Bhagat rasālay*	Devotees absorbed in Him
ਜਿਨਸੀ	*Jinsi*	Species
ਮਾਇਆ	*Māya*	Here creation
ਪਾਤਿਸਾਹਿਬੁ	*Pātsāhib*	Emperor
ਰਜਾਈ	*Rajāyi*	His will

Simply translated this *pauṛi* starts with the oft-raised query as to which is the divine abode and the portal where the Lord sits and tends to the entire creation. The Guru says countless musical instruments, *rāgas* and *rāginis* play in His domain; and countless are the musicians. The winds, the waters and the fires all sing to Him. Dharamrāj and the recorder *Chitragupt* who presents the details of our deeds also sing at His door. *Īssar* and *Devi*, effulgent with His grace, sing to Him. Indra on his throne with the *Devtas* under him also similarly sings. The *sidh* in his *samādhi* (concentrated meditation) and the *sādh* (saintly men) ponder about him and thus sing. The *jati* (men of continence), *sati* (those who give with open heart), and the *santokhi* (contented ones), as also the great warriors, sing to Him. The learned *pandits*, the highest *rishis*, along with their *Vedas*, all sing to Him throughout the ages. The celestial beauties of all the regions sing; heavens, earth and the nether regions sing to Him; the jewels created by Him and the 68 holy places of pilgrimage sing to Him; mighty warriors and created beings from all the four sources sing to Him; the lands, continents and the entire universe which He has created and is supporting sing to Him. Only such can sing to Him who is the recipient of His pleasure. Beyond these listed here are many, the Guru says he cannot even recall, who also sing to Him. The Lord is the Eternal Reality, the True Master and true is His greatness. He is, He will be. He is the One Constant and He is the Creator of all there is. Multifarious are the types of things created by His Māya. Having created it He now watches over it at His pleasure. His actions are not subject to any outside command and He creates as He wills or as He pleases. He is the true Sovereign, King of kings and we must live in obedience to Him. We can in this light now look at the message in more detail and also see what the learned ones have said.

In the previous three *pauṛis*, the twenty-fourth to twenty-sixth, the Guru has narrated for us the impossibility of measuring or describing the Lord. Having told us about the incomparable, indescribable greatness of the Lord and the impossibility of ever finding His measure, the Guru now gives us his own vision of that Magnificence. It is, however, in the form of a question that often agitates the minds of spiritual seekers. In answering that question the Guru has in this *pauṛi* composed a truly magnificent paean to the Divine encompassing in one vision a vast universe consisting of the biggest and the small eternally singing to Him. Our very existence in full accord with the Lord's divine will is our song of praise to Him. This paean is repeated again in the evening prayer, the *Rahrās*. It also occurs again on page 347 of the *SGGS* in the *Rāg Āsa.* There are minor differences in the spelling of the words in all these three cases but none such as to make a material difference to the meaning or to the sense of the high devotion contained in this laudation by the exalted devotee to the True One.

In the first line the Guru exclaims in awe and wonder, and says: "What is the Divine Portal, the Divine Abode where thy seat is located and from where you sit and tend to this entire Creation." The word 'ਦਰ' – *dar* – literally means door or gate. It very often also metaphorically denotes the house or the abode itself. The term 'ਸਰਬ ਸਮਾਲੇ' - *sarb samālay* - literally means 'supports all'. Here, the reference is to the entire creation which is not only supported but has been brought into existence, given the frame work and the laws for its functioning; and also the whole complex interplay of massive forces, as well as the human interactions which the Lord has ensured take place smoothly, and eternally. The awesome Lord who has engendered this mighty piece of work is being spoken of here. How, says the Guru, and from which abode, is this wonder worked? Obviously there is no single abode in the human sense, for the Lord, as the Guru has told us, is Transcendent but, also Immanent in all His creation. Then the nurture and the care are occurring as a part of the Lord's will, present everywhere. The Guru, speaking as a human, in love and wonder imputes human characteristics such as an earthly ruler would have. Note that in answering the question the Guru goes on to describe in sublime poetical imagery the court where the vast creation, each and every part of it, is paying homage to the Lord eternally.

In the second and third lines, the Guru says that within His domain, and singing of His wonders, are the endless *nād* (musical instruments). Innumerable are the *rāgas* and *rāginis* and innumerable the *vāvaṇhāray* (musicians) who sing symphonies to Him. The *rāga* is a term used to describe a classical measure of musical notes and *rāgini* is used to describe the consort of a *rāga*, i.e., a variation within the metrical measure of a *rāga* used to compose music. The word used is ਪਰੀ - *pari* - meaning consort, or here *rāgini*. The Guru is using the term *rāga* not merely as a system of musical notes but as the melody personified. Each *rāga* and *rāgini* in the common Indian belief is given specific characteristics, and often there are paintings depicting these *rāgas* and *rāgini* in human form. All these *rāgas* and *rāgini* are being referred to here as their personification, each singing hymns to Him. Similarly are musical instruments personified as the divine sound resounding through the players in eternal paeans to Him.

In the fourth and fifth lines, and in the many lines thereafter, the Guru returns to listing the many mighty ones, and many forces of nature as sitting in this court and singing praises to Him. Here he says among those who sing to Him are the *pāṇi* (ਪਾਣੀ) - water, the *pauṇ* (ਪਉਣੁ) - winds, and *baisantar* (ਬੈਸੰਤਰੁ) - fire. Dharamrāj also sits at this portal and sings eulogies. *Chitragupt*, who records human actions for presentation before Dharamrāj for judging a man's worth at the end of this life, also sing to Him. In the Hindu cosmology Dharamrāj is the divine personage vested by the Lord with the duty and the authority to judge the worth of a man's action performed in this world. *Chitragupt* is the watcher who is given the duty of actually recording the details of our actions, both overt and secret. In Hindu mythology *Chitragupt* is taken as the son of Brahma whose sole duty is the recording of men's actions. While in mythology he is definitely one person, some commentators among the Sikhs for some reason have taken to saying that Chitra and Gupt are two separate entities, *Chitra* meaning image or something visible while *Gupt* means secret. So it is among these commentators believed that the entity *Chitra* sees and records the overt actions and deeds, while *Gupt* is empowered to see within men and know their secret thoughts and the evils which they may not have indulged in but thought about. This interpretation probably evolved from the Muslim belief of there being two recording angels sitting one on each of our shoulders. Of course, whether *Chitragupt* is one or two entities does not in the least alter the Guru's message in this line. Dharamrāj, along with his aide *Chitragupt*, is pictured as singing to Him. Thus, in these lines are listed the mightiest forces of nature such as water, wind and fire personified, who along with Dharamrāj all sit in attendance to Him singing His eulogies.

In lines sixth and seventh, the Guru lists the other mighty

powers that can be called the guardian powers. The operation of the Lord's domain is in the charge of these super entities created by Him. The Guru says singing to Him are *Īssar*, Brahma and Devi, who are shining with the effulgence granted to them by the Lord. Also singing similarly, the Guru says, is Lord Indra sitting on his throne along with his attendant *Devtas*. *Īssar* is another name for Lord Shiva, who personifies the destructive principle in the Holy Trinity. Brahma is of course another part of that trinity and he is charged with the duty of creation which is then preserved through Lord Vishnu the third component, not listed here but implicit, charged with preserving the creation in accordance with His will. The divine powers personified as *Devtas* are also part of the arrangement and each of them is given power over a particular element. They are then functioning under the rule of Lord Indra, who himself embodies the powers of rain, and is known as the Rain God and also as the wielder of the thunderbolt. Incidentally, the similarity in this aspect to the Norse Odin and the Greek Zeus will be noted, both of whom are the rulers of the gods in their respective pantheons and who are also wielder of thunderbolts. This Indra, the ruler of gods, along with all his court is pictured here by the Guru as engaged in eternal eulogies to Him. The word *Devi* used here in line 6 is for the goddesses, consorts of the gods. It is also used to describe the female principle of the Divine. The consort of Lord Shiva, Parvati is also by herself known by names such as *Sati* or *Devi* or *Durga*, and is often depicted as being more powerful than the gods, and is shown as coming to their aid against especially powerful foes. All these mighty ones are among the singers of His praises, sitting at His portals.

In the eighth and ninth lines, the Guru lists those who are not among the great powers or *Devtas* but are no less revered. These are the humans who have acquired great spiritual status and are to be counted as no less than the divine ones. These are, the Guru says, the *sidh*, sitting in *samādhi* (deep meditation), the *sādh* (saintly men) with minds fixed on Him. There are also the great souls, *jati* (men who have achieved continence), *sati* (who give with an open heart) and *santokhi* (those who have that great quality, contentment). Also listed by the Guru in the ninth line are the *vīr karāray* (mighty warriors). The *sidh* are a class of humans who through great austerity and self-discipline acquires powers called the eight *sidhis*, and with that the capacity to perform miracles. The *sādh* is a seeker who has control over the senses and is able to fix his mind on the Lord. The *jati* are those with superhuman control over their weaker urges – the men of complete continence. The *sati* are those free from greed, who give from the largeness of their heart without expectation of return and the *santokhi* are the contented ones. The Guru's prescription stresses this particular quality, contentment, repeatedly, for he views it as a highly desired quality without which the hunger for material goods will keep eroding our efforts towards uplifting ourselves on the path to godliness. Lastly are listed the warriors. That the qualities of bravery and valour are valued in his world view has been expressed by the Guru more than once. It obviously does not refer to just any strong fighter, as we had discussed earlier also. Consistence in construction demands that these be taken as only those warriors who take up their weapon in support of what is right. Thus, not just a man with strength and fighting ability, but rather the redoubtable hero who brings succour to those who are weak and have been wronged – those are worthy of respect as great as the *sidh*, the *sādh* and the *jati*, *sati*, and *santokhi*. The Guru lists these *vīr karāray* (the mighty warriors) as among the great and worthy ones singing His praises at His portal.

In the tenth and eleventh lines, more of the great humans are listed. There are the *pandits* (the learned ones) and the *rakhīsar* (the highest among *rishis*), along with their *Vedas* (the scriptures) who sing of Him, age after age. The *mohinis* (celestial *apsaras*) who can enchant anyone sing to Him throughout this creation – the heavens, the earth and the nether regions. The singing to the Lord here is in its own way by each category or type of being. The *pandits* sing to Him through their knowledge as do the great *rishis*, the *rakhīsars*. *Rakhīsar* is a composite word from *rishi* and *īssar*, meaning the great *rishis* or 'gods of *rishis*'. It denotes that the mode through which the mighty and greatly learned *rishi*s sing to Him is through the *Vedas*, the holy books of knowledge, from age to age. The *mohinis*, the enchanting women, also sing to Him. These are the celestial beauties (the *apsaras*) as also other women of great beauty. The *apsaras* were the beguiling beauties who resided in the court of Lord Indra and were the entertainers and dancers of the gods. They often were sent to the earth to beguile men whom the gods envied or were afraid of. When Vishwamitra, the *rāj rishi – the royal ascetic* – was attaining great powers such that Indra felt threatened, the *apsara* Maneka was sent, who successfully diverted him. These great beauties, ravishing and entrancing through their devotion to beauty, are singing to Him, says the Guru. Included in the list are other similar beauties who live in this world or in the nether worlds. This line has also been construed differently. Dr. Gopal Singh renders the second half of the fifteenth line to say that: "Sing the earth, underworlds, heavens." However, most others including Prof. Sahib Singh, Bhai Vir Singh, Doabia and Prof. Talib have viewed this complete line as integral and the reference to the various regions of creation as intended to mean that the *mohinis* of all the regions are being referred to. This seems the more appealing construction.

In the twelfth and thirteenth lines, the Guru lists some other great ones as also some wondrous things, and indeed the entire gamut of created beings. He says: "Singing to thee are the *ratan* – jewels created by You, and the sixty eight holy *Tīraths*. Supreme heroes and all the four sources of created beings sing to Thee." The jewels mentioned are taken by some commentators to mean wealth created by Him. More appropriately, and as the *Shabdarth* as also Prof. Talib say, this reference is to the mythical 'fourteen jewels' that emerged from the 'Primal Ocean' when the gods and the demons churned it with the mount *Mandara* as the churner and *Vāsuki*, the *Primal Snake* (also called *Ananta* and identified with *Shesha* on whose back Lord Vishnu reclines in the 'Primal Ocean'), as the churning cord. The mythology, in the Hindu belief system, is that the *Devtas, or devas*, and the *Asuras* jointly, soon after the beginning of creation, agreed to churn the 'Primal Ocean'. How this came about and why is a long story. Suffice it here to say that they did agree and to help them, Lord Vishnu graciously agreed to assume the *Kūrma* or Tortoise *Avatār*, the second of his Ten *Avatārs*. On his back was placed the Primal Mount *Mandara*. Since it was so huge they needed special equipment to do the operation of the churning. They prayed to the 'Primal Serpent' *Vāsuki* who accepted their request, since he was the only 'cord' long and strong enough. For a fulcrum the 'Primal Mountain' was needed and thus was *Mandara* chosen. The *Devtas* held *Vāsuki* from one end and the *Asuras* held the other end. Mighty and difficult was that churning but finally the ocean gave up its best jewels. These were the invaluable jewels numbering fourteen that emerged from this primal churning. Included in these were the miraculous cow, *Kāmdhenu* that could grant any wish; *Amrita*, the Nectar that bestows immortality; and the divine physician *Dhanwantri* who brought the science of *Āyurveda* to this world. These items and things of wonder, says the Guru, sing to Him. Similarly do the sixty-eight *Tīraths* sing. It is the Hindu belief that there are these sixty-eight *Tīraths*, special places of pilgrimage, a visit to which will wash away all sins. The Gurus of course did not sanction such beliefs and deprecated visits to *Tīraths* as a futile exercise when it is not imbued with a feeling of surrender and of total acceptance of the Lord's will. If these conditions exist then a pilgrimage is in any case quite redundant according to the Sikh belief. Further, the Guru says, the supreme warriors in their valour are singing to Him. Indeed the four *Khāṇis* all sing to Him. *Khaṇi* comes from *khāṇ*, meaning a mine or source. It was the common belief that there are four such sources of life, these being *Anddaj, jeraj, setaj, utbhuj*, literally egg born, placenta born, sweat born and earth born. In other words, the entire created world of living things is singing to Him.

In the fourteenth and fifteenth lines the Guru, having listed many living and non-living objects and personages of great worth, now sums it up. He says: "The lands, the continents, and the entire universe which you have created and are supporting sing to Thee. Only those sing to you however as win Thy pleasure and are immersed totally in Thee." The terms *Khandd* and *Manddal* are differently rendered by commentators. Iqbal Singh takes these *Khandds* as continents and *Manddal* as world. Dr. Sangat Singh renders these as: "The continents, the solar system and the galaxies." Prof. Talib renders these as "region, continents and the universe". Prof. Sahib Singh translates *Khandd* to mean part of the universe, i.e., each world, and *Manddal* as *chakar*, a circle of the universe comprising one sun and its attached worlds. He takes *varbhandd* to mean the entire universe. *Khandd* literally means portion and *manddal* is another word for the mystical *chakras* as also for division. The meaning of *varbhandd* is the same as *brahmandd* – the entire creation. Taken either way this line says that the entire creation, each and every part and portion of it, sings to Him. At the end of the list, in the fifteenth line, the concept of all attainments being a gift from the Lord is restated. The Guru says that while all these varied beings in this creation are singing to Him, only those are really enabled to sing who are fortunate enough to be the recipients of His pleasure. In other words, even devotion to Him, which could produce this eulogising, is contingent upon the Lord accepting the devotee and bestowing on him His pleasure.

In line sixteen, the Guru admits his human fallibility. He says that, exhaustive though the list may be, there are yet many others of whom he cannot even recall the details, who are singing of Him. This is a humble admission by a great seer who was a truly achieved a realized soul. He is telling us that the created universe is infinite; the created beings are beyond count and the Lord's mysteries not within human ken. There could be creations beyond whatever the Guru could himself know or enumerate. He admits that his memory is not so perfect as to be able to even recount all that the Lord has created. The Guru says that even those parts of creation which has escaped his memory and whom he cannot recall are equally singing His praises. Here again only those can sing of Him whom He has given this grace. By implication the rest are in oblivion and are lost to Him until they can raise themselves to such a level and earn that grace; be worthy of meditating on the Lord. The ones who are fortunately blessed with His grace are devotees rapt in devotion to Him and they all sing of Him.

In the seventeenth and eighteenth lines, having completed his delineation of this vast cosmos and its creatures singing in total harmony to Him, the Guru now talks directly of Him. He says He is the Eternal Reality – **'ਸਦਾ ਸਚੁ'** (*sada sach*), where *sada* means forever and *sach* means truth, both attributes used often for the description of the Unknowable. It denotes the One Reality – all else being an illusion or a reflection of Him. The Guru, to further underline this point, says He is **'ਹੈ ਭੀ ਹੋਸੀ ਜਾਇ ਨ ਜਾਸੀ'** – *Hai bhi hosi jāye na jāsi* – meaning the Lord will forever exist; He is today, and He will be tomorrow; He is not born nor will He die. *Jāye* here is used in the sense of *Janam* or birth. The Lord is not subject to the human limitation of birth, or the consequent death. The Lord is the Creator who brought all that exists into being. This is the Lord to whom the entire cosmos is singing. This is the Lord, the Guru says in the seventeenth line, who is the True Master and true is His greatness. The phrase **'ਸਾਚੀ ਨਾਈ'** - *sāchi nāyi* - used here is rendered by some as 'name', meaning His name is true. However, Prof. Sahib Singh translates *nāyi* as 'greatness' and others like Narain Singh use it similarly. This even otherwise seems the more appealing rendering and the line means that the Eternal, the True Master is the one also with the true greatness.

Humans achieve from time to time small measures of power, or wealth or stature and seek to pose as great. This is a reminder to all such that the only truly great is the Lord Himself; His greatness is the everlasting.

In the nineteenth and twentieth lines, the Guru speaks of the types of creation. He says of multifarious hues and types are the species that the Lord has through His *Māya* manifested. It is His pleasure that He thus acts and then in His greatness watches over it all. We may note that 'ਰੰਗਾ' (rung) is the word for colour. The word 'ਭਾਤੀ' – *bhāti* – means 'type' and *jinsi* of course refers to 'species'. The Lord in His own wisdom has chosen to bring into existence species each different from the other in size, shape, type and nature. He has chosen to use His Māya to manifest all these. Having brought this great and diverse universe into existence the Lord now watches over, 'ਵੇਖੈ' – *vekhai* - and cares for His creation. Why does He choose to do it? Because, says the Guru, such is His *vaddiāyi* or greatness. In other words, it is a complete mystery to us mortals and the only thing we can say is that such is His pleasure.

In the last two lines, the twenty-first and twenty-second, the Guru adds to this thought further and confirms the above view. He says the Lord has wrought all this because it so *bhāvay* - pleases Him. His actions are not subject to *hukam* or outside direction or command. There is none in existence who could control what the Lord may choose to do, or how He should manifest His will in His creation. Whatever happens is at the sole and exclusive pleasure of the Lord alone. There is none to command Him, for He is *pātsāhib* - the King of kings - the Emperor over all. Total and unquestioned is His sovereignty. He will command what He will, as He wills and when He wills. Therefore, says the Guru, *Nanak rahaṇ rajāyi* - live in total concord with His will. The lesson of this *pauṛi* is here summed up, and the lesson is the same that the Guru has told us before. Surrender yourself and mould your existence in accordance with the Lord's will. Accept Him, love

Him and do not question what or why He does what He is doing.

In this beautiful piece of inspired poetry the Guru has sketched out for us his vision of the divine abode. An abode that comprises the entire universe, an abode where His created beings big or small, mean or divine, and His created things, the world and the wondrous things therein, are all existing in total harmony entirely in character with their own given nature, treating it as the Lord's gift. Each creature, each godling and the Holy Trinity of Brahma, Vishnu and Mahesh, are all in tune with the Creator. The song of their existence is sung in complete harmony without any discordant or dissenting note. And this song is to His greatness. These all exist in total acceptance and surrender to the Lord. The Guru has used this to tell the egoistic human to see the grandeur that exists around him to experience the awe that this mighty and wonderful picturisation should evoke and to learn to emulate this great example. Live in harmony with His way, accept what He has chosen to bestow on you, and attune yourself to His will, as the mighty and the great in this universe have been doing since the day of creation, learn to move towards self-realization, towards *Moksha*, *Nirvāna*. The key, the secret is just one: live according to His will.

So we see in the last four lines of this *pauṛi* the Guru reverting to the earlier theme of the Lord being beyond comprehension. The Guru sums up that He, the Lord, is the Creator, eternally the Truth, forever the Master – the Lord. His creation has innumerable aspects, many categories and multi-farious species that He has been pleased to create. His actions are as He pleases and there is none whose command can work on Him. He is the King of all kings.

There is a belief among some that this *pauṛi* was composed by the Guru soon after he emerged from his three-day absence in the Bein River when he is believed to have been visiting the Lord. More commonly it is believed that the Guru on that occasion uttered the words: "There is no Hindu, There is no

Mussalman", when he came back from his three-day absence. In effect he was encapsulating his message of humanism and of spirituality beyond religion. When exactly was this, the twenty-seventh, *pauṛi* composed is not accurately known. Certainly this *pauṛi* could not have been meant to describe an actual scene in an actual throne room of the Creator. That interpretation would run counter to the Guru's message. The Guru has made no secret of the impossibility of ever describing or measuring the Lord. The Lord does not have dimension or a shape and can never ever be described as residing at any one place or even as having been seen by anyone, including the Guru himself. This, the Guru has himself made clear. Even Brahma, Vishnu and Mahesh have been described as unable to find His limits. To say that the Guru was describing an actual encounter would thus be negating the Guru's clear and repeated message. The real message in this *pauṛi* is of trying to raise our minds towards the Lord's awesome might by describing for us, in awe and wonder the entire gamut of creation including both living and the inorganic, the mortal as well as the divinities of ascending power who supervise the mortal world. The description includes places as also unseen planes of existence. The Guru is telling us that all these are continuing their existence in total accordance with His will and in doing so are in a state of continuing homage to the Creator. The only way we can take this to be an actual encounter is by assuming that the Lord in His pleasure chose so to manifest Himself to the Guru, which assumption is not really necessary to an understanding of the real message of this *pauṛi*.

The Guru has drawn a magnificent picture of how the entire universe of created beings, men, gods, fauna and flora, the great sages, the redoubtable warriors and all the innumerable types of living beings and powers, are in homage and supplication to the Lord. The Guru has in his vision included the created worlds, the nether regions and the heavenly regions as joining in this cosmic prayer and eulogy, thus leaving none uncovered. The

Lord's transcendent form is described by saying that He is the Eternal and the Real Truth, and that he is the only Master of this cosmic show. His immanent form is also described in the form of the material world with its multitude of beings created in a vast variety of forms and shapes as it pleased Him.

In the end the Guru has repeated his constant refrain: *Nanak rahaṇ rajāyi* - remain ever content in His will, sayeth Nanak. This is the crux of the message, occurring elsewhere also throughout the *Gurbāṇi*, and of course it found mention in the very first *pauṛi* which ended with this magic formula: *Hukam rajāyi chalṇa Nanak likhiya nāl.*

33

LESSONS FOR THE JOGIS

Pauṛi 28

ਮੁੰਦਾ ਸੰਤੋਖੁ ਸਰਮੁ ਪਤੁ ਝੋਲੀ	*Munda santokh saram pat(u) jholi*
ਧਿਆਨ ਕੀ ਕਰਹਿ ਬਿਭੂਤਿ।।	*dhyān ki kareh bibhūt.*
ਖਿੰਥਾ ਕਾਲੁ ਕੁਆਰੀ ਕਾਇਆ ਜੁਗਤਿ	*Khinthha kāl kuāri kāya jugat ddandda*
ਡੰਡਾ ਪਰਤੀਤਿ।।	*partīt.*
ਆਈ ਪੰਥੀ ਸਗਲ ਜਮਾਤੀ ਮਨਿ	*Āyi panthi sagal jamāti man(i) jītay*
ਜੀਤੈ ਜਗੁ ਜੀਤੁ।।	*jagg jīt.*
ਆਦੇਸੁ ਤਿਸੈ ਆਦੇਸੁ।।	*Ādeis tisai ādeis.*
ਆਦਿ ਅਨੀਲੁ ਅਨਾਦਿ ਅਨਾਹਤਿ	*Ād anīl anād anāhit jugg jugg eko*
ਜੁਗੁ ਜੁਗੁ ਏਕੋ ਵੇਸੁ।।੨੮।।	*veis.*

Brief glossary

ਮੁੰਦਾ	*Munda*	Ear-rings
ਸੰਤੋਖੁ	*Santokh*	Contentment
ਸਰਮੁ	*Saram*	Endeavour (Sanskrit), modesty (Persian)
ਪਤੁ ਝੋਲੀ	*Pat(u) jholi*	Begging bowl and pouch
ਧਿਆਨ	*Dhyān*	Contemplation
ਬਿਭੂਤਿ	*Bibhūt*	Holy ash
ਖਿੰਥਾ	*Khinthha*	Quilt of patch work
ਕਾਲੁ	*Kāl*	Doom, time
ਕੁਆਰੀ	*Kuāri*	Virgin, Untainted
ਆਈ ਪੰਥੀ	*Āyi panthi*	Of the 'Ayee' sect
ਡੰਡਾ	*Ddandda*	Staff, stick

ਆਦੇਸੁ	*Ādeis*	Salutation
ਜੁਗਤਿ	*Jugat*	Code, system
ਪਰਤੀਤਿ	*Partīt*	Faith

Simply translated this *pauṛi* says (to the *Jogis*) that the earrings you wear should be made from contentment, the begging bowl be of honest toil and the holy ash be made of contemplation. Your patchwork sheet – the *khinthha* – be the awareness of your mortality, keep your person free from taint and let your supporting stick – *dandda* – be deep faith. Let all mankind be your sect and do not be exclusive. Conquer your own self if you want to conquer the world. The Guru says Salutations to Him who is the Beginning, the Immaculate, Eternal and Indestructible, existing Unchanging, Immutable through the ages, forever the same. With this we can now look at it in more detail and also see what the learned ones have to tell us.

This *pauṛi* and the next three have the refrain *Ādeis tisay ādeis, Ād anīl anād anāhit jugg jugg eko veis.* So, like the *pauṛi* no. 8–11 and 13–15, these can also be viewed as a set with a common theme. These are short in length and put together have fewer lines than the twenty-seventh *pauṛi.* These seem to be addressed to some *jogis* who were powerful and widespread during the time Guru Nanak lived. The lessons in these four *pauṛis* are thus built around the belief system of the *jogis*, though the central theme of bowing to the one Lord remains totally unchanged.

It is the Guru's favourite device that we again see in action here. Never did he directly condemn or disparage another's religion or faith. He practically acknowledged the right of each man to choose for himself the path he wished to follow to his own vision of the ultimate reality. But in each case the Guru interposed a caveat that the pursuit of such path or practices must be imbued completely with the acknowledgement of the one God to whom all humans are equally dear. He further prescribed that in any practices that a person may choose, there must be primacy given to the universal criteria of contentment, mercy, love for God and for His entire creation and the acceptance of the unknowability of the Divine Lord. Thus, addressing the Muslims he said:

ਮਿਹਰ ਮਸੀਤਿ ਸਿਦਕੁ ਮੁਸਲਾ ਹਕੁ ਹਲਾਲੁ ਕੁਰਾਣੁ ॥
ਸਰਮ ਸੁੰਨਤਿ ਸੀਲੁ ਰੋਜਾ ਹੋਹੁ ਮੁਸਲਮਾਣੁ ॥
(Mehar masīt sidak musla hakk halāl Korān saram
sunnat sīl roja hoh musulmān)
(*Rāg Mājh Slok, Mahla* 1, *SGGS*, page 140)

And then:
ਮੁਸਲਮਾਣੁ ਕਹਾਵਣੁ ਮੁਸਕਲੁ ਜਾ ਹੋਇ ਤਾ ਮੁਸਲਮਾਣੁ ਕਹਾਵੈ ॥
ਅਵਲਿ ਅਉਲਿ ਦੀਨੁ ਕਰਿ ਮਿਠਾ ਮਸਕਲ ਮਾਨਾ ਮਾਲੁ ਮੁਸਾਵੈ ॥
(Mussalmāṇ kahāwaṇ muskal je hoye to mussalmāṇ kahāwai.
Awall aul deen kar mittha maskal māna māl musāwai)
(*Rāg Mājh Salok, Mahla* 1, *SGGS*, page 141)

It is not easy to be a Muslim and only if you have these qualities then call yourself a true Muslim. Firstly you must have love for the 'Word' and then you must get rid of all your worldly attachments as totally as the *maskal* (an instrument used to remove rust) cleans the iron. The Guru then goes on to say that remaining true to the religion one must give up fear of death and accept the Lord's will above all. He must lose his own self and be in total surrender to the Lord. In the previous lines, on page 140 of the *SGGS*, the Guru had the similar message, that your mosque must be compassion, strong faith the prayer cloth, and honest living your holy scripture. *Sunnat* in Islam means as per the Prophet's teachings, implying righteous conduct. It also refers to the rite of circumcision which is also as per the Prophet's teachings. The Guru is saying that the *Sunnat* must in practice be a hesitation against ever doing anything wrong, the *roza*, a ritual fast during the month of *Ramzān*, must be your kind nature. If you have these then are you a true Muslim. Thus we see that the same message against empty ritual and in favour of an active effort to surrender your will to the Lord and to act always with compassion and honesty is held out for the Muslim if he is to be true to his religion.

Similarly, in the long *Sidh Goshtt* the Guru debates with a group of *sidhs* about their belief system and by acting almost as if he were a *sidh* himself he is able, gently and without offence, to give them the very same message of the one Lord and the equality of all humanity, as also the futility of any ritualistic approach to religion. The essence of true spirituality was imparted in the debate without any offensive denunciation of the practices of the *sidhs*.

In these present *pauṛis* the object of a very similar exercise are the *Jogis* or *Yogis* who were a very prominent presence in the Middle Ages, especially in northern India, the area where Guru Nanak was born and where he spent the major part of his life. The *Jogis* were essentially mendicants who were nevertheless organized into groups or sub-sects, each having a central monastery called *Matth* or *Dera*. There was one chief for each of these, called the *Nāth*. The *Dera* usually had a lady called *Bhanddāriṇ* who controlled the stores and was generally responsible for helping with the administration of the *Dera*. During the tour of the mendicants among the householders and the towns, they all wore a typical dress. All of them wore earrings as the sign of their calling. They carried begging bowls in which the offerings were accepted; these bowls were called *pātra*. The offerings were then transferred to a voluminous cloth-pouch called *jholi*. On their bodies they smeared the ashes from cow-dung pats as a sign of renunciation. Over it all they wore the *khinthha*, a patchwork quilted cloth. The Guru uses the analogy of each of these items of the usual attire and accoutrements of the *Jogis* to drive home further for us his message.

In the first line he talks of the *munda* (earrings), the *pātra* and the *jholi* (begging bowl and cloth-pouch), and of the *vibhūt* (the holy ash) smeared on the *Jogi's* body. He says by all means wear the *munda* but let these be made of *santokh* (contentment). Carry the begging bowl but let it be made of *shram* (hard work), and smear the holy ash of *dhyān* (contemplation) on your body. A similar prescription was given by the Guru to the *pāndda* (the priest) when the Guru in his childhood was asked to wear the 'holy cotton thread' – the *janeu*. The Guru had said then:

ਦਇਆ ਕਪਾਹ ਸੰਤੋਖੁ ਸੂਤੁ ਜਤੁ ਗੰਢੀ ਸਤੁ ਵਟੁ॥
(Daya kapāh santokh sūt Jat ganddhi sat vatt)
(Rāg Āsa, Mahla 1, *Asa di Vār*, page 471)

He was willing to wear the *janeu* if it were woven from the cotton of compassion and the twine were woven from contentment. The holy thread or *janeu* be then made from *Jat* and *Sat*, great self-discipline. We see a similar message here. The outward apparels and the ritual are unimportant. The feeling, the sense with which you approach is the real important thing. So he tells us, addressing the *Jogi* that our life has to be governed by contentment, contemplation and hard work and he does so by addressing the *Jogi* sect and saying these are the real earrings, the true holy ash and the true bowl and sack.

In the second line he carries the same argument further and says, qua the *Jogis*, that the *khinthha* (the quilted patchwork sheet) that needs to be worn is the *kāl*. This literally means Time or Doom. Here the Guru uses the term in the sense of an awareness of our mortality. Combine with this, he says, the effort to keep our bodies *kuāri* (chaste). The *ddandda* (staff) used by *Jogis* for praying should be faith in God. It is the Guru's message to us that if there is in us a constant consciousness of our mortality then evil thoughts will not enter the mind. If we remember death then we will remember God too and if God stays in our minds then evil and wrong doing will never attack us; we will never develop too much attachment to worldly goods, and earthly power will seem as meaningless as it actually is. Secondly, keep your person free from taint. Thus, the smearing of ash on the body to keep away temptation has meaning only if your inner person – your *kāya* – remains pristine and pure. That is the system – the *jugat* – you need to follow. Forget about the complicated practices of yoga and instead concentrate on the purity of the self. The *Jogis* used to sit in meditation with an arm supported on a *ddandda* – forked stick. This *ddandda* was an important aid in meditation. The Guru says forget about the *ddandda* of wood and let deep faith in the Lord be your arm-rest in meditation.

In the third line the Guru, having spelt out the true spiritual requirements for the *Jogi* and having asked him to transform the ritual practices into true spiritual qualities with high ethical standards, gives one more important lesson. He says be of the *Āyi panth,* include all *jamāts* and conquer your mind, which will give you victory over everything. The *Jogis* were at that time divided into twelve *panths* or sects, namely, *Heit*, *Gopāl, Rāwal, Dās, Dhwaj, Dhav, Ramya, Pagal, Kanthri, Bann, Choli* and *Āyi*. Each of these sects, except for the *Āyi panth*, had their own establishment, their own practices and their own *Nāth*, religious head. The *Āyi panth* was the inclusive sect which recognized all the sects and practices. The Guru is thus telling us the high importance of universality of the spiritual, and equality of all mankind. *Jamāt* is an Arabic word meaning sect or group. The *Jogis* in those times adopted this term to describe their various sects. So the Guru says be *Sagal jamāti* - belong to all sects. The Guru is thus gently chiding the *Jogis* for their formalistic exclusivity and reminded them of the one Lord, the one Father to whom all mankind belongs. Discriminating between men or groups for whatever reason is a denial of the Lord. So, he says let your grouping be not with any exclusive *panth* or *jamāt*. Let all mankind be your sect, be universal in your practices and let all men be included therein. Lastly, the Guru says conquer your own self if you want to conquer the world. The *Jogis* through ascetic practices were often said to have possessed certain *sidhhis* or mystical powers. They threatened often to use these to over-awe their opponents. This urge for dominance and for exhibiting supremacy is addressed here. Performing of miracles to influence the layman and thus win more followers is not the right device, says the Guru. Instead, says the Guru, *mann jītay jag jīt* – work on your own mind, conquer its tendency to wander, its constant striving for power and wealth, control your senses and become the master of your own self. The world's material allurement will then immediately lose their power over you. You will have, by shedding the material world and acquiring control over your mind achieved the real conquest.

In the fourth and fifth lines, which are the refrain in these *paur.is* from 28 to 31, the Guru offers salutation to the One Lord. The object of this lesson is still the *Jogi* who had the practice of offering salutation to the *Nāth* of all *Jogis*, Lord Shiva. The Guru says offer salutation only to the one Lord. This is a constant theme in the *Gurbān.i* and the Guru stops to offer obeisance and homage to the one Lord again and again. He says here the offering of salutation must only be to Him, The one who is *Ād* (the beginning), *Anīl* (one without taint), *Anād* (one without a beginning), *Anāhit* (one who is not subject to injury) and He who through all ages has the same form. Having admitted inability to measure, count or describe the Lord, the Guru necessarily still has to take recourse to words when he wishes to speak to us of the Lord. This is done through touching upon some of His attributes but mainly by using the *Neti Neti* (not this, not this) format. Here the Guru says salute Him who is the *Ād* – the beginning. This universe came into existence in accordance with the Lord's will. He said the word and the forms and things appeared as we see them today. Before that moment was:

ਅਰਬਦ ਨਰਬਦ ਧੁੰਧੂਕਾਰਾ॥
ਧਰਣਿ ਨ ਗਗਨਾ ਹੁਕਮੁ ਅਪਾਰਾ॥
(Arbad Narbad dhundhūkāra.
Dharaṇ na gagna hukam apāra)
(*Rāg Māru, Mahla* 1, *SGGS*, page 1035)

Arbad, according to the Shabdarth, is a way of saying *Arab* – ten crores or a hundred million. More often, this is taken as meaning a hundred crores, or a billion. The Guru says *Arab* years ago and then adds *Narbad*, which the *Shabdarth* says is a composite word saying No *Arbad*. In other words, beyond *Arabs* of years ago – meaning eons but implying an unknowable time – there was darkness and chaos. The Mahan Kosh however sees it as *Arbad narbad* meaning from the beginning and beyond man's capacity to describe. The short point is that describing that event, or when it occurred, is impossible. At that time there was no earth, no sky; only the Lord's *Hukam* existed. The moment when the Lord willed this universe into existence is thus for us the Beginning. The Guru describes the Lord as *Ād*, but also calls Him *Anād* in the same line, meaning that while for us He is the beginning but for Him there is no beginning and no end. He also calls Him *Anīl* and *Anāhit*, Sanskrit words indicating 'free from pollution' and 'exempt from injury'. This Lord is unchanging through the ages. In other words, the Guru says salute Him who is the Beginning, the Immaculate, Eternal and Indestructible, existing Immutable through time.

It may be noted that in the first line the word *saram* is also by some commentators used in its Persian connotation of modesty. Bhai Vir Singh therefore renders this line as: "Let contentment be your earrings, modesty the begging bowl and sack, contemplation the holy ash." This rendering is followed by Osho, by Iqbal Singh, as also Prof. Talib. However, Prof. Sahib Singh in the *Sri Guru Granth Sahib Darpan* renders it in the Sanskrit sense as *shram* – hard work – and the meaning alters slightly to: "Let hard work be thy begging bowl ...." Dr. Sangat Singh has translated *saram* as self-respect, probably in the sense of the Persian meaning. The SGPC's *Shabdarth* also renders it as 'hard work' and so has Narain Singh used the term. There is no great offence caused to the general sense of the message in either usage. The term 'modesty' also fits in with the other qualities desired by the Guru of contentment and contemplation. However, *saram* in the Sanskrit sense seems more appropriate. Honesty and hard work was ever the Sikh credo. The Guru here is contrasting it to the *Jogi* practices of acquiring their livelihood through begging. He is saying fill your begging bowl and the sack through dint of honest toil. This would preserve self-respect and will mean that you are no burden on another who is earning his living through hard effort. The sense in which the *Shabdarth*, Narain Singh and Prof. Sahib Singh have rendered this term – meaning honest toil – seems to be the more appropriate interpretation, even though a great scholar like Bhai Vir Singh has rendered it otherwise.

34

WITH COMPASSION IN HEART

Pauṛi 29

ਭੁਗਤਿ ਗਿਆਨੁ ਦਇਆ ਭੰਡਾਰਣਿ ਘਟਿ ਘਟਿ ਵਾਜਹਿ ਨਾਦ॥	*Bhugat gyān daya bhanddāriṇ ghatt ghatt vājay nād.*
ਆਪਿ ਨਾਥੁ ਨਾਥੀ ਸਭ ਜਾ ਕੀ ਰਿਧਿ ਸਿਧਿ ਅਵਰਾ ਸਾਦ॥	*Āp nāth nāthi sabh ja ki ridh sidh awra sād.*
ਸੰਜੋਗੁ ਵਿਜੋਗੁ ਦੁਇ ਕਾਰ ਚਲਾਵਹਿ ਲੇਖੇ ਆਵਹਿ ਭਾਗ॥	*Sanjog vijog doye kār chalāveh lekhay āvay bhāg.*
ਆਦੇਸੁ ਤਿਸੈ ਆਦੇਸੁ॥	*Ādeis tisay ādeis.*
ਆਦਿ ਅਨੀਲੁ ਅਨਾਦਿ ਅਨਾਹਤਿ ਜੁਗੁ ਜੁਗੁ ਏਕੋ ਵੇਸੁ॥੨੯॥	*Ād anīl anād anāhit jugg jugg ekoveis.*

Brief glossary

ਭੁਗਤਿ	*Bhugat*	Food, diet
ਗਿਆਨੁ	*Gyān*	Knowledge, enlightenment
ਦਇਆ	*Daya*	Compassion
ਭੰਡਾਰਣਿ	*Bhanddāriṇ*	Controller of stores, dispenser of food in 'matts'
ਨਾਦ	*Nād*	Sound, musical note
ਨਾਥੀ	*Nāthi*	Tagged, bound
ਰਿਦਿ ਸਿਧਿ	*Ridh sidh*	Miraculous powers
ਅਵਰਾ ਸਾਦ	*Awra sād*	Different taste (here, false satisfaction)
ਸੰਜੋਗੁ	*Sanjog*	Union

ਵਿਜੋਗੁ	*Vijog*	Separation
ਭਾਗ	*Bhāg*	Destiny, lot

Simply translated this *pauṛi* says that, for the *Jogi* the ritual food should be enlightenment and the one who dispenses it should be compassion; while the divine word resonates inside. The real *Nāth* is the Lord Himself who has the universe strung together. The acquisition of *ridhis* and *sidhis* (miraculous powers) is a false satisfaction. Union and separation are inherent in this universe and to each will come the fate that the Lord may ordain. Salutations to Him, he says, who is the Beginning, the Immaculate, Eternal and Indestructible, existing Unchanging, Immutable through the ages. Let us now look in more detail at the message and also see what the learned ones have to say.

In this *pauṛi* the Guru has further addressed the *Jogi* system of beliefs and practices. He speaks here of the system of 'ਮੱਠ'- *matth* - central establishments of the *Jogis* where each particular *panth, jamāt* or sect congregated. These had a *Nāth* ruling over it and a lady called *bhanddāriṇ* who was a sort of caretaker, supervisor and controller of the stores of the *matth*. It was her job inter alia to get prepared the community meals and supervise the service of these to the large number of occupants of the *Dera*. While the food was being served, musical notes called *nād* were sounded.

The Guru cites each of these practices and then offers his message – of how to convert these rituals into a truly spiritual exercise. This transformation of the mundane ritual into something spiritual that could lead you to the Lord, we have seen in the previous *pauṛi* also. So, in the first line the Guru says the true *bhanddāriṇ* should be compassion and the food she offers to you should be enlightenment or divine knowledge. Instead of the *nād* let the music of the worlds – the divine word – resound in every heart. The literal meaning here of 'ਘੱਟ ਘੱਟ'- *ghatt, ghatt* – is 'in each vessel'. The Guru is referring here to the human self as the vessel, the receptacle into which Divine Grace is waiting to be poured – as soon as the vessel has purified itself sufficiently.

As the *Gurbāṇi* says:

ਊਂਧੈ ਭਾਂਡੈ ਕਛੁ ਨ ਸਮਾਵੈ ਸੀਧੈ ਅੰਮ੍ਰਿਤੁ ਪਰੈ ਨਿਹਾਰ॥

(Ūndhai bhānddai kacch na samāvai sīdhai Amrit parai nihār)

(*Rāg Gujri, Mahla* 1, *SGGS*, page 504)

As long as the vessel is upside down, meaning that the human self is not correctly prepared, it cannot obtain anything but let the vessel become right side up and the Lord's word as *Amrit* (nectar) will flow straight into it. In this same sense the term vessel is used here. In each vessel let the divine resonance take place. The *Jogis* ritualized food preparation and service practices are sought to be transformed by the Guru into the spiritual dispensation of the Lord. The divine *langar* (community kitchen) is metaphorically described to tell us that in that *langar*, which comes from the Lord, the food is the divine knowledge, and the Lord's compassion is the 'bhānddarin' (the dispenser of the food); and the accompanying music is the name or the divine word.

In the second line the Guru says that in the world of the spiritual, the real *Nāth* is the Lord Himself. This has reference to the practice of having the *Nāth* of the *matth* present as the music plays and the ritualistically prepared food is served under the supervision of the *bhanddāriṇ*. The Guru says in the dispensing of the food of enlightenment the Lord Himself presides. He then adds that this is the Lord who has strung the entire universe together. The term *nāthi* could also be construed as overlordship, meaning the Lord is the Head of the Universe. The more common rendering is 'strung together' from a Punjabi word meaning 'stitching together'. The Guru then refers to the favourite endeavour of the *Jogis*, the acquisition through austerities and penances of miraculous powers. These *ridhis* and *sidhis* were the end goal of the *Jogis*. The Guru says these are but a false satisfaction. The term *nāthi* means stitching on and also has reference to the nose-string put through the noses of yoked beasts of burden-like oxen or horses. Here he uses the metaphor to say that the Lord holds complete sway over the entire universe. His string runs through and controls all creation. To express his disapproval of this fascination for *ridhis* and *sidhis*, the Guru uses the term *awra sād*, literally meaning different taste, and implying that these are a false satisfaction. He is trying to avoid hurting the *Jogis* and so uses this euphemism, describing their main goal in life as a 'different taste' and not as something contemptible. He is saying you may get some joy from that power, the taste of dominance may for sometime bring a transient satisfaction. However, this is not what the spiritual pursuit should be about. Such pursuit should, as the Guru in the previous *pauṛi* told us – and the *Jogis* – concentrate on control of the mind, of the self so that the world loses its power over us, leaving the seeker the true victor. The Guru gently reminds the *Jogis* that chasing after *ridhis* and *sidhis* is but a diversion from the true path.

In the third line the Guru speaks of the union with God and of separation from Him. He says that *sanjog* and *vijog* - union and separation - are both inherent processes of this universe and to each will come the lot that the Lord may ordain. The universal order moves inexorably as per His command and the apparent joining and separations are all strictly occurring as ordained by Him. These terms seem to refer in fact to all human experience including the travails we face in our daily existence, the constant battle in the human mind between the love of God – which brings union – and the love of material things – which causes separation. It refers also to the ups and downs in our spiritual growth as also in our worldly position that this struggle brings. These are all covered in this march of *sanjog* and *vijog*. Thus we see in action the force of the universal laws as also the outcome of our own actions. We strive, moving often upwards by following the Guru's path; and as often regressing under the impact of our weak minds and greedy senses. Thus do we see-saw in our growth, moving towards union and then sliding back. Doing all this we are also undergoing as per the Lord's law, the cycle of births and re-births where we earn a place on this earth according to our actions, as the Guru told us in the fourth *pauṛi.* In the midst of all this we may pray for the Lord's glance of grace which he may bestow on us if and when He so decides. So the system moves on inexorably and to each man comes, according to this system, such destiny as the Lord may ordain.

The last two lines of the refrain we have discussed in the previous *pauṛi.* The Guru has said in these that salutation be to Him who is the Beginning, the one who is Immaculate, Eternal and Indestructible, existing unchanging Immutable through the ages, through all time.

35

BY HIS WRIT ALONE

Pauṛi 30

ਏਕਾ ਮਾਈ ਜੁਗਤਿ ਵਿਆਈ ਤਿਨਿ ਚੇਲੇ ਪਰਵਾਣੁ॥	*Eka māyi jugut viāyi tin chelay parvāṇ.*
ਇਕੁ ਸੰਸਾਰੀ ਇਕੁ ਭੰਡਾਰੀ ਇਕੁ ਲਾਏ ਦੀਬਾਣੁ॥	*Ik sansāri ik bhanddāri ik lāye dībāṇ.*
ਜਿਵ ਤਿਸੁ ਭਾਵੈ ਤਿਵੈ ਚਲਾਵੈ ਜਿਵ ਹੋਵੈ ਫੁਰਮਾਣੁ॥	*Jiv tis bhāvai tivai chalāvai jiv hovai phurmāṇ.*
ਓਹੁ ਵੇਖੈ ਓਨਾ ਨਦਰਿ ਨ ਆਵੈ ਬਹੁਤਾ ਏਹੁ ਵਿਡਾਣੁ॥	*Oh vekhai ona nadar na āvay bahuta eh viddāṇ.*
ਆਦੇਸੁ ਤਿਸੈ ਆਦੇਸੁ॥	*Ādeis tisai ādeis.*
ਆਦਿ ਅਨੀਲੁ ਅਨਾਦਿ ਅਨਾਹਤਿ ਜੁਗੁ ਜੁਗੁ ਏਕੋ ਵੇਸੁ॥ ੩੦॥	*Ād anīl anād anāhit jugg jugg eko veis.*

Brief glossary

ਮਾਈ	*Māyi*	Māya, illusion, here the Primal Mother
ਜੁਗਤਿ	*Jugut*	Device
ਪਰਵਾਣੁ	*Parvāṇ*	Accepted
ਚੇਲੇ	*Chelay*	Followers, disciples, here sons
ਸੰਸਾਰੀ	*Sansāri*	Creator
ਭੰਡਾਰੀ	*Bhanddāri*	Keeper of stores, preserves
ਦੀਬਾਣੁ	*Dībāṇ*	Court
ਵਿਡਾਣੁ	*Viddāṇ*	Wondrous thing

Simply translated this *pauṛi* says that the Lord caused the Primal Mother through His own device to have union with the Eternal to bring into existence three renowned followers. One is given the task of creation, the other of preservation and the third of holding court. However, they are not autonomous and act in accordance with His will. As He determines, so will the system run. The Lord watches over them all but the great wonder is that He is not seen by them. Salutation to Him, says the Guru, who is the Beginning, the Immaculate, Eternal and Indestructible; existing Unchanging, Immutable through the ages. Let us now see it in more detail and also see what the learned ones have to tell us.

Here again the Guru is addressing the *Jogis* who were staunch followers of Lord Shiva. Their belief system predicated creation being from the Lord Shiva, through mating with his consort *Shakti*. Other sects in Hinduism held differently and for some Lord Vishnu was the supreme deity who brought the world into existence. For most Hindus the belief was that Lord Brahma is the Creator. There would thus often be bitter arguments between the *Jogis* and members of other faiths and sects. The Guru is addressing this problem, something he did elsewhere also in the *Gurbāṇi*.

'ਸਿਵ ਸਕਤਿ ਆਪਿ ਉਪਾਇ ਕੈ ਕਰਤਾ ਆਪੇ ਹੁਕਮੁ ਵਰਤਾਏ॥'
(Shiv Sakt(i) āp upāye kai karta āpay hukam vartāye)
(*Rāg Rāmkali, Mahla 3, Ānand*, *SGGS*, page 920)

The above lines roughly translate as: "Many are saying that this universe came into being from union between *Shiv* and *Shakti*, but this all is a play by the Creator Himself."

The Guru says that there should be no conflict here between these various beliefs. In lines 1 and 2, he says that the Lord caused the *Eka Māyi* (Primal Mother) through His own device to have union with the Eternal to bring into existence *tin chelay parvāṇ* or three celebrated, renowned followers, or offspring. One of these was given the task of Creation, the other of Preservation and the third of Holding Court. The word *Māyi* here is used by the Guru to refer to Māya – the Creative Principle of the universe through whom the one Lord brought into existence the three entities, or sons. The term used is three 'disciples' but the description in the second line clarifies what is meant. These three 'disciples' are 'ਪਰਵਾਣੁ'- *parvāṇ*. This word is taken from the Sanskrit *parvān* which can mean (a) a measure, (b) wealth, (c) proof or witness, and (d) the one empowered or renowned. When in *pauṛi* 26 the Guru said *amul tul, amul parvāṇ*, the meaning was 'a measure'. Here, however, it means outstanding or noted.

The three 'disciples' are then described one by one. The first is the *sansāri*, the one who creates the world *(sansār)* and who is called Brahma in the Hindu belief system. The second here is named *bhanddāri*, meaning the keeper of the stores or the one who provides the world with the wherewithal to exist. He is thus the preserver and is named Vishnu. The third one is called here as the one who *lāye dībāṇ* - holds court. This is the power that has control over the end of existence and in Hinduism we call it Shiva. Thus, the reference here is to the Holy Trinity of the Hindu belief system: Brahma, Vishnu, Mahesh (another name for Lord Shiva). In common parlance Lord Shiva is also called the *Bhola Bhanddāri* for his innocent generosity to his devotees often without considering the consequences. He was also called *Bhanddāri*, the giver of stores, by the *Jogis* for whom he was the creator and provider. *Bhola* means naïve or ingenuous, so the phrase *Bhola Bhanddāri* is for these reasons sometimes used for Lord Shiva. However, that is not the sense in which it is here used. The reference to *Bhanddāri* here is clearly to the preserver component of the trinity, which is Lord Vishnu.

The Guru now adds in the third line the point of his discourse. He says though these great powers exist and are carrying out the function of Creation, Preservation and Destruction, yet do not forget that they by themselves have no independent existence or status. The functioning of this entire system depends not on them but on the One Lord. How the system is to operate is determined by Him alone. And as He determines, so exactly will the system run. The command and the will come from Him alone and not from the Holy Trinity. If Brahma were to wish that instead of creating he will be the judge and the destroyer or that he will be the preserver who upholds the creation – which just cannot happen. Brahma is constrained by the Lord's will to be the Creator and so he is compelled to be. Similar is the condition for the Lords Shiva and Vishnu, as of course also for all the minor gods and godlings, of whom, according to Hindu mythology, the number is said to be thirty-three crores (330 million).

In the fourth line the Guru further stresses the limitations of the Holy Trinity. He says the Lord watches over the entire creation and thus he sees all, including the three Prime Powers. Yet neither these three nor anyone else can in turn see Him. The Guru says this is a great wonder (ਵਿਡਾਣੁ) – *viddāṇ* – indeed. By these words the Guru wants us to see the unique position and status of the Lord Creator, even when compared to Brahma, Vishnu, and Mahesh through whom He is administering the system of creation, preservation, and destruction. He wants us to see where the real control vests – with the Lord Himself, with everything and every entity placed in a subordinate position carrying out His command.

Thus we see the *Jogi* beliefs on creation and on the primacy of one god over another have been addressed here by the Guru and the right picture of a universally unique power, the one God over and above any other god, and without a peer or competition, is presented to the *Jogis* and to us. In the last two lines of the refrain the same thought as we discussed in the previous two *pauṛis* is repeated. The universal religion beyond all sects or groups is highlighted. The *Jogi's* practice of giving ādeis or salutation to the *Ādināth*, the primal *Nāth* or head of *Jogis* – Lord Shiva – is here also touched upon; and the *Jogis*, and through them we, are told to not narrow ourselves down to a mere part of the universe. Rather, give salutation, *ādeis*, instead to the One Lord who is the Beginning, the one who is Immaculate, Eternal and not subject to harm or injury; and the one who is Immutable, ever the same, independent of time.

36

THE DIVINE PROVIDER

Pauṛi 31

ਆਸਣੁ ਲੋਇ ਲੋਇ ਭੰਡਾਰ॥	*Āsaṇ loye loye bhanddār.*
ਜੋ ਕਿਛੁ ਪਾਇਆ ਸੁ ਏਕਾ ਵਾਰ॥	*Jo kichh pāiya su eka vār.*
ਕਰਿ ਕਰਿ ਵੇਖੈ ਸਿਰਜਣਹਾਰੁ॥	*Kar kar vekhai sirjaṇhār.*
ਨਾਨਕ ਸਚੇ ਕੀ ਸਾਚੀ ਕਾਰ॥	*Nanak sachay ki sāchi kār.*
ਆਦੇਸੁ ਤਿਸੈ ਆਦੇਸੁ॥	*Ādeis tisai ādeis.*
ਆਦਿ ਅਨੀਲੁ ਅਨਾਦਿ ਅਨਾਹਤਿ	*Ād anīl anād anāhit.*
ਜੁਗੁ ਜੁਗੁ ਏਕੋ ਵੇਸੁ॥ ੩੧॥	*Jugg jugg eko veis.*

Brief glossary

ਆਸਣੁ	*Āsaṇ*	Place for sitting, here abode
ਲੋਇ ਲੋਇ	*Loye loye*	All the worlds
ਭੰਡਾਰ	*Bhanddār*	Stores
ਏਕਾ ਵਾਰ	*Eka vār*	Once for all
ਆਦਿ	*Ād*	Primal, original
ਅਨੀਲੁ	*Anīl*	Antainted
ਅਨਾਹਤਿ	*Anāhit*	Cannot be hurt, indestructible
ਸਿਰਜਣਹਾਰੁ	*Sirjaṇhār*	Creator
ਸਾਚੀ	*Sāchi*	True
ਕਾਰ	*Kār*	Work

This *pauṛi* says that the Lord's abode is the entire universe and He has filled all His creation with stores of what we need.

This became so with one command of the Lord right from the beginning. Having thus wrought He does not forget but watches over it. The work of the True One is the only reality. Salutations to Him, says the Guru, who is the Beginning, the Immaculate, Eternal and Indestructible, existing Unchanging, Immutable through the ages. Let us now see in more detail the message and also see what the learned ones have to say.

In this, the fourth of the quartet of *paur̤is* addressed to the *Jogis*, the Guru touches upon another practice and belief of that sect. The *Jogis* were the devotees of Lord Shiva, who in their system of belief was the *Ādīnāth* – the Primal *Nāth*. Now like all the super entities Lord Shiva is also supposed to have his own place, called *Shivpuri* just as Lord Vishnu has his own *Vaikuntth*, and the Lord of the *devtas*, Indra, has his *Indralok*. In Shiva's abode, *Shivpuri*, the *Jogis* believed they would forever live in bliss and the place was full of all the good things of life and where all that existed in the *bhanddār* (stores) of the *Jogis* was available in ample abundance. The Guru addresses this belief and says in the first line that the Lord resides not in one *Shivpuri* but in the entire universe. He says the *āsan̤* (seat of the Lord) exists in *loye loye* (world after world), and in each of these are overflowing stores provided by the One Lord. He is asking the *Jogis* to shed their narrow parochial vision and see instead the existence of the one God in the entire creation. The number of worlds is beyond count and the all, and each, of them is the Lord's abode. The great stores the *Jogis* were seeking in *Shivpuri*, the Guru says, in fact exist everywhere throughout all existence. The Lord has equipped and filled each of His abodes with all that humans may need.

In the second line he says these stores in all these uncountable worlds have existed since the very day of creation. The Lord has *eka vār* (with one act of His will) filled the entire universe. This great treasure was provided at the time when these worlds were created. So infinite is this supply that since the beginning His creatures have been using these but these are far from getting exhausted.

In the third line the Guru says the Lord has thus wrought and having brought all this magnificent creation into existence, He has not forgotten about it all or gone on to do other things. He ever watches over what He has created and He continues to be the sustainer of all that exists.

In line 4, the Guru says: "*Sachay ki sāchi kār*" (true is the work of the True One). The term 'ਸਚਾ' – *sacha* – literally means 'true' and is repeatedly used to describe the Lord in the sense of the only Truth, the Essence of all that exists. Thus, we have:

ਇਹ ਜਗੁ ਸਚੈ ਕੀ ਹੈ ਕੋਠੜੀ ਸਚੇ ਕਾ ਵਿਚਿ ਵਾਸੁ॥
(Eh jagg sachai ki hai kotthṛi sachay ka vich vās)
(*Rāg Āsa, Mahla* 2, page 463)

This world is the abode of the True One and He resides therein. The same thought is expressed here. The *sacha* – The True One – has worked this creation into existence and this is also therefore the *sāchi kār* (the real truth).

In the last two lines, the refrain, the Guru again offers salutations to Him who is the Beginning, Immaculate beyond time and Indestructible. With this *pauṛi* the Guru brings to a close his dialogue with the *Jogis*.

To sum up the lesson contained in these *pauṛis*, we can recapitulate the message as a whole. Remember that the *Jogis*, or *Yogis*, were a powerful and numerous sect in the middle ages. These were men who had given up the world and taken to an ascetic mode of life making their way by seeking alms from the towns and the householders. They were grouped into *panths* or *jamāts*, groups of like-minded *Jogis* who lived together in monastery-like conditions in *Matths* under the command of a *Nāth* or chief of the sect. These *Matths* or *Deras* were run in a highly ritualized manner. Prayers were defined and prescribed; even the community kitchen was operated in a well-defined fashion. The serving of the meal required thick flat bread or *rottis* to be baked. These were then broken into pieces and mixed with *ghee*, clarified butter. This meal was called *chūrma*. The members present in the *Matth* would sit on the ground in a row forming what is called a *pangat*. The head of the institution, the *Nāth*, would then come to preside over the ceremony, the *bhanddāriṇ* or *bhanddārī'* the woman or man in-charge of the stores and kitchen, would prepare to serve the meal. A musical note or *nād* would then be sounded. To the sound of this instrument, also called the *singhi*, playing the musical note the meal was then eaten.

In their personal attire also the *Jogis* were subject to a strict regiment. They all had pierced earlobes in which they wore earrings. They wore a patchwork coat or cloak called the *khinttha*. They each carried a begging bowl called *pātra* and a sack or big pouch of cloth called *jholi*. On their bodies they smeared ashes called *vibhūti* as a sign of renunciation.

Their belief system was predicated on the supremacy of Lord Shiva. The creation myth in their system was that Shiva and his consort Shakti were the primal parents who caused this universe and all beings to come into existence. Lord Shiva was the divine *bhanddāri* or the possessor of all material goods and it was their hope that through the right yogic practices and penances they would win the favour of Lord Shiva, the *Ādīnāth*, Primal *Nāth*, and be taken to his abode Shivpuri, or Shivlok, where all *bhanddārs* (material things) would be freely available to the faithful.

The *Jogis*, however, were not a monolithic body and were divided into twelve *panths* as we saw in *pauṛi* 28. Of these the *Āyi panth* is the all-inclusive. Between the *panths* there were differences in practice and belief. The Guru has in these *pauṛis* touched on each of these aspects. He has raised each of these to a spiritual level and to an all-inclusive and universal way of thinking. Thus, he has been able to say to the *Jogis* that their practices are concentrated too heavily on the physical and that they will be able to raise themselves to God-realization only when they start to see the spiritual qualities required. Not earrings, and begging paraphernalia, but contentment, hard and honest toil, contemplation, clean living and deep faith is prescribed. They are told of the One Lord Creator whose sway extends through the entire universe and whose inexhaustible stores are at the disposal of His creation since the beginning. Each *pauṛi* ends with reminding the *Jogi*, and us, of the Timeless One, the True Lord.

37

HIS NAME, THE TRUE MANTRA

Pauṛi 32

ਇਕ ਦੂ ਜੀਭੌ ਲਖ ਹੋਹਿ ਲਖ ਹੋਵਹਿ ਲਖ ਵੀਸ॥	*Ik doo jībhau lakh hoye lakh hoveh lakh vīs.*
ਲਖੁ ਲਖੁ ਗੇੜਾ ਆਖੀਅਹਿ ਏਕੁ ਨਾਮੁ ਜਗਦੀਸ॥	*lakh lakh geṛa ākhiye ek nām jagdīs.*
ਏਤੁ ਰਾਹਿ ਪਤਿ ਪਵੜੀਆ ਚੜੀਐ ਹੋਇ ਇਕੀਸ॥	*Et rāh pat pavṛīya chaṛīyai hoye ikīs.*
ਸੁਣਿ ਗਲਾ ਆਕਾਸ ਕੀ ਕੀਟਾ ਆਈ ਰੀਸ॥	*Suṇ galla ākās ki kītta āyi rīs.*
ਨਾਨਕ ਨਦਰੀ ਪਾਈਐ ਕੂੜੀ ਕੂੜੈ ਠੀਸ॥ ੩੨॥	*Nanak nadri pāyiai kūṛi kūṛai tthīs.*

Brief glossary

ਜੀਭੌ	*Jībhau.*	From the tongue
ਲਖ	*Lakh*	A hundred thousand
ਵੀਸ	*Vīs*	Twenty
ਗੇੜਾ	*Geṛa*	Times, rounds
ਜਗਦੀਸ	*Jagdīs*	Lord of the universe
ਪਤਿ	*Pat(i)*	Literally bridegroom, here the lord
ਪਵੜੀਆ	*Pavṛīya*	Stairs
ਚੜੀਐ	*Chaṛīyai*	Climb
ਇਕੀਸ	*Ikīs*	Become one with the Lord, twenty-one

ਆਕਾਸ	*Ākās*	Sky, heavens
ਕੀਟਾ	*Kīta*	Worms
ਰੀਸ	*Rīs*	Emulation, desire to emulate
ਕੂੜੈ ਠੀਸ	*Kūṛai tthīs*	False boasting

Simply translated this *pauṛi* says that if we had not just one but manifold tongues numbering millions and with each we recited His name a hundred thousand times, then it can become the stairway to the Lord. Hearing the tales of the heavens even worms want to emulate those ascending these stairs, but this can only come from the Lord's grace and these false ones are merely indulging in empty boasting.

The Guru in this *pauṛi* returns once again to the subject of *Nām*, reciting or singing of the Lord's name, something already touched in *pauṛi* 4 where the path to the Lord was prescribed to be through *Nām*, but with faith in the heart and in the right manner.

In the first and second lines the Guru says that if our tongue were not just one but was to become a hundred thousand tongues, not merely that but twenty times that, if then with each of the manifold tongues we could repeat the name of the One Lord a hundred thousand times each. The message implicit is that even those many recitations are not sufficient. In other words, our reciting of the *Nām* can never be overdone.

In the third line the Guru now tells us what the outcome of such an endeavour is. He says this constant repetition of His name is the path to Him, this is the *pauṛīya* (staircase). The implicit message behind this thought here is, firstly, that the path is uphill; it is a climb and hence not to be attained without some hard work. Secondly, this steeply uphill path, this staircase, is built from devotion expressed through constant fixing of the mind on Him. This is the staircase to the Lord and through single-minded devotion only can we achieve oneness with the Lord.

These three lines and the next one have been rendered in other ways also by commentators. The above meaning is the straight-forward and logically consistent rendering and it has so been followed by Prof. Talib, Dr. Sangat Singh and Iqbal Singh. Prof. Sahib Singh in his *Sri Guru Granth Sahib Darpan* also renders the first two lines in the same way and further elaborates to say that, "If a man were to think that by such devotion he is entitling himself to achieving Godhead then it is but the lowly man's empty boast. This staircase can only be climbed by losing your *haumai,* your selfness." The word *ikīs* is rendered by all these learned men as 'union with God'.

This word *ikīs* is however rendered differently by Osho. He uses it in the sense of 'twenty-one' and says that as per the *Sankhya* school of philosophy these are five gross elements: Earth, Water, Fire, Air and Ether born out of the One, which constitute the body. There are five corresponding subtle elements. In addition, he says, there are five organs of the body and these also have corresponding five subtle organs. Thus, for example, if the eye is the organ of action, the capacity to see is the subtle organ of perception. Similarly, for the ear the power to hear is the subtle organ. All these senses and organs then add up to twenty. Osho says God is then the number twenty-one (*The True Name*, Vol. II, pp. 162 to 164, by Osho – discourses on *Japji Sahib*). This concept is also referred to by Bhai Vir Singh in his commentary though he seems to prefer the other rendering.

The *Mahan Kosh* of Bhai Sahib Bhai Kahan Singh also says that learned men have counted the world as being twenty parts and the *Atma(n)*, the God-principle inside as the twenty-first. In this sense these lines can be taken to mean that this staircase makes us the twenty-first part, which is the transcendent condition of oneness with God.

Though the meaning more appropriately seems to be to translate *ikīs* as being one with God, but even if we render it as twenty-one the broad sense of union with God remains the same. The message is that through devotion expressed by way of *Nām Simraṇ* we can move up the ladder to the supra-human state of unity with God. The implied meaning also needs to be understood, that it is not the effort of this recital that can guarantee us any salvation. That has to come from His glance of grace as and when He deems fit to bestow it on us.

Osho puts it beautifully. He says, at pages 151 and 152 of his commentary:

"Thousands upon thousand of ways have been devised to search for God. But whatever a person has attained he has found that He (The Lord) could not be attained through any means. Attainment comes always by His Grace, as His gift; only through His compassion does a seeker arrive. But alas, things become very complex, because without effort on the part of the seeker Grace does not descend."

Osho then gives the example of someone who forgets someone's name and tries very hard to remember. You try a thousand ways to remember and though it is always on the tip of your tongue, it will not come to your mind. You give up in exasperation, start doing something and suddenly it comes in a flash when you least expect it and were not struggling to remember anymore. He says when we try too hard, it becomes a hindrance. Great effort produces great tension in the mind and it becomes constricted and closed and your vision narrows down. God, however, is vast. If a small word cannot be recalled how can God be remembered? And His name is not on the tongue, it is in the heart. When the constriction of concentration is gone, you open up and God enters you. He then adds, "But the irony is that the second happening can take place only after you have truly tried. Without that initial effort and struggle, the intense effort ends in apparent failure, but when you give up, this effort slips into the sub-conscious mind and continues with the same intensity. Then, when you are relaxed, the thought wells up."

"So trying is of two kinds. The conscious effort you put in does not lead to God. When you give up and accept defeat all the effort you had put in now penetrates every pore of your body…Scientists would say it has now become an effort of the unconscious."

So, says Osho, the constant conscious repetition of the name, or *Nām Simraṇ,* or *jāp*, gradually becomes the unconscious effort, the unpronounced repetition, *ajāp*. At this stage it penetrates each atom of your body. You may not hear its music but it is sounding within you. The conscious is therefore essential but only as a passage to the unconscious. This happens only after you accept defeat and surrender. Since at this stage you are making no effort, it is natural to feel that it is His grace.

Either rendering of *ikīs,* as 'twenty-one' or as 'one with God', does not greatly alter the meaning. Logically, however, the latter meaning, that we can become one with God rings more true. The Guru's message throughout is marked by a simplicity and directness fit for the audience he was addressing at that time. The language he used was the everyday language; the idiom used that of the daily toiler, the common man. It is very unlikely that he had used *ikīs* here in the sense of 'twenty-one' expecting his audience to be aware of the deeper teaching of the *Sankhya* philosophy. The meaning here appropriately has to be *ikīs* (one with God).

In the fourth and fifth lines the Guru says hearing tales of the heavens even worms want to emulate those who are thus ascending these stairs. However, the achieving of that blissful state comes only from the Lord's grace and these false ones are merely indulging in empty boasting. The reference here is to the fact that those who do attain the Lord's grace are then so visibly resplendent with it that they become objects of envy. Also, they will want to share their experience, shed their light so that others too can see. They gain in stature and in honour and are esteemed high. All this causes egotistic men of little achievement to burn in envy. They say to themselves that no one could possibly have achieved God-realization ahead of them, because they are men of power or of learning or some other earthly attainment. They are also consumed by greed because they also want to attain the same worldly honours. Thus, the truly God-realized one becomes a teacher, a Guru; and to emulate him there spring up hordes of the false ones, the Pseudo teachers, the self-proclaimed Gurus. These are the ones referred to here by the Guru, *kīṭt* – literally meaning worm, the mean and the lowly; for who is lower or meaner than the one who though actually consumed by greed and envy and spurred entirely by his ego starts to make claims to greatness that he is actually far away from.

The Guru says that such bogus claimants are like worms that in reality are barely able to crawl on the surface of this earth but claim to be able to soar to the skies merely because they have heard the true Gurus speak of that heavenly experience. This claim, the Guru says, is mere 'ਕੂੜੀ ਕੂੜੈ ਠੀਸ' - *kūṛai tthīs* – empty bragging of the false claimant. In reality the Lord can only be realized through His own grace.

The Guru has in this *pauṛi* reiterated that the only efficacious method of reaching Him is to immerse oneself totally in thoughts of Him through *Nām Simraṇ*, repeated recitation of the name. Do it always and soon this will purify your inner-self and you will climb steadily on the upward path towards God-realization. Do not presume that the intensity of your effort will determine the success of your mission. That happy consummation shall come only when the Lord so wills, and His glance of grace descends on you. The hard work of constant recitation is no guarantee of success for the Lord cannot be forced, coaxed or fooled into bestowing His grace. That will happen only if and when He Himself so wills. The effort by us yet is vital and must sincerely be made. It must be done because it will slowly but surely purify your own inner-self. As you progress along that path, the realization will one day dawn that it is our own *haumai* – our sense of selfness, our ego that is standing in the way. That will be the beginning of the state of surrender, the giving up of the egoistic effort, and the flowing with the divine stream will then emerge.

There will be many who will make the false claim to holiness, Osho says, for each true Guru there will be ninety-nine pseudo-Gurus performing cheap magical tricks so as to claim miraculous powers and gain followers, and with that wealth, power and worldly renown. It is hard therefore to find that rare true Guru. Do not worry about these false Gurus for they are but worms hoping to soar like a bird. Concentrate instead on constant *Nām Simraṇ* (recitation of the name) and wait patiently, humbly and with love, for Him to decide when He will bestow His grace.

38

IN TOTAL OBEDIENCE

Pauṛi 33

ਆਖਣਿ ਜੋਰੁ ਚੁਪੈ ਨਹ ਜੋਰੁ ॥	*Ākhaṇ jor chupai nāh jor.*
ਜੋਰੁ ਨ ਮੰਗਣਿ ਦੇਣਿ ਨ ਜੋਰੁ ॥	*Jor na mangaṇ deiṇ na jor.*
ਜੋਰੁ ਨ ਜੀਵਣਿ ਮਰਣਿ ਨਹ ਜੋਰੁ ॥	*Jor na jīvaṇ maraṇ nāh jor.*
ਜੋਰੁ ਨ ਰਾਜਿ ਮਾਲਿ ਮਨਿ ਸੋਰੁ ॥	*Jor na rāj māl mann sor.*
ਜੋਰੁ ਨ ਸੁਰਤੀ ਗਿਆਨਿ ਵੀਚਾਰਿ ॥	*Jor na surti gyān vīchār.*
ਜੋਰੁ ਨ ਜੁਗਤੀ ਛੁਟੈ ਸੰਸਾਰੁ ॥	*Jor na jugti chhuttai sansār.*
ਜਿਸੁ ਹਥਿ ਜੋਰੁ ਕਰਿ ਵੇਖੈ ਸੋਇ ॥	*Jis hath jor kar vekhai soye.*
ਨਾਨਕ ਉਤਮੁ ਨੀਚੁ ਨ ਕੋਇ ॥ ੩੩ ॥	*Nanak utam nīch na koye.*

Brief glossary

ਆਖਣਿ	*Ākhaṇ*	Saying, uttering
ਜੋਰੁ	*Jor*	Power, strength
ਮੰਗਣਿ	*Mangaṇ*	Asking for
ਦੇਣਿ	*Deiṇ*	Giving
ਰਾਜਿ	*Rāj*	Rulership, authority
ਮਾਲਿ	*Māl*	Wealth
ਮਨਿ ਸੋਰੁ	*Mann sor*	Disturbance (noise) of the mind
ਸੁਰਤੀ	*Surti*	Enlightenment, understanding
ਜੁਗਤੀ	*Jugti*	Device, method or plan
ਛੁਟੈ	*Chhuttai*	Be rid off, escape
ਜਿਸੁ ਹਥਿ ਜੋਰੁ	*Jis hath jor*	He who wields, or has, the power

Simply translated this *pauṛi* says that neither our utterances are in our power nor our silence. Our begging or giving is not in our control. Even our life, or birth, and our death are not in our control. Nor can we command wealth or rulership by our will even though the mind makes great noise about it. Achieving of divine knowledge or discourses on it are beyond our control, as is any device or practice by which we could achieve salvation from this cycle of re-birth. The real power vests only in the Lord and by our own effort no one is high or low.

This *pauṛi*, apparently simply-worded and easy to understand, is sometimes misunderstood. It is taken to be an expression of negative passiveness, of pessimism, that there is nothing a man is capable of and whatever happens will deterministically keep happening regardless of human intervention. So why then bother to make any effort. Sikhism is a life-affirming faith and its preaching and practice enjoin upon the true Sikh to always participate, never to withdraw from this world. Hard work, caring for the weak and the needy and sharing with mankind are inherent injunctions for the Sikh. Any such negative interpretation would therefore be entirely incorrect, and inconsistent with the message of the Guru elsewhere. We need to examine it more deeply.

The *pauṛi* has to be read in the context of, and really as a continuation of, the last two lines of the previous *pauṛi* where we were told that only through His grace can we attain Him. This *pauṛi* continues the theme of submission to the Divine Will. By his own egotistic will man can achieve nothing but if he realizes and surrenders to the Lord residing within then he can be himself the achiever. Without this realization and on one's own strength the position will be as described in this *pauṛi*.

In the first and second lines the Guru says our *ākhaṇ* (utterances) are not in our power, nor *chup* (our silences). It is not our own will at work if we are being a beggar or so when we are the donor. Here and in the subsequent lines the stress is on the word *Jor*. This is the Persian word *ẓor* meaning power, strength or might. Some of the earlier commentaries, Prof. Talib tells us, had taken *jor* to mean 'ਜੋੜ'- *joṛ*, which is the Sanskrit for 'union'.

This however does not seem logical, especially in the light of the last two lines of this *pauṛi*. All commentators now are using it in the sense of 'might' or 'power'. The same thought occurs again in the *Gurbāṇi* in *Gauṛi Sukhmani Mahla 5, Asttpadi* 11, page 277 of the *SGGS*:

ਇਸ ਕਾ ਬਲੁ ਨਾਹੀ ਇਸੁ ਹਾਥ॥	*Is ka bal nāhin is hāth.*
ਕਰਨ ਕਰਾਵਨ ਸਰਬ ਕੋ ਨਾਥ॥	*Karan karāvan sarab ko nāth.*
ਆਗਿਆਕਾਰੀ ਬਪੁਰਾ ਜੀਉ॥	*Āgyākari bapura jīo.*
ਜੋ ਤਿਸੁ ਭਾਵੈ ਸੋਈ ਫੁਨਿ ਥੀਉ॥	*Jo tis bhāvay soyi phun thhīo.*

The lines can be translated to mean that man's strength is in reality in the Lord's hand. When this man works in obedience to the Lord then the power becomes his own because his wishes are now the same as the Lord's will. The correct meaning of *jor* therefore should not be taken as 'union', but as 'power' or 'might'.

In the third and fourth lines the Guru further adds that what to speak of utterances and silence or of giving or begging, even man's *jīvaṇ* (life or birth) is not in his own hand nor is man's *maraṇ* (death) under his control. Nor will man be able to command wealth or rulership by his own will regardless of how much *mann sor* – commotion the desire for these causes in our minds. Iqbal Singh attempts an alternate rendering by reading *mann sor* as one word *manshūr* meaning 'manifesto' or 'letter of authority' in which case the meaning, he says, would be: "No power to acquire kingdom, riches and authority". Prof. Talib's commentary also seems to follow a similar line. However most commentators view *mann sor* in the sense of 'disturbance or noise in the mind'. The SGPC's *Shabdarth* as also Prof. Sahib Singh in his *Sri Guru Granth Sahib Darpan* and Giani Sant Singh Maskin in his audio-commentary use it in this sense, as does Narian Singh. On balance this seems to be the more appropriate meaning.

In lines five and six, the Guru says the achieving of divine knowledge or the discourses on divine knowledge are also beyond man's own power. Beyond our power also is any practice or device by which we could achieve salvation from this cycle of re-birth.

In the last two lines, the seventh and eighth, the Guru concludes the discourse by saying the one who wields the power, meaning the Lord Himself, exercises it and by our own effort none is high or low. The seventh line is the subject of different interpretations because of the word '*soye*' occurring at the end of line 7. Giani Maskin in his audio commentary has translated it to mean that if someone has the power then let him exhibit it. In other words, all the things listed in the *pauṛi* are beyond the power of man and if someone claims to be able to do any of these then let him show it. Dr. Sangat Singh also uses the same meaning. But the SGPC's *Shabdarth*, Prof. Sahib Singh, Prof. Talib and Iqbal Singh have a different rendering. Prof. Sahib Singh gives examples from *pauṛi* 5, 21, 26, 27 and 37 where *soye* is used in the sense of the Lord Himself. So the correct interpretation is that having listed man's incapacity in the first six lines the Guru is now saying that the real power vests in the Lord alone and He is the one who is wielding it and by one's own effort no man is high or low.

Prof. Sahib Singh sums up the *pauṛi* to say that men are like manikins in God's hands; all our good and bad deeds, our meditation, even our asking Him for gifts of His name is all as per His wish. At first glance this may seem to mean that all our efforts are essentially useless, and thus be advocating a life of inert acceptance and actionlessness. The message however is quite different. The stress here is on the need to be at one with the Lord's will. The implicit message is about the harmfulness of *haumai*, any belief that you can mould the universe to your own desire. As against any reliance on your own strength the Guru is telling us to humbly accept the Lord's omnipotence which coupled with adoration for Him – strengthened through constant reciting of His name and singing His praises – will create in us the state of mind which will lead us to Him. The message flows seemlessly from the last two lines of the previous *pauṛi*, no. 32, and is in full consonance with the message of the *Japji Sahib* and indeed the *Gurbāṇi* that we have to seek divine grace for which our own self has to be totally subordinated.

As Osho puts it, "All worldly strength proves to be the strength of your ego. If you become helpless God awaits you, for the strong need no support." God is the strength of the weak and the helpless. As he puts it, at page 181, Vol. II of his commentary, "No sooner do you become helpless that the fountain of the supreme strength begins to flow for you. As long as you rely on your own strength and give it importance, your power is not worth a penny."

39

THE TESTING GROUNDS

Pauṛi 34

ਰਾਤੀ ਰੁਤੀ ਥਿਤੀ ਵਾਰ॥	*Rāti ruti thhiti vār.*
ਪਵਣ ਪਾਣੀ ਅਗਨੀ ਪਾਤਾਲ॥	*Pavaṇ pāṇi agni pātāl.*
ਤਿਸੁ ਵਿਚਿ ਧਰਤੀ ਥਾਪਿ ਰਖੀ ਧਰਮ ਸਾਲ॥	*Tis vich dharti thhāp rakhi dharam sāl.*
ਤਿਸੁ ਵਿਚਿ ਜੀਅ ਜੁਗਤਿ ਕੇ ਰੰਗ॥	*Tis vich jīw jugat(i) kay rung.*
ਤਿਨ ਕੇ ਨਾਮ ਅਨੇਕ ਅਨੰਤ॥	*Tin kay nām anek anant.*
ਕਰਮੀ ਕਰਮੀ ਹੋਇ ਵੀਚਾਰੁ॥	*Karmi karmi hoye vīchār.*
ਸਚਾ ਆਪਿ ਸਚਾ ਦਰਬਾਰੁ॥	*Sacha āp sacha darbār.*
ਤਿਥੈ ਸੋਹਨਿ ਪੰਚ ਪਰਵਾਣੁ॥	*Tithhai sohan panch parvāṇ.*
ਨਦਰੀ ਕਰਮਿ ਪਵੈ ਨੀਸਾਣੁ॥	*Nadri karm pavai nisāṇ.*
ਕਚ ਪਕਾਈ ਓਥੈ ਪਾਇ॥	*Kach pakāyi othhai pāye.*
ਨਾਨਕ ਗਇਆ ਜਾਪੈ ਜਾਇ॥ ੩੪॥	*Nanak gaya jāpai jāye.*

Brief glossary

ਰਾਤੀ	*Rāti*	Nights
ਰੁਤੀ	*Ruti*	Seasons
ਥਿਤੀ	*Thhiti*	Lunar dates
ਵਾਰ	*Vār*	Days of the week
ਤਿਸੁ ਵਿਚਿ	*Tis vich*	In the midst of these
ਧਰਤੀ	*Dharti*	The world, earth
ਧਰਮ ਸਾਲ	*Dharam sāl*	Place for worship, literally house of the righteous, here arena of action

ਜੀਅ	*Jīw*	Species of creatures
ਰੰਗ	*Rung*	Colour, but here types
ਅਨੰਤ	*Anant*	Endless, infinite
ਕਰਮੀ ਕਰਮੀ	*Karmi Karmi*	According to actions
ਸੋਹਨਿ	*Sohan*	Are graceful
ਕਚ	*Kach*	Half ripe
ਪਕਾਈ	*Pakāyi*	Ripe
ਗਇਆ	*Gaya*	On reaching
ਜਾਪੈ	*Jāpai*	Appears, is seen as

Simply translated this *pauṛi* says that the Lord has created the night, the day, the seasons and the various special days. He has created also air, water, fire and the *pātāl* (nether regions). In the midst of all this He has placed this earth as a place for us to uplift ourselves (to be able to reach Him). On this earth He has placed beings of various types and has also placed the means of their existence. All creatures will be judged strictly in accordance with their actions, in the True Court of the True One. In that Court are refulgent the elect, who by the grace of the Lord, carry the mark of His approval (on their foreheads). The sorting of the good from the bad will take place in that Court and this will be known only after we reach there. The fitness or otherwise (of the soul) will only then be known. Let us now see it in more detail and also see what the learned ones have to say.

In this *pauṛi* and the next three the Guru is now in a way summing up the lessons imparted so far. These four *pauṛis* describe five *khandds*, literally parts or realms, of spiritual growth. There are differences in the way these have been rendered by the various commentators. All are however agreed that the Guru has divided these stages into five parts, or realms. These are ad seriatim *Dharam khandd*, *Gyān khandd, Saram khandd, Karam khandd,* and *Sach khandd,* with the last one being the stage of being at one with the Lord. It is the culminating stage which the soul attains after it has moved through the previous stages successfully and this is the stage where the difference between the soul and the Lord vanishes; they become as one and there is no further seeking or movement or growth left to achieve.

There are a few different interpretations to these five distinct states. Those who believe in theosophy call these as circles of spirituality existing independently. Others think that this is a vision that Guru Nanak had when his consciousness rose above the limits of space and time, and he witnessed these five realms where people, meaning souls, of different levels of growth exist together. Narain Singh has so stated in his commentary and has then raised some questions on treating these as five successive, sequential stages. He says that at the first stage, *Dharam khandd*, how the *panch* with the sign of His grace could be residing. If they have this *nīsān* (the sign of acceptance) and are already the *panch* (the selected, the accepted), then they are already in *Sach khandd*, the final stage. He says the *Saram khandd*, though the third, is the most significant – the last two *khandds* being dependent on it and the first two being incomplete without it. So, he says, read the first three *khandds* as one in these *paur̤is*. So the first, the *Dharam khandd*, is this earth itself and actions herein determine the place in the Lord's presence. In *Gyān khandd* the outward knowledge of the secrets of the universe will have come to the seeker in the manner of the *Sidh, Budh, Nāth* etc. – all men of high spiritual growth. However, the inner knowledge is not yet there. For that the third stage, the *Saram khandd*, is vital. It is here that the effort is to lift the consciousness beyond and above the material. The hallmark here is great self-discipline and strict control of the mind. The Guru says:

ਖੰਨਿਅਹੁ ਤਿਖੀ ਵਾਲਹੁ ਨਿਕੀ ਏਤੁ ਮਾਰਗਿ ਜਾਣਾ॥

(Khaniu tikhi vālau niki, et(u) mārag jāṇa)

(Rāmkali Mahla 3, Ānand, SGGS, page 918)

The line can be translated as: 'Sharper than the sword edge, narrower than a hair is the path to Him.'

Again, Sant Kabir says:

ਕਬੀਰ ਮੁਕਤਿ ਦੁਆਰਾ ਸੰਕੁਰਾ ਰਾਈ ਦਸਏਂ ਭਾਇ। ਮਨੁ ਤਉ ਮੈਗਲੁ ਹੋਇ
ਰਹਿਓ ਨਿਕਸੋ ਕਿਉ ਕੈ ਜਾਇ॥

(Kabir mukat duāra sankura rāyi dasein bhāye.
Mann tāu maigal hoye rahiu nikso kiu kai jāye)
(*Bhagat Kabir, Slok* 58, *SGGS*, page 1367)

The translation of this line is: 'The door to salvation is narrow as the tenth part of a sesame seed while my mind (with its ego) is like an elephant, how will I pass'.

Thus in the *Saram khandd* hard labour brings the mind into tune with the Lord, and with the ego brought under control the inner-self is so purified as to become a fit vessel to receive His grace. This is then the fourth stage, *Karam khandd*, the stage of divine grace. The seeker has now shed the dross and trained his mind so as to enter into union with God. This is the final stage, *Sach khandd*, where the grace of the Lord has descended and oneness achieved.

Dr. Sangat Singh in his *Japji* says *Dharam khandd* is the abode where truth and virtue are practiced and understanding of the creation is achieved. With this the *Gyān khandd* is entered and in this realm of enlightenment one's horizon is widened about the diversity of creation and of the many religious traditions. *Haumai* is thus weakened and we go to *Saram khandd*, the realm of effort. The inner perception is sharpened and illumination occurs in the mind. Then is *Karam khandd*, the realm of grace, entered and the power of God is seen in oneself. Till here one's individuality is still retained and this goes only in the next stage, *Sach khandd*, where union with God takes place.

Giani Sant Singh Maskin, in his commentary, compares this description with the ancient belief, in *Sanātan Hinduism*, of the three *kāndds*, *Karam kāndd, Upāsna kāndd and Gyān kāndd* – action, worship and union with God. He refers to a similar, but four-stage growth envisioned in Islam called *Shariat, Tarikat, Marfut and Haqeeqat.* The final stage is the destination and the previous stages are the preparation. *Haqeeqat* means 'reality', and similarly in the Hindu faith *Gyān* is knowledge of God, or God-realization. Giani Maskin describes it by saying that Guru Nanak has prescribed four preliminary stages, viz., *Dharam, Gyān, Saram, Karam*, and then the final and fifth stage is the destination, called *Sach khandd.*

We can in this background now see what the Guru has said in each of these inter-connected *pauṛis.* In this *pauṛi*, in the first and second lines, the Guru says He has created the night, the day, the *ruti* (seasons) and the *thhiti* (various special days). He has also brought into existence the air, water, fire and the *pātāl* (nether regions).

In line 3, the Guru says that having created these elements, these regions and the seasons the Lord has in their midst placed this earth, this world we live in. Why has the Guru told us all this again? Because he wants to highlight just how vital this situation is for us. The answer he has given is that all this has been put in place because the Lord wanted for us a place where the individual souls could get the opportunity to uplift themselves, to be able to work to regain that union with the Lord. Earth is therefore placed here as the abode of *Dharma*, the place where cause and effect unerringly operate and which He Himself watches over. It is an arena where we can learn to practice righteous living so that the aim of this birth can be fulfilled. And that aim is:

ਭਈ ਪਰਾਪਤਿ ਮਾਨੁਖ ਦੇਹੁਰੀਆ॥
ਗੋਬਿੰਦ ਮਿਲਣ ਕੀ ਇਹ ਤੇਰੀ ਬਰੀਆ॥
(Bhayi prāpat mānukh dehuriya Gobind milan ki eh teri barīya)
(*Rāg Āsa, Mahla* 5, *SGGS*, page 12)

The lines can be translated as: 'This human form has been granted to you and this is your opportunity to achieve union with the Lord.'

So the Lord has put in place this abode of righteousness, this *Dharam khandd*, for us so that we can learn to do the right thing and live the right life.

In lines four and five, the Guru says having created all this and having placed the world, this earth, therein the Lord has then placed on this earth *jiw* (beings) of various types and has also placed various *jugtis* for their existence. *Jugti* literally means device or practice of *Hattha Yoga* claiming to guide men on the spiritual path. These yogic practices are not an accepted method in Sikhism. Here it is not used in the sense of the yogic practices but rather in the sense of the 'means of subsistence of the created beings'. The sense of this line therefore is 'creatures of various types, living in various different ways, the names or labels of such creatures are *anek anant* - uncountable.

In lines six and seven, the Guru says the Lord's creatures are all judged before Him *karmi karmi* (in strict accordance with their actions). The thought here is that let no one think that he is of high status or has great learning and may therefore find special favour with the Lord. Not so, says the Guru. The judgement will be determined solely by the actions of each creature. Be such actions hidden or overt, all will be registered, evaluated and from these alone will follow the outcome. This will be done in the court of the *Sācha* (True One), whose *darbār* (court) is also true. In other words, the court is strict and impartial and it is only the evidence of our deeds that will be allowed to determine our lot.

In line eight and nine, the Guru digresses slightly to speak of the wonders of this court where judgment will be delivered. He says in this court sit the *panch parvāṇ* (the elect, the accepted ones, the saints). They are refulgent in celestial glory, and on their foreheads they carry the fortunate sign of His divine grace.

In the last two lines, the Guru says the sorting of the good from the bad will take place in that court and this will be known to us only when we reach there. The term used is *kach pakāyi* (the unsound or unbaked). *Kacha* is used to describe something not yet fit for its purpose. Thus, we can have a *kacha* fruit meaning unripe, or a *kacha* person meaning somebody who lacks solidity and worth. Here the reference is to the spiritual readiness of a soul. The ones lacking in merit are the *kacha* and those who have achieved spiritual merit are the *pakka*. However, it is not possible for anyone on this earth to say if he has achieved this fitness or not. Nor can any man make such claim about another person. These are those who assume great airs and believe that because they have performed holy rituals or undertaken great recitation of scriptures, their merit is bound to be high. Such are mere speculations. The reality will come out only when He does the judging. Only when His true judgement is delivered will our true worth become known.

It may also be of interest to know that Osho takes another view, that of the word *Dharamsāl* in the third line as a 'transit inn' and not place of religion. It is of course used in that sense also quite frequently and there are *Dharamsālās* set up by philanthropists for free or highly subsidised use by pilgrims or short-term visitors. Osho says that the Guru meant us to see that our stay in this world is like a tourist, a short-term association. Forming any lasting attachment to things material in this world is thus pointless. Once you accept the truth of the transiency of all things and all earthly relationships your mind will automatically turn to the more permanent Reality, the Lord Himself. This is also an interesting approach and conveys a powerful message quite in consonance with the *Gurbāṇi*. We can thus say that this *Dharamsāl* is our arena of action to earn our nearness to the Lord, but it is not by any means our permanent abode and we must be aware always of the transience of our sojourn here.

40

REALM OF RIGHTEOUSNESS

Pauṛi 35

ਧਰਮ ਖੰਡ ਕਾ ਏਹੋ ਧਰਮੁ॥	*Dharam khandd ka eho dharam.*
ਗਿਆਨ ਖੰਡ ਕਾ ਆਖਹੁ ਕਰਮੁ॥	*Gyān khandd ka ākho karam.*
ਕੇਤੇ ਪਵਣ ਪਾਣੀ ਵੈਸੰਤਰ ਕੇਤੇ ਕਾਨ ਮਹੇਸ॥	*Ketay pavaṇ pāṇi vaisantar ketay kān mahes.*
ਕੇਤੇ ਬਰਮੇ ਘਾੜਤਿ ਘੜੀਅਹਿ ਰੂਪ ਰੰਗ ਕੇ ਵੇਸ॥	*Ketay barmay ghāṛat ghaṛīay rūp rung kay veis.*
ਕੇਤੀਆ ਕਰਮ ਭੂਮੀ ਮੇਰ ਕੇਤੇ ਕੇਤੇ ਧੂ ਉਪਦੇਸ॥	*Ketīya karam bhūmi mer ketay ketay dhoo updeis. (5)*
ਕੇਤੇ ਇੰਦ ਚੰਦ ਸੂਰ ਕੇਤੇ ਕੇਤੇ ਮੰਡਲ ਦੇਸ ॥	*Ketay ind chand, sūr ketay, ketay manddal deis.*
ਕੇਤੇ ਸਿਧ ਬੁਧ ਨਾਥ ਕੇਤੇ ਕੇਤੇ ਦੇਵੀ ਵੇਸ॥	*Ketay sidh budh nāth ketay ketay devi veis.*
ਕੇਤੇ ਦੇਵ ਦਾਨਵ ਮੁਨਿ ਕੇਤੇ ਕੇਤੇ ਰਤਨ ਸਮੁੰਦ॥	*Ketay dev dānav, munn ketay, ketay ratan samund.*
ਕੇਤੀਆ ਖਾਣੀ ਕੇਤੀਆ ਬਾਣੀ ਕੇਤੇ ਪਾਤ ਨਰਿੰਦ॥	*Ketīya khāṇi ketīya bāṇi ketay pāt narind.*
ਕੇਤੀਆ ਸੁਰਤੀ ਸੇਵਕ ਕੇਤੇ ਨਾਨਕ ਅੰਤੁ ਨ ਅੰਤੁ॥੩੫॥	*Ketīya surti sevak ketay Nanak unt na unt.*

Brief glossary

ਧਰਮ ਖੰਡ	*Dharam khandd*	Realm of righteousness
ਗਿਆਨ ਖੰਡ	*Gyān khandd*	Realm of enlightenment or knowledge

ਕਰਮੁ	*Karam*	Practice, characteristic (in this *pauṛi*)
ਘਾੜਤਿ	*Ghāṛat*	Fashioning, making
ਮੇਰ	*Mer*	Mountain
ਕਰਮ ਭੂਮੀ	*Karam bhūmi*	Arena of action
ਬਾਣੀ	*Bāṇi*	Forms of speech
ਪਾਤ ਨਰਿੰਦ	*Pāt narind*	Dynasties of kings
ਸੁਰਤਿ	*Surti*	Divine knowledge
ਸੇਵਕ	*Sevak*	Those who serve
ਖਾਣੀ	*Khāṇi*	Forms of creation, sources of life

Simply translated this *pauṛi* says that having looked at the way of the *Dharam khandd*, the 'Realm of Righteousness', let us now pay heed to the law of the *Gyān khandd*, the 'Realm of Enlightenment'. In that realm exists numberless forms of air, water and fire and as numerous Vishnus and Shivas. Equally numerous are the Brahmas fashioning, as per their duty, varied universes. There are numberless arenas of action, celestial mountain *Sumer* and sermons to (*Bhagat*) *Dhruv*. Many are the Indras, the moons and the suns and as many the lands and solar systems. There are many mystic ascetics, enlightened ones, heads of *Jogis'* sects and many forms of the divine Female Principle. There are many *Devtas* (godlings) and *Dānavs* (demonic forces). Many are the *Munis* (ascetics) who maintain silence to achieve quietudes for spiritual growth. Many are the jewels (like the ones extracted from churning of the 'Primeval Ocean'). Many are the forms of origin of beings, many the forms of speech, many the emperors over men, many are those immersed in the Lord and many the servants of God living as per His prescription. Let us now look at the message in more detail and also see what the learned commentators have said.

In the first line of this *pauṛi* the Guru is first summing up the lesson of the previous *pauṛi* and is saying that what all was described there is the way of the *Dharam khandd*, the 'Realm of Righteousness'. He is saying that the determination of whether you are unripe, half-baked or unfit (*kacha*) or whether you are ready in all ways will be done in the divine court and only when we reach there will the true merit of our actions become apparent.

The Guru in line two tells us to now pay heed to the law of the *Gyān khandd*, the 'Realm of Enlightenment'. The word 'ਆਖਹੁ'- *ākho* - is rendered by the learned commentators either as a question, meaning 'tell us how', or as a statement meaning 'I am telling you'. Commentators have used it in either sense. The SGPC's *Shabdarth* and Narain Singh use it in the sense of a question while most others use it as a statement. This latter seems the more appealing usage. After all the Guru is here edifying his disciples and has thus far in the *Japji* given us his vision of the universe, the Lord's grace and the proper conduct and discipline for us to move up on the path to God-realization. In the previous *pauṛi* he told us about the first stage of the soul's progress on the path to divine knowledge – the stage of the 'Realm of Righteousness', the *Dharam khandd*. He then begins this *pauṛi* by saying such is the way of the *Dharam khandd*. The way he refers to *Karmi karmi hoye vīchār* – that our actions determine how we shall be judged – and says that on reaching His presence *Kach pakāyi othhai pāye* - the difference between the half-baked or unripe, and the ripe ones, those fit for the Lord's grace will become known. So, logically this line has to mean that the Guru is telling us about the next stage, the *Gyān khandd*. The line is not posed as a question but is a positive statement meant to tell us to pay attention and listen to what the *Gyān khandd* is like, what is the way of this *Khandd*. Though, of course, the next lines would follow as logically even if this were assumed to be a question. The Guru explains this *Khandd* in the next lines.

In lines three and four, the Guru says that in this stage of the soul's growth we come to realise that therein exist numberless forms of *pavaṇ pāṇi vaisantar* – air, water and fire. Gyāni Maskin takes this to refer to the various types of air, for instance the subtle air that sustains life, or the forms of air that we see and experience blowing in the world. Similar is the situation for water or fire. Other commentators have just literally translated the words. Logically considered, this seems to be by way of further elaboration of the idea already given to us in the previous *pauṛis*, e.g. *Dharti hor paray hor hor* (there are worlds upon worlds beyond reckoning [*Pauṛi* 16]), or *Pātāla pātāl lakh āgāsā āgās* (there are countless nether regions and as many heavens [*Pauṛi* 22]). A multiverse with countless worlds, each with their own components of air, water and fire are what we are being asked to see. The Guru also adds in this, the third line, that there are as many *Kāhans* and *Mahes*. *Kāhan* is the name used for Lord Krishna, an *avatār* of Lord Vishnu. *Mahes* or *Mahesh* is another name for Lord Shiva. Since there are such countless worlds and universes created by the Lord then all and each of these have their own Holy Trinities of their own Brahma, Vishnu, and Mahesh. The incarnations as Krishna have occurred in these infinite worlds countless times. He elaborates on this theme by adding that equally numerous are the Brahmas carrying out their assigned task of fashioning universes of various shapes and hues and forms. The Guru is telling us that in the *Gyān khandd* the spiritual vision is so widened that, beyond this earth, this *Dharam sāl*, where we are given the rare opportunity to earn merit through righteous actions, we become aware that there exist an uncounted number of universes. The Brahma, Vishnu, Mahesh who are in-charge of our universe, are replicated endlessly in the multiverse the Lord has created.

In the fifth and sixth lines the thought is further carried forward. In this multiverse there are numberless *karma bhūmi* (arenas for action), *Mer* (the celestial mountains) and *dhu updeis* (the sermons delivered to *Dhruva*). Many are the Indras, the moons and the suns, and as many the lands and solar systems. The phrase *karma bhūmi*, literally means arena of action. The metaphysical connotation is of a place where a soul, clad in a human form, gets the opportunity to fight the intense internal battle between good and soil and tries to pass the test for entering the Lord's presence with honour. *Karma bhūmi* is what Lord Krishna called the field of Kurukshetra when serious moral doubts arose in Arjuna's mind after finding his own dear ones arrayed against him in battle. As he sought to withdraw from the battle having lost heart Lord Krishna delivered the stirring sermon called the *Bhagwad Gita* and made Arjuna aware of the importance of surrendering completely to the Lord and entering whole-heartedly into righteous action without the thought for reward, which he explained to Arjuna lies only in the Lord's hands. This *Dharam sāl*, this earth of ours, is every man's *karma bhūmi*. The Guru says that in the Lord's vast creation every world, every place, every man has his own *karma bhūmi* – there are unnumbered such *karma bhūmis*. The second word *Mer'is* short for Mount *Sumeru*, the celestial mountain, and is also generically used for the hills. This, says the *Mahan Kosh*, is that special mountain which according to the *Bhāgwat Purāṇa* and *Vishnu Purāṇa* is made of gold. It is supposed to be 84000 *yojanas* high and it extends into the earth another 16000 *yojanas*. It is topped by a flat plain extending 32000 *yojanas*. This is where the gods reside. Notice the similarity to the Greek Mount Olympus, the supposed abode of the Greek gods. Incidentally, the *yojana* is an ancient measure of distance reckoned differently in various parts of India but generally said to be four *kos*, the *kos* being 4000 yards long. Such *Sumers*, says the Guru, are countless in this infinite universe.

The name *Dhruv* is shortened to the common *dhu* by the Guru. Dhruv was the child who achieved God-realization and for his great spiritual attainment he earned a place in the heavens, where he rests even today as the Polar Star according to Hindu mythology. The story goes that spurned by his stepmother and finding no support from his royal father who was too foolishly smitten by a younger prettier wife, *Dhruv* developed a sense of renunciation for the world and became a child ascetic. He was delivered a famous discourse on the divine mystery by the celestial sage, *Nārad.* Such sermons, says the Guru, have been delivered by a myriad *Nārads* to as many *Dhruvs* under the Lord's canopy. The Guru adds that in all these places there are the Moon God, the Sun God, and their king Indra. This set of gods, and ascetics and great souls are repeated throughout the entire universe an endless number of times. The term *manddal deis* in line six literally means divisions and countries. *Manddal* also is used for the mystic *chakras* - circles or cycles. The solar system is also referred to as *Surya manddal.* Since the Guru is narrating about the infinity of creation, the sense here for this term has to be taken as 'the divisions of the universe'. Thus, we can take it to mean the galaxies, universes, worlds and the countries therein where His created beings exist and fight their inner battles between right and wrong, the good and the evil, within their own selves.

In the seventh and eighth lines more varieties of created beings and achieved souls are listed. The Guru says there are appearing in the *Gyān khandd* many *Sidh*, *Budh*, *Nāth*, and many *Devis*. Many are also the *Devs, Dānavs, Munis* and many the jewels in the ocean. As we have seen earlier also the *Sidhs* are the ascetics who through hard mystic practices achieve miraculous powers called *sidhis*, such as becoming invisible, becoming very large, or very small, being able to control the minds of other persons and being able to force one's will on them, etc. The *Budhs* are the enlightened ones, those who have achieved knowledge of the divine. *Nāth* is a term used for the head of a sect of *Jogis.* So it denotes someone who has highly achieved yogic powers. The 'Devis' are the Female Principle of the Gods, or consorts of the Gods. 'Devi' is also another name for Durga, the divine Female Principle. Prof. Talib renders this word as 'incarnation of the Goddess'. Prof. Sahib Singh, however, renders it as 'forms of Devis'. The *Shabdarth* says this means different 'Devis' like Lakshmi, Durga, Kali, Chandi Bhagwati, etc. as also the Roman Juno or the Egyptian Isis, etc. Narain Singh also takes the line of the SGPC's *Shabdarth*. Further, the Guru refers to the *Devs* and *Dānavs*, which we have seen are the divine powers that stand for righteousness and brute power, respectively. *Munis* are the ascetics who undergo hard penances while maintaining *Maun* (quietude) to achieve spiritual growth. Countless are these in this infinite universe. Similarly, the jewels of the ocean are countless. These are the invaluable gifts that the ocean yielded when churned by the *Devtas* and the *Dānavs* using the mount *Mandara* as the pivot post and the primal serpent *Vāsuki* as the cord. These included the *parijāt* gem, the *kalpa tāru* tree, *kāmadhenu* the wish granting cow, and Dhanvantri the divine physician. Such jewels, the Guru says, have appeared innumerable times from myriad primal oceans in this universe.

In the ninth and tenth lines, the concluding ones, the Guru says just as numerous are the *khāṇi*s, the *bāṇis* and the *pāt narind* (emperors). The *surti* (ones living immersed in devotion to the Lord) and the *sevak* (ones serving Him) are also beyond number. *Khāṇi* is used here to describe forms of origin and these were counted to be four – *anddaj* (egg born), *jeraj* (born of placenta), *setaj* (born of sweat), and *utbhuj* (the flora). Similarly, many are the forms of speech, and so are the emperors who rule over men. *Surti* in common parlance is used for absorption. Prof. Talib says this is from *Shruti*, the Sanskrit term for revelation, the deeper form of cognizance (gnosis). The term has been differently rendered by the learned ones. Narain Singh calls it as 'those who meditate'; Prof. Sahib Singh says it is the plural of *surt* meaning absorption in God. Giani Harbans Singh sees it as the feminine of the next word used here – *sevak* – meaning man-servant; and so he renders it as female attendants. Bhai Vir Singh says it means both the absorption in God as also those who are thus absorbed. On balance, in the present context, the meaning as 'immersed in God' seems the more appropriate. *Sevak* means servant and is used here to describe those who live in obedience to the Lord and serve Him by following His prescription. The Guru says that all these things are beyond the human capacity to count. All this awareness will dawn on the seeker as soon as he achieves the *Gyān khandd*.

Thus, in the *Gyān khandd* the knowledge of the universe descends on the seeker. This, however, is not yet complete enlightenment, which will descend upon the seeker in the future *Khandds* as the soul progresses. Incomplete though this level of understanding is, yet it is a grand jump upwards, a necessary stage before the final state of enlightenment. For that state to be reached there is yet the *Saram khandd*, the 'Realm of Striving', ahead of the seeker. The seeker has by now become aware of this earth and of the purpose of his own existence thereon. He has realized the importance of right action and also that judgement, the fruit of our endeavours, is in the Lord's hands and will depend on the merit we earn through actions, and in the ultimate analysis of the Lord's grace. The seeker has now acquired knowledge of the intent and vastness of the created worlds. He has learnt the humbling truth that he is but one small creature in a huge system where great men much higher than him and divine beings of great power all exist in subservience to the One. Not just that, but also that this huge system is just one in an infinite progression of such systems.

The *pauṛi* concludes here, but the discussion on the *Gyān khandd* will be concluded only in the next *pauṛi* where, briefly put, the Guru will tell us that the seeker's thirst for knowledge will burn bright and he will experience the joy of acquiring the knowledge of Him.

41

REALM OF SPIRITUAL ENDEAVOUR

Pauṛi 36

ਗਿਆਨ ਖੰਡ ਮਹਿ ਗਿਆਨੁ ਪਰਚੰਡੁ ॥	*Gyān khandd meh gyān parchandd.*
ਤਿਥੈ ਨਾਦ ਬਿਨੋਦ ਕੋਡ ਅਨੰਦੁ ॥	*Tithhai nād binod kod anand.*
ਸਰਮ ਖੰਡ ਕੀ ਬਾਣੀ ਰੂਪੁ ॥	*Saram khandd ki bāṇi rūp.*
ਤਿਥੈ ਘਾੜਤਿ ਘੜੀਐ ਬਹੁਤੁ ਅਨੂਪੁ ॥	*Tithhai ghārat ghaṛīai bahut anūp.*
ਤਾ ਕੀਆ ਗਲਾ ਕਥੀਆ ਨਾ ਜਾਹਿ ॥	*Ta kīya galla kathhīya na jāhe.*
ਜੇ ਕੋ ਕਹੈ ਪਿਛੈ ਪਛੁਤਾਇ ॥	*Je ko kahai pichhai pacchutāye.*
ਤਿਥੈ ਘੜੀਐ ਸੁਰਤਿ ਮਤਿ ਮਨਿ ਬੁਧਿ ॥	*Tithhai ghaṛīai surt(i) mat(i) mann budh.*
ਤਿਥੈ ਘੜੀਐ ਸੁਰਾ ਸਿਧਾ ਕੀ ਸੁਧਿ ॥ ੩੬ ॥	*Tithhai ghaṛīai sura sidha ki sudh.*

Brief glossary

ਪਰਚੰਡੁ	*Prachandd*	Ablaze, intense
ਸਰਮ ਖੰਡ	*Saram khandd*	The realm of striving, spiritual effort
ਰੂਪੁ	*Rūp*	Beauty, beauteous form
ਘਾੜਤਿ	*Ghāṛat*	Form
ਅਨੂਪੁ	*Anūp*	Beyond compare
ਕਥੀਆ	*Kathhīya*	Narrated
ਸੁਰਤਿ	*Surti*	Inner awareness
ਮਤਿ	*Mat(i)*	Intellect
ਮਨਿ ਬੁਧਿ	*Mann budh*	Awakening of mind
ਸੁਰਾ ਸਿਧਾ ਕੀ ਸੁਧਿ	*Sura sidha ki sudh*	Awareness which gods and *sidhs* possess

Simply rendered this *paur.i* tells us that in the *Gyān khandd* (which we discussed in the previous *paur.i*) knowledge is resplendently ablaze and in that realm there are soul pleasing amusements, miracles and pleasures. The *Saram khandd* (Realm of Spiritual Striving) is (the next level) where the forms of incomparable beauty are being forged and moulded. The awesome things formed there are beyond anyone's power to describe, and were someone to attempt to speak of it he would soon regret his impetuosity. In this realm are forged the *surt(i), mat(i), mann* and *budh* – the inner awareness, the intellect, and the awakening of the mind. Through this remoulding is attained here the high-mindedness of the *Suras, Devtas*, and of the *Sidhs*, the spiritual adepts. Let us now look at it in more detail and also see what the learned commentators have said.

The Guru, before proceeding to tell us of the *Saram khandd,* recapitulates in the first two lines the marvels of the previous stage, the *Gyān khandd.* He says the glow of knowledge is resplendently ablaze in that 'Realm of Knowledge'. The seeker has, in other words, now great knowledge of the wonders of the Lord's creation and there is in him a burning desire to acquire more knowledge. When he reaches this spiritual stage he is filled with great joy. The Guru says that in that realm there is heard by the successful seeker the *nād*, the music of the spheres, the mystical melody that the godly always can hear and which fills them with bliss. The *Anhad nād* (the unstruck note) is the desired goal of many a worshipper and is said to be heard by yogis when they have successfully gone into *samādhi.* The Guru says in this realm of enlightened knowledge there are for the many soul pleasing amusements, miracles and pleasures. *Binod* literally means an amusement to entertain; *Kodd* is the common form of *kautak* (miracles); and *Ānand* literally means joy. In other words, the Guru is saying that in the *Gyān khandd* the soul is in a state of high bliss such as could be compared to what on earth could partially be attained through entertainments and miracles and wonders of joy. Till this line the Guru was recapitulating and completing the discussion on the *Gyān khandd*, the 'Realm of Knowledge'. Now from the next line he moves to the next *Khandd*.

In lines three and four, the Guru expounds upon the subject of this, the thirty-sixth *pauṛi*, the realm of spiritual striving – the *Saram khandd*. The spirit, aware by now of its place on this *Dharam sāl*, by traversing the *Dharam khandd*, and having acquired the stage of enlightenment about the entire universe and its creatures and its working, in the *Gyān khandd*, is now ready to raise the level of its striving so as now to reach, or seek to reach, the level of inner enlightenment where oneness with the Lord can be hoped for. The Lord in His grace can of course choose to pick up any soul from any stage of its progress; that mystery is beyond us. However, the duty of everyone is to continue to refine one's inner-self through constant *Nām Simraṇ*, recitation of His name. This is the path the seeker followed from step one, the path that gradually brought the seeker out of the morass of worldly attachments and out of the bondage to the senses, to the anger, lust, avarice, attachments and pride that govern most of us. This path properly followed brought the soul to the spiritual spheres we are discussing here. It took the soul to the enlightenment of the *Dharam khandd* and further enlightenment up to the *Gyān khandd* – the 'Realm of Spiritual Illumination'. The same path will now take the seeker to the *Saram khandd* – the 'Realm of Spiritual Striving'. This is a realm of ineffable beauty, the Guru says. The word *bāṇi* is used here not in its sense as 'language' but as 'the making'. The Punjabi word *bunaṇa* also translates as 'to make', 'to weave', from which is derived the word *bāṇi*. Here it is meant in this sense and stands for making or forging. The Guru says that in this stage - *ghāṛat ghaṛīai bahut anūp* - are forged the forms of incomparable beauty. What is being forged is then further explained in the next lines. Why is beauty the predominant theme of this realm? Because it is here that the culmination of a seeker's lifelong efforts can be reached. Having learnt to discipline the body and control the senses, having learnt to recite His name with each breath, having learnt to hear His message with the heart and acquiring true faith in Him, the seeker is now well past the worst shoals of earthly distractions, and should have smooth sailing hence forward. Knowledge of this world, of the purpose of his existence in it; and in the next stage the knowledge of the universe around and of the mysteries of its functioning having been acquired, the true devotee is now advanced enough to start the most difficult, and the most rewarding, part of his journey. He is now ready to undertake the tough task of moulding his own inner-self, his own mind, his own intellect. These have of course already gained from and been much refined by the constant practice of *Nām Simraṇ*; they are now in a state of readiness for the final step. And this happens, the Guru says, in the *Saram khandd.* The uncouth part of us will here be finally polished and what will emerge will be a thing of shining beauty, an inner consciousness fully purified and cast into the form where this vessel is now ready and worthy of receiving the Lord's benediction.

In lines five and six, the Guru expresses his awe at what is being wrought in this realm and expresses his inability to describe it in words. He says these wonders truly beggar all description, and were someone to attempt to speak of it he would soon regret his impetuosity for he would know the task to be impossible, and any description inaccurate and inadequate.

In lines seven and eight, the Guru puts into words precisely what is it that is being forged here in this *Khandd*; what are those things of incomparable beauty? He says these are *Surt(i), Mat(i), Mann Budh*, literally the inner absorption in the Lord or the inner consciousness, the intellect and the 'mind'. *Surt(i),* according to the *Mahan Kosh* of Bhai Sahib Bhai Kahan Singh is that part of the *Antahkaraṇ* which gives us memory. *Antahkaraṇ* is described as that inner consciousness or sense which controls the external senses. It is supposed to have four components – *Mann, Budh, Chit*, and *Aham*. He describes *Mann* or mind as that part of *Antahkaraṇ* which causes thoughts and wishes to emerge. *Budh* or intellect, he says is the component where deliberation or cogitation and decisions take place. *Chit* or awareness, he describes as the part of the *Antahkaraṇ* which enables man to do *Simraṇ* or think on the Lord. The last, *Aham* or the self is the component that links us to the material world. The forging of the mind, the inner consciousness is thus to mould all these components into a controlled form that centres itself totally on the Lord. This is hard work indeed, hence the title *Saram khandd.* The Guru a little later will tell us *Jini nām dhiāyia gaye maskat ghāl* (those who could forge their consciousness to focus entirely on the *Nām* have truly succeeded in their labour). The word *maskat* is the common form of the Persian *mushakkat* which literally means hard labour. The Guru says through the re-moulding of our inner-self we attain in this *Khandd* the awareness levels of the *Devtas* and the *Sidhs.* These semi-divine and greatly achieved souls are the exemplars of high-mindedness and right thinking, of being in complete accord with the Lord's way. The seeker who has reached here now has the mind and the awareness of a *Devta* or a *Sidh.*

We may note that some commentators have rendered the last line to mean "that at this stage is fashioned the genius of the sage and seer in man" to quote Dr. Sangat Singh, or "as also is fashioned the genius of the pious and semi divines", as Iqbal Singh puts it. Also some have viewed *Mann* and *Budh* as separate words here meaning mind and understanding. However, most other commentators have seen it the way we have here discussed, which seems the more appealing view. In this *Khandd* is re-moulded the *Surt(i), Mat(i)* and *Mann Budh* – the inner consciousness, the intellect and the enlightenment of the mind or absorption in the Lord, wisdom and cognitive acuity, respectively.

It may also be of interest to know that the term *Saram,* apart from modesty (Persian) and hard work (Sanskrit), also according to Bhai Vir Singh means 'joy' from the Sanskrit root *sharman.* He translates this term as the 'Realm of Joy', a rendering also followed by Macauliffe. According to most other learned commentators the more acceptable usage is 'hard work' as we have discussed here also. In the context of the *Gurbāṇi* this definitely seems the more appropriate translation. It may be added that Osho in his 'True Name' has used it as modesty and has given an interesting commentary from that perspective in his two-volume work which, true to Osho's style, is well-written and entertaining.

Having in this brief *pauṛi* told us of the wonderful *Saram khandd*, the penultimate stage in the passage to the Lord, the Guru now tells us about the 'Realm of Grace', the *Karam khandd* in the next *pauṛi* which also contains description of the final destination, the *Sach khandd*.

42

REALM OF GRACE: ONE WITH THE LORD

Pauṛi 37

ਕਰਮ ਖੰਡ ਕੀ ਬਾਣੀ ਜੋਰੁ॥	*Karam khandd ki bāṇi jor.*
ਤਿਥੈ ਹੋਰੁ ਨ ਕੋਈ ਹੋਰੁ॥	*Tithhai hor na koyi hor.*
ਤਿਥੈ ਜੋਧ ਮਹਾਬਲ ਸੂਰ॥	*Tithhai jodh mahābal sūr.*
ਤਿਨ ਮਹਿ ਰਾਮੁ ਰਹਿਆ ਭਰਪੂਰ॥	*Tin meh rām rahiya bharpūr.*
ਤਿਥੈ ਸੀਤੋ ਸੀਤਾ ਮਹਿਮਾ ਮਾਹਿ॥	*Tithhai sīto sīta mahima māhe.*
ਤਾ ਕੇ ਰੂਪ ਨ ਕਥਨੇ ਜਾਹਿ॥	*Ta kay rūp na kathnay jāhe.*
ਨਾ ਓਹਿ ਮਰਹਿ ਨ ਠਾਗੇ ਜਾਹਿ॥	*Na oh maray na tthāggay jāhe.*
ਜਿਨ ਕੈ ਰਾਮੁ ਵਸੈ ਮਨ ਮਾਹਿ॥	*Jin kai rām vasai mann māhe.*
ਤਿਥੈ ਭਗਤ ਵਸਹਿ ਕੇ ਲੋਅ॥	*Tithhai bhagat vaseh kay low.*
ਕਰਹਿ ਅਨੰਦੁ ਸਚਾ ਮਨਿ ਸੋਇ॥	*Karay anand sacha mann soye.*
ਸਚ ਖੰਡਿ ਵਸੈ ਨਿਰੰਕਾਰੁ॥	*Sach khandd vaseh nirankār.*
ਕਰਿ ਕਰਿ ਵੇਖੈ ਨਦਰਿ ਨਿਹਾਲ॥	*Kar kar vekhay nadar nihāl.*
ਤਿਥੈ ਖੰਡ ਮੰਡਲ ਵਰਭੰਡ॥	*Tithhai khandd manddal varbhandd.*
ਜੇ ਕੋ ਕਥੈ ਤ ਅੰਤ ਨ ਅੰਤ॥	*Jay ko kathhai ta unt na unt.*
ਤਿਥੈ ਲੋਅ ਲੋਅ ਆਕਾਰ॥	*Tithhai low low ākār.*
ਜਿਵ ਜਿਵ ਹੁਕਮੁ ਤਿਵੈ ਤਿਵ ਕਾਰ॥	*Jiv jiv hukam tivay tiv kār.*
ਵੇਖੈ ਵਿਗਸੈ ਕਰਿ ਵੀਚਾਰੁ ॥	*Vekhay vigsay karr vīchār.*
ਨਾਨਕ ਕਥਨਾ ਕਰੜਾ ਸਾਰੁ॥੩੭॥	*Nanak kathhna karaṛa sār.*

Brief glossary

ਕਰਮ ਖੰਡ	*Karam khandd*	Realm of Grace
ਜੋਰੁ	*Jor*	Might

ਹੋਰੁ	*Hor*	Other
ਜੋਧ ਮਹਾਬਲ	*Jodh Mahābal*	Great warriors
ਰਾਮੁ	*Rām*	Here God
ਸੀਤੋ ਸੀਤਾ	*Sīto sita*	'Sitas', or Ram and Sita (Variously interpreted)
ਠਾਗੇ ਜਾਹਿ	*Thāggay jāhay*	Cannot be cheated
ਮਹਿਮਾ	*Mahima*	Renown, praise
ਸਚ ਖੰਡ	*Sach khandd*	In the realm of bliss, the eternal realm
ਸਾਰੁ	*Sār*	Iron
ਕਰੜਾ	*Karaṛa*	Tough, hard

This *pauṛi* can be translated to mean that this realm of grace has might as its characteristic. None resides there except those rapt in God. Those who reside here are the mighty warriors (who have conquered themselves). Their every pore is satiated with divine awareness. In this realm reside great heroines (like Sita) whose renown is high and whose spiritual beauty because of her complete absorption in the Lord is resplendent. These lucky achievers, the mighty warriors who have reached this level, are then beyond the reach of death and are never *thāggay* (lead astray from the true path [by the wiles of Māya), because the Lord resides in their hearts.

In this *paur.i* the Guru tells us of the last stage of a developed soul, the Realm of Grace where the Lord has now given the successful seeker His glance of blessing. It also tells us of the final destination, the *Sach khandd* to which the previous four realms were the preliminary stages. This is the realm where the Lord's grace has brought the soul into unison with Himself and now the soul and the Lord are as one. This is the realm of bliss, where there is everlasting joy and the soul is now free from the bondage of this world and of the senses that controlled it in the human body. It is the eternal realm where now the soul, freed from the tyranny of the cycle of death and re-birth, is now in *Nirvān.a*, or *Moksha* and is free forever to remain with the Lord.

First the Guru speaks of the fourth stage, the *Karam khandd*, the 'Realm of Grace'. He says in lines 1 and 2 that this stage is marked by might and none resides there except those rapt in God. The word *bāṇi* here is not used in the usual sense of 'language' or 'tongue'. Some commentators, for example Prof. Talib and Narain Singh, describe it as 'expression of'. Dr. Sangat Singh renders it as 'emphasis is on' and Iqbal Singh calls it 'is the attribute of'. Prof. Sahib Singh calls it 'formation of'. The central idea common to all is that this *Khandd* is marked by might. Also, as we have noted earlier too, the term *Karam* is in Sanskrit used as 'action' and in Persian used as 'benediction, blessing'. All commentators agree that the sense here is as in the Persian 'blessing or grace'. Thus, the first line is to be read to mean that in this 'Realm of Grace' the main characteristic is might. The meaning here is that when the soul has attained this stage when the Lord's grace has descended all human frailty is instantly burnt away. What power on earth or in the universe can be mightier than the power of being with God? This is the ultimate power and is available to those on whom the Lord casts His glance of grace. The Guru says in the second line that in this realm none else can exist, or that only those who have achieved this state can exist in this spiritual region.

In lines 3 and 4, the Guru says more on the subject of might being the distinguishing mark of this realm. He says those who reside in this realm are the *Jodh mahābal* (the mighty warriors). They are the ones who have fought the hardest battle and won the greatest victory – the victory over their own selves, and having scored that huge triumph they have got the equally grand prize, God-consciousness in their entire being. Every pore is *bharpūr* (satiated with the divine awareness). Thus are they mighty in their warrior-hood, against their own baser selves and against evil.

In the fifth and sixth lines the Guru says in this realm are *sīto sīta mahima māhe*. This line has been subjected to various interpretations. In the *Mahan Kosh* Bhai Kahan Singh translates it as: "Rām the all pervading God is effulgent every where and the spiritual peace in the form of Sita is in bloom." Bhai Vir Singh in his commentary says that the word *Sīto* means 'Ram' and says it should be seen as *sīta* + *dhāv*' – *Sīto dhāv,* which is written as *Sīto*, on the analogy of *mādhav* being written as *mādho*. He says it refers to Ram as the husband of Sita and the line is to be rendered as 'there are Ram and Sita' highly honoured; though of course he refers also to numerous other interpretations of this phrase which various commentators have adopted. Iqbal Singh translates it as meaning 'cold and hot' in the sense of fully, completely. He probably takes 'Sita' as deriving from *Seet*, a Punjabi rendering of the Sanskrit *Sheetal* meaning cool and soothing. On the other hand, Narain Singh takes it as *Seeta* after *Seeta*, on the analogy of *ūcha* (high), being written as *ūcho ūcha* (very high), or *sūcha* as *sūcho sūcha*, or *amulo amul* used for very pure or very invaluable. Prof. Talib renders it as: "In that sphere reside heroines like Sita." Prof. Sahib Singh in his commentary, and then following the same view Giani Maskin in his audio commentary, takes it to mean 'Completely Rapt'. He has taken the Punjabi word *seen.a* (to sew) as the root here when *seeta* will mean sewn. Thus, he says *Seeto Seeta* means sewn or joined completely together, referring to the soul completely immersed in the Lord. Osho in his commentary takes the reference here as being to Sita, the wife of Lord Rama, and argues that in the previous line the Guru has said that in this realm there is Ram all pervading and hence this line refers to Sita, thus completing the picture by covering both, the masculine and the feminine principles of the Divine. It is his argument that the one without the other is incomplete and so the Guru deliberately used this terminology. The SGPC's *Shabdarth* renders the line as *Seeta* after *Seeta*, the sense similar to that taken by Narain Singh. The *Shabdarth* also says that the Guru uses Sita as an example of valiant women. This is apparently in the context of the *Jodh mahābal* (mighty warrior) used in the previous lines, and the realm having been marked with might as its outstanding characteristic.

There is thus great diversity in interpreting this line. Though the interpretation by Prof. Sahib Singh is also often followed, but on balance the view taken by Prof. Talib, which is in broad concordance with the view agreed in the *Shabdarth* and also the view taken by Narain Singh, seems to be the more appropriate one. He has rendered this line as: "In that sphere abide numberless heroines like Sita …." So the meaning of these lines is that in the Realm of Grace, of which might is the main characteristic, there reside great heroines, whose praise and renown is high. Their spiritual beauty, because of their complete absorption in the Lord, is indescribably resplendent.

In lines 7 and 8, the Guru speaks further of these lucky achievers who have reached this realm. These mighty warriors rapt totally in the Lord, the Guru says, are beyond the reach of death, and never are they *thāggay* (lead astray from the true path by the wiles of 'Māya'). Even earlier in *pauṛi* 13 the Guru had told us *Mannai jamm kay sāth na jāye* (the true believers are not taken by the messenger of death). Here it is put another way and even taken a small step further. *Na oh maray* (they die not), says the Guru, meaning that while the body will die but spiritually they are now forever with the Lord. Already is eternity their abode, for they have the Lord's grace and are ready to step into *Sach khandd*, the 'Eternal Realm' where time or death does not hold sway. These lucky ones are also not subject to the power of Māya (illusion). There is therefore nothing to distract them from their total absorption in the Lord. Till this stage the soul is in a constant state of flux. Its evil or materialistic tendencies keep pulling it down. While the hard work to control this evil keeps raising the spirit upwards towards the Lord, Māya still has great power and is often successful in deluding the seeker away from the right path, with illusions of wealth or power or pandering otherwise to the anger, greed, attachments and pride within us. But this is no longer a danger for the resident of the *Karam khandd*. This exemption, this freedom has come about, the Guru says in the eighth line, because the Lord Himself permeates every bit of their minds.

In lines 9 and 10, which are the last two describing the *Karam khandd*, the Guru says that in this realm there reside *bhagat* (devotees) assembled from *kay low* (the many worlds), and they are in *ānand* (high bliss) because the True One resides ever in their hearts. The concept of a 'multiverse' is touched upon repeatedly by the Guru, for instance *Dharti hor paray hor hor* (there are Worlds after Worlds) in *pauṛi* 16 refers directly to a multiverse. Again in *pauṛi* 19 the Guru says *agam agam asankh low* (countless are the worlds, one beyond the other). Similarly, the Guru has told us that in each of these worlds, and universes, there are an equal number of divinities, Brahma, Vishnu, Shiva, Indras, etc. and an equal number of worshippers and achieved souls. Here we are told that the *bhagats*, the devotees from each of these various worlds, are equally following the path to union with Him in their own distinct ways. And just as in our world, there are many who are able to traverse the hard road to God-realization; these *bhagats* from all these myriad worlds, the Guru says, reside with the Lord as can be seen in this realm. Equally sublime is the bliss in the heart of each of them, for the Lord permeates each such heart from whichever world it originated. Here is a thought beyond compare against any exclusivist tendencies. Those who may be tempted to boast that theirs is the only true religion or the only true path to oneness with the Lord are not truly seeing the Lord's design and purpose. The paths and ways of reaching Him are innumerable, and as long as the basic key of attachment to Him alone, and total detachment from the false and the egoistic exist all true devotees will reach Him, following any of these paths. The multiplicity of religions and sects in this single world of ours should itself be proof enough that there is indeed a universal religion of the spirit. Do not look down upon any path just because it happens to be different from your own and accept and honour the validity of each such guide as long as it leads to uplifting of the spiritual level and cleansing of the material dross from the soul. Any such religion will help reach the true devotee to the *Karam khandd*. For the true Sikh the path of course is as prescribed here in the *Gurbāṇi*, and in the *Japji Sahib* itself.

The Guru now, in the eleventh and twelfth lines, onward tells us of the *Sach khandd*, the ultimate destination of the true devotee. The four main stages of this journey have been described by the Guru in the previous three *pauṛis* and in the first part of this one. The successful pilgrim has now arrived and the Guru tells us what it is like, this *Sach khandd*, the 'Realm of Eternity'. The Guru says the Lord Himself resides in this *Khandd* – stage. As the Guru has made clear repeatedly this is not a person or an Anthromorphic entity he is talking about. This is also not some sort of a magnificent palace where a refulgent shining being sits, though it is always possible for that Infinite Power to so appear to a devotee. What the Guru is telling us is that once the soul has achieved this stage of spiritual growth, and as the Guru says, received the glance of grace from the Lord, then the soul and the Lord are as one, or that the Lord Himself resides in the heart of the devotee in this stage. The soul, in complete attunement with the Eternal, can obviously see nothing but the Eternal once it has reached the *Sach khandd*. This is further clarified by the Guru implicitly when he uses the word *Nirankār* here. The one residing in the *Sach khandd* is the Formless One. As the tenth Nanak says in the beginning of the *Jāp Sahib*:

"Chakra chihan or baran jāt or pāt nāhin jeh. Rūp rung or rekh bhekh kou kayh na sakat kay".

(Neither ritual signs nor caste, nor a form, nor colour nor a recognition symbol does He have. No one can say what He is.)

This *Nirankār* Lord that the tenth Nanak describes is the

One referred here, who resides in this eternal region. The seeker is now one with this *Nirankār* - the Formless Lord This power, however, is not a disinterested entity just because it is formless. The Guru says the Lord *kar kar vekhai nadar nihāl* (creates and fashions and looks upon it all with a loving eye). The Lord's transcendent form – *Nirankār* – is equally supplemented by His immanent – *Sargun.a* – form; and He is involved; He creates, makes and watches with affection the flowering of His creation and He nurtures it.

In lines 13 and 14, the Guru says in this realm are contained all worlds, solar systems and universes, and in such an endless succession that were one to attempt description he would find it impossible to reach the full count thereof. The vision of the successful devotee has in this region become the vision of the Lord Himself, for they are as one, in complete unison. To this devotee are visible all parts of creation. In this stage of development the devotee's consciousness encompasses all the various created universes, with all their infinite solar systems and worlds. The number of these is beyond human capacity, a thought the Guru has driven home to us repeatedly. No man can hope to attempt a count of these, for how do you put a number on the Infinite.

In lines 15 and 16 the same thought is re-stated. The Guru says the devotee having reached this far will now see the *low low ākār* (forms of worlds after worlds) and all this infinite system, beyond man's ken, moves in perfect harmony *jiv jiv hukam tivay tiv kār* (complying completely with the law – the will of the Lord). All creation performs its appointed functions in total obedience to His will. This phrase *jiv jiv hukam tivay tiv kār* can be taken as the key governing all existence. Nothing moves; no action is performed except in accordance with what He ordains. Again, we may caution ourselves and understand that this is not to be an alibi for passive inaction. The Lord's will for the soul specifically requires that there be action and He has granted free will to each one of us to the extent that we are free to choose between good and evil. Thus is our journey controlled by us ourselves through our own actions. This freedom is also strictly in accordance with His will. In His benevolence He wishes the soul to do good, follow His path as shown by Gurus and prophets over the ages, and succeed in making its way through the *Khandds* to Him, and reside forever with Him in the realm eternal.

In the last two lines, the seventeenth and eighteenth, the Guru says again that the Lord watches over His creation; there is none over whom His glance does not fall. He ponders over His creation in joy and pleasure and is ever *vigsay* (in a state of bloom). Describing all these mysteries is as hard as *kathna sār* (trying to chew on iron). The thought here again is to tell us of a Lord who is not distant, aloof or indifferent. Far from it, He constantly watches over what He has wrought and each part of it is constantly on His mind. What he sees gives Him pleasure, and so beholding His creation He delights in the contemplation. The last line is a re-statement of the impossibility of describing, counting or measuring the infinite Lord. Hard as chewing iron is the task. In other words, it is just not possible for a human.

Thus we come to the conclusion of the journey that commenced with *paur̤i* 1 where the Guru posed the vital, the only really important question in the life of a human, *Kiv sachiāra hoīyai kiv kūr̤ai tuttai pāl* (How is God-realization to come to us and how do we break through this veil of falsehood and illusion). Throughout the *Japji Sahib* the Guru sought gradually to uplift our understanding and repeatedly he told us the magic formula. Live in total surrender to Him, train and control your senses, bring your own mind under your sway. And throughout runs the theme – recite His name, endlessly, constantly and as much as you have capacity for, until it becomes a part of your consciousness and then one lucky day each and every pore of your body starts to recite His name without your conscious volition. Each breath you take is rapt in His name and you ingest

His name with each morsel you eat. When you can successfully do this hard work the awareness of the Lord will be bestowed on you in successive steps.

The first stage, the *Dharam khandd*, will come to our awareness and we will know that this world we live in is one among an infinite number and it is placed here for us to train ourselves on the righteous path. The knowledge of the universe, at a conscious level, will emerge in the second stage – the *Gyān khandd*. This will lead us to the *Saram khandd* where the harder task of shaping the inner consciousness will be performed and if successful there, will emerge a mind, a soul re-moulded into a form of great beauty. Now will the devotee be ready for the Lord, and in the fourth stage, the *Karam khandd*, His grace will have descended. The knowledge of the universe which at the conscious level was achieved in the *Gyān khandd* will now permeate every atom of the devotee's being. All powers will be his, and the effulgence of reality will shine through. Thus will the destination be reached, the *pāl* of *kūṛ* be pierced and eternity in unison with the Lord become His gift to the devotee.

43

FORGING THE TRUE WORD

Pauṛi 38

ਜਤੁ ਪਾਹਾਰਾ ਧੀਰਜੁ ਸੁਨਿਆਰੁ॥	*Jat pāhāra dhīraj suniyār.*
ਅਹਰਣਿ ਮਤਿ ਵੇਦੁ ਹਥੀਆਰੁ॥	*Ahraṇ mat(i) ved hathīyār.*
ਭਉ ਖਲਾ ਅਗਨਿ ਤਪ ਤਾਉ॥	*Bhāu khala agan tapp tāu.*
ਭਾਂਡਾ ਭਾਉ ਅੰਮ੍ਰਿਤੁ ਤਿਤੁ ਢਾਲਿ॥	*Bhāndda bhāu amrit tit ddhāl.*
ਘੜੀਐ ਸਬਦੁ ਸਚੀ ਟਕਸਾਲ॥	*Ghaṛīyai sabad sachi taksāl.*
ਜਿਨ ਕਉ ਨਦਰਿ ਕਰਮੁ ਤਿਨ ਕਾਰ॥	*Jin kau nadar karam tin kār.*
ਨਾਨਕ ਨਦਰੀ ਨਦਰਿ ਨਿਹਾਲ॥ ੩੮॥	*Nanak nadri nadar nihāl.*

Brief glossary

ਜਤੁ	*Jat(i)*	Control of senses
ਪਾਹਾਰਾ	*Pāhāra*	Goldsmith's smithy, his work area
ਧੀਰਜੁ	*Dhīraj*	Calmness and control of mind, poise
ਅਹਰਣਿ	*Ahraṇ*	Anvil
ਵੇਦੁ	*Ved*	Knowledge
ਹਥੀਆਰ	*Hathiyār*	Tool, weapon
ਭਉ	*Bhāu*	Fear (awe)
ਖਲਾ	*Khala*	Bellows
ਤਪ ਤਾਉ	*Tap tāu.*	Heat of austerity
ਭਾਉ	*Bhāu*	Loving devotion
ਢਾਲਿ	*Ddhāl*	To forge
ਸਚੀ ਟਕਸਾਲ	*Sachi taksāl*	The true mint
ਨਦਰਿ	*Nadar*	Glance of grace

ਕਰਮੁ	*Karam*	Benediction, blessing
ਨਦਰੀ	*Nadri*	The Lord (of grace), through the glance of grace
ਨਿਹਾਲ	*Nihāl*	Blessed

Simply translated this *pauṛi* tells us that (using the analogy of the goldsmith's shop) control of the senses should be the *pāhāra* (smithy), of *dhīraj* (deep poise) the goldsmith. Our *mat(i)* (awareness or intellect) be the anvil and *ved* (knowledge) the instrument for hammering. Fear and awe of the Lord be the *khala* (the bellows) and *tap tāu* (the heat coming from austerity, spiritual energy). The loving devotion to the Lord will be the *bhāndda* (vessel), the crucible in which the nectar of the name, *Amrit*, will be moulded. In such a *sachi taksāl* - true mint - is the name cast within us. However, this will come not just through our effort; rather it will happen only when the Lord so casts His glance of grace on us. These lucky ones will be blessed indeed.

In this concluding *pauṛi* of the *Japji Sahib* the Guru sums up what it takes to forge the True Word within the consciousness. A question could arise as to why the Guru added this final *pauṛi* when the path to the ultimate destination, the *Sach khandd,* had already been spelt out and in a way the lesson had been taken to its logical conclusion starting from *Kiv sachiāra hoiyai kiv kūṛai tuttai pāl* to *Sach khandd vasai nirankār*. Is the Guru now adding a new issue, a new point to what he has told us thus far? The answer is, no. The lesson is, indeed, complete. This *pauṛi* is now added only by way of summing up of the previous thirty-seven *pauṛis* and the Guru gives herein a short, pointed exposition of what the devotee needs to do if the Word, the True Name is to be his companion, his support on his upward journey.

The Guru has repeatedly, throughout the *Japji Sahib*, told us that the only device, the only tool we can use in this endeavour is *Nām*. What does the devotee need to do before this tool, this marvellous magic key to the divine kingdom, can become available to us. Just parrot-like repetition of the scriptures, the daily prayers is not sufficient by itself. Even such a repetition is not entirely useless, for even this much will help set us on the path away from evil thoughts that would dog the human mind otherwise. However, the Guru is saying now that there are certain personal disciplines and training that we must impose on ourselves, which we must sincerely undertake before the mind comes under enough control. All faculties given to us by God are to be called into action for the forging of the True Name within our inner consciousness. So what are the faculties and disciplines the Guru asks us to bring into play?

In the first line the Guru says make the control of the senses, the *pāhāra* (smithy), and *dhīraj* (deep poise) the goldsmith. The analogy the Guru has used in this summing up is that of a goldsmith's shop where the smith forges the gold into beautiful ornaments. The analogy is very apt because the refining and the remoulding of the inner consciousness involves shaping a very precious raw material, an invaluable inner resource into an ornament of surpassing exquisiteness such that it is worthy of receiving the most wonderful of all gifts, the Lord's grace. Using the example of a goldsmith's shop, the Guru gives the inner human equivalents of the equipments normally used in that shop. The first is the *pāhāra* which is used both for the display of the jewellery as also for the furnace in which gold is moulded. The sense here is that of 'furnace', the analogy is doubly apt because as the Guru told us in the *Saram khandd*, hard toil is necessary for the remoulding. The heat of that tough labour is the furnace, and in human terms where does it come from? From *Jat,* says the Guru. *Jat(i)* is achieved by the control of the senses, right thinking, not letting the eyes see evil, not letting the tongue speak ill or falsehood, keeping the mind focused on what is good and kind and right. Not letting anger, greed, lust, false attachments and pride determine your conduct takes great effort. Maintaining this state makes you *jati,* one who has acquired *Jat(i)*. Acquire this first of all and it will become the furnace in which the refining of the consciousness is now possible to attempt. And who is the goldsmith to control this furnace? *Dhīraj*, says the Guru. This word stands for patience, poise, calmness of the mind. This is in the Guru's word the controller. If there is impatience governing us, the refining process will get immediately disrupted. When patience is there we will wait with a calm mind for the process to be completed and for the Lord's grace to descend, of course only as and when He so wills it. Keep up the process under the control of *dhīraj* and one day in the fullness of time the Lord will turn this glance of grace toward us.

The second line says make *mat(i)* (intellect) the *ahran̥* (anvil), and *ved* (knowledge) the hammer. The word *mat(i)* is translated as awareness, understanding or intellect. Prof. Talib called it 'mind awakened'. Since we are being told of the inner qualities to be used for this refining, the correct meaning should be intellect or understanding. Use this as the anvil and beat the raw material with the hammer of *ved* or knowledge. The word here is in the singular and thus does not refer to the four *Vedas* of Hindu scripture. It stands for knowledge, which the Guru says, is to be hammer. The word *hathiyār* literally means tools but the smithy being the analogy here, the sense has to be that of the hammer used by the goldsmith to do the forging by beating on the anvil. Of course the goldsmith does use smaller and finer tools also, so the generic meaning 'tools' rather than merely hammer can be accepted here. The anvil is the part of the process that accepts the most beating. It has therefore to be truly strong. So the Guru is telling us to stand intellectually firm, accept the blows that come from the growing knowledge of the Divine as it hammers on you to shape, form and re-mould the gold that is your inner consciousness. The Guru has thus told us that while deep and abiding faith is a basic prerequisite, the intellect immersed in that faith is also to be used fully and it has to be exposed to the new knowledge of the Divine. This hammering after heating the consciousness in the furnace of self-control, under the influence of patience and poise, is a necessary step in this journey.

In the third line the Guru tells us about what is going to provide the heat for the furnace and what is to keep the fire going. He says let *bhau* (love and awe of Lord) be the *khala* (bellows) and the *tap tāu*, the heat from your austerity. Thus, a life-maintaining *jat* has to be supplemented by single-minded focussing on Him and giving up of pandering to the senses. In Sikhism austerity as a device in itself is not encouraged. It is a life-affirming religion and requires its followers to fully participate in the world. Live the life of the householder and family man, be involved in the earning of an honest livelihood but through all of it maintain a detachment born of awareness of the divine purpose and of the true nature of human relationships. So, austerity here is not to be understood as withdrawing from the world, retiring to the forests and castigating the body. Austerity here means abstaining from all excesses, keeping the senses under strict control and living in the manner prescribed by the Guru, with every action imbued with and imbibing the love of the Lord and submission to Him. Observing the prescribed practices of reciting His name with each breath, and doing no action under the influence of the ego, is the austerity prescribed for us in Sikhism. The Guru carrying the analogy of the goldsmith's forge further says the spiritual heat that such self-discipline generates will provide the necessary energy for the transformation of the inner-self, but only if this heat, this energy is constantly directed at that one object. The bellows which will provide the blast of air to keep this heat going and properly directed will, in the spiritual context be the fear, the awe of the Lord. This is the fear that keeps us from straying; so, unlike earthly fears it is a positive, uplifting emotion. This is the one fear, which removes all earthly fears from our hearts and minds. If we are afraid of God we will not be able to do wrong and we will not need to fear any earthly power. It is the fear that turns gradually into love and worship of the Lord, and from *bhai* or *bhau* (fear) arises *Bhāu* – love and adoration.

In the fourth line the Guru says the loving devotion that will have emerged in us will become the *bhāndda* (vessel), the crucible in which the smith casts the gold after it is melted and ready for moulding. The casting of the *Amrit* (nectar of the name) will be done in this vessel – this crucible. The need for preparing suitably the vessel to contain the invaluable gift of the Lord's name has been referred elsewhere also in the *Gurbāṇi*. For instance, as we earlier also saw: *Ūndhai bhānddai kich na samāvai, sīdhai amrit pavai nihār* (The inverted vessel will catch nothing but once it is straightened it will be filled with the nectar of His grace). The right vessel is thus getting shaped now from the *Bhāu* of the Lord, the soul's loving adoration and yearning for Him, what is getting shaped in this process is the True Name itself. Commentators have translated these lines in slightly different ways but the sense remains the same. Dr. Sangat Singh puts it as: "Devotion the pot, immortality the mould." Prof. Talib says: "In this crucible forge the immortal vision." Iqbal Singh puts it as: "Loving devotion the crucible and melt God's name therein." Narain Singh translates it as: "Cast the Nectar of the Name in this crucible." Prof. Sahib Singh says: "In this crucible cast the Name of the Lord which is Nectar." Essentially the sense is that the divine, nectar-like name is getting shaped in this crucible through this process which the Guru has spelt out for us in this 'pauṛi'.

In line 5 the Guru has made it clearer. What is being cast is the Name. This is used here in the sense of divine consciousness. Within us, through control of the senses, a patient calm mind, personal austerity, fear of the Lord growing into love and adoration, is getting shaped the inner consciousness wherein the divine name is cast which will now resound and echo within us leading to union with Him. The human consciousness has through these exercises become the holy mind, which then is capable of casting that priceless jewel, the divine consciousness.

In the last two lines, sixth and seventh, the Guru again puts forth the familiar caveat. He says this fulfilment is the destiny, of only those whom the Lord chooses to bless. So do not let 'haumai' govern your efforts. These efforts are necessary and useful, but the fruit will become available only to those on whom the glance of grace falls. And, says the Guru, these lucky ones are *nihāl* (blessed indeed).

Summing up, we see in this *pauṛi* the Guru using the analogy of the goldsmith very aptly because no jewel, no ornament is more precious than *Nām*. The Guru prescribes that the equivalent of the smithy of the goldsmith in us will be continence. Control over the senses and a life of strict self-discipline is the first and basic requirement. Use your intellect and knowledge as the anvil and the hammer or the shaping tool. Light within that spiritual fire through austerity and controlled living in strict accordance with the Guru's prescription in the *Japji Sahib*, and feed this fire through the bellows of the fear and awe of the Lord. When this furnace is fully charged in this fashion use loving adoration of the Lord as the crucible in which the nectar of the Lord's name can then be forged. This is the true mint, in which the true coin – the Lord's name – will be struck. All this will happen not merely by one's own volition, but only by the Lord's grace. Truly blessed are those on whom this glance of grace has been cast by the Lord.

This *pauṛi* has also been read by some commentators as a recounting, or re-statement by the Guru, of the previous four *pauṛis* describing the crucial final steps of the soul's upliftment. The *Khandds* or realms of spiritual growth are, according to them, here referred through a different analogy within the five lines of this *pauṛi*. The *Dharam khandd* is the arena of bringing righteousness to our conduct – the first line here gives what change in conduct is needed for this task and we are told to cultivate continence, self-control and equipoise of mind. In the second, the *Gyān khandd*, knowledge was the theme. The second line here asks us to enlighten our intellect and make of it the anvil, and use knowledge as the tool or hammer. In the *Saram khandd* the hard toil of refining and re-moulding the inner-self was spoken of. The third line here talks of austerity needed for providing the heat and the fear of Lord fanning this heat to keep the furnace burning bright and hot. The next two *Khandds – Karam khandd* and *Sach khandd* – are now re-stated in lines 4 and 5 and clarified in lines 6 and 7. The fourth line speaks of the *Amrit*, the nectar of the name coming to us, permeating us. This growth of the name from the inner consciousness is our becoming one with the Lord. The fifth line is a reference to the *Sach khandd.* That the *Karam* (benediction) will come from the Lord at His will is re-stated clearly in line 6 and the ones spoken of in the seventh line are none other than those who dwell with the Lord in *Sach Khandd.* However, the more accepted interpretation is that this *pauṛi* is meant as a summing up of the lesson imparted to us by the Guru in the *Japjī Sahib*, and thus really of the *Gurbāṇi.*

44

SALVATION THROUGH HIS NAME

ਸਲੋਕੁ ॥	**Slok**
ਪਵਣੁ ਗੁਰੂ ਪਾਣੀ ਪਿਤਾ ਮਾਤਾ ਧਰਤਿ ਮਹਤੁ ॥	*Pavaṇ guru pāṇi pita māta dharat mahat.*
ਦਿਵਸੁ ਰਾਤਿ ਦੁਇ ਦਾਈ ਦਾਇਆ ਖੇਲੈ ਸਗਲ ਜਗਤੁ ॥	*Divas rāt doye dāyi dāya khelai sagal jagat.*
ਚੰਗਿਆਈਆ ਬੁਰਿਆਈਆ ਵਾਚੈ ਧਰਮੁ ਹਦੂਰਿ ॥	*Changiāyīa buriāyīa vāchai dharma hadūr.*
ਕਰਮੀ ਆਪੋ ਆਪਣੀ ਕੇ ਨੇੜੈ ਕੇ ਦੂਰਿ ॥	*Karmi āpo āpṇi kay neṛai kay dūr.*
ਜਿਨੀ ਨਾਮੁ ਧਿਆਇਆ ਗਏ ਮਸਕਤਿ ਘਾਲਿ ॥	*Jini nām dhiāyia gaye maskat ghāl.*
ਨਾਨਕ ਤੇ ਮੁਖ ਉਜਲੇ ਕੇਤੀ ਛੁਟੀ ਨਾਲਿ ॥ ੧ ॥	*Nanak tay mukh ujlay keti chhutti nāl.*

Brief glossary

ਧਰਤਿ ਮਹਤੁ	*Dharat, mahat*	Earth, great
ਦਾਈ	*Dāyi*	Nurse-maid, baby-sitter
ਦਾਇਆ	*Dāya*	Male baby-sitter
ਵਾਚੈ	*Vāchai*	Reads out
ਕੇ ਨੇੜੈ	*Kay neṛay*	Some are near
ਮਸਕਤਿ	*Maskat*	Hard work, toil
ਘਾਲਿ	*Ghāl*	Successfully done

Simply translated, this concluding *slok* says that the vital air is the Guru, water the Sire, and earth the Mother. The day and night are the female and male attendants for us. Our good actions and bad will be recorded and read out in the Divine Presence, and strictly as per the worth of our actions will the reward be, and some will earn proximity to the Lord for the good, and the bad deeds will banish us away from Him. Those who followed the path of *Nām Simran̤* strictly have earned through this hard labour, and their faces will radiantly shine and they will have achieved liberation. Not only they themselves but because of them many others too will achieve liberation from the cycle of re-births.

This *slok* concludes the *Japji Sahib* and is the epilogue, sealing within the thirty-eight *paur̤is* that had commenced after the 'Mool Mantra' and the opening *slok* of *Ād sach jugād sach* – an introduction to the Lord for the devotee seeker setting out to reach Him. The Guru gave us the brief and very broad vision of God, the Eternal; He then took us through the journey gradually exposing us to the vast and magnificent mystery that is the Lord. He also kept nudging us and guiding us to the path we needed to follow to make ourselves worthy of consideration by the Lord. We were told to practice *Nām Simran̤* to purify ourselves and to move away from false attachments and allurements of Māya. He told us to listen with the inner ear, to have firm faith. He told us of the great variety of created beings and then taught us to stay humble and think not that we are exceptionally deserving; to have patience; to wait for the Lord's glance of grace; and to live ever in fear of going against the Lord's will; to build within ourselves love and adoration for the Lord; and through strict and hard austerity, develop our inner consciousness to be worthy of Him; and to be ready for Him. He told us of the destination, the *Sach khandd,* and all through he told us that our efforts are vitally important but that success, if at all, will come only when the Lord in His own wisdom decides to cast on us His glance of grace. In this epilogue the Guru takes a parting look at the lesson and re-states the salient part by way of an overview of all creation, of the actions necessary for the seeker, and also the process of judgement and the reward that hopefully will ensue.

In the first line the Guru describes man's connection to his environment both in a physical way as well as by way of spiritual metaphor. He says the vital air is the Guru, water the Sire and earth is the Mother, and these together have made our existence possible. Since the time humans achieved consciousness above that of the beasts, the earth has been referred to as the mother. This is true of practically all cultures and we all refer even today to our lands of birth as the motherland. The earth as mother is worshipped in most cultures. Water is also a necessity before the earth can produce anything. The living beings however need air to continue existing. Thus are these three referred by the Guru as the three components that make up the created beings on this earth. Spiritually speaking, the Guru is the most vital part. While the Sire and the Mother together can bring life into being but this is a life of no durability and little value. That is acquired only when the vital air courses through. Only then is the life process viable. At a spiritual level the Guru is the entity that will connect the human to the Divine. Without the Guru, who for the Sikhs is the *SGGS* and the 'Word', the message contained therein, the journey from the worldly to the sublime cannot commence.

In the second line the Guru says the kindly Lord having brought us into existence has now created day and night to tend to us. The usual practice at that time was to engage a nurse-maid who often even fed the newborn her breast milk, but in any case was with the child through the night singing lullabies when they would not want to sleep, and watching over their safety. She was called the *Dāyi*. Similarly, the waking child had a male companion to keep watch and to keep the child entertained. He was called the *Dāia* or *Dāya*. Here 'night' with its restful, restorative connotations is called the *Dāyi* and the 'day' with its activity and amusements is called the *Dāya*. In the hands of these two the world is looked after and its needs met.

In lines 3 and 4, the Guru reminds us again that our actions performed in this world are recorded and read out in the Divine Presence and we shall be put to judgement in that righteous court. The judgement will be to weigh our actions and reward us according to their worth with nearness or distance from the Lord. We may especially note the fourth line which spells out the consequence of our actions quite unambiguously. Strictly, as per the worth of our actions, it says, will the reward be. For good actions we will earn proximity to the Divine, and for the bad deeds will we be distanced from the Lord. This is in the Sikh world-view the equivalent of hell and heaven, *narak* and *swarag*, *jannat* and *jahannum*. Proximity to the Lord is the highest heaven and distance from Him is progressively harsher hell.

In the concluding lines, fifth and sixth, the Guru tells us of the outcome of following the path he had prescribed, the path of *Nām Simraṇ*, with a rigorous fixity of mind and steadfastness of faith. Here he says, those who followed his guidance and were immersed in reciting His name have made successful the hardest labour. The word *maskat* (hard labour) is here well chosen for these are few tasks harder than control of the mind and training oneself to see the Lord in everything and to have faith unshaken through success or failure, through joys and troubles. There are many things men do to train themselves for worldly tasks for achieving success in one field or the other of human livelihood. We feel greatly elated when we succeed in any such endeavour and are able, as a result, to achieve high position or great wealth. The difficulties in even such mundane endeavours sometimes defeat all but the most determined. There are thus only a few able to reach the level of PhDs and Doctorates in any sphere of human knowledge, art, and science. The difficulty of attaining success in the spiritual field is indescribably manifold more. The Guru's lesson if understood and followed diligently will lead us to win control over our own minds. The effort required is incredibly hard, because the prize is also incredibly attractive. The prize in fact is beyond all compare and greater than this prize there are no prizes left to strive for. The efforts required are therefore rightly called *maskat*, which is the common form of the Persian *mushakkat* (rigorous labour). But, says the Guru, this labour is successfully completed only by those who faithfully follow the prescription and reach the state of proper *Nām Simraṇ*. These successful students will have reached the Divine Presence, of course then also only if His glance of grace falls on the seeker. Their faces will radiantly shine with the glory of this success, and they will have achieved liberation. Not only will the successful ones be themselves rewarded but because of them many others too will achieve liberation.

The concept here is that these successful toilers are what we call saints, and their sangat (companionship) can help refine our coarser, less-refined souls. The importance of *Sādh-Sangat* of course occurs at numerous places in the *Gurbāṇi*. In fact the *Sukhmani Sahib* has at least one full *ashttpadi*, the seventh, entirely on the benefits of the company of the saint. It starts with:

"Sādh kai sung much ūjal hote. Sādhsung mull sagli khote."
(In the Sadh's company our faces are radiant.
In the Sadh's company our evil shed)
(*Gauṛi Sukhmani, Mahla* 5, *SGGS*, page 271)

Sādh in Punjabi is another term used for saint, and it literally means one who has achieved control of himself. *Sādh Sant* is used to describe saints. The Guru says these saintly ones, their faces effulgent with the divine light, will become the support for many others to liberate many from the cycle of birth and re-birth. The liberation – *chhutti* – spoken of here is the cessation of the circle of life and death, of birth and re-birth. This in all Eastern schools of thought is salvation, *Nirvāna*, and *Moksha*. The lucky few who reach this level are one with the Lord and reside with Him in the *Sach khandd*.

With this epilogue the Guru has brought to conclusion the discourse he commenced with the 'Mool Mantra'. We see that he gives an overview of human life and it is presented as a play, a game played out in this world. Sired by water on the Mother Earth and nurtured and sustained by the Guru the vital air, the breath of life, the entire world is tended to by the nurse-maid *Dāyi* the night, and watched over by the *Dāya* the day. Playing this game the Lord expects that we will play it according to His rules and will order our living and conduct in accordance with what he has prescribed. The world in its play is also forewarned that obedience to the way will be rewarded and transgressions punished. We are told that a watch is being strictly kept on how we play the game. Our actions, our doings, our thoughts are subject to constant and rigorous recording. This record will be read out at the end in the Divine Presence. Dharamrāj will then be empowered to assess and evaluate the worth of our actions. At that time it will no longer be a game, but there will instead be a strict accounting. The worth of our actions only will then determine our fate. Worthy and righteous actions will be rewarded by allowing us to be in the close proximity of the Lord. We will be near Him, and enjoy the eternal peace, the liberation from hardship, to the extent of our closeness. Bad actions will bāṇish us away from Him in loneliness to suffer the pangs of separation. As the Guru said: "*Jini nām dhiāyia gaye maskat ghāl, Nanak tay mukh ujlay keti chhuti nāl.*"

APPENDIX A

[Refer Chapter 3, p. 66]

Extract from 'The Encyclopaedia of Sikhism'

Vol. IV, pp. 243 to 247

In the Sikh system, the word 'Guru' is used only for the ten prophet-preceptors, Guru Nanak to Guru Gobind Singh, and for none other. Now this office of Guru is fulfilled by the *Sri Guru Granth Sahib*, the sacred book, which was so apotheosized by the last Guru, Guru Gobind Singh, before he passed away in 1708. No living person, however holy or revered, can have the title or status of Guru. For Sikhs, Guru is the holy teacher, the prophet under direct commission from God – the Ten who have been and the *Sri Guru Granth Sahib* which is their continuing visible manifestation.

Guru Gobind Singh manifested the 'Khalsa' in 1699. In 1708, he supplied another permanent, and final, feature in the evolution of the Sikh faith when he installed the 'Holy Scripture' as Guru. This is how the Bhatt Vahi Taluda PaRāganāh Jind describes the event: *"Guru Gobind Singh mahal dasman beta Guru Tegh Bahadur ka pota Guru Hargobind ji ka parpota Guru Arjan ji ka bans Guru Ram Dass ji ki Surajbansi Gosal gotra Sodhi Khatri basi Anandpur parganāh Kahlur muqam Nander tat GodaVāri des dakkhan sammat satran sai painsath kartik mas ki chauth shukla pakkhe budhVār kay dihun Bhai Daya Singh se bachan hoya Sri GranthSahib lai ao bachan pai Daya Singh Sri GranthSahib lai aye guru ji ne panch paise narial age bheta rakha matha teka sarbatt sangat se kaha mera hukam hai meri jagāh Sri Granthji ko janana jo sikh janega tis ki ghal thaen paegi guru tis ki bahuri karega sat kar manana."*

"Guru Gobind Singh, the Tenth Master, son of Guru Tegh Bahadur, grandson of Guru Hargobind, great-grandson of Guru Arjan, of the family of Guru Ram Das, Surajbansi Gosal clan,

Sodhi Khatri, resident of Anandpur, Parganāh Kahlur, now at Nanded, on the Godavāri bank in the Deccan, asked Bhai Daya Singh on Wednesday, 'shukla chauth' of the month of 'Kartik', 1765, Bk (6 October 1708), to fetch the Sri Granth Sahib. The Guru placed before it five pice and a coconut and bowed his head before it. He said to the sangat, 'It is my commandment: Own Sri Granthji in my place. He who so acknowledges it will obtain his reward. The Guru will rescue him. Know this as the truth.'"

According to Giani Garja Singh, who discovered this entry, the author was Narbud Singh Bhatt, who was with Guru Gobind Singh at Nanded at that time.

Bhatt Vahis are a new source of information discovered by Giani Garja Singh (1904-77), a dogged searcher for materials on Sikh history. The Bhatts were hereditary panegyrists, genealogists or family bards. (A group of them were introduced to Guru Arjan by Bhatt Bhikkha, who himself had become a disciple in the time of Guru Amar Das. According to Bhai Gurdās, *Vār* XI.21 and Bhai Mani Singh *Sikhan di Bhagat Mala*, he had earlier visited Guru Arjan with the 'sangat' of Sultanpur Lodhi.) Those of them who came into the Sikh fold composed hymns in honour of the Gurus, which were entered in the *Sri Guru Granth Sahib* by Guru Arjan.

These Bhatts also recorded events of the lives of the Gurus and of the members of their families in their scrolls called *Vahis*. Some of these *Vahis* are preserved to this day in the families, especially at the village of Karsindhu, in Jind district of Haryana. The script in which they are written is called *Bhataksri* – a kind of family code like *lande* and *mahajani*. The only known scholar to have worked with these materials was Giani Garja Singh.

Apart from this new testimony culled by Giani Garja Singh from the *Bhatt Vahis*, another contemporary document which authenticates the fact of *Sri Guru GranthSahib* having been invested with the final authority is a letter issued by reference of Guru Gobind Singh's wife, Mata Sundariji. To quote from the original, which is now in the possession of Bhai Chet Singh, of the village of Bhai Rupa, in present-day Bathinda district, to whose ancestors it was addressed: *"Ik Onkar Wahguru ji ki fateh, Sri Akalpurkh ji ka Khalsa yak rang jina dithia Wahguru ji chit avai. Bhai Sahib Dan Singhji Bhai Duni Singh ji Bhai Jagat singhji Bhai Gurbakhsh Singhji Ugar Singhji Bhai Ram Singhji sarbatt Khalsa Wahguru Akalpurkhji ka pase likhtam gulam Khalsa ji ka Kahn Singh Nival Singh Mul Singhji Sujan Singh Gaja Singh Maha Singh Sarbatt Khalsa Wahguru Akalpurkh ka Wahguru ji ki fateh vachani khusha karṇa ji Wahguru Akalpurkhji har dam chit avai sukh hoye Khalsa ji ka bol bala hoi ardas tusadi marfat bhai Dulcha Singh kay hath pāhuti parhkay Khalsa ji bahut khushwaqat hoya tusadi bab Khalsa ji dayal hoya hai hath jore kai jo rakhya hove. 'Jo janu harika sevako hari tiskay kami.' Guru Guru japna Wahguru ang sang hai fajal karkai rakhia hovegi Khalsaji Bhai Kahn Singhji kau Mata Sahibji ne gumastgiri Amritsar ji ki mukarar kiti hai Khalsa ji ne gurmata karkay Harimandar ate bagh di murammat imarat ka kam shuru kīta hai sri Mata Sahib ji ne likha hai ki Wahguru Akalpurkh ji ki nagri hai langar jarura karṇa … Khalsa Sri Wahguru ji ka suchet bibek budh chahie jo sivai Akalpurkh duje no janai nāhi Dasam Patshahian tak jamai paidhe yarvin barvin Banda Chaubanda Ajita vagaire te aitkad lei avana hatiya hai. Hor hatiya Guru japan nal dur hosan, par ih hatiya guṇah bakshiaiga nāhi jo manmukh kay jame upkar aitkad karenge, 'Mukh mohi pherial mukh mohi juttha hoi.' Khalsaji tusan sivai Akal duje no manana nāhi. Sabad dasvin patshaji tak khojna, 'Sabad Khoji ihu gharu lahai Nanak ta ka dasu.' 'Guru ka nivas sabad vich hai.' 'Guru mahi ap samoi sabad Vārtaiya.' 'Jian andar jiu sabad hai jit sahu milava hoi.' Wahguru jiki fateh. Bhai Mehar Singh tahlia Bhai Bule ka pattar kay khasmane vich rahina Guru nal gandh paisi.'*

'Ik Onkar Wahigur ji ki Fateh.'"

"The 'Khalsa', of the timeless Himself, immersed in the one, and whose sight brings 'Wahiguru' to mind. Addressed to Bhai Sahib Dan Singhji, Bhai Duni Singhji Bhai Jagat Singhji, Bhai Gurbakhsh Singhji, Ugar Singhji, Bhai Ram Singhji, the entire Khalsa of Wahigur, the Timeless One. From the slaves of the Khalsaji, Kahn Singhji, Nival Singh, Mul Singhji, Sujan Singh, Gaja Singh, Maha Singh Wahiguruji ki Fateh to the entire Khalsa. May you be rejoiced in constant remembrance of the Timeless Wahiguru. May prosperity prevail: may supremacy belong to the Khalsa. Having received your missive through Bhai Dulcha Singh, Khalsaji is highly pleased. Khalsaji happily prays with folded hands for your security. He who to Lord surrenders himself, his affairs the Lord will set to rights. Repeat always the name of Guru. Wahiguru is by your side. He will extend to you His grace and protection. Khalsaji, Mata Sahibji has appointed Bhai Kahn Singhji to the superintendence of Amritsarji. The Khalsaji, through a gurmata, has taken in hand the construction and repair of the Harimandar and the garden. Sri Mata Sahibji has written that langar must be run in that place which is the abode of God Himself…Wahiguru's Khalsa must always be alert, possessed of discriminating wisdom. The Khalsa must believe in none other than the Timeless One. There have been only Ten Masters in human form; to believe in the eleventh and twelfth, Banda Singh Bahadur, Ajita (Ajit Singh, adopted son of Mata Sundarjit) etc. is a mortal sin. Every other sin can be had cancelled by repeating the Guru's name, but this sin of believing in human forms will not be remitted. "The faces turned away from the Guru are faces perverted." Khalsaji, you must believe in none other except the Timeless One. Go only to the Ten Gurus in search of the Word. Nanak is the slave of him who by seeking the Lord's Name obtains his goal." The Guru resides in sabda. "The Lord hath merged His own Self in the Guru through whom He has revealed His word: "The Word is the life of all life, for, through it, one experiences God." Victory to the Lord, Bhai Mehar Singh, the messenger, son of Bhai Bula: keep the letter secure in your custody. You will gain the Guru's favour."

From this letter it is clear how the Sikhs after Guru Gobind Singh believed that the 'Guruship' had passed to the 'sabda', i.e., the 'Word' as contained in the *Sri Guru Granth Sahib*. None in the human form after the ten Gurus was to be acknowledged by the Sikhs as Guru. Those who, like some of Banda Singh's or Ajit Singh's followers, called their leaders Gurus were committing a mortal sin. All other sins, says the letter, could be forgiven by repeating the Guru's name, but not the sin of believing in a living Guru after the Ten Masters of the Sikh faith.

Several other old Sikh documents also attest the fact of succession having been passed on by Guru Gobind Singh to the *Sri Guru Granth Sahib*. For instance, the *Rahitnāma* by Bhai Nand Lal, one of Guru Gobind Singh's disciples remembered to this day for his elegant Persian poetry in honour of the Gurus. In his *Rahitnāma* or code of conduct, Bhai Nand Lal, who was at Nanded in the camp of Emperor Bahadur Shah as one of his ministers at the time of Guru Gobind Singh's passing away, thus records his last words in his Punjabi verse:

> "He who would wish to see the Guru,
> Let him come and see the Granth.
> He who would wish to speak with him,
> Let him read and reflect upon what says the Granth.
> He who would wish to hear his word,
> He should with all his heart read the Granth,
> or listen to the Granth being read."

Another of Guru Gobind Singh's disciples and associates, Bhai Prahlad Singh, records in his *Rahitnama*, the Guru's commandment:

> "By the word of the Timeless One,
> Has the Khalsa been manifested.
> This is my commandment for all of my Sikhs:
> You will acknowledge Granthas the Guru."

In *Gurbilās Pātshāhi 10* (author Koer Singh; the year of writing 1751), Guru Gobind Singh is quoted as saying:

> "This is no more the age for a personal Guru to be anointed.
> I shall not place the mark on anyone's forehead.
> All sangat is owned as Khalsa now, under
> the shelter of the Almighty Himself,
> They are now to the Word attached.
> He who believes is the Sikh par excellence.
> On the Guru Granthshould he put his reliance,
> To none else should he direct his adoration.
> All his wishes the Guru will bring to fulfilment,
> This he should believe,
> Casting away all dubiety."

Another authority that may relevantly be quoted is Devaraja Sharma's *Nanakacandrodayamahakavyam*, an old Sanskrit manuscript which has recently been published by the Sanskrit University, Vāranasi. It records Guru Gobind Singh's proclamation that the scripture would be the Guru after him.

> "While the Master lay on his deathbed, Nand Lal (?)
> came forward and asked the following question:
> 'Who shall be the object of our discourses?' The Master
> replied, "The Granth, which itself is the doctrine of the
> Guru, shall be your teacher. This is what you should see;
> this is what you should honour; this is what should be
> the object of your discourses."

This point has been laboured somewhat lengthily for the reasons that cavil is sometimes raised. Certain cults among Sikhs, still owning personal Gurus, ask for authentic evidence to the effect that Guru Gobind Singh had named *Sri Guru Granth Sahib* his successor. No archival testimony can be presented, unless the *Bhatt Vahi* entry is included in the category. But evidence bequeathed through tradition, written as well as oral, supports this fact. This is what has come down through Sikh memory. Had there been the 11th Guru, the name could not have been effaced from the pages of history. Guru Gobind Singh brought to an end the line of personal Gurus and declared the 'Holy Word' Guru after him.

Along with the *Sri Guru Granth Sahib*, the 'Khalsa' was now the person visible of the Guru. The word 'khalsa' is derived from the Arabic 'khalis', meaning pure or pious. Guru Gobind Singh used the term in its symbolic and technical sense. In official terminology, 'Khalsa' in Mughal days meant lands or territory directly under the king. Crown-land was known as 'Khalsa land'. As, says a contemporary poet, Bhai Gurdās II, Guru Gobind Singh converted the 'sangat' into 'Khalsa', Sikhs were the Guru's 'Khalsa', i.e., directly his own, without any intermediary or local 'sangat' leaders. On that point, we have the evidence of *Sri Gur Sobha* by Sainapat, a contemporary of Guru Gobind Singh and Guru Gobind Singh's own 'hukamnamas'. To quote from the former:

> "A day preceding the event, i.e. passing of Guru Gobind Singh
> The Sikhs gathered together and began to ask:
> 'What body will the lord now take?'
> The Guru at that moment spoke:
> 'In the Khalsa will you see me;
> With the Khalsa is my sole concern;
> My physical form have I bestowed upon the Khalsa.'"

Guru Gobind Singh, in his *hukamnāma* issued on *Phalgun* 4, 1756 Bk/1 February 1700, to the *sangat* of Pattan Farid, modern Pakpattan, refers to the '*sangat*' as 'his own Khalsa'. *Hukamnāmas* are letters written by the Gurus to *sangats* in different parts of the country. Some of them have been traced in recent years and two collections were published in 1967, one by Dr. Ganda Singh (Punjabi University), Patiala and by Shamsher Singh Ashok (Shiromani Gurdwara Parbandhak Committee), Amritsar. Most of the *hukamnāmas* are common to both Anthologies. These *hukamnāmas* are another valuable source of information on the lives of the Gurus and on the Sikh communities forming in far-flung places.

That *Sri Guru Granth Sahib* is Guru Eternal for it has been the understanding and conviction of the Sikh community since the passing of Guru Gobind Singh. In their hard days of exile, soon afterwards when they were outlawed and had to seek the safety of the hills and jungles, the Sikhs' most precious possession, which they cherished and defended at the cost of their lives, was *Sri Guru Granth Sahib*. The 'Holy Book' was their sole religious reference, and they acknowledged none other. To quote the *Prāchīn Panth Prakāsh*: "Thou Guru Granth art the true Presence. Impart to the Sikh sangat the true counsel." This is how the Sikhs address *Sri Guru Granth Sahib* as they assemble at the 'Akāl Takht' to seek its guidance before launching an attack on the Pathan citadel of Kasur. In the time of Maharaja Ranjit Singh, who established sovereignty in the name of the 'Khalsa', personal piety and court ceremonial centred upon the *Sri Guru Granth Sahib*. As contemporary records testify, Ranjit Singh began his day by making obeisance to *Sri Guru Granth Sahib*. On festive occasions, he made pilgrimage to Amritsar to bow before *Shri Guru Granth Sahib* in the Harimandar. For the Sikh in general *Sri Guru Granth Sahib* was the only focus of religious attachment.

None other existed otherwise, either in human form or symbolically. In all Sikh literature after Guru Gobind Singh, the 'Holy Book' is uniformly referred to as *Guru Granth*.

The personal 'Guruship' was ended by Guru Gobind Singh himself. Succession passed to the *Sri Guru Granth Sahib* in perpetuity. This was a most significant development in the history of the *panth*.

The finality of the 'Holy Book' was a fact rich in religious and social implications. The *Guru Granth* became Guru and received divine honours. It was acknowledged as the medium of the revelation descended through the Gurus. It was for the Sikhs the perpetual authority, spiritual as well as historical. They lived their religion in response to it. Through it, they were able to observe their faith more fully, more vividly. It was central to all that subsequently happened in Sikh life. It was the source of their verbal tradition and it shaped their intellectual and cultural environment. It moulded the Sikh concept of life. From it the community's ideals, institutions and rituals derived their meaning. Its role in guaranteeing the community integration and permanence and in determining the course of its history has been crucial.

The 'Word' enshrined in the 'Holy Book' was always revered by the Gurus as well as by their disciples as of divine origin. The Guru was the revealer of the 'Word'. One day the 'Word' was to take the place of the Guru. The line of personal Gurus could not have continued forever. The inevitable came to pass when Guru Gobind Singh declared *Sri Guru Granth Sahib* to be his successor. It was only through the 'Word' that the Guruship could be made everlasting. This object Guru Gobind Singh intuitively secured when he pronounced *Granth Sahib* to be Guru after him. The *Granth Sahib* was henceforth – for all time to come – the Guru for the Sikhs.

APPENDIX B

[Refer Chapter 12, p. 129]

Extract from 'Hindu Mythology'

by W.J. Wilkins, pp. 353 to 355

[Published by Rupa & Co., 1981]

The three main divisions of time employed in the Hindu scriptures are 'Yugas', 'ManvAntaras', and 'Kalpas'. These will now be described.

There are four 'Yugas', which together extend to 12,000 divine years. Their respective duration is as follows:

The Krita Yuga = 4,800 divine years

The Treta Yuga = 3,600 divine years

The Dvapara Yuga = 2,400 divine years

The Kali Yuga = 1,200 divine years

One year of mortals is equal to one day of the gods. As 360 is taken as the number of days in the year:

The Krita Yuga = 4,800 x 360 = 1,728,000 divine years of mortals

The Treta Yuga = 3,600 x 360 = 1,296,000 divine years of mortals

The Dvapara Yuga = 2,400 x 360 = 864,000 divine years of mortals

The Kali Yuga = 1,200 x 360 = 432,000 divine years of mortals

One 'Mahayuga', or 'Great Age', including the four lesser 'Yugas', therefore, being 12,000 divine years = 4,320,000 years of mortals. "A thousand such Mahayugas are a day of Brahma," and his nights are of equal duration; a 'Kalpa', therefore, or Day of Brahma extends over 4,320,000,000 ordinary years. "Within each Kalpa 14 Manus reign; a ManvAntara, or period of a Manu, therefore, is consequently one-fourteenth part of a Kalpa, or day of Brahma."

"In the present Kalpa, six Manus, of whom Swayambhubva was the first, have already passed away; the present being Vaivasata. In each Manvantra (Period of a Manu), seven Rishis, certain deities, an Indra and a Manu, and the kings, his sons, are created and perish. A thousand systems of the four Yugas occur coincidentally with these fourteen Manvantra, and consequently about 71 systems of four Yugas elapse during each Manvantra, and measure the lives of the Manus and the deities of the period. At the close of this day of Brahma, a collapse of the universe takes place, which lasts through a night of Brahma, equal in duration to his day, during which period the worlds are converted into one great ocean, when the lotus-born god (Brahma), expanded by his deglutition of the universe, and contemplated by the Yogis and gods in Janaloka, sleeps on the serpent Sesha. At the end of that night he awakays and creates anew."

"A year of Brahma is composed of the proper number of such days and nights, and a hundred of such years constitute his whole life. The period of his life is called *Para*, and the half of it *Pararddha*, or the half of a *Para*. One *Pararddha*, or half of Brahma's existence, has now expired, terminating with the great Kalpa called the Padma Kalpa. The now existing Kalpa, or day of Brahma, called Vāraha (or that of the boar), is the first of the second *Pararddha* of Brahma's existence. The dissolution which occurs at the end of each Kalpa, or day of Brahma, is called *naimittika*, incidental, occasional, or contingent."

The dissolution of existing beings is [according to the *Vishnu Purān̩a*] of three kinds: "incidental, elemental, and absolute." The first is *naimittika*, occasional, incidental, or Brahmya, as occasioned in the intervals of Brahma's days; the destruction of creatures, though not of the substance of the world, occurring during the night. The second is the general resolution of the elements into their primitive source, or Prakriti, the Prakritika destruction, and occurs at the end of Brahma's life. The third, the absolute, or final, Alyantika, is individual annihilation; Moksha, exemption forever from future existence."

APPENDIX C

Article IV, Rehat Maryāda.

(Reference page 77)

(1) A Sikh should wake up in the ambrosial hours (three hours before the dawn), take bath and, concentrating his/her thoughts on One Immortal being, repeat the name Waheguru (Wondrous Destroyer of darkness).

(2) He/she should recite the following scriptural compositions every day:

"a) The Japu, the Jaapu and the Ten Sawayyas – beginning Sarāwag Sudh – in the morning

b) Sodar Rehras comprising the following compositions:

   (i) nine hymns of the Guru Granth Sahib, occurring in the holy book after the Japji Saib, the first of which begins with "Sodar" and the last of which ends with "saran pare ki rakho sarma",

   (ii) The Benti Chaupai of the tenth Guru (beginning "hamri karo hath dai rachha" and ending with 'dushtt dokh te leho bachai",

   (iii) The sawwayya beginning with the words "pāe gahe jab te tumre",

   (iv) The Dohira beginning with the words "sagal duār kau chhādd kai",

   (v) The first five and the last pauris (stanzas) of Anand Sahib and

   (vi) The Mundawani and the Slok Mahla 5 beginning with "tera kita jato nahi"- in the evening after sunset.

c) The Sohila to be recited at night before going to bed.

d) The morning and evening recitations should be concluded with the Ardas (formal supplication litany)."

SELECTED BIBLIOGRAPHY

1. Sri Guru GranthSahib Darpan
By Prof. Sahib Singh
(Raj Publishers, 1972)

2. Shabdarth Sri Guru GranthSahib Ji
Sharomani Gurdwara Parbandhak Committee, 2000

3. The True Name (English)
New Age International Private Limited, 1997

4. Japji (English)
Dr. Sangat Singh
(Hind Pocket Book, 1987)

5. Japji Sahib (Punjabi)
Narain Singh
(Bhagat Purāṇ Singh All India Pingalwara, 1981-82)

6. Japji and other Sikh Scriptures
Iqbal Singh (Allen, McMillan and Endersion, New York, 1986)

7. Sri Guru GranthSahib (English)
Prof. Gurbachan Singh Talib
(Vol. II, Publication Translation Bureau, Punjabi University, Patiala, 1988)

8. PajGranthi Steek
Bhai Vir Singh
(Khalsa Samachar, Hall Bazar, Amritsar, 1988)

9. Gurshabad Ratnakar
(Mahan Kosh)
Bhai Kahan Singh
(Punjab Languages Dept., 1974)

10. Ascent to Civilization
John Gowlett
(Alfred A. Knopf, 1984)

11. Collin's Atlas of Archaeology

12. Adi Sri Guru GranthSahib Steek
Reprint Bhasha Vibhag Punjab,
1989 (Punjabi), Vol. I
(Faridkot Wala Teeka)

13. The Encyclopaedia of Sikhism
Editor in Chief:
Harbans Singh
(Punjabi University,
Patiala, 1998)

14. Santhya, Sri Guru GranthSahib Ji
Bhai Vir Singh
(Khalsa Samachar,
Hall Bazar, Amritsar, 4th
reprint, 1981)

15. Sacred Nitnem (English)
Harbans Singh Doabia
(Singh Brothers Mai Sewan
Bazar, Amritsar, Edition 1995)

16. Nitnem Steek (Punjabi)
Prof. Sahib Singh (Singh
Brothers, Mai Sewan Bazar,
Amritsar, 8th reprint, 1989)

17. Japji: Meditation in Sikhism
Swami Rama
(The Himalaya International
Institute of Yoga Science and
Philosophy of the
U.S.A., Hovesdale,
Pennsylvania, 1987)

18. Japji Katha
Sant Sangat Singh Ji Maharaj,
(Kamaliyewale Parbhandak
Trust, Yoga Astha Sriman
Sant Sangat Singh Ji Maharaj
Kamaliyewale, 1978)

19. The Japji (English)
Harnam Singh, Sardar
Surinder Singh
(Santosh Cottage 2-12, Sant
Patel Nagar, New Delhi, 1957)

20. A Popular Dictionary of Sikhism
W. Owen Cole and Prem
Singh Sambhi
(Rupa & Co., 1990)

21. Sri Guru GranthSahib (English, Vol. I)
Dr. Gopal Singh
(World Book Center,
Asaf Ali Road, New Delhi,
International Edition, 1989)

22. Jeevan Birtant Guru Nanak Dev Ji
Prof. Sahib Singh
(Singh Brothers, Mai (Punjabi)
Sewan Bazar, Amritsar, 6th
reprint, 1990)

23. Jap Nirnai (Steek)
Gyāni Harbans Singh
(Gurbāṇi Sewa Mission,
Patiala, 3rd reprint

24. The Oxford Dictionary Of World Religions
Edited by John Bowkayr
(by BCA, First Reprint 2003)

25. Sikh Reht Maryāda
Dharam Parchar Committee
(SGPC, Amritsar,
July 1997)

26. Gurbāṇi te Itihas Baray
Prof. Sahib Singh
(Singh Brothers,
9th reprint, 2002)